MAD TO BE NORMAL

People believe quite different things about R.D. Laing, and the views it is claimed he held. Equally, there are many opinions about his intellectual worth. These opinions have come, mainly, from two sources: gossip and vivid stories concerning his personal life and state of mind; and his books, lectures and psychiatric practice. No coherent rounded portrait has yet emerged. Much of what is attributed to him is in fact the beliefs of others.

What is incontestable is that in the 1960s Laing wrote a number of books including *The Divided Self*, *The Politics of Experience and the Bird of Paradise* and *Sanity, Madness and the Family* that rocked the foundations of conventional psychiatry and galvanized the imagination of millions of ordinary readers. For the next twenty years his books were translated into every single major language in the world, and many more. His collection of short poems, *Knots*, enjoyed huge international success and was performed on television and the stage.

His existential approach to madness angered many people as much as it sensitized others to matters of individual liberty and the importance of the social context of 'illness'. Through his fame he was almost reinvented, hence the burgeoning of the controversies that surround his work. The greatest accusation he has borne is that he idealized mental misery. Laing consistently denied this, arguing that to recognize that a patient's intelligibility exists and has to be discovered and understood, was neither to romanticize madness nor to deny its existence. However, his views were unequivocally against the grain of conventional psychiatry and the stories circulating about his personal life and the company he kept amongst famous people, only served to undermine him and eventually to marginalize him. He died in 1989.

Mad to be Normal presents Laing's own words, about his work and about his life. It is the most complete record on Laing, by Laing. Entertaining, maddening, surprising, impressive, occasionally scurrilous, and evoking a compelling portrait of the heady and sometimes self-regarding mood of the 1960s and early '70s, this book necessitates a reassessment of Laing and his work; work which is part of a lengthier and on-going process concerned with the routine care of those disturbed in mind.

Dr Bob Mullan is a documentary film maker and author of a number of books, including *Are Mothers Really Necessary?*, a study of John Bowlby and attachment theory.

MAD TO BE NORMAL

Conversations with R.D. Laing

Bob Mullan

Free Association Books / London

Published in 1995 by
Free Association Books Ltd
57 Warren Street, London W1P 5PA

Copyright © *Mad to be Normal*, Bob Mullan, 1995
Copyright © The words of R.D. Laing, the R.D. Laing Estate, 1995

A CIP record for this book is available from
the British Library

ISBN 1 85343 395 0 pbk

Impression: 99 98 97   6   5   4   3

Text and illustrations designed by Ray Addicott
Cover designed by Jutta Laing

Typeset from the author's disk in 10 on 12pt Minster Book

Printed in the EC by The Cromwell Press

CONTENTS

Though your face is beautiful, the
cage of your soul is of wood; run away
from me or you will burn, for my
tongue is a flame.

Jalal al-Din Rumi [1]

PREFACE

The main fact of life for me is love or its absence. Whether
life is worth living depends for me on whether there is love
in life. Without a sense of it, or even the memory of an
hallucination of it, I think I would lose heart completely.

R.D. Laing The Facts of Life [2]

R.D. Laing has a number of reputations. People believe quite
different things about both him and the views it is claimed he
held, and equally there are a variety of opinions as to his
intellectual worth. His reputations arise, mainly, from two
sources: gossip and vivid stories concerning his personal life
and state of mind; and his books, lectures, and psychiatric
practice – such information often of a secondhand nature,
already having been selectively interpreted before being
passed on. The sheer range of often contradictory reputations
that have been attributed to Laing remind us of the blind
men in Rumi's famous story. When they were made to touch
an elephant, each described it according to the part of the
body his hands had touched; to one the elephant appeared
like a throne, to another like a fan, or a water pipe, or like a
pillar. But none was able to imagine what the whole animal
would look like.[3] As is the case of R.D. Laing, no coherent
rounded portrait has yet emerged.

It was with this in mind that, in early 1988, I approached
Laing and his literary agent with a request to take on the role
of official biographer: I was seeking access and cooperation,
without any ultimate veto on Laing's part once the book had
been written. After a number of meetings and a stream of
synopses, I was pleasantly surprised to receive their blessing.
R.D. Laing, or Ronnie as he became known to me, was
always forthcoming in information, documentation, memory,
time and support. He was *always* at pains to point out that it
was *my* biography, and that he was merely supplying help and
his version of the events I was interested in.

I felt I was making good progress when he unexpectedly died
in August, 1989. Soon afterwards it became apparent that I no
longer would be afforded the continued generous access to

papers, correspondence and all those items necessary for the biographer's task. After a number of acrimonious exchanges, I left the stage and quietly sulked.

To the executors of Ronnie's estate I handed over boxes of precious material which indeed did now belong to them, although originally they had been given to me for my use. However, there were a number of tapes I kept which were recordings of conversations with Ronnie that had taken place in Kitzbuhel, London and Glasgow. There were indeed hundreds of hours of taped conversations, as well as hundreds more carried out off the record. It was only when I learned of forthcoming biographies of R.D. Laing that I decided to edit these *taped* conversations and publish them.

Why? A number of reasons. Ronnie only managed one *formal* memoir, *Wisdom, Madness and Folly*,[4] which took the story only up to 1957, three years before the publication of *The Divided Self*.[5] There are, of course, fragments elsewhere as well as disguised autobiography in other volumes, but no formal continuation of the story *from his point of view*. His own version of the R.D. Laing story would provide material and a starting point for biographers as well as contradictory arguments and memories. Additionally, I decided to pursue the project because the tapes provide an insightful description of modern social and intellectual history, a period which he partly created and in which he was a visible and prominent participant.

Why R.D. Laing in the first place? As a psychology student disenchanted with learning theory, physiological psychology, laboratory experimentation, statistics and so on, when my interest was in understanding the human condition, his books – especially *The Politics of Experience and the Bird of Paradise*[6] – seemed a revelation. His anger at the inhumanity of the psychiatric profession, his description of 'normal life', his analysis of family life and his understanding of the dignity of subjective experience struck a resonance with me. It was the spirit in which he wrote that so appealed, a lone voice in the psychiatric profession speaking of oppression *and* liberation. And it was the power of the writing itself: the words, sentences, phrases. He woke me up.

It is in this context that I have followed R.D. Laing's career over the years, and have assessed him thus not solely in terms of the specific issues surrounding the aetiology of schizophrenia and patterns of family communication. Rather I have come to see him as a radical thinker attempting to grapple with some of the taken-for-granted yet complex issues of human experience in an increasingly regimented and disenchanted world.

It is worth noting that many people came to know R.D. Laing not so much through his books but rather in his consulting rooms. There they did not seek his psychological perspective or even his therapeutic disposition. Rather what they sought was *him*. It perhaps cannot be emphasized strongly enough that the true legacy of R.D. Laing is contained in the lives of the people he touched with his insight, actions, advice and presence. He truly was a lover of people. He was also the first to admit that he was no saint.

I wish to acknowledge the help of Helen McGregor who painstakingly transcribed the tapes, and Jutta Laing for the photographs included in the volume.

Finally, I have had to check the innumerable names, titles, and words that Ronnie used which were not of common parlance. I hope I have done him justice, but any mistakes that remain are obviously mine.

Note
Throughout the text *italicized* words in Laing's speech (other than publication titles or foreign words) are where he seemed to be placing emphasis.

ACKNOWLEDGEMENTS

The publishers are grateful to John Haynes for permission to reproduce the photographs that appear on the book's cover and for photographs 3, 4 and 5 which appear in the book. Similarly, thanks are given to Dorothee von Greiff for her permission to reproduce photographs 1 and 2 which appear in the book.

The publishers are especially grateful to Jutta Laing for her design of the book's cover and for her help throughout.

INTRODUCTION

Mental hospitals and psychiatric units admit, routinely, every day of the week, people who are sent 'in' for non-criminal conduct, but for conduct which their nearest and dearest relatives, friends, colleagues and neighbours find insufferable. This is our society's only resolution to this unlivable impasse. If they refuse to go away, or can't or won't fend for themselves, it is our only way to keep people out of the company that can't stand them.

R.D. Laing, *Wisdom, Madness and Folly*

R.D. Laing represents a number of different things to different people as perceived through the pages of his books, the lectures he gave and the clinical practice he engaged in. From imaginative and compassionate analyses of schizophrenia; to libertarian views on the rights of crazy individuals; to the explication of the patterns of family relationships, both 'normal' and potentially destructive; and to the psychological poetry of *Knots*, controversy has always followed. Sadly, it is his critique of conventional psychiatry alone of his corpus that he will almost certainly be remembered and judged by. *Sadly* because much of what is attributed to him is, in fact, the beliefs of others. Perhaps more tragically is the fact that the experiment he was involved in – Kingsley Hall, London, a medication-free asylum – ended in chaos, and will be seen as evidence of his irrelevance. Too few people pause for a moment and imagine the courage and sheer innovation involved; the modern western world is a drug culture, yet here was an attempt to do something different for the benefit of those suffering mental misery without psychopharmacology. To evaluate places like Kingsley Hall fairly, we would have to live for a number of decades within a quite different culture and socio-economic environment.

What did R.D. Laing *actually* say about the institution of psychiatry? In a few brief but tightly argued pages in *Wisdom, Madness and Folly*, he attempts an exercise in clarification.

The problem of conventional psychiatry centres on an issue he has placed at the centre of *all* his writings, namely the objective/subjective disjunction. 'Psychiatry tries to be as scientific, impersonal and objective as possible towards what is most personal and subjective' is the way he describes the disordered suffering which psychiatrists attempt to treat. Such suffering, Laing asserts, 'has to do with what are our most personal and private thoughts and desires' (1986:146). It is not merely a matter, however, of conceptual confusion or pure scientism. Within the context of western medicine, psychiatry alone is quite unique. It is the only division of medicine that insists on treating people in the absence of any known physical pathology; it 'treats' *conduct* alone, in the absence of symptoms and signs of illness of the usual kind; and it is the only division of medicine that treats people against their will, in any way it likes – to the point of imprisoning patients.

The accusation that Laing idealized mental misery has fallen heavily on his shoulders. His counter-claim is that he has never 'idealised mental suffering or romanticised despair, dissolution, torture or terror'. In the same passage he also claims that he never said that parents, or society, 'caused' mental misery, genetically or environmentally: 'I have never denied the existence of patterns of mind and conduct that are excruciating. I have never called myself an anti-psychiatrist' (1986:8). However, he is at one with such so-called anti-psychiatrists in believing that, by and large, conventional psychiatry functions to exclude and repress those elements society wants excluded and repressed. Laing further clarifies his own position in the following passage:

> If I were being driven frantic by mental and emotional torment that nothing I or anyone or any drug could stop I might beg for electric shocks. Other people might beg to have electric shocks. The critical issue is the politics of the matter. Who has the power to do what to whom against whose will? (1986:23)

Laing has consistently argued for alternative perceptions of mental misery and alternative 'therapeutics'. Much of his disagreement with conventional institutional psychiatry comes from his belief that the core features of psychiatric practice belong to the sphere of social power and structure rather than to medical therapeutics. Such elements may well be 'therapeutic' but, argues Laing, there is still no clinical, scientific or medical evidence of any kind to support their use.

In the early part of his psychiatric career he expressed the desire to treat his patients in ways different from conventional methods. He wanted, quite simply, to see what would happen if he did so. His attitude was frowned upon, and he was, it was said, abdicating his medical responsibilities: 'It's like refusing to give a diabetic insulin. To encourage a schizophrenic to talk to you is like encouraging a haemophiliac to bleed' (1986:19).

Conventional, institutional, establishment psychiatrists and non-conformists like R.D. Laing do not appear to engage in any meaningful or constructive debate with each other. Unwarranted accusations and claims are regularly advanced: for instance, Martin Roth and Jerome Kroll in their combatitively titled *The Reality of Mental Illness*[7] claim that writers like Laing often ignore the 'very tangible devastation which mental illness imposes upon patients and their family. Job loss, family disruption, economic hardship, loss of educational opportunities, and social drift downwards are all frequent consequences, rather than causes, of serious mental illness' (1986:2–3). Such naïve yet mischievous arguments have become the currency of the debate, a debate which concerns the understanding and 'treatment' of those disturbed in mind.

R.D. Laing: An Introductory Sketch

Ronald David Laing was born at 5.15 p.m. on 7 October 1927 in Glasgow. In the highly descriptive prose which characterizes much of his writing, he notes that he lived through the 'end of gaslit streets and horses and carts, the Spanish Civil War' and, of course, the Second World War. He adds that, in the year before his birth, tanks were out in the streets of Glasgow, on Winston Churchill's orders.

Compared to many of the individuals and families who populate his studies and writings, his childhood was one of relative contentment: 'For most of the time ... provided I looked all right, as long as my thoughts were good and my heart was pure, I was as free as a bird' (1986:35). Early life was divided between school, home, music, Sunday school and play. He did not neglect his prayers, though he constantly thought about what belief in God really meant. The young Laing read voraciously and widely, especially in European literature and philosophy.

He commenced his medical studies in 1944 at Glasgow University, and within the same year he had been inside a mental hospital for the first time when, with other medical students, he paid a traditional visit to the Royal Gartnavel Mental Hospital, although Laing considers that his first actual psychiatric encounter was with his father – his 'first patient' as he put it. In his last year at school his father suffered a 'nervous breakdown' and was subsequently laid off work for three months. Laing recalls that for the most part of that time his father lay in bed, without medication, and that he diligently 'sat beside him for some time every day'. Indeed, David Laing spent the last 10 years of his life confined in a Glasgow psychogeriatric unit. Again, Laing's reflections on his father's fate are instructive: 'During the whole ten years nothing in the way they treated my dad rubbed me the wrong way. He was no exception'. He adds that he therefore knew that 'psychiatric institutions need not be inhumane' (1986:79).

After failing all of his medical examinations the first time round, Laing spent six months before retaking them as a full-time unqualified intern at the psychiatric unit at Stobhill Hospital, Glasgow. Among the experiences gained was a first-hand view of the survivors of *encephalitis lethargica*, 80 men and woman who had caught what was then thought to be the influenza in 1927. In fact, they were victims of an epidemic that swept Europe, which started off just like the flu, but which in fact was an inflammation of the brain that either killed or caused the victim to linger on for years demented, drooling, contorted and paralysed.

On graduation, the newly qualified Dr Laing took up an internship in a neurosurgical unit, skipping the usual two postgraduate years in the practice of surgery and general medicine. This unit, at Killearn near Loch Lomond, he described as being in one of the 'most beautiful parts of the world, comparable at its sweetest and most delicately lyrical to Kashmir'. At Killearn he encountered a man destined to be his mentor: Joe Schorstein, 18 years his senior, the son of a Hasidic rabbi from near Vienna, who became Laing's spiritual father and invaluable guide to European literature.

In 1951 Laing was exempted from military service because of his asthma. Consequently, he expected to go instead to the University of Basel after a fruitful correspondence with the Swiss psychiatrist and philosopher Karl Jaspers. However, a change in British Army rules saw the inclusion of medical grades, so he was to spend two years in the army.

On conscription he chose psychiatry over neurology and made his way to the Central British Army Psychiatric Unit at Netley where he worked in an insulin unit as well as neurotic and psychotic divisions. In *Wisdom, Madness and Folly*, Laing recalls that at this time the idea of 'death comas' was constantly being talked about. In deep insulin-coma the patient comes very close to actual physical death, and indeed sometimes dies. Hence the question was asked, 'might not this near-death be therapeutic?'. As Laing explains, 'The brain is chemically poisoned in some way and the mind is full of unintelligible gibberish. Wash it out, wipe it out, clean the brain and cleanse the mind; how about a fresh start, a new beginning, a rebirth, a resurrection?' (1986:92).

His days were spent in the traditional army mental hospital type of ward environment: neurosis, psychosis, alcoholism, battle neurosis, psychopathy and other categories. It was at this time that he began to 'hang out' with patients alone in their padded cells. Laing believed that despite the rantings of manic thought-disordered patients, he could almost understand what they were actually getting at. At the same time, however, he became uneasy at the so-called 'therapeutic' value of insulin and electric shocks, not to mention the fearful lobotomy. Despite this unease, his urgent fascinations with mental misery and its understanding did not diminish.

After a spell in charge of the psychiatric wards of Catterick Military Hospital he left the army in 1953, at the age of 26. His next destination was Glasgow's Royal Gartnavel Mental Hospital. Unlike army psychiatry which was not involved with long-term custodial care, he encountered patients at Gartnavel who had been hospitalized – incarcerated – for 10, 20 or more years and some since the previous century. He began to experiment with treatments which allowed patients autonomy, self-control and freedom. They were taken from wards and given a day-room experience instead.

Two years later, Laing moved to a post as Senior Registrar at the Southern General Hospital, Glasgow, in the Department of Psychological Medicine. Here the writing of *The Divided Self* began. It was here too that he saw the answers to 'why a lot of people in hospital are to be found only outside hospital', and that a stethoscope, tendon hammer, pocket torch and ophthalmoscope would not further his understanding of mental misery. In 1956 he moved to the Tavistock Clinic in London to see day patients and to undergo four years' training at the Institute of Psychoanalysis.

What may be termed the 'existential tradition' lies at the core of Laing's writings. Common to all existential thinkers – Kierkegaard, Heidegger, Buber, Tillich – is the basic principle: 'The person is more than a thing and cannot be adequately formulated in the terminology of natural science' (Lomas, 1968:119).[8] The person is to be seen as a whole being, and agent of his or her actions.

The Divided Self was published in 1960 while Laing was working at the Tavistock Clinic researching family dynamics and doing clinical practice. In an analysis of an interview with a patient (carried out and described by Kraepelin), Laing demonstrates that the psychiatrist is too preoccupied with *categorizing* the behaviour of the patient to notice that the 'psychotic' utterances of the latter are 'reasonable, if disguised, objections to being merely classified and not treated as a person'. (Lomas, 1968:120). Laing concerns himself with those who are treated as a thing, rather than a person: and with the schizoid, alienated states which *result* from such treatment.

In his attempt at understanding such schizoid, alienated states Laing develops the central notion of *ontological security*. The basically ontologically secure person will encounter all the hazards of life – social, ethical, spiritual, biological – from a centrally firm centre of his own and other people's reality and identity. If life experience has not enabled the person to acquire this 'primary ontological security', he or she is forced into a continuous struggle to maintain a sense of their own being. In this weak position they may fear *'engulfment'* by others, fear the *'implosion'* of external reality, and fear *'petrification'* – of becoming no more than a thing in the world of the other. The total 'embodied self', faced with disadvantageous conditions, may split into two parts; a disembodied 'inner self', felt by the person to be the real part of themselves, and a 'false self', embodied but dead and futile, which puts up a front of conformity to the world.

It was not merely the application of the existential perspective to schizophrenia and other psychotic states that singled out Laing's approach, additionally there were the practical implications involved – the patient's intelligibility existed and had to be discovered and understood, not routinely dismissed. This view went unequivocally against the grain: conventional psychiatry had neither the time nor the patience, nor seemingly the desire to partake of his view.

Self and Others,[9] first published in 1961, continued Laing's explorations into the nature of individual and interpersonal experience: 'I shall try to depict persons within a social system or "nexus" of persons, in order to try to understand some of the ways in which each affects each person's experience of himself and of how interaction takes form. Each contributes to the other's fulfilment or destruction' (1961:9). A number of years later Laing co-authored *Interpersonal Perception* (1966)[10] in which the 'person perception psychology' of *Self and Others* was further developed in order to describe human relationships. At the time, it was apparent that there was a danger of this useful and imaginative method becoming lost or submerged in mathematical formulae.

The controversy which has surrounded Laing began in earnest with the 1964 publication of *Sanity, Madness and the Family*,[11] co-authored with Aaron Esterson and based on research at the Tavistock Clinic on families, one of whose members had been diagnosed as schizophrenic.* Once again Laing was at pains to understand and support the patient's point of view, which he felt was often nearer the truth than that of the rest of the family. 'Delusions' of persecution were, in fact, picturesque accounts of what was actually being done to the patient by her family at a certain level of experience. Her identity was being crushed because the family colluded in quite subtle ways to invalidate her experience of life, causing her to doubt the evidence of her own senses. Faced with insufferable circumstances and strange experiences, she herself comes to behave in a strange way, but the best solution as far as the 'victim' is concerned: making an intolerable situation tolerable, if somewhat bizarre.

Laing and Esterson's description of the pathogenic influences exerted in the here-and-now by the family challenged both traditional theories about the origin of schizophrenia as well as psychoanalytic accounts which were still preoccupied with early life experiences, particularly of infancy.

Laing was seen to be blaming parents, pointing the finger at families, and refusing to acknowledge the part the patients

*The study was confined to female schizophrenics.

themselves might well contribute to the situation. He himself
now began to be given the label of 'troublesome'.

Kingsley Hall, London, was an experiment which began in
1965 with Laing as one of its prime innovators. A house where
the division between staff and patients was somewhat blurred
(and indeed where such labels were deliberately not used), it
was a medication-free zone where people attempted to live with
and through their 'illnesses'. It was also a chaotic zone and yet
another activity which estranged Laing from his more conventional colleagues. The experiment was to last five years.

The culture of the 1960s and R.D. Laing appeared to be a
marriage made in heaven. A lonely hearts ad in New York's
Village Voice read 'Two chicks who dig Coltrane, The Dead
and R.D. Laing seek compatible mates', and for a while he
undoubtedly was centre stage and seen as arch-seer and
prophet-in-chief.[12] The 1960s and 1970s were also the decades of the development and use of hallucinogenic drugs;
again stories quickly spread that Laing was using such drugs,
especially LSD 25, in 'therapy' and otherwise. Robert Hewison ironically notes, in his essay on art and society in the '60s
that one of the 'unwritten books of the sixties is a projected
collaboration between [Alex] Trocchi, William Burroughs and
R.D. Laing on a definitive anthology of "Drugs and the
Creative Process" ...' (1988:128).[13] Jonathan Green mean-
while reports an incident when Syd Barrett of Pink Floyd was
taken to Laing with his LSD 'problem': 'Laing didn't say
much. We tried to take what he said literally, we tried to use
the inner meaning of what he was saying, we tried to change
the objective situations' (1989:167).[14] The strand of '60s
libertarianism coincided with Laing's psycho-political theories,
and it gave him plenty of opportunity to express them: 'One
lunchtime Laing said, "where can you scream? It's a serious
question: where can you go in society and scream?" ...'
(Durden-Smith, 1989:209).[15]

Laing's reputation and international fame peaked in 1967
with the publication of *The Politics of Experience and the Bird of
Paradise*, the latter an essay *reputed* to have been written while
the author was on LSD. On the one hand, the volume became
an American campus classic and Laing *the* world's most 'controversial psychiatrist', while others saw the book rather as an
unfortunate fall from grace: 'There is certainly nothing in the
original insight of *The Divided Self* to necessitate the stance of
The Politics of Experience ... [with the] ... obsessive fixation upon

the familiar objects of radical discontent – upon the family, the bourgeoisie, capitalism, the established moral order, upon morality itself' (Scruton, 1985:46–47). This critique from the avowed conservative perspective of Roger Scruton continued the attack, claiming that Laing's 'facile doctrines', cant words, and 'above all its unscrupulous sentimentalization of individual experience', adapt it 'perfectly for the market in cut-price ideas' (1985:52).[16]

Other critics argued that Laing had romanticized psychosis, turning a tragedy into a potentially fulfilling transcendental experience; a mere 'episode' into a journey. Laing was certainly determined to reconceptualize psychoses: 'Madness need not be all breakdown. It may also be break-through. It is potentially liberation and renewal as well as enslavement and existential death' (1967:110). This truism was perhaps couched in an unfortunate turn of phrase.

The Politics of Experience and the Bird of Paradise did not read like a conventional psychiatric text – with his use of poetry and rhetoric, in addition to argument and research – hence its readership was wide and varied. Laing's earlier theme of attempting to understand and describe an individual's experience as mediated by their interactions with others was expanded in this book, whereby the societal straight jacket of conformity placed on every child became the focus:

A child born today in the UK stands a ten times greater chance of being admitted to a mental hospital than to a University, and about one fifth of mental hospital admissions are diagnosed schizophrenic. This can be taken as an indication that we are driving our children mad more effectively than we are genuinely educating them. Perhaps it is our very way of educating them that is driving them mad. (1967:87).

Such utterances were seen by some as wisdom, by others as cliché. Laing's work was now seen as centrally *psycho-political*, an impression reinforced by his involvement in a two week congress, the 'Dialectics of Liberation', held in the summer of 1967 in London. Participants included Herbert Marcuse, Stokely Carmichael, Allen Ginsberg and Lucien Goldman. Thousands paid the price of admission. Laing's own contribution, the ironically titled 'The Obvious', was wide ranging and concerned the context of social events. In his lecture he talked of the range of social contexts that exist, including the ultimate 'total social world system', and how such contexts do not 'exist out there on some periphery' of social space; 'they pervade the interstices of all that is comprised by them' (in Cooper, 1968:15).[17]

This version of psycho-politics not only appalled the right, but it did also not impress the left. Peter Sedgwick, his chief critic, consistently and relentlessly argued that, while Marx held the view that 'social being' determined 'social conscious-ness', Laing was never able to accept such a view. Indeed, according to Sedgwick, the 'largest social unit that Laing is able to handle is that of the extra-familial personal network of a family, a potential face-to-face assembly which the good therapist will strive to reconvene' (1982:114). Sedgwick argued that while Laing talked of connections between large social structures and individual experience, nothing concrete was spelled out.

In 1971, as the Kingsley Hall experiment was coming to its predictably confused and chaotic end, Laing left, dramatically and unexpectedly, for what was then Ceylon. There, and, later, in India, he continued and developed his intellectual interest in and practical understanding of yoga and Buddhist meditations. On his return the following year, he soon became an almost reinvented individual; his best-selling *Knots* had been published and, resplendent in pinstripe suit, he lectured to large audiences and engaged in private practice.

Knots (1970)[18] was a somewhat short and playful volume concerned with the nuances of interpersonal behaviour, couched in poetic language: aspects of what Laing considered to be the deadly duologues that silently mar relationships. Some loved it, others saw it as evidence that R.D. Laing had now retired from the serious psycho-political arena. Nonethe-less, *Knots* achieved a wide ranging and international success and was performed on stage and recorded. Laing became the Harold Pinter of psychiatry.

But whether Laing's books and ideas have affected the routine care of those disturbed in mind is an almost impossi-ble question to answer. He certainly rattled the cage, and many therapists, social workers and the like have been undoubtedly sensitized to matters of individual liberty and the importance of the social context of 'illness'. However, the establishment itself closed ranks 'and psychiatrists and politi-cians adopted a defensive position' (Ramon, 1988:11).[19] It is not, however, a closed chapter. The arguments and the tentative, small-scale experiments of Laing and others are merely part of a lengthier process, the outcome of which is yet to be settled.[20]

A concern with all aspects of *biopolitics* is how Laing has described his post-1970 writings: most notably, *The Facts of Life*[21] with its concern with issues of power over and descriptions of the birth and pre-birth experience – 'if you were to die now, and be reconceived tonight ... which woman would you choose to spend the first nine months of your next lifetime inside of?' (1976:31) – and *The Voice of Experience*[22] in which he continued his life-long attack on scientism.

Laing's last *published* book – his memoir, *Wisdom, Madness and Folly* – is an account of aspects of his life up to and including the writing of *The Divided Self*, his first book. Further memoirs, articles, collections and volumes were to follow: as throughout his life he had it all planned.[23]

1. FAMILY LIFE

In this first set of conversations, R.D. Laing talks about his childhood in 1930s Glasgow. He reflects on such matters as discipline, his health and state of mind, and the values taught him by his parents. In particular, he discusses the nuances of the marriage of his parents, David and Amelia.

Memories of his adolescence and first loves are recalled as are his student days.

Finally, he talks of the families he has himself created, especially his first marriage to Anne which produced five children and, subsequently, to Jutta, a marriage which resulted in three more children.

Wisdom, Madness and Folly is a vivid and at times unsettling account of an interpretation of a life up to the age of 30. Laing's selection of events and incidents is, in itself, instructive. For instance he tells, in great detail, of the 'sound thrashing' he received for eating a forbidden Jelly Baby, while he also recalls the tragedy of being told that Santa Claus was in fact his own parents: 'Santa Claus was them. I hated Santa Claus and them for being the same ... I was physically panic stricken. Why? It was an extreme intellectual crisis in a five year old' (1986:41).

In Wisdom, Madness and Folly *you picked on particular things like Santa Claus and the Jelly Baby incident. What do they tell you about your childhood?*

In *The Bird of Paradise*, I had a sentence there of wandering through one of my many childhoods. I've got many childhoods, you might say, they are all one, but I think every child has, this vast number, and looking back its as if there's a whole world of them, and in one gaze when you look back at a particular sequence of events you recall, or a particular type of event that you organise together, one reminds you of the other. In *Wisdom, Madness and Folly*, I was picking on three or four what I would call epitomizing instances or paradigm examples of what from the point of view of my subsequent life as a psychiatrist at the time of writing the book, looking back in a sense on, both my time as a psychiatrist in the '50s up to the '60s and the making of that creature from 1927 when I was born, there seemed to be a number of things in my childhood that came to mind – Santa Claus, sweeties, all sorts of issues about what is the case and what is not the case, what is real and what is not real, what is true and what is false, what is being honest and what is being dishonest and in what sense such issues are important to some people and not to others and in what sense they became important to me, personally, and with this array of things, our relationships with each other. With this array of personal interest I became engaged in the theory and practice of what is called psychiatry. So I continued to look at what I saw in the domain of psychiatry in the light of these things that had come to be important to me, and one of the things that quickly became apparent to me that these things that were important to me personally did not seem to be important to psychiatry, in theory or in practice, but they seemed to be very important to the people called patients, who seemed to be occupied, many of them preoccupied, with very little else than these things ...

What kind of basis is there in your childhood for your later writings on family pathology? Must everybody go through those experiences because of the simple fact that they are in a family?

Everyone's got to go through whatever experiences they have to go through from the time of conception to whenever they're picked up as doing what, and no one comes to any walk of life whether it's psychiatry or not as a *tabula rasa*. Psychiatry has itself already established a form, a mode, it's become an institution, it has corporate bodies, it's got its own initiation ceremonies, where you cannot be a psychiatrist except by the ways you have to become one and you bring in to that your self as it has formed so far, intellectually, emotionally, libidinally and every other respect. To say that does not imply any assent to a particular theory of, say, transference, a particular type of fashionable psychoanalytic type theory of the nature of the relevance of one's past to one's present, that the whole of one's life, past present and one's future intentions were without – well, as I would say phenomenologically – that I'm not sure whether some definitions, like Foucault rejected Husserlian phenomenology completely because of its, you might say, unsocial character, but when you say that Bowlby was very English, well you couldn't say that I was very English. I am indelibly very Glasgow, very much the southside of Glasgow. Anyone in Glasgow knows I'm not from Bearsden, anyone who's a Glaswegian can place me in the southside of Glasgow.

What are southside Glaswegians like?

[laughs] I don't think I can say that, I can say much more what someone from Kelvinside is like, you might say, than what someone from the southside of Glasgow is like. There is a great deal of parts of the southside of Glasgow; just on the south of the Clyde where I grew up was the area generally designated as the Gorbals, a very heavy slum area which extended for about a mile and a half or so south and then from one side of a street to the other you moved out of that territory into lower middle class, that's the working-class people who liked to regard themselves as lower middle class but not working class. Then another layer of that past Queen's Park up to further south, you got into a sort of middle-class outlying area of Glasgow – you couldn't quite call it a suburb – and then beyond that you were out into the country, a car drive from the Clyde, say, in the middle of central Glasgow in under half an hour.

Glasgow is almost unique I think as a city in having so many different dialects between one side of the street and another side of the street. Someone who doesn't know these two dialects in Glasgow might not be able to understand. I have to be in a Glasgow pub talking to a Glaswegian and I could switch into one or two. I can speak two or three Glasgow dialects which is almost say, more than a European can speak two or three languages ...

What was the address of where you lived?

21 Ardbeg Street, Glasgow – there is an island called Ardbeg. About 10 years ago, 12 years ago maybe, a Canadian film team made a documentary series of films called *People In Cities*; Anthony Burgess and Rome, Mai Zetterling and Stockholm, Peter Ustinov and Leningrad, and R.D. Laing and Glasgow. The film won a second prize at a Czechoslovak television festival and it has been shown in Glasgow. The film maker got a lot of footage, went round Glasgow and he filmed 21 Ardbeg Street and up the first landing.

Is it still standing now?

Yes ... It's a Corporation, red stone ground floor, one-up, two-up, three-level tenement building which is very much standing now. These schemes that were built in the '20s are still well kept up by the – they've been selling them now, as they have been all over the place – Glasgow Corporation. The radical Labour left has objected to the selling off of these things that were meant for the Glasgow Corporation employees and working people.

In the house were there any objects – artefacts – particular things that were significant, important, interesting, colourful? Books, paintings, furnishings, carpets?

Everything was carefully chosen, and everything that was in the house, as far as I know, had been bought with my mother's money. When she died a few years ago she left £20,000. I didn't know, I knew she had a little bit put aside, but I was surprised at £20,000 – well she spent practically nothing on herself or anyone else. She did buy the furniture and the curtains and the blinds and the carpet and after that my father bought the linoleum that surrounded the carpet in the living room and the bedroom and the hall and the other room. I loved the furniture.

My mother kept three pieces of the furniture in the flat that she and my father moved to when I was in the army. They moved from the house I was born in to a comparable flat in a comparable Corporation development that was two or three miles further south of Glasgow and much the same type of flat. They had a thing that was called a couch, or I think we would call it a settee, with a back and arms made of wood and upholstered, with a braiding between the upholstery and the wood with these round-topped pins that went round it and a small amount of the wood was curved. I don't know what you call the name of these chairs that have got that shape of leg, I loved these curves on the settee and that shape of the chair legs, there were four of them for the table in the room.

There was a black, baby grand, Challen piano. It was like a cello – well again, I don't have to explain what the shape of a baby grand piano is but like the shape of a violin, like the shape of a cello, the shape of a baby grand piano – I think that's a lovely shape and the piano was in what was called the front room. One up, you entered the door, there was a small lobby, front bedroom, front room, kitchenette where there was a washing line, a pulley, an oven and a washing gas round boiler for washing clothes, a small sink by the window. On the right-hand side there was the bedroom, front room, on the left-hand side kitchen and then between the kitchenette there was a passage which was called the bunker. Coal was stacked in the house about half-way up. Coal on one side of it stacked up, and then a bathroom, bath, WC and basin.

I had no idea that there were other plumbing arrangements, that a bathroom might be a room in which there was just a bath and not a WC. There was a bath, WC and bath and the back room which was a small room and was my father's room and later became mine. There were two pictures hung up on the wall of the front room, the living room facing the fireplace. As you walk in, there is the bedroom, the front room, kitchenette and the back room. The back room was where my father was, the bedroom was where my mother had a double bed and I had a single bed and there was a bedroom suite which was walnut or – I remember later – it wasn't the same wood all the way through, it was some veneer that would come up in bubbles as it got older. Well the bed was a double bed facing the window and at the window there was a dressing table with an oval mirror and a small dressing table – that was my mother's. There was a wardrobe which had two doors, one door opened and there was a full length inner wardrobe mirror on the inside of that door and a space and some drawers at the bottom of that compartment that this door opened and shut.

What were you saying about mirrors?

I was fascinated not so much by my personal mirror image – I'm careful who I say this to because in my world, looking into a mirror too much is supposed to be, you know! [laughs] I don't know whether you know that in 16th century Italy, you had to have a licence in a papal state to possess a mirror. It was like hashish is nowadays. You could be busted for having a mirror in your house if you didn't have a licence to own a mirror because it was condemned as smacking of heresy. There was a suspicion of heresy about owning a mirror. If you look up the history of mirrors in the West, in

Italy mirrors became much more available domestically, until then mirrors were rather expensive items that were reserved for the rich because they had developed a fashionable practise of speculation – speculation was a sort of possibly slightly heretical gnostic thing of looking in the mirror as a so called meditation exercise – gazing in a mirror for too long was called speculation. The original word speculation is for looking in the mirror. Well of course I didn't know that at the time but I speculated quite a bit.

What were the paintings of?

There were no paintings. There were these two portraits of – quarter length portraits of, fair sized sepia faded or brownish tint – of the two photographs of my mother and father reproduced in the *Wisdom, Madness and Folly* book. I don't remember the presence on the wall of anything else. The walls had a border, a little wooden strip, and every so often, I think it was expected to be once every two years – my father would never dream of paying a painter to paint – there would be the business of scraping off the old wallpaper and laying out on the table the strips and cutting them up and I used to do that as I got older. You put a border on and a little floral thing at the edge; we boasted, as the saying goes, that we had a standing lamp with a lamp shade. For a while we had a budgie in a cage.

Who chose that, your mother?

Yes, that was another thing. I got attached to this budgie and I got home from school one day and the budgie was ill and she had thrown it out, taken it up in a newspaper and thrown it out in the rubbish in the back green.

Was there anything on the mantelpiece?

Oh, on the mantelpiece there was – I don't remember whether the wood was walnut – but there was an oval-faced clock with a white face with two keys that were kept under the clock and you opened the front thing and you wound the clock up. I don't know why it had *two* keys. Beside the side window, on the window sill, was a radio and my father, of course, in his capacity as an electrical mechanical engineer could repair radios and knew about valves and stuff like that. In the kitchenette he stored his tools in a tool box. I suppose they were simply the tools of a professional workman with files and screwdrivers and so on. I wasn't allowed to touch his tools; I regret that I was headed off from that and I hadn't enough sort of persistence to find my way into that via school lab or somebody else's house.

When I got married in the first place and hadn't any money at all, I had to for the first time make a real point of getting a screwdriver, and I also papered, and even laid a cement path in Harlow New Town in the garden, but I never got into being a handyman to say the least of it. I remember the first time I was in Paris in my first year at university to visit Marcelle [first girlfriend], and this was the first time I had ever been out of Scotland. Took a bus down with some students, and one of the lights blew with a fuse gone and my father had never let me mend a fuse. So it seemed as though, I suppose in those days, the man, the male student, would mend the fuse and I didn't know how to do it. I think I must have blushed crimson and so one of the French girls took it from me in impatience and did it herself.

Some commentators make a big deal out of the fact that you slept in the same room as your mother. Did your father sleep in there as well?

No, no.

He never did?

They had stopped sleeping together after I was born. There are couples who stopped sleeping in the same bed together ...

That was normal?

That's normal, especially as you get older, you stop sleeping in the same bed together and my mother liked the double bed to herself and there was never any idea that I might crawl into her bed.

Not like they do these days?

Never any thought. I never saw my father and mother naked.

You undressed in the bathroom and came out with your pyjamas on, I didn't undress in front of mother. You wore pyjamas and you tied your pyjama cord decently so your penis wasn't hanging out or anything like that. So there was a bedroom, it's a rectangular room. Supposing that's a bedroom, this is the front window, this is the door, this is the wardrobe, this is the dressing table, this is my mother's double bed and this is my single bed.

That was it?

That was it. And when my mother dressed and undressed she did it as she saw fit without doing a striptease for my benefit. It wasn't repressed, there was no prurient play of sexual arousal, there was nothing sick about it at all. People who have not grown up in a working-class or lower middle-class background in Britain have no idea how simple it is, nothing arises.

Was it both of them who decided they didn't want to sleep together or was it predominantly your mum because she had had a baby?

They never talked about that in front of me. When I was in my late 20s and 30s, and before my father retired; when I had gone to London and I came back to Glasgow sometimes, I asked about that and he said, 'oh your mother put the bar up on that' and that was it.

I read recently that Philip Larkin said that his mother and father were awkward and that these things 'rub off' on you ... what rubbed off on you?

Well, in a way I wasn't a south Glaswegian because my father's father came from Aberdeen and he ended up in Glasgow from Aberdeen via Edinburgh. On my mother's side, her grandfather, my great grandfather had gone to Australia in 1852 so my mother was really an Australian. Her father left Australia and went around America and gravitated to Glasgow and I don't know why, by the end of World War I. She never regarded herself as a Glaswegian.

And as I say my father's family always saw themselves as Aberdonians and I was an only child who never went out to play with other children *at all*, outside of the front door, until I went to school, I was never out in the street playing on my own ...

The children came into the house?

No. No children ever entered this house. It was a very unusual childhood. Not so unusual in Glasgow; there is a type of Glasgow family that lives in a tenement and they have a child, or two children, and no one enters the house, except the family.

... even working-class children?

This family *I'm in* is not defined as by themselves. I mean, they didn't read any sociology. My mother took the stance of an embittered woman who had married my father who could have but *didn't* earn enough money to get her and us out of this hell that she was living in, where a guy upstairs went to work in the shipyards. This was a disgrace as far as my mother was concerned, that she had to live in a block of flats, that even if it had a bannister, even if it had a wooden railing, it hadn't any stained glass windows on the first landing, that she had to live under these circumstances. My father wouldn't address himself to earning money that at least would take us to a decent flat in Moss Park, a quarter of a mile further away from the Gorbals. So I was brought up in this family tension. The only child of my age or of any age that I remember as far as I know ever came in through our front door was my cousin who is an income tax inspector in Glasgow now. I'm three months older than him, he's the son of one of my mother's elder sisters, who for a while lived nearby in Glasgow. I did play with children, taken with my mother or my father to what was called in Glasgow a 'swingie' or children's playpark where you've got roundabouts and swings.

Why didn't they want children to come into the house? Because they were ashamed of the conditions? And why didn't they want you to play on the street?

Well I think there were three reasons. One is that my mother never had any friends, I don't think she *ever* had any friends. She might have things that are called friends as a girl but by the time I was born I don't think she had any friends; I don't think there was another woman that she ever visited to have a cup of tea in the afternoon, she never ever went to the theatre with any friend, or with anyone, she never went out with anyone to anyone's house.

Was that deliberate, I mean was she self-punishing or ...

Oh she didn't regard it as punishing. It would have been punishing to her to spend an afternoon with another human being. [laughs] A lot of people think my mother must have been terribly depressed and miserable and catatonic and, no, not at all. She went out shopping, there were one or two people she met in the street and talked to in the course of that activity once a day, and once a fortnight or so visited her mother and younger sister in Cathcart a couple of miles away and that was about the only house that she ever entered, I think, literally, except once a year she entered the door of my father's father's flat at New Year. So one reason [was that] by virtue of her marriage to my father, she had sunk down in the world; she just detested all the local environment and the people in it. So none of those people would come to the house, if there was someone who came from a proper house, like when I went to Hutcheson's Boys' Grammar School, most of the boys in my class came from proper homes, proper houses. For one thing everyone came from different parts of Glasgow, it wasn't a regional school, so that would be a big deal for one of them who came from a proper house to be brought round to this place, that would be a matter of shame. Either she was above one lot or she was beneath another lot.

I remember when I went to school at the age of five in the first place, there was one chap I brought round to the house and we looked at my *Pitt's Encyclopedia of World History* while my mother sat in her chair and he said two things that counted irrevocably against him. One was the only thing he could think of in all the questions, about all these little pictures of battles from Mongolia in the 13th century, which was great food for me considering my horizon ... [He said also] 'who were the goodies and who were the baddies?' I tried to explain to him that there were either no goodies and no baddies or I didn't know who were the goodies and who were the baddies; and the other thing was that he had a cold and a runny nose. The back of his hand had sort of slime on it, so he was never to enter the door again, or set foot in the house.

*Was he there in the first place only because he was of a lower
class?*

No, he was a friend of mine from class and I had vouched for
him, so she agreed to have him round, but never again. So
there was never anyone else that I invited or thought of
inviting round to the house again.

*Why was your mother bothered at the talk of goodies or baddies,
did she see herself as liberally minded?*

She thought all that sort of thing including God and belief in
God and all that as a whole lot of nonsense.

How would goodies or baddies come into it?

She never explained. [laughs] No, it was just 'a lot of nonsense',
sort of trash. She thought it categorized most of the things that
people thought, a whole lot of nonsense. The main thing was
the snobbery.

You say she was an embittered woman ...

Well, to say that she was an embittered woman is a bit too
vague, she wasn't embittered in every respect in her life, but
in terms of social position. I think I could safely say that –
she didn't make any bones about it – she did not like the
circumstances which she had to live in because of her
marriage with my father. I mean there's two sides to the
story; from my father's side there is someone you should go
and see, she is a delightful woman, my aunt Ethel, she lives
in Largs. She's 76, never married, she's my father's younger
sister. I've got two letters from her that she wrote me last
year which depict her memory of me as a baby and as a little
boy and what sort of life I had in that house at that time with
my mother and father. They are very vividly written ...

Did she disapprove of your mother?

Well, she is a very undisapproving person. She's got very clear
Scottish, Ayrshire, sort of Aberdeen blue eyes and I don't
think I've ever heard her say a bad word against anyone, she's
got a remarkably even, chirpy, cheery, equanimity about her. I

asked her a few questions about what she thought about mother and father when I was writing my memoirs and she didn't want me to put my mother down but at the same time she sees her, I think, very clearly.

Of course she sees my mother from the exact other point of view from me, because her whole view of my mother is of the mother she met which was always the mother outside of the house, and mother as a girl in Glasgow that was a total disaster for David, her big brother, to get married to. Why does he have to get married to her, when he was very popular, he sang, he was charming. After the musical soirees that he must have had in Alexandria in 1917, 1918, he was a year delayed in getting out of the Royal Air Corps and back to Glasgow, after all that, to come back to the southside of Glasgow and marry a moaner. You know, we thought he was going to marry someone who was just right for him, but he went and married her.

She was too dour?

Well, she was very beautiful. I don't think she ever said very much and I don't think he had any idea of what he was getting, when he opened the paper and found what was underneath it.

They were married for nine years before I was born and my mother always protested that she had no idea how it ever happened ...

If she was embittered solely about her social status, was her relationship with your father satisfactory then, or was he too mingled up with the fact that he was the reason for her low social status for her to enjoy him properly?

She never at any time got off on sexual pleasure, that must be a very big consideration.

But that wasn't unusual, or was it?

No, not at all, and a woman like Ethel, my aunt – I don't think she ever had a love affair, she had some boyfriends, I don't know whether she ever had sexual intercourse, it certainly hasn't dried her up or made her bitter or anything – she's one of these, a rather rare type, a very alive and engaging person. You wonder whether they ever a long time ago ever, they didn't obviously do it very much, but it hasn't affected their flesh, or their manner, a completely different type of woman. My mother had absolutely given up sexuality and I think this was a component ...

When you say it was nine years before you were born and she hadn't a clue how it happened, are you saying they didn't have sex for nine years or just very infrequently?

I'm sure they must have had sex for some time, but according to my mother, she didn't like it and ...

She told you this?

Oh yes, she told me this, she just didn't like it and she said *no* – what my father's expression is, she put the bar up. She did two things, she put the bar up on sex and she put the piano lid down. She used to accompany him on musical evenings, she played the piano quite well, if she ever played it at all. So this bond with him might be quite important to him as a singer, to marry someone who played the piano. Well she cut that out, she denied that completely, she never accompanied him. I don't remember ever as a child, her accompanying him, it was one of the motives of me getting into the piano to accompany him.

You consciously did it for his sake?

For the fun of it, because there he was singing and occasionally he had someone round to the house to rehearse and it was great, one of the things I saw myself doing was playing the piano.

It's too strong to say you felt sorry for him?

No, I didn't feel sorry for him at all. I had no sense of feeling sorry for him, or for her. They never asked me to feel sorry for them, I mean they never laid it on. My mother's way; I want to do justice to this, she was not miserable, I never felt that I was in the room with someone who was being miserable and depressed, it was quite clean energy. I didn't want to hang around her particularly, you know I was very glad to get out of the house.

What constituted her life, if she was embittered about her status? Were you her life in the end?

I seemed to be to me, a great deal of her life, but I don't know. For a number of years probably a great deal of her focus was on giving me the best of everything – was one of the expressions, from her side of it – but she spent the last 20 years of her life doing amazingly nothing, well, appearing to. Because I never see her when there's no one to see her, or when I'm not seeing her I don't know what she did when I wasn't there, but she seemed to spend a great deal of her time simply sitting in a chair in front of the fireplace, and keeping the house fairly impeccable. She was very particular about her three-room, small Corporation flat, and what she was thinking about I've not the faintest idea. She never read, I don't think there was a single book, I mean literally never read at all. She read the Glasgow newspaper and there were some programmes on the radio that she listened to and that was it. She never went to church, I never heard her singing, or whistling, or emitting any other sounds than words and very few of them. [laughs]

Can you clear up one thing. I think it's in The Facts of Life. *The report in there of other people's accounts of your father not wanting to admit that you were born, 'your mother going into decline' and you being looked after by nurses. Can you just clear that up, because you don't mention that in* Wisdom, Madness and Folly.

No. It's very interesting, it never occurred to me when I wrote it, some people took that to mean that my father didn't want me or didn't want a child, it wasn't that at all. He was absolutely delighted at having a child but after all these years of being married, nine years, he was embarrassed for it to become a declared fact that he now had a child.

Because they would have had to admit what had happened in the early years?

Yes, and what had happened now. [laughs] I think maybe the both of them had given up, and of course he would have had to admit he had a fuck which I think he had got out of, you know.

He never drank at all, still less my mother. My mother's father had died the year before I was born and my mother's mother and my mother and elder sister who had separated for the time being and had gone back to stay with her mother – there was no question in those days of divorce but my mother's sister had gone back to live with her mother and then the father had died – they came to stay in this three-room flat when I was under a year old.

There was my grandmother until about eighteen months old, my grandmother, mother's mother, my mother and my mother's younger sister, I think my mother's elder sister just touched in there and then got a place for herself very quickly. When I said 'decline', I never heard anything more than just that referred to. No doctors were called in, there was no question of anything like that. She expended some of her savings to get a woman in, to help out and this was referred to once or twice. There was never any big deal made out of it.

I gather from my mother that this woman drank Guinness, she was working class, she was Irish and she regarded it as perfectly normal if she came to have a bottle of stout. I don't think there was any question of anything more excessive than that but that would be absolutely out as far as my mother was concerned. After a while, which couldn't have been so long, my grandmother and Aunty Mysie turned up, my mother's younger sister, and so there was a certain division of care for wee Ronnie, between these three women. There was always a bit of edge about how I had been treated according to my mother. My grandmother never said anything about my mother nor did Aunty Mysie but my mother was a perfect exemplar of the ... which when I say this to people now – I haven't said this to anyone actually for years – but when I have said it they think that my mother was peculiar but her philosophy of food was that which is espoused by millions of people now. No white bread, starchy food, no cheap jam, no margarine, no overeating, and no tea for a baby, for a child. So I was fed on milk and water, as much water as I cared to drink out of the tap which came from Loch Katrine in those days, and rusks, brown toast, butter, honey, apples, oranges and bananas, and anything else than that was beyond ordinary means. A pineapple would be a special treat and I remember the taste of a pineapple for the first time or the taste of a melon, because she didn't usually buy melon, or the taste of a lemon. I absolutely loved oranges.

When I went to school my mother would always be trying to urge me to eat a bit more because it became a joke that that's all I wanted, apple, banana and orange and cup of milk and I went off to school. She was worried that I wouldn't last out until lunchtime when we had school soup. But in winter I would have a plate of Scots porridge oats, salted. My father was a Scottish deviant in that respect, he ate his Scots porridge oats with sugar. I favoured salt, with the creamy top of the milk bottle. I had two-thirds of that because my father wasn't particularly into cream so I was able to get cream and would take care that there was that layer of thick cream on top.

Being on your own a lot, do you think it possibly benefited you in learning to value solitude, aloneness, the imagination? Or do you think you just lived a lonely life?

I never felt that it was a lonely life. I wasn't pining for brothers or sisters. I was delighted when eventually I went to school. I went out to play, and spent as much of the time as I could in the swing parks and was very physical. I was fully out to play with other kids when I went to school. That's quite common in Glasgow, you were kept in the house with your parents until you went to school and then you went out to play; in fact, I think that was probably the norm in the streets where I lived, children out to play in the streets, the back courts, the back greens up and down the city.

Were there any friends you made at school who have become lifelong friends? Was school so mundane that there is not really much to say about it?

Oh, it depends how inventive you are. I think anyone's school days, if one has got a flair to tell them, have got schoolboy episodes. There was nothing in the ordinary sense of the word particularly outlandish, it was very straightforward. I went to school in the morning, I wasn't late for school. I got up and I didn't have to be prised out of bed, I went off to school, I came back from school and *later*, because I wanted it to be. We played rugby after school at Hutchy once a week and on Saturday mornings, otherwise I came back from school and I had a music lesson once a week in the early evening; I practised the piano for an hour. The routine was an hour a day after school I practised my pieces that I'd got to learn and went over a bit of musical theory and did my homework and read the home reading that was given and had tea ...

I still call it tea ...

At half past six. My father came home between half past five and six o'clock and about half past six we sat down and had tea, and I did some homework or played the piano after tea and then went to bed at a proper hour, which I think was the average hour; I think earlier on it was nine o'clock, half past nine, ten o'clock, half past ten, by the time I was 16 or 17. Then after that it was left to my discretion. I would go to my room and my parents would be concerned but they never made a number of it, that I was getting enough sleep. Of course it became routine, every night, that my light would be on; they never came into my room. I would shut the door, wouldn't lock the door, but I would go into my back room to read.

Your father at that time used to sleep on the sofa?

In the front room – well the sofa was a converted bed, so that was his room.

What about friends at school?

I had several friends at Hutchy. There were about three particular friends that I would later go to the pictures with on a Saturday afternoon. I would always go to the pictures on a Saturday afternoon and I would have a friend I would go with. There were about half a dozen boys that I was quite friendly with and two or three that I was particularly friendly with. One of them that I saw from time to time died about 20 years ago; he died of a heart attack, young, for no apparent reason. One of them is now a psychoanalyst in psychiatry in Glasgow – he lives in Largs.

And his name is ...?

Jimmy Templeton, and you are free to look him up if you care to. And I had two other particular friends, one was called Jean-Paul [laughs] who was very good at Greek and Latin and went to Oxford – I went to Glasgow University and he got a

scholarship to Oxford – and I remained friends with him until
the last time I met him which was in the British Army. I visited
him in hospital, he had a touch of tuberculosis and went from
Oxford to I think it was Argentina; he got a university
appointment in classics in the Argentine and I never heard from
him since, but Marcelle – *George*-Paul – Marcelle's still in touch
with him. The two of us fancied her and he fell in love with her
desperately. So we vied with each other for her favours and I
won, and George went off. There was another boy who
disappeared out of my ken – Alastair Kennedy, who went off to
Africa to be one of the last Scottish missionaries – that I haven't
heard of since, for years and years and years.

*Were there any friends that you met at medical school that you've
continued with over the years?*

There were three friends. Jimmy Templeton, who went into
the Indian Army from school; an army talent scout came
round the sixth form and he was seduced into joining the
army and he came back to Glasgow University and so was
two years behind us. This separated us off a bit in that
respect. There were two friends from those days – there are
others but there are two in particular who remain close
friends of mine – both of whom are the people I would stay
with when I go up to Glasgow. One is a doctor in Glasgow,
again you are welcome to get in touch with him, he knows me
pretty well, he's a general practitioner called Leonard Davidson, naturally of my age, and he was a houseman at the same
time I was at Killearn. He stayed on in Glasgow. The other is
a chap called John Duffy who was not a doctor but – I don't
know how it came about – he was into mountaineering and
we fell in with each other and he hung around my crowd of
students. He went to the student union and went in and out
as a student, I think he even had a student card, but he was
actually not a student, he was a ship's engineer.

*How would you describe the personalities of your parents, how
would you begin to describe them as people?*

Well, my father lived the life of a mains engineer for Glasgow
Corporation. At the age of 14 he was apprenticed at Mavers
and Colston Shipyards, at 17½ he went into the British Army
in the Tank Corps as a private, and came to the notice of a

senior officer and was picked out of the ranks and put
through officers' training. He was in the tanks and was
primarily a mechanic, mechanical engineer, but I think the
Tank Corps side of it for him must have been related to
maintenance of airplanes and he became a lieutenant, eventually in charge of a small Royal Air Corps depot. He had the
option of staying in the service in that capacity, specializing in
the maintenance and design of aero-engines. He could have
moved into a career in that respect, he could have come out
of it and got his membership of the electrical engineers.

You see, this was a thing that was always held up that he
didn't do, he went through everything and didn't take the last
exam so he was an associate member of the Royal Institute of
Electrical Engineers in the capacity of maintaining power
stations and St Andrews power stations in the southside of
Glasgow. Shift work, 24-hour mains engineering, so he was,
when he was not at home, or out with leisure, out and about in
the world.

His nickname when I was at university was 'laying of the
mains'. He was principal baritone of the Glasgow University
Chapel Choir and had an office in Byers Road; a number
of the people on the university staff knew my dad, my
father – 'Oh your father is laying of the mains and he's the
principal baritone'. So he had that world, internally, the side
that I, maybe, knew more of, he was more introverted than
he may have appeared. He was, I think, moderately popular, a well-liked man in that position that fitted him quite
comfortably.

He was never interested in money for its own sake, he'd
got this Corporation flat, there were good schools nearby,
he'd got himself attached to the university in that capacity, a
top-class international repertoire he loved. So why take a
four-figure-a-year job in Manchester that he was offered –
three times as much as he'd got there as an electrical
engineer – when, if we were very careful about the money
and the superannuation, there was never anything to want for,
we didn't have a car and there was a difference between a
farthing, a halfpenny and a penny and he kept a record of
in-goings and out-goings every week, never owed anybody any
money, but it was, he thought, a good life.

And I thought so too. When I compared myself with a
lot of the children that I walked past going to grammar
school in the middle of the Gorbals, I mean I never

thought with that expression – what the fuck are they doing? I thought that what was really important was what I learned at school, this business of arithmetic and writing and reading and music. Music, the mind behind it. When I heard the first piece of music on the radio, I was absolutely amazed, I'd never heard anything like it. The radio wasn't on all the time, there was no television. And in the house there were a few records, I think they were practically all singing. There was a Bible and very quickly – putting it in the language – I really wanted to assimilate what was called culture ...

Did they talk to each other a lot, did they go out, did they have jollity in the house?

I think they did all these things, the usual pubs that existed and all that culture, they lived ordinary social lives, they went to each other's houses; my father went to a dance hall on a Saturday afternoon, they went ballroom dancing. Many people, couples, all ages, went to ballroom dancing, that's the only kind of dancing there was, or Scottish country dancing. Or my father was always out singing at this or that musical evening for which he'd get a small fee, in a church hall for a social, or he would occasionally sing on Scottish radio. He was a professional singer but he didn't earn enough and didn't devote himself wholeheartedly enough, he said he'd never take the risk and he always warned me off music as a career.

It sounds much happier, their relationship, than the book suggests ...

Well, it's very difficult to paint in what you don't write. From another point of view it was, I suppose, very bleak, but a great deal of the time my mother seemed in my middle, early childhood, to be quite content. My father was doing his number and my mother seemed to be doing her number and they weren't laying any numbers on me and I was doing my number. When I describe the facts as best I can, which I never felt impelled to do to very many people, they say 'oh it must have been awful' and 'your mother must have been psychotic' or 'what did your father do, did he have affairs?' or 'you must have been so lonely and melancholy', and it was nothing like that at all.

The musical evenings and the singsongs around the piano you've talked about ... was your house only 'jolly' when there were lots of other people there?

Look, mother was not eaten up. In my memory of her being a bitter woman because we had come down in the world and weren't living in Moss Park, that was something she certainly held. My father certainly had a buoyant nature and good cheer and all the rest of it. Every so often, I would think it was two or three times every three months, I don't think there was any regularity to it, Aunt Ethel would be round and a woman who was my piano teacher and accompanied my father for his rehearsing and when he sang at a social or a miner's concert. Gladys ...

Yes, I don't understand about Gladys. I'm not sure about the mystery surrounding Gladys ...

Oh, well I can tell you about that if you want to know, but it's not a great saga. There was Gladys and then there were one or two others – there was this or that soprano or contralto, there was an occasional violinist. A musical evening was a musical evening in that there would be maybe three or four people who would come round, sit in the sitting room, tea would be served and Gladys might play a short piano piece and Ethel might sing a song from an operetta, and my father would sing a Victorian ballad. Then maybe Isor and my father or another singer would venture a duet from an operetta, and that would go on for two-and-a-half hours and people would depart and I thoroughly enjoyed these musical evenings.

Occasionally, the carpet would be rolled back, literally, you had to lift the piano completely, and there would be a bit of dancing. That would be dancing to a piano being played, a waltz or a quick step or Charlie Kunz. It was Henry Hall's 'Guest Night', big band music of the British variety that came across the radio, it was accepted as music. So there was Ambrose and his orchestra, and Jack Payne, Joe Loss, he was, I think, thought to be a bit vulgar in his choice of pieces.

My father went dancing every Saturday afternoon and the joke was, he said he went for the exercise and my mother said, it wasn't for exercise it was just to dance with women. But I don't think he did anything, he was always back, he was

never late or out at night. He would go out to other people's
houses to sing and my mother didn't like going out and said it
gave her a headache. She said that everything like that gave
her a headache. She would stay in and I would – when I
became old enough to be wearing long trousers and playing
the piano for my father – occasionally go to these musical
evenings in other people's houses and it was very exacting, I
mean they really meant it.

I've got a record of my father when he was about 75 or
78, when he had given up his singing at the Glasgow
University Chapel Choir. I was up in Glasgow and I took him
into a recording studio and got two sides of an LP of him
singing things like Dvorák and his favourite Victorian ballads.
Which was interesting to me because I hadn't heard him sing
for about 20 years and he hadn't sung really for I think about
10 years, he just went straight to the studio and I hadn't
played the piano for a long time and it's not too bad. You can
well imagine his voice 10 years, 20 years earlier with a bit of
rehearsal, it was quite professional.

*Why exactly didn't your mother, 'play [the piano] for your father
again'?*

... I think it might have been because she was embarrassed
about her own playing. She was very, very shy and I don't
think she ever enjoyed playing in public. I remember my
father asking her if she would accompany him and she said
get someone else, she didn't want to play the piano. She
never played it anyway, when I was in the house. I only
remember her sitting down and playing the piano for her own
delight and amusement on maybe two occasions. She played a
Chopin mazurka that she had learned. She wasn't a very good
player, she was good enough to play a rather simple piano
accompaniment of a Victorian ballad.

*Gladys ... I've read everything there is in the book about her but
again I'm still not sure I understand what it was all about.*

Gladys and my mother were friends for many years and then
something happened and I asked my mother later what happened. My mother was very sensitive to what she called cheek
from any woman or anyone stepping out of line, and apparently I had been ill or had flu or was in bed or something and

there was some altercation about – maybe about my piano lessons – she said Gladys had said something to her. She never told me what is was, which was by way of a criticism of the way she thought fit to treat me. She said something which she thought was a piece of cheek on Gladys's part, and I'm not going to tell you, I'm not going to pass on that.

I could see – this was maybe when I was about 13 or 14 – that a sort of frostiness had come over my mother in relationship to Gladys but she never said anything. This is my mind – as she would say, 'my evil mind' at work – she put together a holiday package which when we went to Prestwick as usual and Gladys came, she hadn't fallen out with Gladys. There was myself, my father and my mother. Gladys and my mother shared a double room in the hotel on the seafront in Prestwick and my father and I shared the other bedroom. My mother would sometimes make a remark about my father, 'he was such a vulgar man' and it was not necessary to say what that meant because I knew and she knew what that meant and I was not a vulgar boy. When he did the cord up of his pyjama trousers, before he went to bed and came in to say goodnight, there were buttons in his pyjamas, you could see his penis maybe, coming though the trousers, [laughs] and Gladys was a high Anglican, an Episcopalian, and my father came into the room to say goodnight with his pyjamas on and I saw my mother just look at Gladys because she was not going to tell my father to ...

Put it away ...

And Gladys saw this organ and fell back on the bed in a faint, [laughs] so my mother gave me a look, that was her pay off to Gladys.

Female voice [Marguerita]: But Gladys was in love with your father wasn't she?

No no, I don't think so. I mean she admired David like Ethel admired David, because he was good looking – well, not, I think, because he was good looking – because he was a very nice singer, and a very nice man. He was a handsome man, that photograph shows that, I think, he was a handsome character, well put together and fit because he played golf in all sorts of weather and went out for his constitutional on a Sunday afternoon.

Were they in any way physical parents, you know in the sense that we are today, we pick up our babies, we cuddle them ...

No. I don't remember my mother ever putting her arms round me spontaneously from her point of view, *ever*, or ever kissing me. As a baby my father certainly had taken me on his shoulder and things like that but again there's nothing unusual about that in that part of Scotland.

Did your mother talk to you about being pregnant, or when she had you?

I don't know anything about my birth, I'm not even sure whether it was at home, I always assumed it was at home because everyone was born at home in those days and I imagine it was uneventful. I've taken acid and had various birth-type dramas under acid that we could perhaps maybe talk about. But it wasn't caesarian, it wasn't forceps and I don't think my mother was in danger, I don't think I was in danger and I don't think there was any great drama about it.

Presumably you were breast-fed until nine months or something like that?

Yes. I think it was a mixture and the schedule was influenced by Truby King and the ideas that you quote in *your* book was very much like that. Every baby I think of that time, of that upper working-class, lower middle-class, healthy sturdy Scots wain, was that New Zealand ideal – you weren't a big fat slob by the time you were six or seven months and there weren't folds in your legs and you didn't waddle and you were alert and nippy. You wouldn't be skinny but you wouldn't have any excess and you were bright and alert and engaged and that's how I remember myself very basically enjoying the experience of being alive. I've had experiences with analysts and particularly Californians who draw me out to tell a little about my childhood and they say 'oh, what a miserable childhood it must have been for you and how bleak and never any child came in' and I tell them it wasn't like that at all. But they don't believe me and they think that I'm trying to defend my mother or defend my parents or having a denial, or a hyper-manic denial amnesia of how horrid it was for me.

You have said that your life is 'part of a thesis'. Precisely what does that mean?

I was saying that in view of you being here writing a book about R.D. Laing and these books by R.D. Laing and the fact that R.D. Laing is still alive, that among the many things that I haven't written about is the whole field of existential philosophy and what life as a human being is all about if it's about anything. Whether there is a bottom line or is *no* bottom line of nihilism or whether there are things that give life value or whether life has value, what it means and what it's all about, etc., etc.

Karl Jaspers made a distinction between Galileo and Luther, I think – or it could have been Giordano Bruno, an exact contemporary of Galileo – the truth that Galileo was talking about didn't depend on Galileo, the objective scientific information data and the hypothesis relating to them. The sort of things that Bruno was talking about and writing about and saying, Luther is talking about, you've got to stake your own life on it, 'cos it's about the truth or falsity of the way one lives, it's not about the stars. So there is relevance there to what I'm writing about in the way I live. You have to put your money where your mouth is. [laughs].

So you are saying that – as I understand it – everything you have written about has a double check; it is theoretically true and the double check is that it accords with your life experience?

No, I wouldn't say that about *Sanity, Madness and the Family*, that's a report on what I found. I would say that so far a great deal of what I've written doesn't matter who Ronnie Laing is, who the author of that is. I don't think it matters. It doesn't matter to me what sort of guy Apuleius was who wrote *The Golden Ass*. I mean it's quite interesting that he came from North Africa, he must have imbibed this, that and the other but he must have been some sort of guy that was relevant to writing that sort of thing, though it doesn't really matter who you are. You don't really need to know anything about him. In one sense I think that's true for anything that's written at that level; it's a statement out there, it's got a life of it's own. There's one sense in which there is nothing that happens to me now that I would say would invalidate what I've written, or validate what I've written.

Can you explain that ...

Well, I can't get away with being anonymous. I mean through you, my life is to some extent being turned inside out. I don't mean grossly, terribly traumatically and so forth, but there is a private, inner face of my life that is going to be mythologized to the external world to some extent, whether I drop dead now or not – maybe even better from that mythologizing point of view if I do. So I'm playing a part now, Ronnie Laing is playing a part in the mythologizing of R.D. Laing.

What do you think about whether ultimately each individual life is nihilistic and meaningless or whether it does have value?

It depends who I'm talking to. All the words that are the collection of words that we have to use in that zone, from God, Jesus Christ, the whole Christian rhetoric, the Buddhist rhetoric, the Sufi non-rhetoric – any form of words that is available to us to talk about what we refer to as what life's all about – these words are understood by everyone on their own terms. One reason I found for not wanting to take on trying to write about that sort of thing directly is that the distribution of meaning of all the words disappears into other people – the reception of these words by other people – and I haven't a way that satisfies me, in that I could say what I wanted to say which I could expect to resonate with other people in a way that they would recognise what I would like to them to recognise, as (you know) where it was coming from.

If I was a composer with the status of any of the great composers I would feel that you can express a sensibility as long as there is still a convention of hearing through the musical form. But to combine that with discourse of language without becoming sheer lyrical poetry or some other poetic form that is part of the 20th century ... it can't be an epic these days, there isn't the coherence to sustain that and there isn't an agreed world view, a consensus mythology. The end of metaphysical systems – and there's no-one else with the possible exception of the early work of Heidegger and then Adorno really, you know that little book of Adorno – and the jargon of existentialism is a devastating criticism of that rhetoric so there isn't a rhetoric to hand for me. If there is I've got to very largely invent it myself, and I don't want to invent a whole lot of neologisms.

I want to use the simplest everyday language in a coherent way. That's what I'm trying to do just now. So that it's both accessible to anyone who can read, whether or not they've got a university education. So feeling under constraints of that order, it's not surprising I haven't written a book on existential philosophy or theology. I got very imbued with a sort of literary minimalism and after you read a certain amount of it, these hundreds and hundreds and hundreds of books, and if you look at any page of them, I mean what are they saying? Foucault and Nietzsche, the sharpness of Kierkegaard at his best, but these are like needles, you can't really make a whole haystack out of needles, if I could I would, but I haven't had the inspiration to do that.

A lot of your work is interpreted as being either wildly pessimistic or painfully optimistic ...

Well I think when we get to this *level* of talking or writing that it very much runs into silence, that the sounds and symbols we are using and the distinctions we make in terms of language, make it very difficult. I don't think it's entirely impossible but I find it very, very, difficult to say what I want to say, though I'm not going on about it, but I've got to take stock of the extent to which I regard myself as, so far, very misunderstood.

There are two ways of dealing with that. If too many people misunderstand you, you just shut up, but I don't particularly want to. I'm not dedicated to shutting up but I want to write what I write in such a way that people eventually can refer back to the text, and there is a chance that the text is actually saying what it is saying so that if a really clear-headed reader comes along and says 'oh that's not what he is saying at all, this is what he is saying', you can point to the text as a means of clearing up the misunderstanding. I mean there are a great deal of the things that I'm said to have said that can be refuted from what I've said because I either haven't said it or I've said other things which don't seem to agree with what people say I've said. Well that's at least something.

You wrote about your father's hero being Gandhi. Was he a man who was interested in many figures or just Gandhi?

My father, like my mother, read very few books. Albert Schweitzer – he was very impressed with a meeting he had with Schweitzer when I was a boy. Schweitzer came to Glasgow and conducted the Glasgow University Chapel Choir and on that occasion my father went out for a walk with him. Gandhi was a name, Bertrand Russell was another name or thinker that he respected. He read another book that I gave him when I was 14, I found it in Woolworths, a six-penny; the Rationalist Press in those days published little red books, one of them was by Julian Huxley, *Religion without Revelation*, a handbook of early 20th-century scientific humanism. My father maintained he was a Christian and at the same time espoused Julian Huxley's scientific humanism and we had endless arguments for several years about this. My argument was that you couldn't endorse two incompatible positions and he didn't see why this should be.

Did your mother join in?

No, she sat and listened and sometimes she would say 'who won?' before we went to bed that night. He had no relationship to Marx or the Webbs or political theory of any kind at all.

Why do think Gandhi attracted him?

The branch of the Laings that came from Aberdeen, there had been among them my great-aunt who was a teacher of classics. I think my grandfather's – my father's father – either my father's uncle or my grandfather's, someone that I called a great-uncle, I'm not quite sure whether he was a great-uncle or a great-great-uncle had a record. He was the oldest person ever to graduate from Aberdeen University. He had been a lay preacher all his life and at the age of 72 he went to university for the first time when he retired and at the age of 75 he collected an M.A. from Aberdeen University.

... Father took it for granted that God is a spirit and those who worship him worship him in spirit and in truth, and that meant in the way you live, and the way one lived had something to do with living according to the way we were meant to live. God put us here in order to live a good life, in a pretty perennial philosophy sense of the word of good, to live correctly; you might have to find it, it might not be given as a grace or a revelation, you might find out you're not living the way you should. Definitely a *should*, should I or not, and correct or not.

A favourite expression of my father's for that sort of thing
was clean. He wasn't suffering from a Freudian anal reaction
formation, he lived a clean life, he hadn't got into what he
would regard as the filth and dirt of a great deal of ordinary
living. He had a sort of clean-cut life and one of those things
was that money gave you enough to live in our society in such
a way, but he would never have thought of changing what he
wanted to do for the sake of money. I grew up with all that
taken for granted and these are still the values that I've got.
If my father was here at my age now, age 60, 61, and we
were talking to each other about these sorts of things I don't
think we would have anything very much to disagree about,
nor my grandfather. Scottish Presbyterianism, inflected with
that 19th-century religious atheism. He never voted in his life.

And your mother didn't vote?

I think my mother sometimes voted Conservative, only Conservative. I think she was sometimes picked up by a car and
taken and I think she voted Conservative, but she would never
told me who she voted for. My father had the view of many of
his generation who had been through World War I that the
ordinary population was simply canon fodder and factory
fodder for the people who were making the decisions, God
knows what they were playing at. He wasn't a Communist or
socialist or Labour supporter, but he thought that the only
rational thing to do is that the major nationwide or interna-
tional-wide things like the telephone system, communication
systems, the electricity system, railways, major transportation,
etc., should all be public enterprises. The National Health
Service, he saw that as simply logical common sense.

If he had had to get into an argument about a sort of
Augustinian Pelagiun argument, he wouldn't have known
which way to go, he would have gone both ways about free
will or original sin. He had no time in between for things like
football or Rangers and Celtic. I don't think he ever went to a
football match or followed the game. He played a lot of golf,
he started golf when I was about nine and we played a lot of
golf on the Glasgow Municipal golf courses. It was a working
man's game, golf, in Glasgow – all through my life, great
Glasgow golf courses, great Glasgow parks, that I took
completely for granted as a public amenity. Queen's Park,
that's a beautiful park. I spent by choice quite a lot of my

time playing with other kids in these parks. I never particularly developed a vocabulary of trees or birds or flowers or that side of it, but I played around these parks, I took that for granted as a habitat.

How would you summarise your father's values?

God is everything. Father didn't know about negative theology but if he could have translated George MacLeod, and Paul Tillich's *The Courage to Be* sort of theology, he would have gone along with that. There had been a central design somewhere, it is not random and it is not nihilism. What the affirmative statement is, is difficult to say. It's an affirmation, it has got something to do with not inflicting intentional pain for glee or delight on other people, it's got something to do with being harmless. This is my father: 'God helps them that help themselves'. He insisted you could find that in the Bible.

I went through the whole fucking Bible, for two shillings and sixpence, which in those days was quite a lot of money, and I had already read the Bible once. I think this was the second time. I'm sure it wasn't in the New Testament, I'm sure it wasn't in most of the Old Testament. It wasn't in Proverbs, it wasn't in Psalms, it was not in the Bible, 'God helps them that helps themselves'. Don't complain to God, don't waste God's time with your whining and prayers and whatever, get your arse in the saddle and get on with it. So there's that – that study of Samuel Smiles, *Self-Help*, a bit of that too.

I wouldn't lay that on anyone else. I retain that sort of thing that if I can't drag myself to get up in the morning, I needn't expect anyone else to pull me out of bed. It's always very nice to get a little help from one's friends from time to time. I think that my family, coming from non-urbanized Aberdeen, always regarded themselves as Vikings, coming from the north, Norway, and not Highland Scots, not Celtic, not Lowland Scots, so carrying that ideology, that ideology of sturdy self-reliance, being inner directed. Of course if you read Tawney, *Religion and the Rise of Capitalism*, you can see that that was to some extent a capitalist put-on to the working class, to work away and save and put money away in the savings bank, slave away for the rest of your life making profits for them, etc. But there is something other than that, that I think was quite healthy about it.

One thing I'm not clear about through reading Wisdom, Madness and Folly *is the religious environment of your childhood.
What did your parents believe in?*

The religious denomination was Church of Scotland. Both my
parents were nominal members of the communicant, you talk
about taking communion in the Church of Scotland and being
communicants of the Church of Scotland. In Glasgow ...
there is a place called the Langside Monument, ... there is a
church up there called Langside Parish Church, about two
miles from where we lived. Neither my father nor my mother
ever or very, very seldom went to that church because my
father was a principal baritone at the Glasgow University
Chapel Choir and so that entailed him going to church on a
Sunday morning for the Sunday morning service, the Sunday
evening service and a rehearsal in the week on a Thursday
night. My mother claimed deafness and never went to church
as far I know.

My Aunt Ethel, whose two letters you've read, was about
15, 16 years older than me and a little younger than my
father; yes she's 77 or something like that now. She was a
young woman in her early twenties when I was coming on for
three, four, five, six and I was sent to Sunday School which
was a common thing to be sent to on a Sunday afternoon. I
never went to church because my father's number was on the
other side of Glasgow and it was out of my ken, Glasgow
University chapel; and I never went to church with my
mother as far as I remember or anyone else, but I attended
Sunday School regularly every Sunday.

I think I mentioned in *Wisdom, Madness and Folly* that I
won my first prize at the end of the first year for reciting the
books of the Bible faster than anyone else, and for a year's
perfect attendance. Ethel was one of the teachers I remember. It was a common thing for an unattached woman, who
hadn't got a family and husband and children to look after, to
be a Sunday School teacher.

When my mother put me to bed she taught me, before I
can remember, to say my prayers every night – you say your
prayers and there was a standard prayer you say before you
go to sleep. There was no saying of grace or any outward or
visible signs of religious observance or piety or anything like
that, devoutness or whatnot in the house. It would be
completely outlandish for either my father or my mother to

get down on their knees and hold a prayer meeting. I wonder
if – I don't think we ever said grace – I wonder how I ever
got to know about saying grace? Anyway I'm pretty sure it
wasn't part of the family system. There was a Bible in the
house, of course, along with not very many other books; an
edition of Shakespeare and the Bible.

They had two contacts with the external and outside world,
the morning and evening newspaper, the Sunday morning
newspaper and the radio. Neither my mother nor my father
switched on religious broadcasts in particular. When I got
hold of the Bible – I think [I] must have been about 10 or 11
– I started reading the Bible at home, on an extra-curricular
basis. I mean more than I needed to memorize a few verses
for Sunday School. I remember having an unspoken feeling
that that was not quite done, there was a great sort of
unspoken kudos placed on sound Scottish common sense and
getting 'religious' or getting converted or becoming a Roman
Catholic or taking it really seriously, unless you were going to
be a minister yourself, was all a wee bit excessive. So I was
rather shy about actually reading the Bible in front of my
parents, and first of all I hadn't a room of my own so all my
studying work was on top of a baby grand piano in one sitting
room. When my father vacated his dog kennel to me to let
me have a room of my own to work in, particularly at night,
and slept in the sitting room, then I confined all my Bible
reading to the privacy of my own bedroom.

We never talked about these things particulary until I
started taking it pretty seriously; I realize now that I actually
took it seriously as we were supposed to. I stopped going to
the Church of Scotland Sunday School and under the auspices of the Hutcheson's Boys' Grammar School there was
the Scripture Union and the Crusaders, and the Crusaders
had a regular Sunday afternoon meeting that I switched to
instead of the Sunday School meeting. I played the foot organ
which was in a tennis club in Moss Park at the Crusaders, a
joint Scripture Union, Crusaders Sunday School.

I remember an occasion when I was about 14 or 15 when I
turned up there and the teacher wasn't there and I sat down as
usual to start the hymn for us all to sing and then go through
the routine, but everyone disappeared to go out to play since
the teacher wasn't there. No one ever dreamt of going through
the Sunday School number. I had internalised it, I wasn't doing
it routinely and I wasn't doing it because the teacher was there.

I still went to Sunday School in order to sing hymns, read the Bible and pray. But they all scattered and evaporated.

I mentioned in the book that at about 14, 15, 16, I took the question of the existence of God seriously, and came to be extremely doubtful of the existence of God as I understood it. You could be a Christian agnostic, pretty well everyone was, but to be a declared atheist which was rather heavy, that would be different. My music teacher was a Roman Catholic from Berlin and had studied music at the Berlin Academy. It was a very good choice in one respect for a music teacher because she was right in the most élite-piano-European tradition of being taught by someone who had been taught by someone who had been taught by at least Franz Liszt. You know things like the way you hold your hand on the thing and all that. You are supposed to have that imparted to you by people who had been taught by people who had been taught by people who had been taught.

When I was 17 or 18, she was concerned about my spiritual welfare, it came to her notice that – I wasn't getting up on any proverbial soapbox but I had said to my father or mother – that I didn't believe in God and I don't think I told her but she was very worried about that and she said that would I – her brother was a dentist but had spent two or three years as a fully-fledged Franciscan – would I agree to go along and see her brother. He prevailed upon me to go along and see him once a week to have a spiritual discussion about the existence of God. Of course I knew Latin, I think I was between my last year at school and first year at university, and took as a text to reason with me about the existence of God, the proof of the existence of God as expounded in Thomas Aquinas's *Summa Theologiae*, which is basically Anselm's proof of the existence of God and we never got further than that. But I went to see him, there was nothing belligerent about it. I always put that proof in suspense in my mind, I wasn't sure whether it was reasonable, I wasn't sure whether it was as absolutely compelling, which it is supposed to be, I mean it's a necessary, God is the most necessary of all things you can imagine or think of ...

And what do you believe now?

I like to regard myself in the best orthodox Roman Catholic theological tradition of negative theology which the present Pope is known for, so it depends as far as I'm concerned on who I am talking to. I'm not a theist in the positive sense of requiring a concept of God which I believe in. Well, at the end of my book called *Sonnets*, there is a passage from Dionysius the Areopagite which I would go along with, not this, not that, you know, what is God, you can't say he's a number or measure, or that which, or power or ...

With reincarnation I would have to say that I certainly do *not* believe in it and I'm not happy about saying that I do not *not* believe in it, but I haven't got a positive belief in it.

The Buddha was traditionally asked a number of questions, about 14 questions, one of them being about previous lives and so on, all of which he refused to answer which you can take different ways and I like to believe the reason why he refused to answer these, or he had nothing to say about these questions, was because he didn't know any better than anyone else.

What about your mother's views?

I took it all more seriously, I think, than both of them. Free thought, free thinking was another sort of thing, take it absolutely for granted, absolutely. What we call freedom of thought, freedom of intellectual position in relationship to *weltanschauung*. My exploration of these things that they gave to me, I never talked about this with my mother. I mean talking about the subjective idealism or the position of Aristotle or Plato and so on, that wasn't the domain that I lived in with my parents at all.

What about simple rules, like how you should behave to other people and how men should behave to women. Did they talk about those types of things?

You should treat women with respect, you really shouldn't have sexual intercourse before you get married, if you do, be careful. We never had a conversation about the facts of life.

In Wisdom, Madness and Folly *you talk about when you were 15 and your mother was in the bathroom and you were frightened of her seeing your pubic hair, does that suggest that no one talked about sex at all?*

There was never any explicit conversation about sex in my teens. The occasional reference to this or that, but never a formal conversation or never a developed informal conversation between me and my parents about that sort of thing. The idea was that you'd get married and you'd have children. They would keep up with the times and my mother prided herself on having no sentimentality, so I don't think she would have been anti-abortion now, but she would have regarded it as maybe a very serious thing. I mean in the early '50s, '40s in that part of the world, an abortion was a major event.

Was there much in your life when you left home that they disapproved of, relating to their sense of values they thought they had installed in you?

We never had any arguments about these things. There was quite a lot of things to do with respectability and ideas of respectability were changing rapidly. When I got married in the first place and then later in the '60s when my first wife and I separated, all that sort of thing was blown really. I mean it wasn't a disgrace to get divorced, but I also had quite an open sexual life with women in between monogamous relationships before getting married and in between getting involved with my second wife. These are only two phases that were relevant to my parents. They didn't know anything about my life in that respect *at all*.

My mother seriously thought that I was gay. There is one of the stories that are not in this book [*Wisdom, Madness and Folly*] that she went round to see Anne, my first wife, and confided to her 'don't you know that Ronald is homosexual and don't you realize that when he says he's out at clinical meetings at the Southern and General Hospital, Stobhill and so on, that he is carrying on with ...' She seriously indented this into Anne's mind for several years, it was so shocking to Anne that she never said anything about it to me for two or three years after my mother said that to her. I don't know whether that was sheer maliciousness on my mother's part or whether she really believed it.

When it came round to me sitting my final medical examinations, I failed them all totally. When I came home, I was still living at home, my father was so ashamed of this event that he couldn't go to the office that day, and my mother couldn't go out in the street and I thought – well, fuck the pair of you. My father had to come home and he was going to give me a lecture on failing my examination and we didn't actually have a thing but what I felt was that was the absolute end with the two of you and I'm finished, and I walked out and never ever spent a night in my parents home after that. I got a job in the hospital and I graduated six months after that, and after that they knew virtually nothing about my life. I visited them about two or three times a year and stuck it out for two hours or three hours.

When I came to Glasgow after coming out of the army there was a certain interplay between my father and my mother and my first wife Anne and the children. In the early '70s when my second daughter was 15 years old – she died when she was 21 of leukaemia – when she was 15, no, 16 she [Susan] said to me in Glasgow, my daughter, 'Your mother has told me that she has, and she showed me, a little doll she's made called Ronald that she is sticking pins in in order to give you a heart attack'. So I thought, well I'm going to get her, my mother, for this. So the whole five of us, Fiona, Susan, Karen, Paul and Adrian, I took them round to my mother's house, in Newlands, Glasgow, for Sunday afternoon tea. This performance with the teacups. Chairs that have got no side arms around the thing for tea. We are all going to be on our best behaviour. With afternoon tea you'd have one leg with heels and toe pointed out like this, and that way the back is straight and you rest, the tea saucer is resting on your hand which may or may not rest on your knee and you lifted the teacup up with your thumb and one finger and not at all with fingers splayed, like that. Mummy was just starting the operation of getting the teacup up to her mouth, 'Susan tells me you've got a little doll called Ronald that you're sticking pins in in order to give me a heart attack'. [laughs] She got the teacup up to there and without any shred of anger turned around and said 'Ronald, we don't talk about that sort of thing', and that was the end of that.

Why homosexual?

My first wife Anne told me that this is what my mother told her, that when in the first six months after I had graduated, I brought Joe Schorstein, he wanted to meet my mother – 'cos I got quite friendly and involved with Joe Schorstein. And I brought him and a chap called Charles Macartney who was the superintendent of the Glasgow Ear, Nose and Throat hospital, and a chap whose name I forget now who was a consultant child psychiatrist. He was about the only child psychiatrist in Glasgow, he wasn't a paediatrician, he was an actual psychiatrist. I got to know him because I used to teach piano lessons and his wife came to see me for piano lessons.

Anyway, Charles and this guy were gay. I didn't think it was at all obvious. But the guy who was the child psychiatrist later committed suicide. He was appointed to some hospital job and made out a report to the regional board of some abuses that were going on in the nursing staff and the chief male nurse, or one of the other male nurses implicated, got back on him by blowing it that he was gay and in the face of this disgrace he committed suicide. I think that what happened is that my mother read it in the bulletin and she made up this story and went round and told Anne. Because he had been one of the people that had come round, with Joe, this guy and Charles Macartney.

Why was she feeling so bad about you at the time?

Well I had gone 'evil' for reasons that I don't know. I didn't invite her and my father to my wedding. I didn't invite her or my father to my graduation, I didn't even tell 'em. Since my father was too ashamed to go into his office and my mother was too ashamed to go out into the street because they didn't read my name in the *Glasgow Herald* when it appeared that morning, well then they could fucking well read my name in the *Glasgow Herald* and that was an end of it for me. We never ever quarrelled or said anything about it, but there was a real sense, more on my part in relation to both of them, that in one sense that was an end of it. So I think that my mother took that as internal fury and rage and revenge.

Why do you really think you failed your exams? Do you really believe in the speculation you wrote?

About talking out of line in my year dinner with the professors? Well, I did make a mess of one oral examination. I'd always had a thing about Yale and Harvard and Oxford and Cambridge and grams and grains. I used to have a thing about left and right, I still muddle up Harvard and Yale and doses of drugs in grams and grains. I was in my medical oral examination and I was asked about doses of barbiturates and different drugs and I got into a terrible mess and got completely disconfabulated in terms of doses, even for a dose of aspirin and things like that. There was no mercy in something like that, there were no allowances made, it was like an interrogation and part of the competence that you are supposed to be able to exhibit is to keep your mind clear under pressure and I made a mess of that.

But the rest of it, I thought that I knew the subject and answered the thing. I was failed in everything, *absolutely everything*. It was very unusual to be failed in everything; the usual procedure was that you were told you failed in this and you have to repeat this course. Well, I was just failed and I wasn't told what to do, just to appear in six months and sit the whole fucking thing again. So the fact that I hadn't been told to attend as a student to anything enabled me to apply for a post-qualification job as a houseman at Stobhill where, because I hadn't got my degree, they payed me half a houseman's salary for not being qualified, and I did a houseman's job in Stobhill and went back, sat the whole exam again and passed without comment.

At that final year dinner I was giving one of the speeches and I was sitting beside the senior professor and I said some things that were definitely out of order, over the claret and the port and the whisky. I thought fucking hell, it made me cringe. I think it's within reason that they might have decided to teach me a lesson, obviously I was cheeky but I'm not paranoid about it.

When you said well, fuck them, and never spent the night there ...

That's not absolutely true, I did spend a few nights there, on leave from the army.

Was it an accumulation of things or was it that one thing that dreadfully upset you or was it merely the final straw ...

Well, it was an accumulation of a number of things. Before that a friend of mine in Glasgow – who is still a friend of mine – he's about my age, quite a well-known Glasgow character called Johnny, he was a ship's engineer on oil tankers and he was away from Glasgow for months on end. When he was away, I discovered when he came back, he had written me several letters. When I challenged my mother about this, and my mother had to admit she had opened them and they were full of 'such filth', that was her expression, that she had thrown them out and not told me. I was absolutely scandalized. Then about the same time, just before graduation, a friend of mine had written me another letter, in which he had detailed a particular sexual encounter he had had with a woman up in Loch Lomond, and my mother had read this and it was 'absolute filth'. Well I was absolutely scandalized that I was living in a house with a couple of parents who would open my mail and told them that.

And on two or three occasions in the course of my medical career, the only exam I had ever failed was anatomy and physiology in second year and I felt absolutely alienated from them, this was the first time I had ever failed anything, the way they treated this as *my fault*. It was exactly as later, walking along the road with my father in Glasgow in the late '50s, with my eldest child who was about one-year-old walking along ahead, and toddling tripped over and fell. I ran ahead and picked her up and so my father turned to me and said 'you know, your mother would never have done that if that had been you, she would have given you a good smack for falling'.

So I was fed up with it. So that was it on my part. If you imagine the take my mother must have had at that separation it must have been 'evil, filth', and the fact that I became a psychiatrist was absolutely awful for her, that I was devoting myself to this, this was her word for it, *filth*.

Psychiatry?

Filth. This was the filth, all the filth in people's minds, you know filth and madness, instead of becoming a surgeon. Instead of becoming a brain surgeon.

Did your father think differently?

Well, he didn't know what psychiatry was.

But your mother thought ...

She didn't know what it was either, but she thought it was filth, this filth. I've often thought, when I've seen so many people get locked into fights with their parents, they go on and on and can't stop it. And my way of dealing with it, well just fuck you, finally, you know, right or wrong, I can live without ever seeing you again. The last letter I ever got from my mother was a number of years ago, when I went round with my eldest daughter, Fiona, who was at that time about 28. I got a note in pencil, unsigned, unaddressed, undated: 'I want you to promise me that you will never visit me again before I die or after my death'. So I got a piece of white paper, put a heart on it and said 'I promise'.

And sent it back ...

Yes, and that's the last I ever saw or heard of her, my mother. *That was it.*

Was there any reconciliation between you and your parents?

No. It's very difficult to convey the quality of the relationship. This story that Susan told me, that my mother had told her that she had a little doll called Ronnie she stuck pins in in order to give me a heart attack in London, where I was in the '60s. I found that very difficult to believe. Susan was a very tricky young girl, who was quite capable of making up a story like that, on the other hand she was quite capable of not making it up and my mother was quite capable of doing it, so it's undecided.

When your career developed, you wrote your books, became quite famous, married and divorced and remarried. Did that affect your parents as far as you know?

I think it compensated my mother. I was bit of a rascal as far as my father was concerned, and evil as far as my mother was concerned and it compensated my mother that she now thought she had given birth to a genius. [laughs]

Where did this come from? Why wouldn't a lower middle-class mother be proud that you had actually got to medical school? Why wouldn't that satisfy her?

It was taken for granted. It was a disgrace that, the way I got to medical school, I made a terrible mess of my university scholarship exam and I ended up 25th in the first hundred for a free scholarship to Glasgow University. When a guy I

had beaten all that year at school came in third, I ought to
have come in first. And a girl from Hutcheson Girls' Grammar School came in first, and I was 25th. It was almost
impossible for them to go out of the house because I had
come in 25th instead of first to get into medical school.
Actually 25th was enough. The only way I could get to
medical school was to win a complete scholarship to pay for
everything, and that was enough.

That was no honour and then when I started to run for
Glasgow University and never had asthma at that time, a
chap they knew – I think called Jimmy Paterson who was at
the time the world champion high jumper – he held the world
record for a while and there was a guy who was in my class
at school won the Scottish half-mile, what was I fucking well
doing? Couldn't run a half-mile under 2.6, 2.8. Any of these
things that other people would regard as achievements didn't
appear as achievements to me as mediated by them.

*Did you put it down to the fact that their lives, or in particular
her life, were empty therefore you had to fill it all up and that's
why you became so important?*

Oh yes. When I was three, four, five, as I remember, about
two years before going to school and about two years after,
my father and mother used to have what I remember as
frequent rows where both of them would shout and scream at
each other. My father never hit my mother and, as far as I
know, my mother never hit my father but voices were raised
and one of the things was *me*. That my father, who had been
consigned to the dog house – the dog kennel – and I was in a
bed in my mother's bedroom and father would frequently
inveigh my mother: who did she think I was, that she was
completely spoiling me and I was Little Lord Fauntleroy. This
was his expression that I was being treated like Little Lord
Fauntleroy, and at that time I just wanted to keep out of the
way of it.

There was one particular moment which led me all the
more to want to keep out of the way. My father and mother
were going to a department store in Glasgow, called Paisley's,
now defunct, then supposed to be one of the best department
stores in Glasgow. She had got me a little red dressing gown
with a ribbon and a couple of tassels, and in one of his rages
with my mother, he picked this up – and [I] was very glad

that I wasn't in it – and threw it in the fireplace and how she was out of line in the way that she was treating me like that.

The usual way of interpreting that was that my father was very jealous of my mother's attention being lavished on me, which it was. At the same time she would betray me – I gave her cheek, what she called cheek. One afternoon, I said something to her, or it could have been an expression on my face, and 'you take that face off'; remove that face. So I had to wait up until my father came back at night, to get a thrashing from him. She would report to him 'he has been giving me cheek this afternoon' and then he would give me a sort of going over. So I had deep reservations about both of them.

In The Facts of Life *and* Wisdom, Madness and Folly, *you talk about a sound thrashing and being 'smashed to pieces' by your father; presumably your father was no more or no less physical than any other father at the time?*

Oh, I think he was rather less. I was very frightened at that, the feeling of going to pieces was not the immediate physical effect of actually being smashed, no bones were broken, no blood was drawn, no bruises were produced but red marks would be produced on the skin. He never used a belt or a strap and he never used his knuckles, he never used the flat of his hand, and he didn't do it very often and when he did it he meant it and I don't think he did it other times that I don't remember. I don't think that that amounted to more than four or five times in my whole life before the age of five and then by that time I was past it. He hit me once I think in my teens, slapped me across the face for something that I said that he took exception to. There was a teacher at school who asked us at Hutchy – when I must have been about nine – he asked for a show of hands of how many boys in the class had been hit by their father as chastisement and pretty well everyone put their hands up.

You say in Wisdom, Madness and Folly *that you learned to live with a queasy sense of corruption, that it was terrible to have to pretend you loved someone when you didn't ...*

That was primarily my mother ... My mother said to me that I had given her mother cancer of the breast because she had picked me up on one occasion and I had hit her on the breast and that had given her breast cancer.

Did she choose a moment to tell you this?

Oh yes. Aunt Ethel has got a story about when I was a toddler. I was showing off with my mother and my mother's mother, and my mother's older sister, Aunt Ethel, my father and my father's Uncle – 'come to Aunty, come to Granny'. So I was going to them, and my mother said 'come to Mummy' and I ran out of the door and she ran after me and brought me back and gave me a slapping in front of them for running out of the door, when she'd said 'come to Mummy'. So I didn't run out of the door when she said 'come to Mummy', I went to Mummy, and I smiled and gave her a kiss in future. I didn't like having to do that, I was very clear that I was doing that. I don't think I ever confused my mind that if I wanted to keep out of trouble I had to conduct myself in a way that was expected of me and, again, a lot of people seem to think 'oh that's terrible', but I mean that doesn't drive anyone crazy ...

Some people think that children just get used to the way they are treated, and they don't reflect on these things.

Oh, *I* reflected on these things. From about the age of eight or nine, I thought the piano was a way out and, if someone like Diaghilev could be walking along Calder Street and hear me play a Chopin étude or a polonaise, maybe I would be discovered. There was going to be some way I was going to get out of that house as quickly as I could, even though I realized it might take me over ten years to do so. There seemed to be a chance at the beginning of the war. My mother's brother, Uncle William who lived in Boston, offered to take me and I jumped at that. The only time I ever saw tears come in my mother's eye [was] when I said 'oh OK, OK', and her eyes filled up with tears.

But you didn't go?

No, she didn't let me go, they didn't let me go. The other chance was going to London in the middle of the war, the blitz. I came up for a music exam at that time and proposed to my music teacher and my parents that they allow me to go to London, when I was 11, 12, to study music full time and that was turned down. I would have gone off and possibly done things in music.

No one's made any particular connection between your childhood and your work. What you've been saying about your childhood and some of your later work do seem very close ...

I'd have thought so. I never made any secret of it, I put quite a bit, more than most psychoanalysts or Freud ever put about his self, in the first two chapters of *The Facts of Life*, but I didn't want to write about that sort of thing when both my parents were alive. I think that's fair enough.

In the Anthony Clare radio interview that I did, I said some of the things that I've told you just now and my mother might have heard that. I know – also it may be the worst thing for me – everything I'd written until I went into the army, I left at home, which was quite a lot. All gone when I came out of the army, she had no idea where they were. The baby grand piano that was then hers, she told Susan that she had taken an axe and smashed it up so we wouldn't sell it, which was the piano I played. And all the books I had, and everything I'd written; I'd written a thing like a *Diary of a Madman*, after the manner of Gogol, up to the age of 24.

She burned it all?

Yes. I mean I had the belief I would keep that and look at it as juvenilia and some of it might be worth something as literature. That went.

And you confronted her?

No, I didn't. Well, they had moved house and I said, 'well where is it?' – 'oh, no idea'. She was so small, if I'd taken her and thrown her out the window she'd have drifted off like a feather. I had settled that policy of war with my parents that I was never going to have that sort of punchy interchange on my part.

Did you go to their funerals?

Yes.

And your father died first. Was it easy going to your father's funeral with your mother being there?

Well ...

He was an invalid, wasn't he, before he died?

Well, he wasn't so much geriatric as suffering Alzheimer's disease, senile dementia. Extreme loss of memory. There is an episode in *Do you love me?* of the return of the prodigal, a sequence which is almost word for word my last visit to my father at home ... But, I decided at my father's funeral that I'd give my mother a present of impeccable behaviour. The crematory – its a crematorium and a mechanical chugg chugged up the coffin, the funeral guests are in the small chapel and the coffin is there. There's an everlasting bonfire and the minister presses a button and the coffin starts to chugg chugg chugg chugg and this disappears and the door closes. My father put in a request years back, it might have been in his will to have – I can't remember which one it was – but his favourite song in Italian sung at his funeral on a record. So my mother decides to have it as short as possible, she arranged the whole thing and again I thought all these things that my mother had done with sort of minimalism. Both of us were looking straight ahead, I turned round to her and said 'don't you find this somewhat moving?'. And she said, 'Ronald, think of something else'. That was the only remark I ever made to my mother about the death of my father.

What exactly happened to your dad in his last 10 years?

When I was 17 or 18, he had a nervous breakdown and was laid off work at the point of getting promotion and that's when he started to tremble and took to bed for a while. In the course of listening to him talking about his boss – who was retiring [and] whom he thought was going to put him down so that he would be passed over for promotion which he was entitled to under ordinary circumstances, and someone else would get the job – I remember being struck that there were some similarities between the way he was worked up about his boss, Inglis, whom I had met. So I said to my father that I didn't think it had anything to do with Inglis, he was talking about his dad, about Old Pa who he had always had a thing about; Ethel thinks very much that my father had a warped view of his father and that she didn't think was justified.

Anyway, my father recovered and got himself together and it wasn't held against him that he had this nervous breakdown and he got the job actually ... That was way back in the 1940s. He and my mother continued to live together. When he was in his late 70s, I was in my early 30s – this is according to my mother, I don't know whether I've put this story in one of the books – he fell and hit his head and this did something to his immediate memory and he would become very absent minded and misplace things. He was by no means broken down in bodily functions, but on one occasion, according to my mother, in Marylee in Glasgow in the flat, as usual he put on his homburg or bowler hat and took his umbrella [and] went out of the door to go round to the local public library which he did every morning to look up according to my mother, the birth and deaths columns, the deaths column to see who had died – you know as you start to do in a place like Glasgow where you look up the death columns to see who's left – everything was perfectly in order except that he had forgotten to put his clothes on. [laughs]. I mean that was not in any way funny, that was the end, so she got the doctor round and he was put away in the psychogeriatric unit of the local mental hospital.

It was a new psychogeriatric unit; he had a bed and dressed himself, got up and pottered around. As one of the intact characters, he was let out in the grounds for several years but was not expected to walk out of the grounds but occasionally he did and was brought back. The sister told me on one occasion he got lost and was brought back by the police and she thought it was quite touching, what the police had told her, that he went into the police station and said, 'I am an old gentleman, I have forgotten my name and I've lost my way'. So they twigged where he might have come from and brought him back. The latter year or so he got frailer and faded away after being there for the last 10 years.

Did this sadden you?

Saddened. I was particularly saddened and the irony of it, of course, it's one of those things that are very double edged. My father had said on a number of times to me, 'I hope your mother dies before I do because I wouldn't like to think of her living alone without me', little idea had he that that she had no compunction. She – well I don't know whether it's fair to say she was glad to get rid of him and have the house to herself – but she probably *was* glad to have the house to herself.

I don't want to sound stupid, but what exactly *is a 'nervous breakdown'?*

That's one of your arch disclaimers, nervous breakdown in quotation marks. It was called a nervous breakdown. If I was putting my clinical hat on, it would simply be an acute or sub-acute anxiety neurosis. Anxiety neurosis, and that's a perturbation of quite sweaty, trembling – the person goes into a rapid trembling, they feel very frightened and very often their heart is beating, they are in a state of fear, and very often the anxiety is free floating, non-specific. A non-specialist probably wouldn't refer them to a psychiatric out-patient department, they would give them a tranquillizer today. In those days it would be nembutal, a barbiturate.

Father didn't, I don't think, take anything, didn't want anything as far as I know. The doctor was called in, wrote him out a prescription, to take some time off work; 'over-work', it was called. It was the end of the war and he had been stretching himself and singing and all the rest of it and so it wasn't put down as a psychiatric number, just that he needed a rest, and the Corporation let him have his rest and then he got back into his promotion.

Since that time, did you look at his illness in any way other than simply over-work and stress?

Well, I looked at it in a way I looked at it at the time, without having read Freud in detail. But, I mean, it occurred to me he always had this thing about Old Pa, his father, being a bit of a bastard. One of the things that my mother brought up, that my father had got to within three weeks of sitting his membership of the Institute of Electrical Engineers, he was a AMIEE – Associate Member of the Institute of Electrical Engineers, he was just on the point of sitting the exam for membership and it would only have cost him £50 and his train fare down to London, but he didn't take the exam. Old Pa said to my father that it was sheer funk, he was a coward and if he had taken that exam and become a MIEE instead of AMIEE he would have been qualified for a higher paid bracket of job and got my mother out of this 'pit' that she had been condemned to.

This moment at promotion is sometimes called promotion neurosis and there are two forms; at the threshold of promotion or after promotion, some people get depressed and this is interpreted because they have made it and the guilt that kept them back overtakes them after they win the prize which is unconsciously their mother which they are guilty about getting. Then they go into a depression. In my own work I've come across a number of people who suddenly, not suddenly, but there is a threshold where they got what they've always wanted, and suddenly the world has collapsed for them and they become very very depressed without knowing why. When they've got what they wanted eventually, it's a dangerous moment.

My father was just about to get what he wanted and went into this anxiety – Inglis and his father – the exam for the MIEE that he didn't take just at the moment that he might have; maybe the thing about marrying my mother instead of the woman that he might have – who was up the road, that Ethel refers to who was the sort of woman for him – and maybe at that moment he didn't quite go for the prize and went for my mother instead.

Later, we used to play one of these meta games of golf, you know the last putt, have you played golf? You know the sort of number; well, my father and I played it, you stand and three-foot putt, [laughs] he wasn't terribly good at that finish. It was also a feature of his voice as a baritone, he had said half jokingly – by the time that he had been in Glasgow for a number of years – that his musical ambition, that the height of his musical ambition would have been principal baritone not at University Chapel Choir but at Covent Garden.

I don't know if it was true, he put it in his own retirement notice in the electrical electricians' journal, he wrote his curriculum vitae, that he sang the first song in Italian over Scottish radio. I've also got a side of me in relationship with George Cunelli, who said you ought to set up a studio next door and you teach music and I'll teach them voice production, and I thought that was very nice of him to say that. When you've to go for the note that absolutely tells, the thing that separates the Caruso from the guy who's a stand-in, his voice would just take on a slight – it didn't quite crack, there was a very fine edge to my father's, it was very subtle, he was a very competent professional singer but he could have had a major career. I mean a minor major career, I think, as a singer in opera.

What did I get wrong about the transference?

You condensed the two episodes, the thing about his father which was the anxiety stuff and the geriatric number at the end. You said he was projecting his father on to me. It wasn't so much that he projected his father on to me, as I thought there was a switch in the relationship that when he took to bed and I sat beside his bed I in a way became his father ... He treated my opinion sometimes, after that, well between a young man and – I had an education that he hadn't had – he treated my intellectual opinion with surprising respect. I mean he never became a little boy in any respect in relationship to me but he would take me seriously.

What about your mother's last years and death? Again, you weren't that much involved, were you?

No, I went to visit her and said very little, just a few words and left. One of the occasions that I visited her in her last years she lived alone in a flat in Marylee in Glasgow.

Did she ever ask you for money or, indeed, anything?

No, no, and she cut me out of her will completely. She left £20,000 but left all of it to the next-door neighbour. However, in Scottish law she's not allowed to do that so I got £10,000, they took the other £10,000. I didn't feel like arguing with her. The neighbour took her over some soup and so forth, in the last few years when she got very frail. I was up at northern New Hampshire at the time, word got to me via my eldest son, who put together the funeral arrangements and I flew over for the first time by Concorde from northern New Hampshire first to New York, then to Glasgow Central Station Hotel – which must be the worst hotel in Britain – and stayed a couple of days for the funeral and then went back. As far as my mother was concerned, she didn't want me to even know that she had died, according to the neighbour.

And her funeral presumably was quite different from your father's; they'd both gone and she wasn't there to see you ...

Her funeral was just attended by my first family, who knew her as Granny, though they only knew her as Granny as very small children, when my first wife and I separated in '64 or so.

Anne, who was a State Registered Nurse – we met in the army – helped my mother with my father somewhat before he went to hospital and my mother claimed to me bitterly that she had given Anne, to help her out, a loan of £1,000. When she asked to get it back, Anne told her that she was never going to get it back. So my mother would never have anything to do with Anne after that, and so the children never saw her, she never went round to the house, that was about the last eight years of her life. I don't think she met anyone except the neighbour and my Aunt Ethel in Largs who went to visit my mother two or three times a year, and myself. When I was up in Glasgow I would always go round to see her for an hour, it would be about as long as I was prepared to stick it out.

Doesn't that sadden you at all?

Well, it's just ....

Sad in the sense that they couldn't see what they were doing ...

It's sad that relationships with my parents turned out that way, particularly with my mother but, well, no it *is* sad, there's no but, I'm not qualifying it. Joe Schorstein, after he met my mother – I think he only met her on one occasion – he never said this directly to me but to a fellow doctor who told me, he said, 'Doesn't Ronnie realize that his mother's mad?'. Well, there are two sides to that, certainly very relevant to the position I developed as a psychiatrist. I could certainly see that if a chap like Joe Schorstein, a sophisticated man of the world from not far from this part of the world [Kitzbuhel], in a way not far from Vienna, looking at my mother, would say she is mad, I could see that. I think she had been mad probably from before I was born.

Interruption [Marguerita]: Oh no, you don't think she was really, you said there were two sides to that.

I'm saying that side of it, that sadness about it, this with-drawal of my mother from all contact with anyone, I think, except the neighbour who was a very tactful woman who saw my mother simply as an old woman living alone in a flat with no one to take care of her and too frail to go out sometimes in the middle of winter. And I don't think there was anyone else. She got rid of practically every little thing in the house that she had, so it was just white walls, perfectly simple chairs, no record player, but she did have a television set. She said the television set had changed her life, for the first time in her life she saw through the television what the world was like outside of her room.

She said that she thought when I was 17 or 18 or 19, her mother had had a dream and come round to the house, and told her that I had turned evil. Her mother never set foot in the house for about 18 years, came round to our house to tell my mother that she had had a dream in which I'd turned evil. Which my mother believed. And she now softened up about 30 years later and my mother was doubting it and she said, 'you know that I think I was going about 85 per cent mad at that time and you helped me to become only 15 per cent'.

In Aunt Ethel's letters, she says these days your parents wouldn't last a minute because they were so incompatible. Did that strike you at all, or were you simply a child who never looked at them in that way?

I never looked at them in that way. I see what she means now, but maybe they weren't so incompatible at home as she thought. She didn't realize how much my father liked his solitude, he went into his room and he worked. He wasn't desperate for company or desperate to go out of the house to find it or round the pub or round to other people's houses.

He devised an instrument that he never made a number of because he was a Corporation employee, he turned it over to the Corporation and I remember him saying that he would have made a fortune out of it if he had kept it to himself and marketed it. His main job, during the period of my childhood, was an on-call mains engineer so there was a telephone in the house installed by the Corporation for his purposes and he would be called out when he was on duty. There would be a fault and two or three streets would be shut down. This meant that there was a fault in the electrical supply between electric pillar boxes with street fuses and cables under the street to the houses. Well that required you to determine where the fault was and when he began his work it was not an uncommon thing to find a part of a street all dug up, to find the fault. He devised and made himself a little ampli-meter that you could monitor above the ground where the current was disconnected so you could foreshorten the work by digging down there, instead of digging up the whole thing, between one fuse box and another which made it more efficient. Maybe other people had done that at the same time but he devised this and introduced it to the routine work at Glasgow Corporation.

If you were saying that you thought your mother was in a sense mad before you were born, are you also suggesting that, the grandmother talking about the evil, that she herself was mad?

Ordinarily, the life of women of that type of woman includes dreams of things like this – mothers and daughters. On the other side of it, my mother would not be mad at all in terms of the clinical psychiatric classification in an ordinary sense. In the sense of some psychodynamic Sullivarian interpersonal psychiatry she was a very withdrawn woman, and would bring up some ambivaletory schizoid stuff and so forth. But she never exposed herself to that; she had to go into hospital when I was 15 or so, yes, maybe about 16, to have a gall-bladder operation and said to me at the time: 'If they ask you anything about me, where I come from, or what my address is, don't tell them anything, it's none of their busi-ness'. OK. So the houseman there said, 'you know your mother, she won't tell me what her address is, or how old she is, she just says it's none of my business'. So I told him her address and where she was born, her birthday and so forth.

It's not normal, to stick pins in a doll called Ronnie. Could she have done it?

It surprised me and saddened me, and slightly frightened me that if Susan, my daughter, was not having me on – she is extremely mischievous, she could just be capable of making it up – especially from what she heard about my mother from her mother, when they fell out, as Anne had absolutely no time for my mother at all. Completely different stories; she said she had five children to cope with, your mother's got all sorts of money in the bank she's never told you about and £1,000 for her grandchildren, and we were very hard up and so forth, etc., etc., and then she wants it back. 'Well, the bitch is never going to see it again, I gave her much more than £1,000 worth of helping out'. So you see that doesn't surprise me. Well, it wasn't a world shattering revelation.

Eczema and asthma, can you remember the onset?

Well, there was only one class in medical school that I came out at the top of my year, skin diseases. Undoubtedly skin eruptions, of which there are many varieties and most of which the causes unknown, are intimately related to the interface, interskin relationships of human beings with human beings. Compared to many children, but not particularly to Scottish children, the relationship was not one of cuddling and touching and stroking and all the rest of it. One of my mother's stories about me, in retrospect, was that I was evil, and one of the things that proved that was that I was black in the face. This is her expression, 'black in the face' for the first year of my life, this was the evil coming out of me.

I was brought up in the Truby King method, 20 minutes every four hours a day, eight hours at night. When I told this story to Winifred Rushforth – can you place Winifred Rushforth? Prince Charles went and visited her before she died – she died when she was 99, two minutes before her 100th birthday, when I was in Iona. I told her this story and she said at least they didn't beat the life out of you, which is what could have happened to some children. Black in the face, no doubt, with frustration and terror, and I thought for a number of years that part of my sensitivity to states of complete disintegrated loss of body ego comes from my experience of going to pieces, fairly regularly two or three times a day for the best part of a year, the first year of my life. When that phase got over, it went into skin. After about a year or two and I think I started picking up these water blisters, so if you punctured them, or they burst, they ran, and I was always told by my mother that I was ruining her by doing this.

Every week I was taken by her into the Glasgow Savings Bank in Ingram Street off George Square, while she drew out her savings to buy lint and bandages to bandage up my arms and legs; both my arms and legs up to my knees with these running sores. So off and on for about two or three years, maybe three or four years, from about a year before going to school for about two years after school, this was attributed to … eating sweets, which were poison, sweets and [laughs] and this is what ordinary human beings ate, who were 'the trash' that I was not one of. Mary Douglas would be a perfect gloss on that, *Purity and Danger*, the absolute boundary of particular food – never eat anything that anybody gives you. It was one reason for not going into houses; my Aunt Ethel had gone into a Jewish house when she was 12 years old and that's why she was deaf in one ear, she'd got a Jewish germ. She was told by her mother that she went into the house of a Jew and became deaf in one ear. [laughs]

The eczema was there from, unknown reasons, from I think the age of about three years, because I remember myself without having that and I seem to have ran into it just before school and I was in this intense eczema number for two or three years. Not bandaged all the time, but I have a familiar memory of these bandages and how the fluid would seep through the white lint into the bandage so that it all stuck and my mother always did this sensitively, got the bandages off, with this weeping eczema. That evaporated and was replaced with a chronic runny nose; my nickname at school was 'sniff' because I was always sniffing and ruining handkerchiefs, which were absolutely sodden wet. I also had a number about putting handkerchiefs in my mouth and chewing handkerchiefs, ends of my hankies would be shredded from chewing them. I couldn't bite lead pencils because that would mean a thrashing for putting lead in my mouth. And then when I was 18, asthma came on.

That's quite late isn't it?

The asthma came on absolutely specifically. The first asthma attack was at the end of my last year at school sports, I ran a half-mile, I never ran track or never thought of running but I won that race, hands down, in 2 minutes 12. In those days you could run at Ibrox Park or in a stadium on 2.12, with a handicap, it was certainly ratable running and so I was picked up by a trainer.

I joined an athletics club and started running around the track and that summer there was a very intense training race, just within the club, a three-mile number and I was given a handicap of about 100 and the best guy in the club was off round the track about two miles into the last three times round when I realized that I was coming to a threshold. Could I keep my feet going one after the other? They were getting heavier and heavier and heavier, my whole body system was becoming intolerable, my will could keep on saying – I already had bronchitis – I had bronchitis all through my childhood, but I hadn't had asthma and I had a bit of a cold that day and it was in the evening, in September and chilly. Asthma; I never dreamed of what that was like but it came over me and completely knocked me out. I just had to get off the track and fall down and that was the first time that I had a real attack of asthma. It went away after about 20 minutes or so, and thereafter asthmatic attacks began to come on every so often, so if I was running a race I would have to take half of ephedrine half an hour, 20 minutes beforehand, and then it would be all right.

I had a sort of nocturnal asthma, which I went along to our family doctor about. He examined me first of all, and found in my lungs a bit of bronchitis and a couple of weeks later I got this really bad attack of nocturnal asthma, and I went round to his surgery immediately afterwards. He put stethoscopes on and he apologized to me, he didn't believe I was making it up but when he examined my chest, he thought I might have been exaggerating it, but he had got me this time just after an attack and realized that it was pretty bad. Inhalers were unusual in those days, it wasn't for several years that I took up with an inhaler, I never had to be whipped into hospital or anything dramatic but it was a feature of my life until I was about 38 or so and then it evaporated for no reason.

How psychosomatic is asthma considered to be?

Ah, well, you've got two schools of thought but if you read the literature of psychosomatic medicine, asthma is a highly-rated psychosomatic sort of thing. There is every sort of psychoanalytic type of psychodynamic interpretation, attacking the maternal bad breast, thwarted rage, residues of a birth trauma, it's everything you can imagine that people say about it.

What do you think?

It didn't seem to me to be very specifically related to these emotional, relational matters in relation to this or that specific person. I saw it as an extension of my childhood, of my university days at home, and after university, what I ran into in the British Army, what I ran into right through, from Gartnavel, Glasgow Psychiatric Department, the Tavistock Clinic, the Tavistock Institute of Human Relations. I'd an overall sense, which was not vague, it was very specific, related to how I got into getting married in the first place, but mostly intellectually, *of being suffocated.* In a suffocating world where you had to be very careful if you didn't want to end up like Jesus Christ on the cross or one way or another of 'how you said what, to whom, about anything'.

So I had a tremendous drive to get myself in some position in the world where I could feel I could breath more freely, symbolically speaking and literally speaking and I had a feeling that I was gonna keep on [gasps and wheezes] until or if I could get out into that space and I wrote myself, to some extent, out into that space. The asthma was related to that sense of social and existential and emotional suffocation.

The way you characterize your adolescence in Wisdom, Madness and Folly *is jazz, drink, nude photo's – that's how you talk about that period of your life.*

No.

No?

No, no, where did you read that?

It's in the book.

Well show me the passage and we can directly refer to it.

Well let's start with jazz. You began to get interested in jazz ...

As I said, the big band music, Jack Payne, Joe Loss, came over the radio, but Julia, my music teacher – I never referred to her as Julia, I mean she was Miss Ommer. Her sister taught the violin and cello and she taught the piano and later formed the Ommer College of Music that was affiliated to the Glasgow Academy of Music and when I got an LRAM and ARCM – a

Licentiate of the Royal Academy of Music and Associate [of the] Royal College of Music; I think still the youngest in Britain at that time to get these two degrees from the two Royal Colleges, performers' degrees, you didn't expect to get them until you were 22 or 23 – I got them when I was still at school.

I gave piano lessons at the Ommer school of music and later taught at home a few people, a few students and a couple of music teachers in Glasgow now were taught the piano by me. When the Warsaw – what you call it, the Warsaw Concerto – I got the score of the Warsaw Concerto and took it round to Julia Ommer to play the Warsaw Concerto and she could barely tolerate the vulgarity of the music. A rip-off of Rachmaninov, and she didn't like me dipping into that sort of music. Richard Addinsell, after Scriabin and the way she had brought me up to you know – da da da de – you know and as far as she was concerned it was Horowitz and Moyeowicz.

I mean to take seriously a pianist like Art Tatum, she wanted me to stay away from that and be completely classical. The whole of the Glasgow Royal Academy of Music was in the same vein, that you played the classics and you didn't dabble in jazz. It was also music that if you really had good taste you wouldn't really listen to. There was no television and the only records were records that were bought. I went into the main Glasgow music shop which I frequented, went into a booth and listened to a record of Louis Armstrong and I wasn't immediately taken with it but it was so different from what I was used to. That sort of gravelly voice and that trumpet, I can't remember who was on the piano, Lester Young was on trombone and it was 'Down a Lazy River'. You know the Louis Armstrong of that time.

Well, in the students union there was a piano in the cafeteria and I couldn't play that music at home. There were piano arrangements that were well known in those days, and music aficionados of that period will remember Billy Mayall, and Charlie Kunz was also acceptable. Jazz is a very disciplined medium and of course I wasn't interested in slopping around, I found that I had been so trained only to play from memory or internalize from the music – I was also expected to be able to improvise formal composition – but to play jazz was another matter and I was very upset because I couldn't just sit down at the piano as some guys could ... I felt terribly a musically third-class citizen because I wasn't up to sitting in and playing a Saturday night stomp and just jazzing with them. I could do that on my own but I couldn't do it well enough to join a company and that was because I had been so streamed classically. That was jazz.

Are you one of those people who would give up anything, give up all the books and everything, if you had composed certain pieces of music?

I wouldn't have given up anything to be Horowitz, I'd have given up everything to be Chopin, or Scriabin. If I could have been a world-rateable composer and performer, I'd have gone for that absolutely. But I wouldn't have regarded that as exclusive, I mean there are very accomplished musicians who actually write. But if I could have been Schoenberg, I mean with a talent like [that] you couldn't be anything else because even with the moderate musical talent that I had, when you are gripped by it, it's very difficult to tear yourself away. Even with a moderate musical talent, at a certain point people will tell you that you've got to make your mind up and some people give it up because you become too addicted. I had a very strong feeling that unless my talent was more than it was, I wasn't going to spend overmuch time on it cutting into what I might be able to do better. I felt that what I ought to go for was what I could do best and that was a combination of the investigation of life and writing.

Do you think there is any connection with your musical sensibility and the form *of some of your writings?*

Oh, very much so. I mean that piece that I've given you that you are photostating about therapy – the sound of the voice as well as the content of the voice, the rhythm and volume and timbre and so forth. When I've had people in supervision as students to be prospective psychotherapists, they've never listened to the sound of their own voice. Not only what they say but they don't listen to how it sounds.
    A number of years ago I went for singing lessons, with a guy called George Cunelli in London, he's dead now but was in his 80s then, he tutored Rex Harrison to sing for *My Fair Lady* and he would have people flying in from the Metropolitan Opera in New York and so on. The sort of top soprano who had gone out a bit would come just to be tuned up by him. He would take on

people whether they could sing or not, as he regarded singing as a special instance of the voice, a cultivation of the voice. Everything was music, the sound, the volume, the timbre, whether it's pleasant or rasping. I'm very conscious of that, the sound of my own voice and other people's voices. Say for instance the voice production comes from different parts of the body, the rasping thing from the nose, other people from the throat, other people from different ways. When I'm talking just now, for instance, the sound is coming from between the throat and the heart. If I wanted to try and explain that to Californian New Age people I would say it comes from between my throat and the heart Chakra. If I got into a certain sort of mood, the timbre of the voice would change. Jerry Lee Lewis sang from his face.

And what about the form *of writing?*

Well, the rhythm of a sentence. I will read my ordinary prose to check out that the sentence flows. You ought to be able to read it, anything, you should cultivate that in what you write; also, *you* ought to!

It ought to sound all right, as you read it through to yourself, that you don't trip up over it. You know you can read it visually, but it doesn't work. I'm not saying you should write as though you are speaking but it's something you should bear in mind for style. I've got these criteria of style, say what you want to say or can say in the fewest words of the fewest syllables with the simplest construction, that is an impeccable criterion of taste.

So you had a 'normal' adolescence, interested in jazz, occasional drink, girlfriend?

The drink was pretty occasional because I had no money at all and didn't feel like more than an occasional drink. The Glasgow Mountaineering Club crowd or two or three people that I, with a haversack, rucksack, hitchhiking up the Lomond Road and staying at a youth hostel and going to a local village pub in Craianlarach on a Saturday night and all one could afford – I mean six pints would be the absolute limit. I don't think I could afford that to start with, it would be a couple of pints. If you had one whisky that was one's tram fares gone for half a week and that wasn't every week.

When you were at medical school you met Marcelle. She was your girlfriend?

No, she wasn't at medical school my girlfriend. At that time she wouldn't consent to sexual intercourse.

But she was a friend?

Yes, and I fancied her very much. The first time I actually had sexual intercourse was with her in the springtime in Paris. We were both virgins and I had an absolutely dream three weeks in Paris in the spring with her. She was by that time in Paris so we corresponded. She has still got letters she's kept all these years which I wrote her from Glasgow, which I never read but I met her a few years ago and she mentioned these letters. She said they were great letters.

At medical school, you talked about the Nazi films that were shown to explain X-rays. You were one of the only people who complained ...

Two people ...

Did that give you an insight into the kind of people who were going to be your colleagues and the profession you were entering?

Well, I had a very sheltered education in a grammar school where I was in the A form while the war was on and there was an occasional raid in Glasgow. I went to school, I stayed at home, I practised the piano and did my homework, played golf with my father. I was now fourth form, fifth form, sixth form and then first year university. The level of culture, you might say, after Latin and Greek among the 200 medical students was pretty – I mean they were a pretty rough crowd. Everyone was a stranger to everyone else except the three or four boys that came from my school and who were in my year at university and who, as it happened – none of us had been particularly friends at school but not enemies – we were quite friendly. I found my way into friends, a group with fellow medical students that were quite congenial, and there was a minor culture shock in the move from the grammar school to medicine.
    Glasgow University is a very compact place. The students union is just across the road from the main university

buildings and there was a lot of student societies and I frequented my share of that and fell in with this or that student who studied physics and mathematics. I was in no way thinking of becoming totally enveloped in the medical school world so I had contacts outside the medical school and with two or three others wanted to have a forum to talk about things that were of interest. To question rather than answer. The forum not being a sort of punchy debating society. We put together a short constitution, sent it to the university – you had to have a new society approved – and formed a thing called the Socratic Club. I think the Socratic Club in Glasgow is still in existence.

From your initial formulation?

Yes, from our initial formulation with Bertrand Russell as the first president. Every month or so we held a meeting in the women's union. This had a small room that housed about 10 to 20 people comfortably and people came along to this and a number of times we invited a few people. I invited Waddington, I remember, the geneticist from Edinburgh, and invited a guy from Oxford who was a specialist in chemistry who talked about alchemical history. I remember we invited Hugh McDiarmid to talk about poetry. Sometimes we chose a subject and discussed it ourselves or invited a lecturer from the anatomy department or invited a lecturer if not a full professor from anywhere in the university who fancied coming to talk about his subject.

And the Nazi films incident itself?

I was shocked at the way people went along with it, but I wasn't entirely outraged. With John Owens, who was my friend and who felt strongly the same way as me, we asked to see Professor Hamilton who had shown the film. He saw us and we said that there was an ethical objection that we wanted to raise with him about the showing of these films.

It seemed to be not the right thing to do, these films ought to be destroyed or if they were to be kept for a historical record to be kept but it was offensive for the victims of these films, for them to be displayed like this and shown as teaching material to us. His response was that he agreed it was horrible and terrible and so on, and that virtually as it were for their sake, for the people that had died in this way, who had been treated in this way, meant that they hadn't died entirely in vain if we could use their death in some constructive way. He wasn't dismissive and he was perfectly serious and presented us with that argument and that stymied it.

Can you talk about your first marriage?

Well, I'll just rattle through the *dramatis personae*. There's my mother and father, referred to as Mummy and Dad, there's on my father's side, there is my father's father, called Old Pa, my grandfather, and my father is the eldest of four children, the next one to him is a sister called Isobella and Isa, then Uncle Jack and Aunt Ethel. On my mother's side, my mother's father died before I was born, there's my mother's mother who was a real person in my life and who died when I was 18, 19, 20 or so, and an older brother of my mother called Archie, another older brother called William, and then my mother and then a younger sister called Mysie.

My first wife's name is Anne. She lives in Glasgow now, she's 60 years old. I met her in the army, when I was in psychiatry at Netley near Southampton, which was in those days the central British Army psychiatric unit. She was a lieutenant in the Royal Army Nursing Corps, she had joined up and volunteered having done her nursing training at Edinburgh Royal. She joined the army in order to see the world and found herself in Netley. We met, she got pregnant, and I was posted to Catterick in Yorkshire, and she was posted to Germany, but had to resign her commission by virtue of being pregnant.

What kind of age was she?

Twentyfour, 25. Without the immediate prospect of getting married, I was having an intense affair for three years with Marcelle. I still know Marcelle, she's originally from Annecy and was a French student over in Glasgow learning English when I was a student, and at that time I thought that my future life was going to be with her. When Anne got pregnant I was so guilty about the prospect of being an illegitimate father, the code of honour and so on. It never occurred to me that we would get married, and I don't think it ever occurred to her. But when she got pregnant we got married and she had the baby,

my eldest daughter, Fiona, in Teignmouth in Devon where her
parents lived, and then moved to Glasgow. She got a flat in
Glasgow when I was in the army in Catterick and when I came
out the army, we embarked on living together with Fiona.

While first working at Royal Gartnavel Mental Hospital
and then after 18 months or so of that at the Southern and
General Hospital and during my time in Glasgow, over a span
of three to four years, she had another three children, about a
year apart. Fiona's the eldest, she'll be 36 now and lives in
Glasgow, with her boyfriend, in Springburn; the next eldest,
Susan, Susie who died when she was 21; next eldest, Karen,
who is married to a chap called Tommy Heenan, who is, in
his generation, quite a well-known Glasgow character. He and
his mother own what used to be the largest dance hall in
Glasgow, Denniston, which he's turned into a massive
snooker palace. I'm told it's the biggest in Britain. They have
two children, William and Mark. William is about 12, 13
years old and Mark is about three or four years old and she's
having another child in May. So I've got two grandchildren.
And I've got a son, Paul, who's about 18 months younger
than Karen who works on the oil rigs, he is a cement mix
consultant; I've got another son who's the fifth child of that
first marriage called Adrian, who until last year was a
barrister in the Temple, and together with his wife, Deborah,
who is also a barrister, has written a book on television
contract law. He lives in Muswell Hill. And she's having a
baby about the same time as Karen, in May. These are four
surviving children out of an original five children by my first
marriage with Anne.

My second wife's name is Jutta, she lives in Highgate, and
I had three children with her. Adam, who's 21; Natasha who
is 18; and Max, who is 13. Adam left home last year, he was
a skiing instructor, in France, this year he's living in London,
I don't know exactly what he is doing, he's not interested in
university or anything academic or anything like that – I'm
not sure what he's addressing himself to. Natasha is over in
India as of now, at a big Hindu festival, she's drawn to India;
and Max is at the International School in London. He lives
with Jutta.

I've got a four-and-a-half-year-old son by a woman called
Sue Collier who is a psychotherapist, family therapist and
couple therapist who lives in London, with Benjamin ... I was
around when he was born and saw him when he was a baby

in the first year of his life and visited them. Then I left
London. I've been away for two and a half years and I visited
him the last time I was in London, a couple of months ago,
and so that makes nine in all, and now Charles. That's it.

They all know each other, I think. Marguerita has met my
first wife, Anne, and she's been up to Glasgow several times
with me and met Karen and Tommy. Sue Collier, she's a
German woman in the first place but she's lived in London for a
number of years, she actually comes from Munich, but I never
met her outside of London. Now she knows Jutta, they seem to
have a quite friendly relationship and visit each other.

Ten children is unusual.

It's out of fashion now. My great-great-grandfather in Australia had 24 children ... The family, both families, missed a
beat in terms of reproducing the line. At my parents level,
I've only got two cousins on my mothers side and no cousins
on my father's side; my father was the only one of four
children who got married and the only one that had a child.
So there might have been, that sort of momentum of making
up for it and me as the only child. But if there's something of
that order, it's not a conscious deliberate decision.

The women that I got involved with, none of them wanted
to have abortions. When they got pregnant, they all wanted to
have a baby and I never felt sort of imbued with feeling that
they had to have an abortion. I felt that was up to them.

You had thought you'd spend your life with Marcelle. Was there
a change of heart that led you to having five children with Anne?

Well, I was into *The Divided Self* at that time and I didn't
know what it was going to turn out to be, but I had to get my
DPM, that is my Diploma of Psychiatric Medicine which
pre-dated present membership. I was working in the hospital,
I was absolutely shocked with the inhumanity and the disgrace of what was going on in psychiatry. Talk about concentration camps and what we had done to the Jews and what
we had done to the native American-Indians, and now what
we were doing to these people! There was fury and indignation and outrage working in me. All this stuff that I was
seeing and there was no R.D. Laing then, there was no
Thomas Szasz even. There was no voice.

So I wasn't thinking of contraceptive devices or anything like that, that was up to Anne and she felt that she hardly ever saw me, except in bed. I was reading or writing or working and she absolutely loved having a child and she wanted another child and then another one and another one. I mean, she lapped them up, and was keeping up with her eldest sister who had four children, just before she did, so she was on for children and it was fine with me if it was OK with her. They played around, and I was Daddy and I didn't find that difficult. I never came from a background that required the consumer goods of a contemporary middle-class person, and she didn't worry about that sort of thing either, so we just mucked along and got on with it. I got on with it and she got on with it and suddenly there were five children.

What about Marcelle?

Well, that was, for me, absolutely heartbreaking. That was one of the most intense emotional catastrophic things that I'd run into. But in a sense it had happened before I met Anne. Because when I went into the British Army, I would have liked Marcelle and I to get married at that point, but she had no notions of marriage in the Scottish Presbyterian sense of marriage, her father was – I don't know what this expression means to you – he was a relic of Léon Blum, French socialist. He played an active part in the French resistance movement. He had an entirely secular mind. Marcelle was the first woman I'd ever met who had read Kafka. She had never read the Bible. The Bible to her was like Greek mythology. I mean it meant absolutely nothing, the French completely secularized culture so a convention like marriage meant nothing to her and she wasn't about to follow me around wherever the army took me.

We both appreciated that our relationship might be one that didn't include actually living together, but I had a very strong feeling for her. I thought when I went into the army – and, you know, the Korean war was on, that was why I was conscripted – that it was quite likely that we would never see each other for years or maybe ever again. So getting married in that way with Anne, in virtue of her having a baby, put the seal on that relationship being carried forward as a relationship of lovers.

But in terms of women in my adult life, Marcelle would

have to be the first one, then Anne and then for a year with
another woman that you might have come across – she works
in London as a journalist – a woman called Sally Vincent.
Then Jutta, and then when that crumbled about seven years
ago, we continued living together for a while and then I was
out and about in the world of the sexual arena for several
years and eventually settled into the relationship that I now
have with Marguerita.

Sue Collier. That wasn't a long relationship?

That went off and on for about 18 months or so, but I don't
think it was ever in her mind at all or in my mind at all that
we would ever live together. This is the only child she has
ever had. I don't know whether she's still married. She's been
separated for a number of years, whereby she takes the name
Collier. But she very much wanted to have a baby.

So which divorces did your parents know of?

Just the first one. Jutta only met my mother once before we
got married. We didn't get married until we had been together
for about eight or nine years. We got married for all sorts of
reasons but it was largely to simplify things with Adam and
Natasha. Adam and Natasha were of course both very much
born by the time we got married and Max was born in the
first year after getting married.

What about Susie, your daughter who died?

It was very sudden, she was sailing along, absolutely fine and
then, within a week or so, she wasn't well, sort of non-
specifically. This is how very rapidly developing leukaemia
generally happens, you don't know what it is – no energy and
so you go along to the doctor – he gives you a tonic, go back,
get a blood test. It was a variety of lymphatic leukaemia, no
one known has ever recovered from that, you die within three
months to two years. You can be put up on an oxygen
cylinder and a continued circulated drip which might keep
you alive for, say, two and a half years maximum rather than
being dead in three months. She was in a hospital in
Glasgow. There were some terrible scenes over that. The
consultant, Anne, the whole family and her boyfriend and the

nurses were all in a complete conspiracy not to tell her she was suffering from a condition that no one ever recovered from. She was just 'ill'.

This was a conspiracy of silence to 'protect' her?

Not to tell her that she was dying. Or what she was suffering from. Well, I almost had to fight my way to the nursing sister. I went up one Sunday afternoon and decided I was going to tell her. She was in this oxygen tent permanently, hardly able to lift her head off the apparatus that took – I forget the name of it – it's a continued circulation of blood, blood is drained off and blood is put in, so it's recycling but you can't get out of that, if you're disconnected you die in about three weeks maximum. The nursing sister said, 'Dr Laing, you're not going to tell her'. *Fuck off.* I told her. I just told her the facts, as I knew them, and she elected to be disconnected and taken back to her boyfriend's flat. Her boyfriend asked me if I would come and stay there when the end was in sight.

So after two or three weeks, the end was in sight and I went up and stayed there for the last three weeks. She died in his flat and she was glad that she had been told. I mean, she said that she was very glad that I had told her and thanked me very much for telling her. It divided the family, I mean murder was in the air; Anne, Karen sided with Anne to some extent and Fiona didn't know what to think, and Paul and Adrian and her boyfriend thought that I had – the boyfriend said – 'you have killed my girl, you have destroyed her by telling her'. This is what he thought in the first place but he got over that. He wanted her kept alive for as long as possible in the hope against hope that the clinic might find a cure for it if she was kept alive long enough.

This was the argument of the consultant. Since I was, as you know, a fellow doctor – he'd never heard of R.D. Laing, he was a haematologist – but I was a psychiatrist of his age and status and he said, well, he couldn't have done that. He said he'd only told two people in the last thirty years that they're going to die, it's against the policy of the National Health Service in Stobhill to tell people that they are going to die. He only told two people and he said one of them was a Roman Catholic priest who he thought, you know, was used to it, but said he was very upset. This was the argument for not telling him. He'd told the Roman Catholic priest and the other person he had told was a male nurse whose job it was to wrap up the people who died and take them down to the morgue and he thought he would be so used to it that when he told him he was going to die, he wouldn't be upset, well he was very upset. So he never told anyone.

When you look back on your families, in both symbolic and practical ways, how were they involved with your work?

Well, two things. One is the relationship as a man that one develops with women in the course of one's life, something I haven't written about but I'm writing about *now*. Well, everyone in a sense has it all to learn but I had no sisters and it was a process to make contact with women, and relationships with women was something that I had to learn. I hadn't any women really to model myself on. The relationship of my mother and father was not a role model for me to adopt, or my Aunt Ethel. This is a major area of exploration in life both in the most intimate, personal way and in terms of what life is all about.

You can live it as an aesthetic in that tradition, and not undertake any physical, intimate, emotional relationship with other creatures at all, and a lot of people have advised that that is the simplest and best way to go through life. If you have anything to do with that sort of thing, then keep it in place and don't allow it to become too important and don't go overboard with it. David Hume's advice was that – unlike those bachelor philosophers like Kant – he had relationships with women but they shouldn't be allowed to colour the whole of life or dominate one's life. All sorts of things like that one has got to discover, what importance they have and what importance you hoped they would have, or could have and so forth. And children, what sort of strategy might one adopt as the caretaking person for one's own children or other people's children, negotiating on their behalf their first years in this very complex world that we live in. And these considerations have always been alive.

I felt that I'd been too much of a learner in that respect, but it has always been on my agenda that if I lived long enough and came out into a space where I felt that I had something that I wanted to say in that domain, I would have a go at it. And in the latter part of my life having what I would call a balanced life, where I am actually engaged in something as well as reading and thinking and writing and meditating and hanging about in a domestic situation and whatever, that there was something to engage in, then the idea of cultivating a sort of specific focus in relationship to the relational aspect of child development, using the intimate, personal domain as the area in which to study in a model way, not in a distant, subjective, and depersonalized way, but some sort of way that could be an example of the sort of way of doing this, that if I read it as a parent, or prospective parent, I would find that useful, that's what I'm turning to just now.

How have the emotional crises in your different relationships affected your work?

I'm perfectly glad to address that question. It's a difficult question, however, to answer in a few sweeping generalizations because if you consider my writing career as beginning in my teens, by the time I was moving from school to university I had, like Sartre said in one of his autobiographical writings, that he never had an ambition to become a writer, he *was* a writer.

I think he says that in *Words*. He *was* a writer, and so he had to fill in that timeless thing. I felt that I was some sort of intellectual by the time I was 16, 17, 18, 19. I was some sort of intellectual, not necessarily modelled on what had gone before, but I was entering into that destiny in my generation and that certainly entailed writing which at university I felt I could practise. I mean I could read and whatever happened I was going to put first stake down in the writing arena, by the age of 30.

So I was a bit behind time with – well I was just about on time – I had imagined first publication by the age of 30; I'd kept the schedule pretty well by my own manuscript. For reasons that were out of my control the publication of it was delayed because no publisher was prepared to accept it and then the Tavistock publishing house became bankrupt, and it was two years before they got themselves together. But I did not regard any degree of emotional pain, of the ups and downs of love affairs or – these could be excruciating. But this I could expect to be coming to anyone. I wasn't particularly grimly pessimistic, but the literature that I was imbued with was not a prospect of good news and the world, of that time, was much darker than it is now, in a more obvious way. Hardly anyone that I knew didn't assume that there was going to be another war and it was going to be worse than the last one and might be the war to end all wars.

The turmoil of the period of moving out of the establishment in one sense and into Kingsley Hall put a lot of pressure of all sorts on me that made intensive writing over the period of the latter '60s very difficult.

I did a series of lectures in New York, the Alanson White Institute where Erich Fromm and Rollo May were, which is a manuscript I never published, I never felt I got it quite together enough. They very much wanted me to publish that. There was that and there was the volume, *The Politics of the Family* and *Knots*. After *Knots* there had been all the emotional stuff of the divorce, first wife and the loss of the five children largely, which meant a great deal to me, and I had a feeling of being unable to catch up with myself. I was now into a relationship with Jutta and she had got pregnant with Adam, she got pregnant a second time, and I felt almost completely misunderstood ...

Badly judged?

Mainly, I was being badly judged in the way I was being taken up, and the feedback I was getting from the world was very largely what I had said was being completely ignored. And what I had not said, I was being attacked for, and, I felt, for all sorts of reasons – I was just going at this almost continually, since birth, since going to school, right through to Kingsley Hall, and I saw it was not going to be taken up as a model. I didn't see that that was a successful pragmatic actual centre as I had imagined it as a possibility of being. The Italians were all, as far as I could see, totally fucked in what they were on about. The whole way the Americans were caught up in Vietnam and Cambodia and so on was just so insufferably wet and sickening in its hypocrisy of that whole generation, especially those who used me as a justification for their attitudes at the time.

I thought I'd take a sabbatical year, clear out for a year and do as little as possible and seriously cultivate the art of meditation. I did this for a year, came back and during that time I was away I hardly looked at a book except Pali. I learned Pali and Sanskrit but I read no books and I wrote nothing except Pali, and the odd entry, the occasional entry in a journal, not because I deliberately was trying to withhold, but it just evaporated.

When I came back, re-entered, my relationship with Jutta almost immediately became agonizing. She was off having affairs, and I didn't want to live with a woman who wanted to see the relationship that way; she was perfectly entitled to do so, but not while we were living together. But I couldn't bear to give up Natasha and Adam, that would be giving up seven children. So I was involved then for the first time in an excruciating emotional, sort of personal, intimate, emotional – I really couldn't talk about it to anyone, couldn't write about it. Then for the first time I had real difficulty in writing and I wanted to get into writing again but I couldn't.

What I had written in the '60s was my past, what I wanted to try and get to, I found very difficult to find the voice, the tone. I wanted to give it an expression of a certain vision, a certain sensibility; anyway what I did was *The Facts of Life* and *Do you Love Me?*, *Conversations with Children, Sonnets*. I was now living and working at home and being very unhappy at home in the most intimate way and was cutting into my intellectual life. My place of work had always been outside the home up to then, it was a whole new lifestyle. So I sort of grinded through that. There were various projects that never came off, there are whole unpublished manuscripts. I've got three manuscripts that I've still got that were turned down, didn't come off and the synthetic vision that I wanted to put together, which was quite extensive, I eventually did everything I could to concentrate on that.

My experience was so different from most people. There was no psychiatrist that I knew who had spent anything like the length of time for years and years that I had spent with extremely disturbed people who weren't on drugs. It was impossible to talk to these guys, they just had no idea of what I was talking about, about relationships between myself and various people, they had no connection. 'Growth and develop-ment' people, like Janov and Grof, had no fucking idea of working with seriously disturbed people, they were taking people on trips of some sort of psychedelic trip, some sort of workshop weekend. Re-birthing; they'd not the faintest idea how to last two minutes with someone who's seriously in it. Well, that's what I was doing all the time. Until I left London. Two and a half years ago. It still hasn't come to me how I could share that with other people, that experience, convey that. I've done workshops and seminars and sometimes with professionals and so on and I very much get the feeling when they go away they don't get it and it's very difficult to show them *it*.

You were asking me particularly about the vicissitudes of writing and these considerations, you know, influence what one feels drawn to try to write. I mean, the inner compulsion is a dialectic or a relationship with the environment that one's writing into, that one's addressing. I'm glad now that I didn't try to say a number of the things that I wrote notes about, that I didn't work it up into a book form, about this and that in the '70s because I felt ... from the early '70s to the last year or so, that's when the 20th century has really changed. It wasn't World War II, something has, a new era, the computer world, a new era is just coming now. Well I'm quite fresh for that.

Also I realized that I was lamenting too much within myself a world that I saw disappearing. I was in danger of that attitude of this whole era, the going down of the western world, the loss of this, the loss of that, that sort of lament that was going on in the '60s and '70s and I was getting caught up in that. I never got completely caught up in it, but it was something that I sensed and had to fight against. Well, I don't feel that now. I think there has been a transition, a qualitative transition, and the children of Max's age, they don't know anything about the whole world that was my world. For them the world began yesterday and there is everything to live for in the future and they are not interested in carrying on into the future a great deal of the things that I felt I couldn't imagine life without.

I've got through to now, so from now on in, without denying or forgetting the past, I've got a different relationship to it now than I had three or four years ago. I adopted a policy in the year I was away that I would adopt – I don't really know whether you know about technical terms of Buddhist meditation – of what is called Vipassana meditation, you just observe and don't stop–start. Often I wished that I would get out of this space, would move and I'd very much prefer another one, or do I fight to get out or do I endeavour to keep a position of clarity through the fug and the fog. There could have been several books, there were certainly several manuscripts, several separate books that got crushed into *The Voice of Experience*. After *The Voice of Experience* I just managed to get out the *Wisdom, Madness and Folly*, and then after that until really about the summer this year, I haven't had any internal, consistent drive. I've made notes, I've written quite a lot of things but nothing systematic or anything on the horizon that I could see what the picture or shape could be. So I had the choice of polishing up this bit and that bit or keeping them at a penultimate state and just playing along 'til hopefully some proverbial lightening or, in terms of a writer, I'd see an opening and could go for that, which I hope is what I am now involved in.

2. INFLUENCES

In these conversations, Laing discusses the intellectual influences on his thought. For example, he talks of his interest in Marx and especially the debate concerning the so-called 'young Marx' of the 1844 *Economic and Philosophical Manuscripts* and the more 'mature' writings of *Capital*. Similarly, he shares his thoughts on the value of Freud, Jung and Adler.

The influences most central to his development, however, lay in existentialism and phenomenology, those philosophical traditions somewhat excluded by mainstream English philosophy. Laing was self-taught in these most complex and difficult philosophical languages, in itself quite a considerable achievement.

Existentialism was attractive to Laing for a number of reasons. For one thing, there is its hostility to abstract theory for obscuring the roughness and untidiness of actual life; while its religious sensibility would have undoubtedly appealed. Existentialist thought is sometimes profoundly religious, as in Kierkegaard, and sometimes overtly atheistic, as in Sartre. But even in existentialist atheism there is discernable an almost obsessionally religious note.

Kierkegaard (1813–55) sought to introduce – against the widely accepted presuppositions of the academic world of his day which emphasized rationality, objectivity, and essentialism – the importance of concepts such as subjectivity. However, the most important among modern existentialists and one who immensely influenced Sartre is Heidegger (1889–1976), who emphasized all the great existentialist themes: freedom, authenticity, and 'others'.

Sartre (1905–1980), the most radical exemplar of nihilistic existentialism, deeply influenced Laing's analysis of the human condition. For Sartre there is no distinction between 'essence' and 'existence'. When one asks who is the 'father' of existence the answer must be *le néant*, 'nothingness'. Man must create his own essence. He recognises a distinction between an authentic and an inauthentic life. Since in Sartre's view there is no God and no absolute standard of ethical conduct, each person must choose what he or she is to be and live accordingly with total involvement. Borrowing heavily from Heidegger, Sartre distinguishes between the *en-soi*, the existence of a thing, which exists in itself, and the *pour-soi*, the existence of human beings who project themselves to values and aims.

Phenomenology is the philosophical outlook developed initially by Husserl (1859–1938) and which is characterized by a preoccupation with the fundamental character of subjective processes. The aim of phenomenology is to delimit the entire endless realm of experiences, in all their types – perception, phantasy and so on. All belief in truths of any kind are suspended ('bracketed') and we are left with the experiences themselves, and with the objectivities meant by them. With all beliefs placed in abeyance as a matter of method, one can then speak of 'pure subjectivity', or of 'pure experience'.

Much of Laing's time was spent in the understanding of and appreciation of aspects of Nietzsche's (1844–1900) thought. In Greek tragedy, Nietzsche found the mingling of two elements equally important: Dionysian passion and ecstasy, and Apollonian serenity and calm. Accordingly he considered that he had found a means of uniting the classical and romantic elements in European thought and culture. Nietzsche also called for a 'transvaluation of values', to express the need to conceive of new understandings that would lead men to a stage beyond, that of the *Übermensch* – the noble, compassionate, 'superman'.

Can you tell me the context in which you read Marx, and how you think that people can read Marx in your work?

That question has caught me slightly by surprise. I think it was at the end of my second term at university. I frequented Glasgow 'street oratory', from my school days, every Sunday: there were several places where people got up on their soap boxes in Glasgow, just off Sauchiehall Street and Renfrew Street. The other one was up the road where I lived and I heard Willie Gallacher speaking in Shawlands, who was still an M.P, and was the only Communist M.P. He was talking about the revolution. I went to street meetings, there was quite a lot of that at the end of the war and every year there was the May Day Procession that went up from Eglinton Toll in the southside of Glasgow, went up Victoria Road to what

was called locally the Queen's Park recreation ground where
the rally was held. From a boy I was aware of this movement.

From the end of the war I was very imbued with my own
mixture of a sort of insistent atheism – that this was all a put
on, God and the Christian Church and all the rest of it –
which I had got more from Nietzsche in the first place, and
Kierkegaard. Somehow or other at university I picked up a
complete contempt for the Labour party and Beveridge and
that type of thing ...

Because they were reformist?

Reformism, and I'd also been very sentimentally attached to
the Communist and Anarchist side of things in the Spanish
Civil War. The Spanish Civil War was sort of acted out in the
playgrounds at school. People took sides at school, it was
very interesting. It was a whole passage that I didn't put in
Wisdom, Madness and Folly that as the war began to take a
turn and it was evident that Franco was going to win and the
long siege of Madrid, the balance of the fights that went on in
the school playground began to tilt with the fate of the war ...

*Why would Glasgow children be so interested in the Spanish Civil
War?*

I don't know, it's that sort of cultural diffusion system that, at
Hutcheson's Boys' Grammar School, among the children were
reflected the nuances of the socio-economic and political
positions of their parents. I thought at that time the only
logical society was one of one class of people – this was
without reading Marx – one class of people who had no claim
to right. We were brought up on history at school, the history
of treaties and wars and the divine right of kings and the
succession of dynasties ...

Remember, I was into this thing about the *truth* so it was
all a lot of fucking lies, that they taught, and I was indignant
about these lies that had been put over like *Santa Claus*.

God suddenly seemed to be just the biggest collective
put-on, the opium of the people and the unemployment and
slums, factories, things that I didn't know anything about but
I lived around where people who worked and lived in these
things. And the Spanish Civil War, the Russian Revolution,
World War II, the Nazis, concentration camps and the atom

bomb, and if things went on this way there would be contradictions in society.

So where did you learn of Marx?

Where I got it from was conversation, the odd thing that I came across from reading, and then I addressed myself to stuff that was published by the Marxist Leninist Publishing House. They were blue books and this was Lenin in some ways more than Marx. A practical man, who had, with logic as it seemed, just wiped out this ridiculous empire of the Tsars. Over a period from the late spring of the first term at university through that summer into the next year, I'd read all that stuff. In that first year I couldn't stand the forums, I looked into the Glasgow University Student Debating Society and people were just not talking about anything, so I founded a thing called the Socratic Club in Glasgow. I wrote to Bertrand Russell and asked him to be the President and I got a letter back and he accepted. It's a letter I've still got somewhere. This was a small group of my friends and people, intellectuals, a Chinese guy who was most intelligent, struck me as the most intelligent person of my age that I'd ever met. He came from China, he spoke, he read German, he made me terribly ashamed of myself, that this Chinaman spoke perfect English and German, had read Hegel and Marx in German, and assumed that you read a fucking thing in the original.

Two or three of these people I met through the Glasgow Mountaineering club; I don't think I ever paid any subscription to the Glasgow Mountaineering Club but I fell in with people. Every weekend we'd hitchhike from Glasgow, up to Craianlarich or past Oban and walk up one of the mountains and stay in a youth hostel.

I went along to the Centre of the Iona community which was located in Clyde Street, and I got to know a guy called Penrys Jones there, who was two or three years older than me and he was a sort of lieutenant of George MacLeod. For about 20 years he was chairman of television religion censorship, and he went to live on the island of Iona years ago. There was also the movement of worker priests which had surfaced in France, Roman Catholic priests who interpreted the Christian message as Jesus Christ has no other hands but ours, we have to put ourselves on the line, you know Jesus

Christ wasn't crucified in a cathedral between two candle sticks, he was crucified in a town garbage heap between two thieves. They were opposed to all this sort of sickening Christianity of the kind where people go to church with their hats and fur coats on.

I got into discussion and arguments there while hanging about and I became aware of John Maclean – I don't know whether you know that story? John Maclean became my first literary project, I decided I was going to write a biography of him. John Maclean had been a friend of Lenin; the first Communist consulate to be set up after the October revolution was in Renfrew Street in Glasgow and he was the first president of that. He was arrested, put in Barrlinnie Prison, died three months later under suspicious circumstances and some people thought he was poisoned or starved to death. I came to meet occasionally, over a pint in a pub, with some of the guys who had fought in the Spanish Civil War – Jimmy Kerrigan, members of Glasgow Communist Party and other people who were anarchists of that vintage. They were all men who were about 15, 20 years older than me.

I imagine those guys were not aware of the so-called 'young Marx' of the Economic and Philosophical Manuscripts ...

That early Marx that was claimed to be a sort of existentialism, a humanism, Marxism as humanism. These guys had no time for that at all. I don't think I ever particularly brought it up but I remember Willie Gallacher using that favourite expression, the first time I heard it: 'you can't make an omelette without breaking eggs'. You can't make a revolution without killing people, this ridiculous bourgeois sentimentality about the sanctity of human life.

I was impressed by these guys because they seemed to mean it, and I mean they weren't just talking. Nothing had happened in Glasgow, it had been nipped in the bud with John Maclean. I read Tom Johnson's *A History of the Working Class in Scotland* and I began to feel that Scotland was itself a colony. All the investment capital in Scotland came from outside Scotland. Scotland wasn't capitalist, like England was, I mean the English capitalists owned England and they owned Scotland as well; look what had happened to the Highlands and the clearances. I realized it had to do with a specific socio-economic historical analysis of specific circumstances and we couldn't rely on what Marx had written over 100 years ago simply applied to different circumstances.

I gave an occasional lecture or seminar when I was at that age, 18, 19. The first one I gave was to the Gorbals Debating Society. I went along and gave a talk on some aspect of Lenin's theory. And I read *Capital*.

Apart from the fact that these guys 'meant it', were you impressed by the rigorous so-called scientific analysis of capitalism; was that the stuff of Marx that interested you?

Well I had a sufficient self-training. No one ever taught me, I had no mentor in this, I had a sufficient self-training to realize that. This is what I thought then and still feel now. Practical material contradictions, not logical contradictions, which clashed with each other in terms of the historical process, seemed to me the only *motor of history* that I had come across.

I read a bit of the classics of economics: *The Wealth of Nations*, I went through Adam Smith and Ricardo, and pre-Marxist stuff of the 17th century. I came across Maynard Keynes and I was aware that there was a type of economic and theoretical analysis that I didn't have very much time for.

My most vivid reference to the Stalin era was Arthur Koestler's *Darkness at Noon*, but I had enough intellectual awareness to realize that if I was going to be really serious about this path I would have to teach myself the whole discipline of economics and a few terms like 'surplus value' and 'scarcity' and 'means of production' and 'modes of production' and a simple-minded view that the more you produced the more you end up yourself as out of work was not going to go very far unless I took it further. I got to the point of looking at economic graphs and diagrams and fluctuations and I became very puzzled as to what is money, what is capital, what is actually this stuff and the whole process of extraction industries world wide.

And the secondary literature didn't stand up very well. There was Christopher Caudwell's *Illusion and Reality*, a book written in the mid-'30s which was a serious effort but if I read these self-styled Marxists they all had a simple-minded formula and then they turned the handle and applied it to anything. I mean after being a born-again converted Christian I wasn't about to become converted to atheism as another creed, and I wasn't about to espouse a sort of political activism on the basis of a Marxist ideology that I found ...

Was it too evangelical for you?

Well, I don't like abandoning the word evangelical. I don't like abandoning the word mythology for a lot of superstitious nonsense. There is a good word that the Pope could use for evangelical, isn't there? I mean there is a good sense of the word evangelical, there's a good sense of the word mythology, and there's, yes, evangelical in a sense. I mean I don't mind being evangelical about something that I could imagine would be worthwhile really campaigning for, and trying to get as many people to agree with you about something.

Did you take anything from Marx which is evident in your work? People like Peter Sedgwick have criticized you because of your lack of following, what he considers, a 'correct Marxist' line ...

Oh yes, I mean my attitude to that is go fuck yourself ...

Sure ...

I thought that Peter Sedgwick in particular, his absolute impertinence, to accuse me of not following a correct Marxist line where as far as I'm concerned Marx is an important intellectual and very important figure in the world that we live in, that I respect. But I never would have regarded myself as committed to following a correct Marxist line, and especially after World War II. What the fucking hell is a correct Marxist line?

I mean we're aware that so-called Stalinism had taken over Russia, this was a vast system, whether what was going on in Russia had anything to do with Marxist purity is hard to say. And anyway, I never could see how you could extrapolate Marxist apocalyptic revolutionary writings of the 19th century to the present-day world. I was at any time looking to read a contemporary person in the Marxist tradition giving me a really good rundown on the present state of affairs at that time. There is nothing that I came across or heard of, which met that criteria of a certain amount of rigour. I had a contempt for these ideological amateurs who'd get a few juicy phrases and think they turn around the world. So it wasn't getting me anywhere.

You realized early on that what you were interested in was human suffering and human misery. When you were reading Marx had you decided by then why you were reading these things with those preoccupations in mind?

Well yes, I was reading Marx as I was reading everything else, in order to find out what the hell was going on in the world that I was living in and beyond my immediate sense data which was all I'd got – and reading a newspaper here and reading the print of a book – what was actually going on in the world. I'd never been to England, I'd never been across the border, I'd been about 30 miles to the Ayrshire coast and about 60 or 70, 80 miles up to Fort William and over to Edinburgh. *That* was my horizon on the fucking world.

I realized that I couldn't apprise myself of everything, and I hadn't all that curiosity to go too far into sheer abstraction, too far into sheer abstract logical theory, too far into sheer, pure arithmetic and mathematics. I sort of lost it in the complete play of abstraction. I realized that these operations of mind were behind the world that I lived in in the technological fall-out of mathematics, and physics and chemistry and all the rest of it; that side of it was *anchored to*, I wanted to know about the human body, anatomy, physiology, and particularly the nervous system, where things meet and intersect. What is this central nervous system, the human nervous system?

Well, Marx hadn't anything to say really about that. Of course I was interested in Pavlov and immediately couldn't see how people could take Pavlov so deadly seriously. What had that got to do with the concrete reality of human beings in the socio-economic circumstances? I mean, that sort of way, the Marxists were always saying you've got to come back to concrete socio-economic material reality and not go away off into bourgeois subjective idealism.

Who did you read before coming to Marx? In various books you mention Kierkegaard, Nietzsche, Hegel, and Marx. Who were the others?

Well, apart from the stuff that was efflorescence from school which was very important. That's Plato, the dialogues of

Plato, which weren't expected school reading, but you just
sort of touched on it and I dipped through into *The Republic,
The Phaedo, The Symposium*, and a touch of that debate, the
laws and political thinking from there and a little bit of
Aristotle. There was Henry George, Adam Smith, no, I read
Adam Smith after Marx. There was, however, a completely
other world – Kierkegaard, Freud and Nietzsche.

Before Marx?

Yes.

Why Kierkegaard? I mean how on earth did you come across him?

Because he was K in the reference library that was just across
the back green from where we lived. The Govan Hill Public
Library. I made my way through the library. From about the
sixth form at school I was eating my way through the library,
I mean I was looking at all the books and I was looking up
the card index and I was working my way from A to Z. That
was my idea of continuing to educate myself.

I hadn't any primary interest in medicine. I mean, the way
physics and botany and zoology and the other subjects were
taught in medicine was pretty mindless.

There was Darwin, in the sense of *Origin of the Species*, I
still hadn't read *The Ascent of Man*, which is a thing I keep on
wanting to read, and a complete edition of *The Expression of
the Emotions in Man and Animals*. There was a sort of
evolutionary materialism of a broad span which I was aware
of, in which the compression of human history into a few
hundred years expanding into two or three thousand years of
all we knew of that relationship to the prehistorical origins of
culture. The vast timescale of zoological time. I knew of
D'arcy Thompson on the growth of forms, and Sherrington on
the integration and function of human nervous system, and
Cannon on the physiology of human emotions.

That side of a materialist thesis had to be integrated to the
human form and function embedded in a social and economic
context, with the immediate delivery of ideological conditioning in order to make so many people behave in such
destructive ways towards each other against their own best
interests. It is amazing how people apparently were prepared
to kill and die as long as they believed that they were doing

what they were supposed to be doing. The question of the propensity for obedience became, and has always remained, a sort of extraordinary question mark for me.

Also at the end of the war when there was a big contingent of ex-servicemen who had been four years or so in the war and some were prisoners of war who came back. They were a special class of student, were four or five years older than the rest of us. Quite a lot of them were marked obviously; they were different, they had seen what they had seen, we were just schoolboys. All they could think of as far as I could make out was getting through the exams, it didn't seem to induce in any of them a questioning – 'what the fucking hell is all this about and when's the next time coming?'.

Well, I couldn't see how Marx – getting back to Marx – explained the fact that everyone just took that, whether you were rich or poor or whatever socio-economic class. There's a metaphor of Kierkegaard of the ridiculous sort of attitude epitomized by a guy trying to stop the course of history in a railway compartment, throwing himself against the rear wall of the railway compartment in the idea of stopping the train. That's absurdity.

So let me get back to Kierkegaard, Nietzsche and Freud, that you read ...

In lousy translations ...

Presumably it was quite amazing that you were able to read Freud, Nietzsche, Kierkegaard and so on, in a small public library in the 1940s?

Yes, I suppose it was. There was no one else I knew that had read these things but nevertheless Govan Hill Public Library had a copy of *Either/or*. I mean, the first major thing of Kierkegaard that I read was a big book *Concluding Unscientific Postscript* and that was one of the peak experiences of my life. I read that through, without sleeping, over a period of about 34 hours just continually.

With difficulty?

Well, I got so caught up in it. I never felt impelled to go back and do an in-depth study of it but I was caught up by the clarity of his mind and with irritation with the translation – after all he wrote in Danish. I was reading a translation that I wasn't convinced I could trust. But nevertheless it was a great experience in those years to come across things like that in Govan Hill Public Library. I'd never seen any reference to him, I mean it's not as though I'd read this or that book, as you say, that directed me to it. It was just this complete vista that I'd no idea that that type of mind and that type of thinking existed.

What did he say to your heart and your mind that made you continue to read him and want to know more?

Well, it's difficult to answer. Because I didn't ask myself when I was reading, 'what is he doing to my heart and mind?'.

Because I didn't *hear* music, most of the music that I played as a boy, I never heard – I learned it from the music, I never heard it anywhere. I had never heard it at concerts, I never heard it on records, I never heard it at home, it was music that I bought from a shop and then learned to play it. Chopin's mazurkas, Chopin's scherzos, Chopin's waltzes. Well *Kierkegaard* was like a sort of musical, intellectual Mozart, a combination of Mozart and Chopin. It just absolutely fitted my mind like a glove, my mind, my sensibility, here was a guy who had *done it*. I felt somehow or another within me, the flowering of one's life.

If I had the sensibility, the education, the opportunity and dedication, the hard work and the genius backing up those sort of elements of sensibility in me, I'd have written that, I'd have written the Chopin corpus, I'd have written a great deal of Mozart. There it was, the same creature, the same God that I'd created. The amazing network whereby there was Kierkegaard over a hundred years ago, writing this stuff down that – the cohesiveness of our civilisation that – over a hundred years ago in another country, it was still in Europe. You know there are Chinese texts or old Hindu texts and so on – this can get to one, this sense of some absolute, very profound common factor in being human. Despite the fact that most human beings didn't have any sensibility for it at all, nevertheless some had, because this had got into the Govan Hill Public Library.

*He affected your sensibilities and so that is the best way to talk
about him influencing your work, simply that it comes into your
mind, it is not forgotten, it slowly shapes your sensibilities?*

Oh, I'm not saying that. I mean you'd have to ask me what I
mean by sensibility and I would have to write a book on what
we mean by the *word* sensibility. I don't mean sentimentality,
I don't mean what, in a certain stream of contemporary
writing, means affect or emotion divorced from cognition and
intellect. I imagined the mainstream of my interest was that I
was going to be a scientist doing work that was relevant to
human beings in relationship to the way we suffer. I didn't
feel all that unhappy. There was a double thing, there was all
this misery and ugliness and brutality and inhumanity to man
and so forth, and there was this beauty, this elegance, this
rigour and elegant beauty of a mind like Kierkegaard's and a
mind like Mozart's or Chopin's.

*Let me put it differently. In terms of the conceptual framework
with which you approached the world and which fires your
writings, is there anything from Kierkegaard that is discernable in
this conceptual framework you have continued to use from the
early days?*

This a preliminary answer to that, and it's not that I haven't
thought about it but I haven't addressed myself to a sustained
attempt at revision. The distinction in *Either/or* between the
aesthetic, the ethical and the religious opening out into the way
one organizes a *weltanschauung* and the way one construes the
whole situation that one calls it situationism – it was called that
by some people and still is – that in thinking about trying to
come to terms with the ethical issues that are not abstractly
theoretical, the answer to these questions have to do with
whether I smoke this or whether I don't. It's not just a
chemistry of nicotine, it's whether this gives me cancer and
whether I want to live or die or stay healthy or whatnot –
existential flesh and blood decisions. Most of our existential
flesh-and-blood decisions have not got any objective correlative
data to justify or not to justify them. We make our decisions, we
act and live according to whatever you want to call it –
assumptions, things we've been taught, things we believe in. The
embeddedness of all that in our socio-economic positions,
money, self interests, bias, thoughts, and so on.

Kierkegaard and Marx and Freud and Nietzsche were united. Nietzsche had absolute contempt for 'The Lie', as he called it. The last words that he wrote, certainly the last words that were published in the definitive Nietzsche volume, were 'I deny the Lie'. Then after that it's silence. 'I deny the Lie'. That sense of demystification, right into our physiological system, our flesh and blood and the way that our body operates, embedded in this mass of confusion that is put over as the truth.

These people from different angles seemed to clarify that, also in the contemporary French writings of that time, of Camus in particular. Not the sort of movement of contradiction and thesis and materialized thesis and antithesis, movement to a synthesis. A sort of piece of elementary conceptual machinery, sheer unalloyed and irremediable, unredeemable *absurdity*, the confrontation of absurdity; how can you live because this challenges one's sense of vitality, that there is a possibility of boggling under that, of fading away under that, of forgetting it all, of just smashing it all up, or going berserk, or killing yourself or going mad. There is something about the human mind that seems to want reconcilability and harmony; conflict is all right as long as it, through time, goes through a process that intertwines and resolves and comes back again and so forth.

So from different positions also since I was, to some extent, like a sort of Camusian judge and jury of all this, I would read Freud, read Marx, Kierkegaard. Kierkegaard and Nietzsche were very similar to each other in various ways. But these were the main horizons. I didn't come across Hiedegger really until, it was really Sartre's *Being and Nothingness* that introduced me to Hiedegger and Rousseau.

Nietzsche seems more important to you than people possibly imagined, or was he just another ingredient for that sensibility?

No, there was one paper that was quite a good one by, I forget his name, Dan Goldman perhaps, called 'Nietzsche and Psychiatry'. It was an academic paper written in the late '60s, picking up on Laing, and he said the thing that people had missed is the influence of Nietzsche in this set of writings, particularly *The Divided Self* and *The Politics of Experience*.

Can you elaborate?

Well, we'll take it somewhat chronologically. I was reading, I
think, first of all Ludovici – I think his name was – who did
the first translation of Nietzsche into five volumes and it was
chronological, *The Birth of Tragedy*, ending up with *Ecce
Homo*. And maybe some pieces picked out of his last several
years of unpublished writing and posthumously collected
under *The Will to Power*. The distinction which I first came
across, between *Dionysian* and *Apollonian*, was a major distinction, in my mind, that separated two types of mind, and
two types of my own mind. People would now to some extent
trivialize that by talking about left and right hemisphere
dominance; Dionysian is obviously the right hemisphere, the
dominant type thing; what I almost sort of breathtakingly,
before in *Ecce Homo* it became excessive where you had to
make certain allowances for this guy. In *Zarathustra*, the
amazing, *the transvaluation of all values*. For someone like me
who had this great propensity to be devout, if I could be, just
be given the chance to justify, the nerve with which he
rejected that, and my horrified terror at what the destiny of
thinking in this way might turn out to be if one thought these
things as far as he did.

At that time I would read Nietzsche and I'd a pencil and I
would tick off an aphorism, giving him 100 per cent for that,
you know, you've got a mixture of both being in a sense the
absolute pupil of his and at the same time a judge of his. I
recognized that that was correct, he had hit the nail on the
head, that was correct. I wasn't entirely reading it as a
revelation of why I had never thought of that. No, somehow
he had put an expression that was latent as a seed in my
mind that hadn't come to the surface and I recognized it. I
mean I was just following my nose, my instinct, I had no
curriculum that I was bound to, like why did I go into
medicine, why didn't I study the humanities, or literature or
philosophy and so on. I thought this was an absurd idea, I
had access to all this sort of thing directly from the top guys,
I didn't need this mediocrity in between telling me what I had
to read and what the right answers were, or how to write an
English sentence. I would do that myself.

So I was right out in the open just following where my
sensibility took me. Like, since I didn't go to Musical
Academy, I didn't have to listen to and study and analyse and
compose music that I didn't like. I had a very belligerent
sense of, you know I had one life to lead and it might not last

all that long and I was going to go for just what I wanted to
go for, I didn't know where it was taking me. I'd have been
very surprised, I think, at that time if I had been told that the
first book that I was to write was going to be *The Divided
Self*. I'd no idea that I was going in that direction, though
retrospectively it makes sense but I didn't think so at the
time.

Can you be more specific about the influence of Nietzsche?

Well, the Apollonian and Dionysian distinction from *The Birth
of Tragedy* was one thing and then the transvaluation of
values. That was mainly spread out over two volumes. There
was all the writing about Christ and the Anti-Christ. In fact it
was the same thing that got Foucault about Nietzsche. I don't
know whether you've read very much of Foucault, he hasn't
written very much about Nietzsche but he expressed his debt
to him. There wasn't structuralism in those days, and we
weren't taught mathematics in terms of set group and latticework theory, but I was aware that there was something like a
sort of grid. That one's mind was operated in terms of this
being good and that being bad and this being correct and that
being incorrect, a binary system. The whole thing could switch
and give you another take on it and there was a tremendous
embedded physical sense of guilt and anxiety about switching
these things around. You were told you're going to die if you
did so, or you're going to be damned if you did so, and these
were the way things were and these were all constructs,
constructs of the mind, they are all socially and historically
conditioned. Whether by the predominance of the means of
production and material distribution of goods in the market or
whatever the theory of it was, there was no doubt that one's
mind was operating in terms of these things.

Wittgenstein, and *The Tractatus* in the first place, was
important. I don't think the logical *Philosophical Investigations*
were published just at that moment, but that, and Freddie
Ayer's book, *Language, Truth and Logic*, was an influence. This
was another mind that was looking, as it were, with the mind
that we had at the terms in which one thought, and seeing
them all to be in another way relative.

Nietzsche was born in 1844, only 12 years before Freud,
in 1856. Nietzsche's sister, Elizabeth, didn't die until 1938. If
Nietzsche had lived to be 80 or 90 he would have overlapped

with me. I was born in 1927. If Nietzsche had lived, he was only 12 years younger than Freud. I had very much the sense of Nietzsche being a contemporary. So there was this precursor of a structuralist mentality, a structuralist interest that I had from Nietzsche that I didn't have the intellectual equipment to take it into a formal declaration of a structuralist framework but I was thinking in those terms in my 20s, influenced by Nietzsche.

Now I came across Buddhism when I was 18 or 19, a very curious translation by a Japanese guy of *The Platform Sutra* of Hui-neng, sixth Ch'an patriarch which was the seed sutra that goes from Ch'an Buddhism into Zen ...

This was in the library?

No, this was Smith's bookshop. The Buddhist Publication Society published it. This was a Japanese guy who became imbued with Zen Buddhism and translated it from a Japanese translation – originally Chinese – into English, though he didn't know a word of English. He looked up every single word as he went along and translated the Japanese into English, and so learnt English by translating *The Platform Sutra*. I developed a technique of reading translations. A great deal of what I was reading was translations and I would make allowances for the translation as I was reading it and intuit what he meant to say from what I understood he was trying to put across. Well, there was this Ch'an Zen type of Buddhism which I read before I came across Mahayana.

And indeed before I came across Schopenhauer and this enervating pessimism of 19th century. Matthew Arnold and his 'Dover Beach' sensibility, and bits of Tennyson, coming through into T.S. Eliot's *The Waste Land*.

Nietzsche was translated by Ludovici as the *Joyful Wisdom* but he took it in Italian, *The Gay Science*. There was a sort of ebullience and buoyancy and clear blue sky in *Zarathustra*, 'you look up I look down'. That undeterred – call it arrogance – you know, fuck you, the lot of you, the slave morality. Slave morality; that's bourgeois morality, that's slave Christian morality, that's depleting yourself of everything and putting it all onto God. Get back down on your bended knees, worshipping your own idol – that is not God. So there was this attitude of Nietzsche, blended with this Ch'an Zen Hui-neng Dharma that I didn't care whether it was Taoism or Ch'an

Zen. The way that you call the way is *not* the way, and that sort of bafflement you run into in the best of the Sufi, that says it as far maybe as you can say it and after that, baby, you tread the air for yourself.

What of Freud did you read first, his First Lectures, the Psychopathology of Everyday Life?

Well, at the library there were five volumes of the Hogarth Press ...

Good library, that's all I can say!

Well, I don't know who the librarian was, but they had all that stuff. Anyway there was a university translation of Nietzsche and there was this first version of Freud in five volumes. I read Freud while still at school, very rapidly so that in my sixth form at school [I] went through Sophocles' *Oedipus Rex* in Greek. I was told at the end of my school days by my classics teacher that I could walk through an M.A. in Latin and Greek and English, in other words that I was ordinary M.A. standard when I left school.

I actually read Freud before, no, I read them about the same time, Sophocles' *Oedipus Rex* and *Antigone*. I didn't read *Oedipus at Colonus* until a few years later, for some reason or another I had consigned that to a not very important play. But the person that I had read most, or the corpus that I mostly got into, being able to read it with a translation available, was Homer. I read a certain amount of Homer and Sophocles so Freud presented me with two things. One was that at that time, and this happened before I read Freud, my father had what he called a nervous breakdown, he was trembling, and lay in bed quite a bit with this tremor and I sat beside him quite a bit and he was ...

I know, but can we ...

... but this was very relevant to Freud. I can't remember the exact paper of Freud but there was the Oedipal complex thesis of Freud, there was *The Psychopathology of Everyday Life*, there was his study of Leonardo da Vinci, there was his study of Moses, not the *Moses and Monotheism* but the piece on contemplating Michelangelo's *Moses* in the Vatican and there was a number of other papers. There was 'Mourning and Melancholia' which impressed me, there was quite a bit about the primal scene and Oedipal situation in 'Mourning and Melancholia'. So there was my father and there was the original Greek of the Oedipal story, it was a very powerful story and quite early on I didn't read very much of the Freudians but I read Ernest Jones on Hamlet.

The first paper I actually wrote to present to anyone else was a paper I wrote when I was 20 years old which the Institute of Psychoanalysis has still got in their library. I saw on the university notice board a notice offering a prize of £20 for a student essay on any subject relating to psychoanalysis, so I sat down that weekend and wrote about a 20-page paper on 'health and sickness', which won. A couple of months later I got a cheque for £20 and a letter from the psychoanalysts saying I'd won this prize in London, that it showed a great deal of talent and promise and would I be interested in coming down to be interviewed by them. So I went down to London.

You never mentioned that in Wisdom, Madness and Folly ...

It wasn't particularly personally important, it was £20 as far as I was concerned. I was so intellectually arrogant, you might say, that the fact that these characters of London thought highly of that essay was an encouragement, but I was operating in the company of Freud and Nietzsche and Kierkegaard and I wasn't really thinking about who I had never heard of in London.

I looked it up in their library a number of years ago because I hadn't got a copy myself, and they gave me a photostat of it. 'Health and Happiness', I think it was called. It started off with the quotation from John Donne, 'There is no health; Physicians say that we, At best, enjoy but a neutrality. And can there be more sickness, than to know that we are never well, nor can be so?'. If there had been a Nietzschean society that had asked me, I would have preferred to do that, but I rattled that off in the psychoanalytic direction. I think that was when I was twenty. If you get a hold of that, that will give you a fair summary of the zone I was in.

You mention your arrogance ...

I say that with due irony because I don't ...

Was it arrogance, or just enthusiasm?

Well, I'm saying that the level at which I was – since I wasn't particularly talking with people – I had no companions in this respect, it was all on my own and I had this intellectual life derived from books and *Les Temps Moderne* which could be purchased in Glasgow. Also the *Hibbert Journal* from my scouting around in Smith's bookshop, in the University Bookshop in Glasgow, the best theological journal of the time.

At that particular time was Freud no more important than Nietzsche and Kierkegaard?

I'd made a mark of Freud, because Freud was the only one who had been smart enough, I thought, to translate his preoccupations into a way of earning money out of it, the idea that you could earn money from it.

Did you really think that?

Yes, *yes!* Was I going to work in a laboratory? Was I going to work in a hospital? I saw myself in a hospital, as I didn't see myself working as a family doctor. I thought my life was going to be in a university research department, researching the state of art neurology, neuropsychiatry, neurophysiology, and all the metaphysical, ontological, existential, socio-economic problems that converge on the way one's physical system delivered all this to one's consciousness. All the problems of that.

I was going to get a Nobel Prize, I was going to make my mark scientifically. All this stuff had laid the groundwork, but there was obviously a place now that somebody had to come along and it might be somebody else but it might be me, who would get all that together and do some specific research. It wouldn't be just a lot of words in the air, it would be relevant to the 20th century. Who had done that? Sir Charles Sherrington? No. Pavlov? No. Freud? Well, he should have stuck to neurology, nevertheless he had a brilliant idea of just a room, a couch, himself, and could get people to pay him money for some hours a day to analyse them. So I made a mark on that. He was different from Nietzsche and Kierkegaard and I wasn't going to be a professional revolutionary in the style of Trotsky or Gramsci by that time, so this might be worth bearing in mind. There was a practical economic side to Freudian theory.

Jung doesn't appear in your work much, does he?

No, well he does actually, in *The Politics of Experience*. I don't say very much about Jung but I do note that [he's] the first person, as far as I've come across who, in *Symbols of Transformation* ... envisaged a parallel between what was called a psychotic episode and a mythological journey or transformation of the soul, and he called that *metanoia*, borrowing that term from the New Testament word for conversion or repentance as translated.

Well, I got very impatient with Jung as a stylist, compared to Freud's elegance and wit and irony and sharpness. But the first thing I read of Jung which ought to go along with Freud and the rest was his *Psychology of Religion*, his six Terry lectures he gave in America. In it he has some consideration of Nietzsche whom he regards as psychotic, suffering from general paralysis of the insane, with disintegration of his mental functions, the falling apart of his clarity.

I detested Jung for adopting that stance in relationship to his *frère*, his brother, and I never believed that story. A study of Nietzsche which is a thing that I've got as one of the things that I haven't done yet. I got the records from Basel and the other mental hospitals that Nietzsche was hospitalized in; he wasn't suffering from syphilis, it was a story that was put out for complex reasons that I would have to track down in terms of his biography. But that put me off Jung and I'd also heard that he had done the dirty on James Joyce and I'd heard that he had said that Picasso was psychotic.

There was something about Jung entrenching himself in the justification of being the sane authority, the pontificating post meta-psychiatrist that he never gave up. Jung had distanced himself from the people that took their *chances*. Like Artaud, like to a lesser extent André Breton, like Rimbaud, like Nietzsche and the rest of them. I felt there was something potentially very corruptive to entrench myself in an authoritative surround, through which I could judge people like that from that position.

Karl Jaspers was someone I was originally very taken with. I was very taken with a publication of his, the first collection I got of his were his radio broadcasts in Switzerland, a translation of *Modern Man in Search of a Soul*. I liked that at the time but then there was something again, an element of doughiness, not like the Sartrian type of clarity, of intellectual cutting, not like Ch'an Zen.

Was Adler a man that you read?

Adler. I read a touch of Adler in my university days, more than now. When you thought of that world it was Freud, Jung and Adler ... Freud represented the unconscious, sex theory, developmental stuff and the Oedipal complex and Jung represented the self, the collective unconscious and synchronicity and Adler represented the inferiority complex and the striving for power. He emphasized power, Freud emphasized sex and Jung emphasized the self and the integration of the self.

Well, I hadn't been drawn to Adler as sharply as the others. I didn't quite regard Jung as in the same class as Freud, he was a beta figure. Freud was an alpha figure but Freud wasn't in the same class as Nietzsche. Nietzsche was past Freud and before Nietzsche – as Nietzsche felt and I felt – Spinoza, that type of mind. We are talking about the top of the Himalayas in the field of philosophy. Well, when I read Adler he didn't seem to be in the same class as Freud.

Or Jung?

Or Jung. Actually he seemed to be doing not much more than footnoting Nietzsche. And everything that has been written about Abraham Maslow, you know this sickening sort of 'self-actualization' American style, that's all laid out in Nietzsche's aphorisms. He didn't go on and on about it, when he said something in a couple of lines then it's said. As he makes clear in *Der Wille zur Macht* – it is interesting to go through a German/English dictionary – *Macht* he is talking about the *Will to Macht*, Nietzsche, which he made absolutely clear wasn't the impotence of putting on fancy dress and then killing someone, that was an expression of total impotence, the will to *Macht* means, really, the will to becoming as a full human being.

Would Adler have read Nietzsche?

Nietzsche was a household word in intellectual European

circles, I mean he died in 1900. I mean to say did Adler read Nietzsche is asking me whether I had read Freud. I'm sure he read Nietzsche.

Groddeck, *The Book of The It*, have you ever heard of Groddeck? Groddeck, I came across Groddeck and he hadn't very much in terms of content but just the one phrase, 'they say we live a life but we are lived by life'. The ease with which he commuted without any difficulty between extreme physical ailment and life situations, he was better than Freud in that respect, definitely. Freud took Groddeck very seriously, he didn't try to patronize Groddeck, he admits he stole Groddeck's *Das Es*, the it, and turned it into his id. In one of Freud's footnotes he says Groddeck had said to him once, 'oh you've bourgeoisified my it to your bourgeois id'. I'm sure Groddeck could talk like that to Freud and Freud would have no sense that he was the master.

In your books you acknowledge Goffman as being important, but what about Russell Barton, and his Institutional Neurosis? *Was he someone that you thought about, met?*

I never met him and I never read that book until I had left Gartnavel. There was a paper that I'm not the first name on – Cameron, Laing and McGhie – though I did all the work for it and there is a whole story about that, at Gartnavel, of getting people out of the refractory ward ... the institutional literature, of which there was a little bit, I think Russell Barton's book had already been written by the time I did that work at Gartnavel but I didn't know about it and no one at Gartnavel knew about it or put me on to it. I can't remember the year Goffman's *Asylums*, and *The Presentation of Self in Everyday Life*, came out.

'62, '63?

Yes well, all slightly after the '50s. The only person that I really knew about as far as I remember at that time was Maxwell Jones at Dingleton, his idea of the therapeutic community and of opening the doors. Opening the doors was a thing that was in the air.

I went to Dingleton when the word was getting around and Maxwell Jones wasn't there at the time. He was not on the premises. I met his second in command who was very –

whether it was a personal thing between him and Maxwell Jones, but he was a consultant psychiatrist, and he showed me around the wards and 'there's the door open' – well, the impression that he was conveying was well there you see it, it's *no* big deal. I mean there's the door, you can see the grounds and there's the village and that's as far as they can walk, and it's all very carefully taken care of with the local police and it was no big deal.

This was just before tranquillizers, it wasn't tranquillizers that opened the doors of Dingleton, it was – this is what the consultant said – it was the electric shocks that enabled us to open the doors. You know, no *big deal*. I had already opened the doors, with Angus MacNiven's permission at Gartnavel, it was no big deal, we never even published it. And MacNiven was a very old-style conservative psychiatrist. I mean I was a conservative revolutionary, you might say, to some people; older psychiatrists were disgusted at what had started to happen in psychiatry, with lobotomies and electric shocks and the new types of medication. The older humanitarian clinician regarded these blighted people as people under their care and protection and there was a new wave of psychiatry which Sargant was one that they did not like. These were the older men in their 60s and 70s, there was a connection between me and them.

A conservative revolutionary?

Well, you know how Reagan talks about conservative revolutionaries, it's a revolution that brings in the old values. You might call me a conservative revolutionary. I was regarded as conservative first of all because that was the expression, I was conservative, the patois for my stance as a clinician. Well, say, I'm at Catterick military command, captain-acting-major, with some of the responsibilities of a lieutenant colonel, ranking captain in charge. I'm the liaison officer in the Stobhill department of psychological medicine. The neurology and medical departments, if they wanted a consultation with a psychiatrist called in, I would be the one to be sent. Well the expression they would use would be – 'well, Ronnie's very conservative'.

... I did a tour of Sao Paulo, Rio and Bella Horizonte and the chap who was acting as translator for me was a professor of psychiatry at a psychiatric unit in a general hospital in Rio de Janeiro. He spoke perfect English of course, and expressed

himself as an admirer of my clinical work. He didn't like what
he had to do as a psychiatrist. When the surgical unit have a
difficult patient they phone up his department, they go round –
without needing to examine the patient, because their surgical
colleagues are completely competent in that respect – put a
screen round the bed and give the patient an electric shock
which puts them out for six hours without need of any chemical
medication. The patient is not asked permission nor are the
relatives and the patient is never told that they've had an
electric shock. A perfectly normal ordinary patient having
routine medication.

I remember him using that word about me, he was being
apologetic, that I would be *conservative*; in other words that I
would not approve of that sort of thing but this is the world
we live in, and that's the only way you can be a professor of
psychiatry. That is the service that his department is expected
and has to supply on demand to the surgeons.

*Were there men before Sargant, say, who generally thought of
asylums as asylums in the best sense of the term?*

Not very many. You could read the history of The Retreat at
York and Conolly, he was a major figure in the development of
attempts at humane asylums in the 19th century. And I think in
Glasgow and elsewhere there were a sprinkling of perfectly
decent doctors who had become psychiatrists who didn't know
what to do with these people, but the best one could do in the
circumstances was to treat them in a decent human way and
leave them alone and not experiment with them and interfere
with them and not allow the wards to run into neglect. Make
sure that you always do your ward round every day and an
evening round and make sure that the nurses get you to sign the
book. The nurses ran the whole thing and you had to act as an
overseer to see that that morale didn't run down, that people
weren't being allowed to *rot*.

*Let's just leave that for a minute. Can we talk a little about
phenomenology, and the influence of Husserl, Heidegger, Alfred
Schutz, say. Did you read them at the library or at university, or
much later?*

Oh, this was past this, I mean the library was a phase from
leaving school to the early years at university. Then there was

the end years of university and going into Killearn Hospital, the Glasgow and West Scotland neurosurgical unit.

Let me just go back a little. Goffman, Russell Barton and so on, all of them, were very much second-order thinkers. The first book of Goffman's that I came across was *Asylums* and, as far as I remember, that wasn't published until the late '50s or early '60s. It wasn't a primary, seminal, or original influence. None of the American sociological writing as far as I remember meant anything very much to me, it all seemed very wishy-washy. Goffman was an exception but I hadn't read anything that preceded Goffman in terms of what is now called micro-sociology.

But you had assumed what Goffman observed anyway already, in terms of your practice in hospital?

Yes. Goffman didn't tell me anything I didn't know.

OK, those phenomenologists. Were they just part and parcel of the intellectual apparatus you developed or are they more significant than that?

Well, there's the whole process, you might say, of paring away and subtraction rather than addition. Of trying to see things as clearly as possible without what one might call socially-conditioned or acquired projections ... or constructions or socially-determined value systems which are all open to the critique of contingency. They are contingent. There is a reading of Kant, *A Critique of Pure Reason*, and there is a background behind that of scholastic philosophy in terms of particulars and universals and *a priori* categories – is there any bedrock? Is there something you can get back to that isn't a construction one way or another? There is the treacherous phenomena of hypnosis that I mentioned where you can transform the perceptual and cognitive world that you live in amazingly by interhuman influence. This is demonstrable, experimentally, to a remarkable degree.

At the end of my university days and starting my first post-graduate experience in neurosurgery I was coming across in practice brain damage, brain tumours, hydrocephalus, cerebral abscess, all that stuff; the *relationship* of cognitive functions and the construction of reality to the material flesh and blood of one's nervous system. So there was first of all

Heidegger, a translation of several of his essays in a volume published by Vision Press called *Being and Time*. This made me very thoughtful indeed. There hadn't been a text that I had read that seemed to be so contemporarily to the point to me than *Being and Time*. There were peripheral writings of Sartre that I hadn't read. I learned to read French basically while reading *L'Être et le Néant* – I just looked up every word as I went along and similarly I learned to read German by reading *Sein und Zeit*. I just looked up every word as I went along for the first ten pages and then when you've got most of the vocabulary it's very simple basically if you're not German. It's very difficult for Germans to read. Then there was Hegel, coming after Sartre's discussion of the nature of interhuman relationships and the inadequacy of always seeing the other as an object – subject/object relationships instead of seeing oneself as being seen by another as a primary phenom-enological datum of relationships. There was also Scheler's *On the Phenomenology and the Theory of Sympathy* that I had picked up on and there were patchy bits of Husserl.

I was confronted with all these things, for the first time, by another human being, an actual person, Joe Schorstein, who was my clinical chief and he was very imbued particularly with Heidegger and to a lesser extent with Karl Jaspers. I had just read *Being and Time* of Heidegger's and I think I had read everything of Jaspers' that had been translated.

There was of course the latter 19th century textual criti-cism that was really generated by the breakdown of the theology of the New Testament; you know Schweitzer's quest for the historical Jesus, and the textual criticism of the New Testament which led into all that German theorising about the hermeneutics of the text. I think there was one major volume of Dilthey and there was Jaspers; these were the main intellectual components of this which also linked up with, you might call it, English Empiricist Realism – of distinguishing between what hopefully you could regard as given and what you could regard as constructions upon the given.

What about Husserl, Hegel even?

Historically, the first text that I had come across that used the word phenomenology was Hegel's *The Phenomenology of the Mind*, and there were some chapters there – 'The unhappy consciousness' – and a great deal of Hegel was very opaque to me. I still, I haven't felt impelled to get into Hegel on his own terms. There were Jean Wahl's lectures and I was now beginning to read some French, jumping off from *L'Être et le Néant*. There was Jean Wahl's Hegelian lectures at the Sorbonne, and there was Merleau-Ponty, who I think was just beginning to be translated but I found his French a bit too florid. Sartre was much easier, his constructions are much simpler and his vocabulary is much simpler. But in Merleau-Ponty I sensed there was something there.

So all this is around the time of Joe Schorstein and at that time I was influenced by Joe. The question arose 'what was I going to do?' after the six months in neurosurgery because I jumped about two or three years by taking a job. You weren't supposed to take a job in neurosurgery when you graduated, you were supposed to take a job in medicine and surgery. So I would have to double back in terms of constructing a medical career, but on the other hand there were these philosophical interests and there was a German/Swiss school of medical thinking, of medical anthropology, that I knew and still know.

But why not get a scholarship for a year and go over and study with Karl Jaspers? So I wrote to Karl Jaspers and I got the scholarship lined up. I had to go to a review board in Edinburgh, I put this to them. I had become known now as a bright young thing interested in neurology and maybe Queen's Square and maybe an apprentice to Macdonald Critchley who was the leading light in neurology in Queen's Square, London. So there were these professorial people considering how they would groom me for advance in medicine and I was told, 'well, you don't want to go and study with Karl Jaspers, well, he's armchair isn't he?'. What about Stayland and the department of neuropsychiatry, and we want you in the British Army and anyway there was this death coma stuff going on and insulin.

Remember Karl Jaspers had written a book on psychopathology in which he had introduced the term and the notion of phenomenology and also he had written his *Psychopathology* in something like 1906 and had revised it about 20 years later in about 1926 or '27. That second edition hadn't been translated at the time but there was an edition in French of the original edition which was the one that I had read. I thought that Jaspers had been trained in psychiatry. Jung was still alive, Minkowski was known to me, I was able to read

him now in French. I'd got access to the French work with a
bit of an effort and Minkowski's ideas seemed to be about the
best that were going – I actually use a line from Minkowski
as the epigraph to *The Divided Self.* So that's where I was
poised.

You mention Tillich, The Courage To Be, *a great book. And
Buber. Were you interested in them because of their existential
writings or because they were theologians grappling with issues
that you were interested in?*

... I was still following my nose. There *was* Buber, there was a
developing interest in the phenomenology of human relationships. Schutz wasn't around just then, so I wasn't aware of
Schutz and inter-subjectivity. I was only aware of inter-
subjectivity *via* Sartre and Husserl, as a problematic as the
saying goes. Also, I think it was about '54, there was Ryle's
book, *The Concept of Mind,* and this sort of philosophical
problem that I was very impatient with, what was called the
problem of other minds. I developed an idea that I never fully
developed in writing that, with the Descartian split, the
mainstream western thinking had developed a psychopathological streak. I thought there was a curious parallel between
the writings of psychopathology, which attributed a schizoid
split between the self and the body or between the mind and
matter, and the mainstream thinking about the subject. This
seemed very, very strange to me.

   Medard Boss had written *The Psychopathology of Perversions*
and there was a translation a little bit after that of the
Phenomenology of Dreams, by Boss, an attempt to do a
Heideggerian thing. There was no intellectual lever to lever
one out of talking about psychopathology all the time. So I
thought that what we needed was some sort of description
which doesn't just describe what we see immediately in terms
of signs and symptoms because a 'sign' or a 'symptom' of
disease is actually a theory about the disease we are trying to
describe. *We needed some sort of pure description.* Now this was
triggered more than anything by Husserl's book, *Ideas,* and
his British Encyclopedia article in the 13th or 14th edition. In
it Husserl wrote a paper on his own phenomenology. I was
just lifting this. I was trying to get through to the idea that
what is called in psychiatric textbooks 'a description' of a
disease is not a simple description of a reality because calling

something a disease is already part of a theory of accounting for it.

Were you now actually writing The Divided Self?

So I was now – this was before writing *The Divided Self* – aware that you cannot simply describe experience and behaviour in terms of a medical model which distinguished between signs and symptoms, where signs are what you see from the outside, and symptoms are what you feel from the inside. A headache, for instance, is all symptom, no one else feels the pain. Toothache is also a good example. Someone comes along with a pain; the pain is probably a symptom of inflammation. You look for a swelling, redness and tenderness to pressure; tenderness to pressure is a mixed symptom because the feeling of pain is a symptom of the withdrawal, the observable behaviour is a sign. The symptom and the sign together add up to the disease which is probably a dental root abscess or whatever. Well, that model helps you to zone in and is a tremendous boon for everybody to be able to do that. But I couldn't talk about this to any of my medical colleagues because they were so impatient, you know 'get on with it, what the fuck does it matter'. But I saw that you had to suspend the attribution of physiology or pathology, so I was thinking up a phenomenological neurology.

Neurology was an entirely clinical thing. I thought there ought to be a branch of neurology which was equivalent to the neurophysiology of the nervous system, and I was convinced that the neurophysiology of one person's nervous system was related to the neurophysiology of someone else's nervous system. They were not completely isolated, non-connected things. They were related to each other, there was an interplay between your physiology and my physiology. I was convinced of that. The way that people recovered from head injury and came out of coma, I was convinced that they would have died if they hadn't had attention lavished on them by the nursing staff. This was human contact. Human touch and someone, that's the physiology through the skin, nerve endings, affecting vital centres in someone else's physiology, from someone's physiology to someone else's physiology. There was nothing anywhere about this in any study that I could find. There was Kurt Goldstein, but it wasn't *inter*personal neurophysiology. There was nothing.

Did people think that this was a bizarre thing that you were thinking at the time?

Yes. Joe Schorstein was completely unaware, insensitive to this sort of thing. He was a complete clinician and came from a Hasidic Jewish background and culture. You know Heidegger and the end of the world, the Holocaust, the Heideggerian application of philosophy to the technological horrors of one's society, depersonalization, disintegration and fragmentation and alienation and existential Marxism and *blah blah blah.*

When it came down to actual relationships that one had with another human being, the nearest physicians had to that was, of course, Osler. This was the tradition of clinical bedside manner. Sir William Osler was one of the great early 20th-century clinicians who was Professor of Medicine at Harvard University. Have you come across a guy called James Lynch; have you come across books called *The Broken Heart* and *The Language of the Heart?*

Yes.

He mentions Osler in exactly this respect. It doesn't come out so much in *The Broken Heart* and in his last book – I met him in Denver, Colorado, last year – but he has done exactly what I had in mind with measuring blood pressure and people talking to each other. The resting blood pressure has always been the standard way of taking your blood pressure with the doctor putting a stethoscope on so that there's no talking. That has nothing to do with the *ordinary* blood pressure. Blood pressure fluctuates and goes up as soon as you start to talk, goes down as soon as you start to listen, and it's only with the latest monitoring machines that you can get the blood pressure without immobilizing someone. That is not a sample of the ordinary relationship of the blood, and the blood pressure is tremendously interpersonally sensitive.

I was intuitively aware of that and if there had been the instrumentality available that I could have used I would have been doing that. I mean, if there was some way that you could have just tuned into a brainwave while we were talking I would have been fascinated to see how our brainwaves vary with what we were talking about.

So, you got phenomenology from the phenomenologists, but there was no guide to show how this could be translated into psychiatry and for the so-called mentally ill.

Yes, well, I'll give you [it] exactly as I see it. There was this clinical experience particularly, I want to emphasize this, of six months at the Glasgow and West Scotland Neurosurgical Unit and before that I had six months in Stobhill with Parkinsonism. You know, what's his name, Oliver Sacks. *Awakenings.* I had six months of that after failing my finals for the first time. I took a full time job, half-paid, at Stobhill, and I was working in a psychiatric unit and Parkinsonism unit. Well it was amazing, I mean I had never seen that when I was a medical student in such detail, people in that devastated state of *encephalitis lethargica* and God knows what. Artane was introduced to us as a precursor of L-dopa at the time I was actually on the wards. It was amazing the transformation. The first time the Rip Van Winkles, sort of 'broken downs', actually very noticeably changed.

Looking at the recovery process from comas which was so much emphasized in the suicide prevention work in Los Angeles in the '70s, people coming back from near death and so on. It became clear to me how tremendously important it is that there is some human being who, as it were, welcomes them back to life and encourages them to come back to life. *The human factor.* I was very sensitive to the existence of a human factor, but there was no reference points. The one single text perhaps where that had been written about was Martin Buber's *I and Thou.* I had a dream of the relationship between *I and Thou* and the relationship to neurophysiology.

There was *I and Thou* on the one hand, there was that world, there was definitely a relationship between us, human beings, that sort of relationship that was actual, the sort of relationships that Goffman wrote between you being there and me being here and we're talking to each other and looking at each other, and maybe smelling each other subliminally. That immediate relationship exists and when we crumble in some way or another, get ill or diseased, that relationship doesn't cease to exist, it becomes more important than ever. I could have said that, and so I'm imbued with this.

The first research grant that I actually got was to do a study of Nan, a girl's recovery from head injury. A film was made of that and Schorstein and I took it down to London and showed it to television people and William Sargant, who was a BBC medical adviser. They turned the film down for commercial showing because he said it was too depressing for people to see. Though it was actually anything but depressing, it was an amazing recovery from being almost wiped out.

I thought that if I could stick with this, if I could see this through in the field of, I was thinking, of – neuropsychiatry – I didn't believe and I still don't believe there's any what you call psychiatry or study of mental suffering that is properly divorced from taking into account a person's whole being in the world which is one's physical body as well, but not in the split way as practised in medicine which is a double split, which reflects the schizophrenia that they describe in patients. There is the split between me and you and there's the split between your mind and your body, a double schizoid split which I saw reflected in medical theory projected onto people who, when I met them, fully engaged me immediately, however crazy they were supposed to be.

Why wasn't Freud of use to you at the time?

Well, he was *interpreting* all the time. It was all a set of transformations round – I love a man, no I don't love a man, a man loves me, no a man doesn't love me, a man hates me, oh it's not a man it's God, God hates me – so he's deducted, a deductive scholastic piece, a brilliant device, paraphrenia, well fuck it. For one thing, when I actually met people they didn't seem to have repressed homosexual fantasies or stuff like that in particular. It didn't match my immediate empirical relationship with people who were supposed to be in the category that Freud was describing and it said nothing whatever about how you treat another human being.

Are you saying that there was no one around who said that the psychiatrist and the patient must meet as two separate human beings in order to aid the recovery process?

No, the nearest to anyone who was saying that, that I was aware of, was Harry Stack Sullivan. I came across Harry Stack Sullivan for the first time, I remember that extremely vividly, in the medical library at Netley in the British Army. I had come across a sentence of Harry Stack Sullivan quoted by Alastair Cooke in an article he wrote about America in

Encounter, which was 'in our state of society' (Alastair Cooke quoting Harry Stack Sullivan addressing young psychiatrists), 'I want you to remember that in our present state of society the patient is right and you are wrong'.

I never looked into Harry Stack Sullivan, however, until reading through journals, medical journals, psychiatric journals, the British Army's own journal of interpersonal relations, published by the school of psychiatry called *Psychiatry*, I think – a yellow journal – and there was a series of lectures by Harry Stack Sullivan where he says that there is a *mésalliance* between neurology and psychiatry. The subject of psychiatry is disturbances in living manifested in disturbances in interpersonal relationships; the subject of neurology is pathological lesions of the central nervous system. The two have been wedded together since the beginning of western psychiatry and neurology; they don't really belong together especially closely. That was dong, dong, dong for me in the second sixth months after I graduated from medical school.

I'd never come across the writings of Harry Stack Sullivan before, and Freud never said that, he tried in fact to maintain the opposite, he insisted on ploughing away all the time on psychopathology, to the extent that he would spread psychopathology right through into everyday life and everything, into one's ordinary dreams and everything. That wasn't phenomenology, there was a lot of phenomenology in Freud but it was all clothed in his psychopathology. So Harry Stack Sullivan's argument was quite critical because then I was able to say, well, I think there is a *mésalliance* between neurology and interpersonal relationships. At the same time I had been feeling a theoretical and clinical discomfort about the split between interpersonal relationships and neurology, that they were both right – couldn't we have a neurophysiology of interpersonal relationships which would be based on the clarity of the distinction between the two disciplines and it would be a real wedding?

So it was Buber and Harry Stack Sullivan ...

Made Buber operational ...

Sullivan made Buber operational?

Mmm ...

So they were the two other names on the same road as you at the time. There was nothing else?

Goldstein. Kurt Goldstein's books are more or less unreadable but Oliver Sacks refers to Kurt Goldstein. Marjorie Grene has got a book on holism; holism, this organic holism of Kurt Goldstein. But I came to Goldstein particularly through Joe Schorstein. I had come on the one hand with all these bits and pieces of phenomenology and particularly existential phenomenology and the usual equipment that I thought was neurology; Hughlings Jackson neurology and basically the work that had been done with Macdonald Critchley on the parietal lobes, and Wilder Penfield was doing his work at that time on temporal lobe epilepsy. But the nervous system as I had thought of it was a system of hierarchical levels which is still the main way that it's taught. But the notion of the neurological holism of Goldstein was mediated to me through the clinical detail, and bedside manner, of Joe Schorstein.

He was very good at that. He pointed out to me something that impressed me very much. There are people who have got some diseases of the nervous system, and if you turn someone on their abdomen and put the leg up you don't get the Babinski response in that position. That might seem just a curious thing but tracks from the periphery of the body to the central receiving stations and back again are intact or not, and it means that the Babinski response is a partial reflex and I don't think that is still obvious in clinical neurology.

I haven't kept up with the state of the art in terms of neurology but that organic holism was one component to an interpersonal holism and then I was becoming aware of, from another vector – remember this was when cybernetics and systems theory were just coming – the notion that the system you should study is not a one body system, you don't turn to a one body system and look at that object as a system, you look at the relationship between people as the system. So all this was in the air.

What do you think stopped the work of Harry Stack Sullivan becoming as well-known as your work?

I think what he didn't do was write well; he's got a terrible English style. It is not a pleasure to read many pages, or any page. I mean he occasionally gets a sentence and lays down key words like ... I don't know if he invented such an obvious word as 'interpersonal relations', but I mean he's put his name on it, and 'selective inattention' and a few other things. But his writings don't get to many people beyond a particular school of psychodynamic psychiatry, he's difficult enough to read in English, I don't know how far he has penetrated into French and German, Italian or Spanish or Portuguese in translation.

Like in *Self and Others*, the references, the intellectual horizon of *The Divided Self*, he rather seemed to have a very restricted intellectual horizon. He was like Winnicott, who said to me on reading *The Divided Self*, that he agreed with every word of it except one word which was a misprint – an unconscious error – and then he added, he was a bit disappointed that I hadn't given him as much credit as he thought he might have got. And he could never pronounce the word phenomenology, neither could Bowlby. He always used to stutter over pronouncing it ... Because he's intellectually stultified, that's why Winnicott couldn't read or think beyond the immediate thing he's focused on, he couldn't do his own intuition as much justice as he could have. But Harry Stack Sullivan is even more a case in point. I mean I think it's something to do, I also see a politeness, to try to write clearly and there is some serious lack of sensibility in Harry Stack Sullivan, that he could put out that type of language and be satisfied with it.

3. A Career in Psychiatry

R.D. Laing's psychiatric career *proper* began when, on conscription, he worked in the Central British Army Psychiatric Unit at Netley near Southampton. However, before that period he had encountered psychiatric patients first at Stobhill Hospital, Glasgow, where he worked for six months as an unqualified intern, and then in his internship at the Glasgow and Western Scotland Neurological Unit at Killearn, near Loch Lomond.

In 1953, after another army post at Catterick Military Hospital, he moved to Glasgow's Royal Gartnavel Mental Hospital and then a mere two years later he was appointed Senior Registrar at the Southern General Hospital, where the University of Glasgow's Department of Psychological Medicine was located. Much of *The Divided Self* was researched and written while in this post.

Laing's involvement in psychiatry came at a most significant time. The doors of mental hospitals were beginning to be opened by virtue of the increasing and extensive use of technological developments in 'treatment', like ECT, and the psychopharmacological revolution had begun with the widespread use of powerful tranquillizers.

Can we first talk about the psychiatric unit at the Duke Street Hospital, Glasgow?

Duke Street was important to me in a way that I only realized retrospectively. It was my first introduction as an undergraduate to the practice of psychiatry. I went to the Duke Street Hospital for my psychiatric period as everyone did for three months, along with doing the other minor subjects like skin and other things. Psychiatry hadn't been up-graded to the extent that it is in some places now as part of a triumvirate of medicine, psychiatry and surgery. The consultant there was a guy called Sclare.

I say this was retrospective because I didn't realize what it meant at all. Sclare had banned electric shocks, he wouldn't have electric shocks in his psychiatric unit. You see, older psychiatrists still resisted, they were conservative, so my first normative dose of psychiatry was that electric shocks were a barbarous innovation and you don't use them in a tactful psychiatric clinical unit and that was Sclare's attitude. Now I didn't realize that that was very unusual in Glasgow and elsewhere at that time, and only older psychiatrists who were about to retire still kept up a last-ditch stand to resist the latest state of the art innovations and technological treatments of biological conditions.

Stobhill then was the crucial ...

There was nothing crucial.

You were just learning?

Yes. I went to Stobhill because of the existence of this extraordinary colony of 40 men and 40 women survivors from post-encephalitic Parkinsons. And from my second year in anatomy and physiology, I was interested primarily in embryology and in neurology; and neurology in its most extensive sense called at the time 'New Psychiatry'.

I slotted myself in Stobhill as an intern, half-paid, unqualified, and then got a tip-off about this opening in Killearn. That I could get that job though it wasn't usually the sort of job where they would take anyone who was just newly qualified. I must have made a decent impression with the consultant in Stobhill who must have tipped them off. I already knew the professor of psychiatry and they probably tipped off Killearn that I was available as a houseman.

I thought, OK, I'll jump the gun, I'll take the job. I wasn't asked to go through a competitive application, they phoned me up and said look this job is available, would you like to take it. Well, I wouldn't be asked if I wanted to take the job unless the people who were offering it thought they had an idea that they would steer me through my career that way rather than going through general medicine and surgery which I wasn't interested in particularly. So I took the job in Killearn.

In Wisdom, Madness and Folly *you talk about the difficulties of 'keeping an open heart to the suffering and at the same time remain efficient'. Can you talk about the problems of remaining efficient?*

I didn't want to go into the British Army because I felt that it was a clinical letdown, it wasn't quite in the same class as the neuropsychiatric clinic in Basel, and studying with Jaspers. I didn't think the British Army was in the same class for me and I also had this thing about going over to Paris, which would kill two birds with one stone. Of getting a flat in Montmartre which vied with Marcelle and the attractiveness of Paris and getting a job in one of the hospital clinics in Paris which was very appealing.

I thought that that's what I was in for, and that was going to be what I was going to engage in. I mean we got well past that type of clinical barbarism that some doctors practise in hospital, like having an appendicectomy race, and things like that. I had a contempt for that and a disgust for that. When it came to a nine- or ten-year-old hydrocephalic child I wanted to be at the cutting edge of the state of the art of what surgical or neurological finesse and research could contribute to alleviating the condition of hydrocephalus and things like that. Very much so.

Can we talk a little about your time in the army?

When I was drafted into the British Army – before I was sent to the British Army Psychiatric Unit at Netley and the insulin situation that I was not informed about before I was sent there – I was given a briefing with several other people by a member of British intelligence to put us in the picture. The picture was a situation of biological and chemical weapons and he was just giving us a briefing to tell us that it had been decided that this group of us – it wasn't everyone, it was several of us, I didn't know who the others were, I'd never met them, I didn't even know whether they were members of the RAMC – but I was a member of this briefing, there was six or seven of us.

This might still be classified information. At the end of World War II, the British Army did not know why the Nazi regime had not deployed their arsenal of biological weapons which they had – infinitely more devastating than nuclear energy. They had intelligence that German chemists had been working on plague viruses and had augmented the virulence of the virus to at least 20 times it's original potency. They had this in vats that were stationed in the outskirts of West Berlin, hence the German Army – in conjunction with the

American and British intelligence – in the last few weeks, they put all their energy into holding the Russians off who had found out about this store of stuff and were trying to get to it before the British and Americans. The British and Americans got there first.

That was the secret history of the final race to Berlin according to him, that was the name of the game. They found these vats and said that they were in different degrees of sealed chambers, enough to wipe out the whole world population if they just put some of it on a plane and put the plane up and threw it out in the air. It would be enough to end the whole story. Apparently, the German High Command had decided not to use this; they had been given orders to use it and decided not to deploy it and told the British and Americans they had it and to get there quickly. They didn't know what to do with it.

So we had this stuff now, they didn't know what the Russians had been up to, and the Americans had a whole load of biological weapons that they had not cultivated to the same degree. The Americans jacked themselves up thereafter and put a lot of intense research into developing their own arsenal of biochemical weapons because they suspected the Chinese – they had got photographs of stuff in central China. They had to be very careful about the Chinese. The chemical weapons were no surprise to me, chemical gases and such like. Anyway, if anything happened there was nothing that we could fucking well do about it, if something blew it up and this stuff got around, but anyway we would be told what our orders were.

If there was a war and this stuff started to be chucked around, they saw no antidote, because they didn't know what the degree of virulence was. Apparently they had stuff which any living creature – through the sealed walls of concrete where this stuff was – that even an atom bomb dropped on this wouldn't break the store of it and they've still got this stuff which is still in Germany somewhere. They had buried it. But it was totally unusable, it would be total ecosphere annihilation, totally mad. So that put the atom bomb in a place in my mind.

There are three, known to me, methods of species annihilation that have become accessible to the human species in the 20th century: chemical – that is nerve gas, nerve chemicals that paralyze the nervous system and cause death; biological weapons of this order; and the release of nuclear energy and the radiation effects, apart from the immediacy of it.

In Wisdom, Madness and Folly *you talk about soldiers who, in the Army psychiatric wards, talked about being dragged away and beaten up. Was that the beginning of your train of thought about the intelligibility of what other people considered to be unintelligible? Or was it just another example of the inhumaneness of the system?*

It was both. It was part of my job as an officer to see that the people under my command conducted themselves correctly and appropriately and this was outrageous. I reported this to what was called 'A Branch' which was a non-medical Army High Command, and they immediately looked into this and eventually got a couple of guys and court-martialled them. I gave evidence in court-martial along with other officers. I mean it was just out of line in every way.

They thought they would get away with it, of course, because I would never listen to nutcases. *But I was already listening to nutcases.* Maybe it was unusual even for someone who listened to what patients said to take it seriously or to consider that it could not be a phantasy.

You have characterized your army psychiatric career as spending time in a neurotic-psychopathetic-alcohol-battle-neurosis-anything-goes miscellaneous ward. Did you realize early on in your career that a lot of people were just thrown together in rag-bag fashion?

Yes. I was the one that was throwing them together. Well, I wasn't admitting people, people were sent to me.

You develop a sort of institutional hypocrisy; again the thing that was unusual for me was that I took it seriously but it was taken for granted. You know, people who conduct themselves in the army in a certain sort of way, the only thing you can do is put them in the guard house and then you decide whether you deal with them through the medical branch or through disciplinary means. There are only two routes, and in a situation when you don't want to deal with it through discipline you put it through the medical route and the medical route deals with it.

When you were in the army you talked about 'hanging around' in a padded cell with a guy who, subsequently, became 'John' in Self and Others. *Your colleagues in the army presumably thought that was quite bizarre ... or did they just see it as humane ...*

I don't think anyone particularly noticed. I was in charge of the ward, my future wife, Anne, was a sister at that time on night duty, and attached to this ward were two or three padded cells. I quite often went around to see her and hang around there at night-time. I often went round to the ward and into his padded cell and sat down with him and just hung out with him. I mean, obviously pretty strange for an officer to do that, but I didn't blow any trumpet about it and I don't suppose it came to anyone's notice that I did that.

Peter, who you took to your mother's house. That was unusual, I mean did she take that easily enough?

Of course, I had written and asked if I could bring this chap to stay in my room, and I went over there and there was no drama about that at all. You might say he was undemonstrative to the point of being clinically diagnosable as catatonic, but quiet and maybe not saying anything when he was with me. I put him up in a camp-bed in my bedroom and he hardly came out of that for the week that he was there, and the only thing after a while I think that I said was that he would eat sweeties, I think my chocolates. Mother made hardly any comment, she was very sensitive about it, we hardly talked about it, she just got the idea that he needed to have something to eat and that he might like chocolates.

How did you come to terms with having a position in the army which demanded that you exercised authority?

There was very little difference from being a lieutenant in the Royal Army Medical Corps in a psychiatric unit in Netley and being a civilian doctor in any hospital. You're in military uniform but there is exactly the same chain of command and that's what I grew up with. How things were done in medicine and within that system, it is how things *have* to be done. There is no valid place in a hospital for a junior doctor who is coming across all these things for the first time after training, he's got – it's called responsibility and discretion – responsibility and discretion I had as a lieutenant and a captain were pretty well exactly the same.

In the two years of being a conscript in the British Army there were never any major situations that were different from being *not* in the army. You were expected to go on parade and do a few things that you were expected to do but they didn't expect very much of us. They were short of doctors in the army and they wanted us to fulfil that function for two years whether we liked it or not, and that was fair enough.

I had to make my mind up whether I was going to be a conscientious objector on the basis of an overall philosophy of harmlessness and pacifism, not on any immediate political issue. I went through quite a number about making my mind up about that for a couple of weeks and then I made my mind up. I went up to Iona and had a chat with George MacLeod who had been a major in the army in World War I and he didn't see any contradiction between being a combat officer in the British Army and being a Christian at all, in his understanding of both.

Joe Schorstein had been a lieutenant colonel in the medical corps as a surgeon, and both of them pointed out that I needn't make any big deal about this unless I really wanted to because I was under the arrangement – the Red Cross Convention – that it wasn't one of my duties to have to carry a weapon and use it unless I wanted to. I could have done if I had wanted to, but I would not be expected to command people in combat.

I think one of the criticisms of myself is that I wish I had found the right balance between *laissez-faire* in terms of authority. If I ever go into action again in terms of a plan about an institute or centre, I would be entirely authoritarian. I will appoint people that I like for no other reason except that I appoint them if they want to be appointed. And the deal is that I sack them if they don't conduct themselves in a way that I want them to and that would be understood from the very beginning. There would be no question or any argument in that particular project. We are not talking about any theories of organization of society or anarchism or anything like that; if I'm *not* the captain then I'll take orders immediately, absolutely without questioning it, from the captain of the ship.

Your first professional paper, the one you wrote for the Journal of the Royal Army Medical Corps. *Did that excite you, the fact that you wrote something that was accepted by a professional journal?*

The one that was accepted was simply a short review of a few papers on a thing called the Ganser Syndrome. That was the first paper that was published as far as I remember, and I liked being published very much and that's why I wrote it – to be published. I didn't write to give enlightenment to people, I wrote it because here was a chance that came up to write something that could be published in a medical journal.

And the other one that wasn't published?

That was a paper that was jointly written with Murray Brookes.

This was the ENT man?

The ENT man. He is now the director of clinical research at Guys Hospital in London.

It sounded an interesting paper, was it more interesting than the other one as far as you were concerned?

Well, both of them looking back on it now were interesting to me because of the problem that was presented. How could you tell whether someone was having you on or lying or kidding themselves?

Yes, I've got this quote here that 'the issue of malingering covers not only the army's but everyone's attitude to a psychiatric patient'. It was that important?

Well, I was very – I suppose I would say shaken – I was really affected, I was shaken on a number of levels simultaneously by other stories that I put in there. I went up to Glasgow for a weekend leave, I think it was a Saturday morning, I got a train and was to get back for Monday morning. About the last thing I had to do was examine a guy who had been sent along to me by the medic from the medical wards in a wheelchair who was intermittently letting out a scream. They weren't sure what to make of it. You usually expect someone to look ill if they've got cerebral meningitis, you can have cerebral meningitis without having a raging fever but it's not usual. It's like, someone can have a silent pneumonia and really hardly notice it until they've stopped breathing, then they stop breathing again and then they are dead.

But he didn't look ill and I hadn't much time to get into a sort of prolonged number and in any case I wasn't expected to. The medical consultant just wanted me to look at him really, you know 'what do you think of him?'. I would take him back to the ward and write out something like 'kept under special observation ... make sure someone looks at him ... put him under special observation'. So he took him back to the ward and thought, well, we'll do a lumber puncture anyway and see, and they found it full of pus. Well, I thought, so much for clinical intuition; I mean I wasn't an experienced clinician, how could I be at that age? But I mean he fooled everyone, I mean he didn't fool everyone.

It was a bit of a joke [in] the Ear, Nose and Throat department that Murray Brookes was running because it was taking the whole of Northern Command, right across, as far as I remember, to Carlisle as well as Newcastle. Soldiers in the pioneer corps, who were the dimmest but who were still let into the army, really hadn't very much to say except either that they had a pain in their ear or they had a headache or they had gone deaf. Some of them were so obviously stupid they couldn't *fake* it, you know you would say 'when did you go deaf?' and they would say 'yes sir'. [laughs] Read my lips you know, but some of them were a lot cleverer than that. So how do you tell whether someone is actually deaf in one ear? You can be deaf in one ear, you can be half-deaf in one ear, but not in the other and it could be a serious condition, you could have a serious middle-ear infection. So he had asked me to come along. Is this guy simply trying to get out of it? Is this a route out, because obviously if you're deaf you can't hear orders so you're no use for the army. But it's very easy to stand there when the sergeant major bawls at you and you say you're deaf. And the sergeant major can't afford to lose his cool because that would be a court-martial for him, all he can do is report the soldier as deaf.

Was your paper with Murray Brookes more philosophical than the one that got published?

No, it wasn't philosophical, it was very technical. It was no big deal. His side of it was very well done, a state of the art run-through of the tests available to test for deafness in one ear and all the different sorts of deafness – middle-ear deafness or central deafness or functional deafness of this kind and that kind and the tests that there are and the impossibility of deciding if people knew the right thing to say then you couldn't prove them wrong really, or if they were capable of not being startled. You know the obvious thing, you come up behind them and they would blink. [laughs] It's very difficult to cut that out, but you could teach yourself to – you could practise – you could look in the mirror and get someone to bang or shout and get over blinking.

At the time did you think, if they want to fake it, that's acceptable anyway?

I wasn't worked up in one direction or another. I was pretty pulled back and the army wasn't worked up. The army wasn't particularly interested in tracking down the rather scholastic clinical niceties, but the army had two considerations which I think was absolutely fair enough. Obviously, if you're going to run an army you've got to consider morale so you can't have a gaping escape-hatch for anyone to walk out once they're in. It's perfectly clear in a conscript army; no army wants a conscript army really because you've got too many people who don't want to be in the army and are not sufficiently indoctrinated in the army that the morale is going to fall apart. On the other hand, the army didn't want us to casually write out medical discharge notes that would enable these people to get pensions for the rest of their lives due to military service, and that's what some people were also trying to do.

But, as you say, it didn't bother you ....

I was asked at the end of my year at Netley, by the Commandant at Netley, if I was posted to the command of divisional psychiatrist to the British troops in Korea, would I accept? 'Because we never invite anyone who doesn't accept'. I didn't reply to that letter. It was one of the grounds of divorce from my first wife, she thought this was absolutely terrible, to turn down the possibility of an invitation to the garden party at Buckingham Palace. [laughs] I often regret that I didn't snap up the opportunity of going to Korea for the experience.

But I was glad I didn't go because in order to do my job I would have had to do something to myself. The combat soldiers who were back were shattered, suffering combat neurosis and so on. Sent back to base camp. General Patton was in charge of the policy of how to deal with that and he summarized it as: three grains of amytal three times a day, out on the playground at half past four in the morning and back as quickly as possible. And 95 per cent kill themselves in the first year. Which the army was very happy about because it was more cost effective for them to die in battle than to get a lifelong pension or be invalided out of the army on psychiatric grounds. So in a situation like that, an army psychiatrist has got to be an army officer.

You have talked about how useful you found pentothal, which you used for a limited time.

Yes, pentothal facilitates what is called abreaction. There were people in the army and there were later people at Glasgow – one or two miners, I can't remember which mine it was, somewhere between Glasgow and Edinburgh, that had a cave in and there were some guys taken out in shock which was very like what I had seen in the army. I had seen one or two people in Netley who had been through combat in World War II and had broken down about five years later.

A typical image now that comes to mind is of a guy who was a complete soldier, he'd never blown it, he'd never talked about it to anyone and he started to tremble. Then he can't remember anything, amnesia. So we sedate him for a little while and then have him in the bed with a screen round and give him an injection of pentothal and talked. It's the same drug that used to be used as a pre-operative, in a small dosage.

The tranquillizers came in and pretty well reduced the use of barbiturates. Barbiturates were the only things that were anything like that, and if you encouraged the chap to sink into what it was or where he was, then he's walking along the street and the time of day and he would get absorbed in that at the same time and talk about it at the same time, and hear a swish swish swish and it would be German troops. This was one example – the sound of swish – the first thing he recalled;

he was left in an Italian village street and he heard swish swish and the German soldiers coming from all quarters with their coats swishing and the guns held. And he was captured.

You were interested in it as a technique of getting things to the surface?

Well, I was and I still am. It wasn't a matter of principle in leaving a department of an in-patient unit, a department of psychiatry to work in an out-patient department at the Tavistock. I sort of drifted away from that clinical context where it was part of everyday life that there are syringes and vials and drugs to the extent that it almost becomes often thought of that a doctor's expertise is knowing what medication is best for people who are terribly frightened or frantic or so on. I never had or ever had any objection to that in principle at all, *at all.* My only subsequent objection to it was the extent to which it became a mindless fashion of being employed without discrimination.

At Gartnavel you write that 'the females ruffled my hair and undid my trouser buttons'. Was it that unusual to see a male doctor?

Unusual? It was very unusual in that usually a doctor went into a ward and consulted the nurses – you know, 'how's it going, is there anything to report?'. He would stroll around the ward and day room and make sure he'd visited everyone who's for one reason or another confined to bed and see that they are all OK. If there was an examination to do, to do it, and not rush through the day room where a number of people are sitting, but if you were a gentlemanly clinician you'd say 'how are you today', and so forth. Then outside the ward again.

Well, I had made an arrangement with the matron and the staff nurse. I wanted to get some sort of idea of what the ward was like. I promised to be as unobtrusive as possible, in order [to] sample a bit of the ordinary life of the ward when the doctor didn't do his official ward round. Hospital wards at that time were either all women or all men so if it was a man, apart from a workman, a guy doing the windows or plumbing or something like that, to actually be in the ward was very unusual. This immediately was a focus, and I couldn't get away from sitting there. There was a sudden rush at me, what the hell they thought they were going to do – say like deprived children who rush at a thing and they don't know what they'll do when they get it – but that's the stuff of a lot of phantastic anxiety. About 60 women who hadn't been out of that ward or out of the hospital grounds for years and a couple of young nurses maybe in their teens who didn't expect any trouble. Suddenly this sort of fracas, and Doctor Laing fending off raving women. [laughs]

Doctor MacNiven and the experiment. In retrospect – now considering the fact that there haven't been that many serious attempts with control groups – how do you conceive the status of those experiments?

It was published as one of a half dozen or seven or eight papers by *The Lancet* as a booklet of Lancet papers. I think all the papers had been submitted to and published in *The Lancet* over a period of about two years.

The years being what?

This must be 1954. I came out of the army '53, went to Gartnavel '53 to '55 and this was written up in the second year. There might have been some delay in publication by the time the booklet came out, so the booklet must have been published in '55, '56. I think the reason why the editors of *The Lancet* obviously published that was that they must have been getting papers that had started to come their way in the way that sort of synchronicity happens. Remember it was the time of Maxwell Jones. There were other papers – what they called *In the Mental Hospital* – it was a stirring of intelligent interest among younger psychiatrists in their work in mental hospitals and they wanted to encourage that. I don't remember in detail what they specifically addressed but it was all in that direction of a quickening of attention and alertness to what was often called the *milieu*, a variable that had been forgotten about.

You conclude in Wisdom, Madness and Folly *that after 12 months the patients returned and you asked yourself the question, had they found more companionship inside than they could find outside? Did you actually ask yourself that question at the time?*

Oh yes. The work from Chestnut Lodge was coming out and had been for some time. Harry Stack Sullivan, in British clinical psychiatry, and that sort of socio-dynamic orientation that was far more pervasive in America. And American social work and para-psychiatric activities – there was far more going on in America than I was aware of or any of the psychiatrists that I was around were aware of. We weren't terribly alert to what was going on elsewhere. But this was very much in the air.

Stanton and Schwartz had written a book called *The Mental Hospital* which already had, I think, papers to quote from but I think it was – I was going to say the first – but it was a pioneering effort of the time, a sociological look at this type of system and it asked, was this type of mental hospital system, in the organizational form that it had taken, out of the 19th century really as appropriate as it might be to the situation it was attempting to address?

And in the refractory ward at Gartnavel I had made a point of trying to construct my own version of Moreno sociograms. Putting in suspense for the moment the clinical diagnosis – who were the people who were most socially isolated, whom the nurses regarded as the most hopeless, who they spent less time with, gave less attention to than anyone else and from that sociological scale who were the bottom of the heap as far as their place in the social world goes? These were the people that I wanted to see what would happen to if one reversed that unconscious, unintended trend. That's what I did with the 12 people who were selected to go into this day-centre room in the hospital from nine in the morning to five at night from Monday to Friday. The change in them was immediate and dramatic and was sustained over a period of about 18 months or so until all of that group left the hospital and I too had left the hospital by then.

But I was still in touch with the hospital and by another year or so they were all back in the hospital. So what led them to go out of the hospital and what had led them to go back into the hospital? I had already got practically all the grist of *The Divided Self* out of the army and the hospital set-up, including Julie, 'The Ghost of the Weed Garden'. She was included in this group as a special favourite patient of mine, as it were; she wasn't in the refractory ward, she was in the next ward to that. I had met her parents because it occurred to me how it might be interesting to find out a bit about her family, a bit more than an ordinary family history. So I saw her parents at the hospital. I got them to talk to me at more length than was usual, and I was aware that that was one of the things that I wanted to follow up, that here was an opening. I was always thinking of what I could address myself to that someone else hadn't done, what was an opening of ignorance, what was some sphere that was so obvious that no one had thought about looking at this.

And I thought, well, I'll put myself right through this psychoanalytic stuff and I don't think I'll forget about this, I'll get back to this, which is more or less what I did. I thought I would get back to this in Glasgow, I didn't think I was going to stay in London forever as it were. I had to get a higher qualification if I was ever going to be a professor and the DPM wasn't enough. And maybe their attitude would change and they might regard a fully fledged psychoanalyst with a DPM and with some significant scientific contribution.

In 1955 you took a job as senior registrar in the Department of Psychological Medicine of Glasgow University, located at the Southern General Hospital. You were the youngest to hold that rank in Britain at the time. How clever did you think you were?

I was aware that I was clever. I wasn't sure how clever I was; I was very aware that the world that I was clever in was occupied by a lot of very clever guys. A lot of very clever people go into the exploration of the human nervous system, it attracts clever people. I was extremely impressed by Warren McCulloch and seriously disheartened by the extent at which that level of exploration had got to. I had done myself in because I had neglected to keep myself up with the scientific side of it – that's the physics and mathematics of communication – although I wasn't entirely out of it. I wanted to have enough intelligence and acquired know-how that I wouldn't have to take anyone else's word for the state of the art. With every week that goes by there were very clever guys who were at it all the time, going further than you were ever going to be able to catch up on, even if you go on working and not sleep.

In terms of rank, it's extremely important because, in that world, there is this twin thing of responsibility and discretion. A pilot of a plane has got tremendous responsibility for all his passengers and everything, he's got very little discretion most of the time, he must exercise his responsibility within very set parameters of discretion or under some circumstances he'd put on automatic pilot and he's got no discretion at all. Well, I wanted, within the human organization, to work myself as fast as I could through the ranks to a position where I had enough discretion to have options and freedom but of course I would have no less responsibility. I didn't want to give up the hands-on relationship with people.

You were working all the time?

Yes, I was at it all the time. The main frustration I felt was the limitation of my own intelligence, my own capacity. I would have liked to have had, immediately, the information that a man like Kurt Goldstein had as a neurologist and neurosurgeon and at the same time know everything that had to be known about the physics of the physiology and the communicational. I would have liked to have been able to invent and to construct and to make a better EEG machine, that would access closer and closer what was actually going on inside the skull, because what was going on in the skull was affected by drugs. I mean you didn't really call them drugs, these were 'chemical messengers' or molecules of different kinds that obviously affected how you saw things, how you thought and *what* you thought even.

This extraordinary psychophysical meeting place of everything in the body, and the nervous system in particular, I didn't know all that there was then to be known about that. If I could know it then I would have a chance, but a guy like Macdonald Critchley knew far more. I mean I had to read a book or a monograph on the parietal lobes to be told from his digest of where it was at. But I wanted to be able to not to have to read the book myself but to know everything that was behind the book and then I would be able to really get there.

I never did proceed in that field, of course; I couldn't do everything. But I wanted to. I was aware that I would have to sacrifice 95 per cent of what I wanted to carry with me in order to keep on going on the march with a lighter pack. I had to be realistic, I had to find out what my limitations were and this was the name of the game for my life at that time. I wasn't interested in sleeping. I was also wanting to be at it in terms of my family, I saw that as life as well. So I wasn't by any means totally immersed in a clinical world. I was living an ordinary human life at that same time.

There is something about seeing life steadily and seeing it whole, 'the integrated vision' of Thomas Traherne's. I saw a danger of a very sophisticated sort of idiocy of knowing more and more and more about less and less and less and I wouldn't know why I knew this or what it's application was.

Can I change the subject to Martin Buber and the Jewish Society! When you went to see him you were the only non-Jewish person there. Did you think that there was something special about the Jewish sensibility or were you just imbued with Buber's thoughts?

I didn't think of Buber's *I and Thou* as a specifically Jewish sensibility being expressed in the terms that he expressed it. The background that Joe Schorstein had of his father coming from a Hasidic background was important. Quite often we went for car drives in the country from Glasgow, and he would sing while he was driving. Hasidic songs and Buber's tales of the Hasidim was a sensibility I hadn't come across. I found it a very, very heartening and a congenial component of what there was in the world.

There were always jokes among Glasgow doctors because there were three Jews in the Department of Psychiatry. Psychiatrists all a bit more psychodynamically oriented without being explicitly Freudian. There was a standing joke, you know, 'are you still in the Department of Psycho-semites?'

Well, I didn't see within myself at all that contribution to the unconscious and the understanding of dreams as anything especially Jewish. I don't know whether any one else did, it was just an occasion to make a silly joke about it and dismiss it as not really scientific, not really serious compared to real clinical neurology. The people that I associated with in my intellectual network were Joe Schorstein and Karl Abenheimer and John Macquarrie and Archie Craig and a guy I haven't mentioned, Tony Barnett. He was a biologist, he was a guy who I mentioned in a passage in *The Facts of Life* who was doing research into the copulation of rats. He was freezing rats to see how cold they could get and still have a fuck. I thought this was a joke, I didn't realize how much of serious money there is in this. [laughs] How had you to package stuff, and how cold, so the rats wouldn't get at it. But the application of that was entirely lost on me at the time. He took me to his laboratories and he showed me these rats and he had a viewing camera and little bits of cotton wool and fluff so they would collect this .... [laughs]

At the same time in the book as you talk about Buber, there is a passage where you describe meeting a lot of ministers who knew more than you'd 'ever know'. There is this constant thing in your work, isn't there, about religion and about the kinds of things that religious minds might get to know?

Well. Like you were saying of reading my Aunt Ethel's letter about my mother reminding you of *your* mother and father, I'd only attended two funerals in my life, the death of my grandfather and the death of my mother's mother. There is nothing, no fantastic big deal about what I felt at the time and here was I a senior registrar at the Department of Psychiatry, with this course for ministers who had approached the Department of Psychiatry. My job was to rattle through for them Freud's theory of mourning and melancholia, grief and psychoanalysis.

They were not particularly religious about it. Their job was to attend to people who were dying or had died and see their relatives, day in and day out. They thought this just didn't address their work particularly because they didn't think it was a particular generalization that you could make that certainly the Scottish Presbyterian people were not particularly hypocritical. It was about an even chance when someone died, that the nearest and dearest were quite glad to see them in their grave or quite happy to get whatever legacies were going. Sometimes someone died that people really liked, but a lot of people died that had outlived their welcome long ago. [laughs]

I mean they slaughtered it. I remember that evening, you know, they were *absolutely right*. I'd just read this in a *book*. But they weren't preaching to me about Lord Jesus Christ and anything like that, they just talked about funerals they had been to, while I was doing my out-patients clinic. I didn't have anything to say to them at all. I occasionally came across someone who came in because they were in a state of involutional melancholia. It was very obscure as to whether it had anything to do with anyone that had died in their life.

I wish I had had James Lynch's statistics to hand, they would have been very interested in that. There's a high incidence of death among widows and a high risk-factor is being attached to someone who dies. You've got a much greater chance of having a heart attack in the first two or three years after someone dies who you've been living with for a while than if you haven't. But there was nothing like that that I could say to them, so it just stuck in my memory. But it wasn't because they were ministers of religion, it was because their job was a hands-on job.

To go back a bit, the one thing that surprised me in Wisdom, Madness and Folly *is your interest in hypnosis and the paranormal, and you mention that your interest in hypnosis has continued ...*

When I say that my interest in hypnosis has continued, it has in a way but not in the terms of the formal cultivation of hypnotic techniques. That has become very sophisticated nowadays and the institute in Phoenix, Arizona – the Milton Erikson Institute – is maybe the most sophisticated nerve-centre of studying hypnosis in surgical interventions, the use of hypnosis in hospitals. People who are full-time, professional, post-modern practitioners of what used to be called hypnosis are not too keen on the word now, because of its connotation that you put someone into a special trance and make post-hypnotic suggestions.

Neurolinguistic programming was the most popular rip-off of Milton Erikson's work. When the neurolinguistic programming book first came out it became a very popular thing in America, a very highly-paid practice. There were people being consulted by business and corporate bodies and management. They were interested in the degree of interpersonal power possible without people being aware of it.

The first book that the two guys who originated that was called *The Structure of Magic*. They asked Gregory Bateson if he would write an introduction to it but he demurred and put to them and put to me whether *I* write an introduction to it, which I turned down. I didn't like the smell of it. So in a yes-and-no sense, I'm there with people like that in their minds but I don't engage in it in the manner that they do and I don't do formal experiments.

I couldn't help but – early on as a medical student – notice the existence of this technique called hypnosis and I read a few books and papers on medical hypnosis, the history of it, mesmerism, James Braid and the use of hypnosis in surgery and dentistry. Also I read of French hypnotists and Freud's interest in hypnosis with his characterization of moving from hypnosis to a more sophisticated practice and way of putting someone down, relaxing them and touching their forehead.

There was a chap I became aware of who was a professional hypnotist, and who lived just up the road in Arbegg Street in the southside of Glasgow. I wrote to him and he invited me to come and see him. He did some demonstrations free of charge, to popularize what he was doing. At that time I was involved in a student research project that I had going with a couple of other guys. Having been converted at a school camp as I thought at the time, I was carried away by being on the side of Jesus although it didn't stick, but I was aware that this had happened to me at a school camp – how? So I made a point of going along with Mike Todd and another couple of other guys who were friends of mine who were fellow medical students, we used to go to revivalist meetings.

We went along to Billy Graham when he was in Glasgow, and we'd observe what happened and take our own pulse rates. I could feel my own pulse changing at different points of the rhetoric; there was a Welshman I remember, who was into a real revivalist evangelical speech with the blood of the lamb and this florid language. And I went along to a stage hypnotist who I thought was very similar to Billy Graham.

I got half behind the scenes at the Billy Graham meeting. He had this meeting in the Kelvin Hall in Glasgow, it was hypnosis and revival and oratory, this was what I thought. I'd read some of the speeches of Hitler and seen them on the newsreel of course. So I thought, you know, how do you do this, what's going on here?

And you were interested in seances, weren't you?

Seances. Yes I dipped into one or two of these things.

Anyway the techniques of conversion at an event like a Billy Graham meeting are well worked out. They start off with a choir singing and music, then they work people into the mood and then the *pièce de résistance*. You get the preacher and he carries it along. At any meeting they could reckon on a minimum of 10 per cent who would be converted and for that purpose they had interview rooms. You could go along and confess, be converted and then you are told a whole line of patter, that you have not chosen Jesus – Jesus has chosen you. Then the main thing is to hang on to these people.

If you're serious about it, you've got to have an organization that in the next day or two will try to hang on to people.
Most of them fade away as there is a temporary effect of
conversion which doesn't last very long, a sort of conversion
psychosis that fades away. So you get their address, or if
you're really enthusiastic you go round and visit them, to
keep them in the fold. There were other phenomena that were
reported, things like fire-walking and ecstatic trance states
where the body could experience pain or burns, even tissue
reactions that were being induced by changes in states of
mind.

So I allowed myself to be hypnotised by this hypnotist in
Queen's park. I forget his name, he was just a local guy as far
as I know who had set up a practice as a hypnotist and
probably just wanted to make himself a bit more known than
he otherwise would be. Maybe he had put an advert in the
Bulletin or *The Glasgow Evening News*. Anyway, I had looked
him up and there were a number of effects that he induced in
me that I was very impressed with indeed.

There's a number of routine things that are the first
number like the first ski lesson that you go through, any
lessons, that are absolutely standard before you go to greater
depth. One of the first things is the eyelid flutter. Your eye is
looking up at a light or a watch or looking up at anything,
and then your eyes get tired and your eyelids flutter and the
hypnotist gets on to you just at that point as your eyes start
to flutter. So your eyes are fluttering, and then the eyes dip a
bit more and start dipping. He knows that your eyes are tired,
that your eyes are very tired and just as they're closing he
says 'your eyes are closing'.

Now he just follows what he knows, it is just standard for
everyone. He then makes the suggestion just a fraction of a
second before it happens so you're now following him instead of
him following you. And he's got you. Once he's got you in the
first stage your hands are shut and the harder you try to open
them the tighter they press together. You try to open them and
are looking at your fucking hands and you want to do that and
you find you are caught, you're caught in this spell or trance or
induction. Then he'll take you step by step into more and more
peculiar or little things and your hand you feel is resting and it's
quite heavy but then it gets lighter and it gets heavier, and so
on. It's as light as a feather and before you know it your hand is
moving up without you doing anything, just like a feather, or it's

getting heavier and heavier, it's sinking down. The harder you try to lift it up now it feels like a ton weight, you feel your arm getting heavier and heavier and absolutely can't lift it. I was fascinated by all that.

About three of us would meet in my mother's house and we'd take it in turns and to some extent we could do it ourselves. It was very important to eventually cancel the whole effects, that you're out of it and everything is back to normal so you don't get that lingering post-hypnotic suggestion effect. So I played around with that and kept on playing around with it in Killearn. I remember doing it with one guy and actually to my great surprise telling him that I was burning him with a lighter and actually – it was what was called a first-degree burn – the skin does this thing, that is a standard hypnotic effect. You can induce a first-degree reaction by suggestion.

I don't know how far you can go; redness and a slight separation of the skin, by *pure suggestion*. Then there is the other way round of holding a flame to someone – not doing it too much because you can actually burn them – but they don't feel that they're being burned at all.

The paranormal has interested you apparently.

All the stuff with *meditation* and this and that. I have a friendly relationship with a full-time shaman, Gangotri Baba, and am into all sorts of worlds, but I never really felt that anything of that order was anything I wanted to ever write about or publicize.

It was part of my strategy of meditation from the very beginning. In the Buddhist field, there are two paths that you can take, one is the path of the cultivation of *siddhis*, have you heard the term? and the other is the non-cultivation of *siddhis*. The traditional schools of Tibetan Buddhism in particular make a point in the training of monks, they practise different techniques which are said to induce paranormal phenomena at will. This white magic is regarded as, in fact, part of the course and something that you ought to do. You ought to become proficient in these things at different degrees of mind control. The same is true with the Hindu tradition of yoga. Raja Yoga is regarded as the thing to do, to actually practise levitation or engage in thought reading. I myself never felt inclined to engage in that as a practice.

However, there are people who have and do practise that sort of thing. They regard themselves as being able to recognize the degree of development of other people at a glance or not even at a glance. They *know*, you don't have to tell them. They attribute to me – like Gangotri Baba said, after his ceremonial initiation of me to this Kali system – he didn't see why I didn't engage in that when I could. What I can do, according to him, is summon him. I could summon him, for instance, materially to appear in this room if I wanted to.

You'd save me a trip to India if you could!

Well, as a hologram, instead of using the letters, I could communicate with him. By sight and sound and touch and smell – I could produce the materialization of him here if I put my mind to it.

Plate 1 Lecturing in London, 1973
Plate 2 At a conference in Spain, 1979
Plate 3 (opposite) London 1969
Plate 4 (above) London 1970
Plate 5 (overleaf) Hampstead Heath, London, 1969

4. The Tavistock Clinic

In 1956 Laing took up a psychiatric post at the Tavistock Clinic and at the same time began a four-year psychoanalytic training under the auspices of the Institute of Psychoanalysis.

The Tavistock Clinic was founded in 1920 in Tavistock Square, London (whence its name). It was one of the first out-patient clinics in Britain to provide systematic psychotherapy on the basis of psychoanalytic thought. In 1948, the organization of the clinic was taken over by the then new National Health Service.

While Laing was at the clinic, there was a vigorous debate taking place as to the precise value of 'object relations theory', a perspective predominantly associated with Melanie Klein. This psychoanalytic theory focused on the infant's need to relate to objects (i.e. persons), in contrast to classical 'instinct theory' which centres on the subject's need to reduce instinctual tension. In their different ways, Melanie Klein, Ronald Fairbairn, Donald Winnicott and others evolved theories of personal development based on the child's need of, and attachment to, his mother.

For Kleinians, the origins of neurosis are held to lie in the first year of life, not in the first few years. Central importance is attached to the resolution (or otherwise) of ambivalence towards the mother, the breast, and personal development is regarded as being based primarily on introjection of the mother and/or breast. Klein attaches little importance to the infant's actual experience of mothering, this being overshadowed in her view by the infant's difficulties in overcoming its innate ambivalence towards the breast.

Being endowed with both innate envy of it and the need to use it as the recipient of its own projected death instinct, the infant has first to work through its fear and suspicion of the breast (the paranoid-schizoid position). The issue for the infant is seen as the survival of the self against his or her own (projected) death wishes; the defences of psychical 'splitting', 'idealization', 'projection', and 'introjection' make up the survival technique he or she attempts to evolve. The second stage the infant has to work through is its discovery that 'the breast it hates and the breast it loves are the same breast' (the depressive position). The issues for the child are now the survival and restoration of this 'object', the loved and needed figure upon whom he or she depends but whom, because of ambivalence, in phantasy he or she damages or annihilates through envy of her or in anger with her.

Kleinians assume the infant has a much more vivid, violent phantasy life than does classical psychoanalytic theory. Winnicott and Bowlby were far more concerned with actual mothering. Perhaps Winnicott's most well-known contribution is his concept of the 'transitional object'. This is a term for a child's indispensable possession – a doll, a piece of cloth – which stands for the dimly remembered unity of mother and infant self. Contact with it gives security and facilitates switches in identification between mother, self and others. Bowlby, although concerned with *actual* mother–infant relationships (*attachments*), also argued for the introduction of ethological concepts into psychoanalytic theory. The *actual* attachment and bonding process seen in other species was, for Bowlby, instructive for his own theories of maternal–infant relationships.

It was in this somewhat complex, almost esoteric, environment that R.D. Laing was to spend a number of interesting and formative years.

You decided to go to the Tavistock Clinic and ended up having four years of analysis. If you thought that the whole business of interpretation *was against the phenomenological approach you favoured, why did you go?*

Well, you have to take into consideration that at that time, I was working in a neurosurgical unit and was imagining a career in medicine in relationship to neuropsychiatry and the phenomenology of the world that we present ourselves to and which we live in as mediated through our central nervous system. And how that operates. All sorts of considerations seemed very relevant, that I haven't mentioned. One of them was Paul Schilder and the extraordinary phenomena to do with the body image and the body schema, the precise stuff that Oliver Sacks has written about in that book *The Man who Mistook his Wife for a Hat*. Any neurologist comes across this sort of stuff every day, where you'd meet certain people that had this or that set of brain cells out of action.

Schilder I mention in particular because there you have a psychoanalytically imbued psychiatrist. Then there is the work of Paul Federn, again the body ego and physical sense of identity in relationship to other people and objects.

I am now both reading and relating to Freud in the context of being a young professional, working in the British Army and dealing with life-and-death issues and extreme forms of physical and mental disarray. I was taking Freud more seriously then than I took him for a while. I held in abeyance the philosophical, you might say, objections to Freud, like the way that Heidegger completely dismissed Freud as really not worth very much consideration. From a Heideggerian type of mentality, Freud is trivial. Well, there was the nitty gritty of Freud which appealed to me in *The Psychopathology of Everyday Life*, the detailed analysis of dreams, and that attention to specific detail in his clinical studies. Not things like *Civilization and its Discontents, Moses and Monotheism, The Future of an Illusion*, the study of Moses, the study of Leonardo da Vinci and so on. They became less important than Freud as emerging out of having worked with Charcot, and his relationship with Pierre Janet.

So there was the clinical neurological psychopathology on the one hand, then the phenomenology, all that stuff even though couched as it all was. And there was Harry Stack Sullivan, in the language of psychopathology. And Freud coming from that clinical background which was my world, through hypnosis into psychoanalysis as a *method*, as a sort of meta-sophisticated form of interpersonal influence and nego-tiation. And there was the claim of psychoanalysis that you can't really fully criticize and appraise psychoanalysis without apprenticing yourself to the method.

I didn't want to be an outsider to that discipline, I felt I was now in as much as I wanted to stay in the field of neurology. I'd got my foot in there. And I didn't need initiation into philosophy, of course. I could still have gone over to Germany. Schorstein had met Heidegger, he said 'wouldn't you like to come over with me and I'll introduce you to Martin Heidegger?'. Heidegger was so far in a sense beyond my horizon of reality, he was unreal. I didn't actually realize he was just a guy who was a few years older than me, still alive and who I could have gone and met. Who knows what would have happened. I could have gone and met Jaspers for that matter even though I didn't.

I was aware of what seemed to be a movement John Rickman had called 'One Body Psychology', the inter-psychic psychopathology of one person alone in the adumbration of something that reached out to other, the other in the form of object relations theory. Also from the little bit I could glean of that world, there was John Rosen and his 'Direct Analysis' that appeared when I was working at the Department of Psychiatry, Glasgow University. Rosen's work had a remarkable effect on the Department of Psychiatry at Glasgow. I mean, here was a guy who actually used ordinary language and interplay with psychotic patients, not just more or less normal neurotics but real psychotics and talked back in something like ordinary language. This seemed to suggest within the application of psychoanalytic theory a method of relating to other people. I couldn't see, in looking at myself, that Freud's constructions on what it was all about had ever seemed to bear very much relationship to my relationship with my father and mother. And my developing sexual life, my relationship with women.

But my arrogance was counterpoised with a certain amount of humility. It is an uncivilized argument that psychoanalysts were using – that you can't disagree with us unless you become one of us. But I thought, OK, it fits the direction I'm going, it will broaden my range, it's an intermediary position between philosophy and phenomenology and clinical studies. With the example of people like Schilder and Rosen, I thought if Kurt Goldstein had had a bit more psychoanalysis his neurology might have had much more depth. I could either, as it were, go to Queen's Square and get into neurology or I could go to the Tavistock. But neurology is too far away from the relevance of the world of other people in relationships than psychoanalysis.

This is where Wisdom, Madness and Folly *leaves off, isn't it? Lets talk about the theorists and the relationships ...*

Well, before going down to London I was in Glasgow. I was the instigator of a study group that comprised Professor Henderson, who was Professor of Systematic Theology at Glasgow University at that time; Archie Craig, who was then secretary of the World Council of Churches; Ian Cameron, who later went to America – he's dead now, had been in the British Army and a prisoner of war, was a psychiatrist at

Gartnavel, and went to work at Chestnut Lodge – and Karl Abenheimer, who had been a student of Jaspers and was a quasi-Jungian psychotherapist in Glasgow. Finally there was Joe Schorstein and John Macquarrie who at that time was working on his translation of Heidegger's *Sein und Zeit*. We met once a month and gave papers to each other.

The group was called what?

It was just a group, it wasn't called anything, we just met in each other's houses. The paper that I gave that might still be somewhere – it was the first thing I'd written – in some ways it was the beginning of *The Divided Self*, was a paper called the 'Ontology of Human Relationships'. In it I rattled through the philosophical difficulty there undoubtedly was, of being able to talk about human relationships. I can't remember whether Sartre and Camus had quarrelled over the *Myth of Sisyphus* or *L'Homme Révolté* at that time, but it was in the air, it was taken very seriously that Sartre was arguing that we could not use the word *we*, we are, in the same ontological category as *I am*. You can die and I can die and death separates us from that sort of mush of we.

When I went to the Tavistock Clinic, there were a number of people there or associated with it I had heard about or read about from Glasgow. One who wasn't actually working at the Tavistock was Bion. I got imbued with Bion's work theoretically and did Bionesque groups in Glasgow and there was this 'collusion' chapter in *Self and Others*, which was originally a paper I wrote on my experience of doing psychoanalytic group work *à la* Bion in so far as one can do it without having been actually apprenticed to Bion. Well, I was doing all these analytic group techniques before going to the Tavistock. Also, there was Michael Balint, with his work on families. I think he had already published a paper on the 'basic fault' or the primal fault which had something to do with Ian Suttie, that I had come across. I hadn't much time for ethology in terms of the relevance of ethological studies to human behaviour. I had also come across Fairbairn.

What I didn't bank on, what I hadn't realized was that the Tavistock was an exclusively *out-patient* organization. All my work had been done in hospitals, and this was to be the first time since I had left school that I worked outside of a hospital and clinical context. These were ordinary people who lived in Hampstead and all very white and very middle-class, and none of them seemed to be any more disturbed than I was or anyone else. I had a lot of sympathy with the Maudsley argument that they dealt with the really ill, and serious cases, and that the Tavistock was a sort of dilettante outpost of an organization that dealt with normal people.

Even the children?

To a degree. There was a complete split in the Tavistock between the child department and the adult department. Bowlby was all the time at the Tavistock and held a research study group that met every so often to discuss clinical theoretical problems. He was always trying to educate the staff to what he saw as the parent discipline for our work, which he argued ought to be the discipline of biology. What he seemed to really be talking about was social biology – I don't mean E.O. Wilson's brand – but he was talking about social biology, that human beings scientifically had to be seen within the context of all the other biological life forms and that the relationships between human beings should be seen in the context of ethological biology and not the distortions created by sampling behaviour in the laboratory or in isolation but *in vivo* situations. But there was the continued dictum that the only way you could really make any scientific direct study of a species is to study the species. So you have to study human beings, and the relevance of any ethological theory to the human situation has got to be determined by what's going on in the human situation.

In the adult department at that time there wasn't, as far as I remember, any major Kleinian figure. Hannah Segal was brought round on one occasion to give a series of seminars to the staff on Kleinian theory. Henry Ezriel – does his name ring a bell? – well, he was on the staff, and there was Jock Sutherland who was Director of the Clinic who had been an analysand of Fairbairn, and Charles Rycroft who was about 12 years older than me. He was about 40, 41 by the time I was about 28, 29 and it turned out that I was to be in supervision with Winnicott and Marion Milner. So I began an ordinary full-time job as a registrar at the Tavistock clinic.

What kind of people were you seeing?

I was seeing characterological disorders and, you know, obsessional neurosis. They rigorously excluded anyone who had any gross psychopathology. It took a day to screen someone and then they went into groups. They mainly did groups and a certain amount of one-to-one, but mainly groups. I quickly got myself a group of so-called 'borderline' people that would otherwise not have been accepted. So I had a group of borderline patients, plus I was doing ordinary Tavistock groups and assessment interviews.

I would interview someone, take a history, a more detailed history, neuropsychodynamically oriented, and then a clinical psychologist did their number and then we had a case conference with the staff in which you presented your findings about a patient. There was a general discussion and all that. From very early on at the beginning at the Tavistock I felt sort of 'fuck this', I had really fucked myself up here. I was shunted into doing this out-patient work, seeing people in an office, of a kind that, compared to the extremity of distress that I'd seen in the army – and neurology and Gartnavel and the department of psychiatry – this wasn't what I wanted to be doing. There was no integration of this with the body and disturbances in the body, just all sitting and talking, and that's where I felt I went down the drain in my career.

I had to do something about this and make the best of it. I was now cut off from the Maudsley. I'd got into the wrong street. I hadn't got the energy and the time to keep up a contact with Queen's Square and the mainstream. I thought the Tavistock Clinic was sort of lost in a miasma of human relations and the Tavistock Institute seemed to be lackeys of business organizations and were doing things like studying what sort of lavatory paper to market – whether people wanted to have rough-grain paper or whether it was to clean you or soothe you. Character types, stuff like that.

At the Institute of Psychoanalysis, Willie Hoffer – the Secretary of the Psychoanalytical Society – gave the first clinical seminar I attended. He came from Vienna: 'you have to all realize that you have been contaminated by your background'. So there was this deep contamination, and a process of Freudian 'cleaning up' that we were getting. 'Who's read Freud?' Not a single person. Well, actually three people put their hands up. This was the first year of psychoanalysis. I didn't put my hand up at all, I thought fuck, I mean he wouldn't have lasted 30 seconds in other company.

He gave a lecture on the anatomy of the psyche. Freud had discovered, for the first time, the anatomy of the human mind which consisted of the ego, the superego and the id, and these were three parts of the mind. These were all the things that he had discovered, the economics and the dynamics and the structure of the central nervous system. He went on like this!

Rycroft was simply Rycroft. He's an urbane, intelligent man who had no major scenario that I could make out that he was laying on me. I realized what the name of the game was, so I went in and laid down on the couch and he didn't have to tell me what to do. I simply started talking, addressing myself to what I had been dreaming that previous night. He made very, very few interpretations of a psychoanalytic kind. Occasionally he expressed an opinion with a reservation that he was going to express such an opinion. I had an undramatic analysis.

Being analysed by Charles Rycroft was undramatic? Was that proof to you that it was a waste of time?

No, no, I didn't feel that. I was thinking about the tone more than the content. It is very unjust on the Tavistock and Institute of Psychoanalysis in a way. Since we've got a certain amount of time, and I don't have to say both things at once – for me, I can hardly think of anything that for me hasn't got two sides to it. There was one side of the Institute of Psychoanalysis and the Tavistock lumped together which were my sort of professional world. There was no real conversation in them. But at the same time, I was among very intelligent people who were, as far as I knew then and as far as I know now, among the best of their generation, of their time. Ernest Jones was a bit out of my ken as a first year student, but I had seminars from people like Bion, Melanie Klein, Winnicott, and Paula Heimann. Joan Rivière had just died, so I had missed her in person. It was a great experience. But I did lose the connection in my life with neuropsychology and neurology and, from a clinical psychiatric point of view, cases of extreme hospitalization and the physical treatments which included tranquillizers that were just being introduced.

Tranquillizers were introduced when I was in the Department of Psychiatry at Glasgow University and as the registrar
in the department, I got a report together on the latest advent
of tranquillizers. When I first went to the Tavistock I was in
touch with the development of that. I very much wanted to
keep in touch with that, but I got into something else so what
I was talking about was the gain/loss measure.

Of course what I gained was a type of patient. A client at
the Tavistock wasn't of the kind that I had seen in Glasgow
as that sort of person didn't go along to the out-patient
department in Great Western Infirmary in Glasgow. *The
Divided Self* was practically entirely based on Glasgow up to
the end of my time at Gartnavel. The last chapter of that
book is about a woman in one of the refractory wards – Edith
Edwards, 'The Ghost of the Weed Garden'. That personal
experience with her simply consisted in meeting her in the
visiting room of the hospital at Gartnavel, with her talking to
me about herself and of me entering into her world. She
really, more than any other person, initiated me into *The
Divided Self*. I think one of the reasons why that book has got
something special is the sense of pathos that I had about her
existence. It was the main dynamo of writing it and the mood
of the whole thing.

The thing that may be difficult to realize for anyone who
hasn't been at the Institute of Psychoanalysis is that there is a
definite common factor in the method. Fairbairn had proposed two chairs and this was a major issue. The British
Psychoanalytic Society stuck to the couch, while the Jungians
had already gone to chairs. I mean, it would be completely
out of the question to put an ashtray beside a patient because
analysis was to be conducted under conditions of maximal
frustration. Even a glass of water, you know. So that the
discomfort might arise from the impulse to ask for that. Such
aspects were looked at in detail, very, very carefully. There'd
be seminars in technique, there would be seminars on the
technical problems of 'splitting' and 'introjectory identification'
and so forth.

Apart from the method, I had very little in common with
someone like Ezriel who believed in the complete here-
and-now type of interpretation, and other people who believed
in a mixture of, technically speaking, interpretations and
constructions. And little in common with people like Winnicott and Marion Milner and Rycroft who I don't think had

any comparable system of interpretations that they operated with like the Kleinians did. The Kleinians would ask themselves 'who am I?' in terms of am I a good object or a bad object at this moment in time and what is he or she putting into me or taking out of me at this moment in time?

But you obviously learned what the others believed in?

It became second nature that you could construe any moment in those terms and of course you were expected to. I'd already learned it, for myself. I was self-taught, but you had to learn to recognize what is called your countertransference reactions. Debates still go on as to whether countertransference is limited to the analyst's reaction to the patients transference. Or can you call transference everything – *Übertragung*, the original term for what you carry over – *Übertragung* was Freud's German word for transference. It is an ordinary conversational term for what you carry over into the present from the past. Well, in the object relations theory you are considering in what way the other person is projecting upon you parts of themselves or parts of their repertoire of good or bad objects. That's where Klein and Fairbairn were seen to come quite close to the Jungians. Michael Fordham, for instance, found Melanie Klein the closest to his position. I think he felt much closer to them than they maybe felt to him.

So I was participating in that world. I think the only criticism Winnicott ever explicitly made to me in my supervision sessions was on one occasion when I'd shown him a manuscript of *The Divided Self*. This was early on in my relationship with him. I don't think there was any bad feeling about it and I didn't say it to him the way I am saying it to you, but I had to point out to him the following: Karen Horney had written about the false self and there was a soft type of American sociology that talked about this before Jules Henry talked about sham culture. Anyway, before I went down to London, when I was writing *The Divided Self*, Winnicott was not a major figure in my intellectual horizon, with *his* notion of false self and true self. Maybe I *should* have given him more credit, but I didn't think so. Mine was more a translation of the Heideggerian notions of authentic and unauthentic. Winnicott said he agreed with every word of *The Divided Self* except one word: 'You said the *conscious* self and it was a misprint or typing error for the *unconscious* self'. He said he was sorry that I hadn't mentioned him more, or words to that effect, and he had a certain amount of irritation about phenomenology and false and true self.

What about your supervision sessions with Winnicott? What were they like?

I think it was the second time I went to see him in supervision, he always opened a bottle of wine. He was the only professional person that ever offered me a glass of wine. It was usually about five o'clock in the afternoon and I presented to him what I was doing with someone in analysis and he never actually adopted the attitude of teaching me anything. Rather, some point would arise and he would say something or discuss it in his terms. I was very specific. I always made meticulous notes of all the sessions that I was doing and would give him either a detailed account of one session or characterize the whole week, then put a microscope down on one aspect of this. His remarks were also addressed to the type of thing that he was concerned about. He was concerned about 'the stage of concern', he was concerned about Melanie Klein's 'depressive position'. He didn't like the schizoid-paranoid position as a concept, he wanted to talk about a stage of primary un-integration, with non-differentiation of self and other.

Charles Rycroft wrote a paper a year into my analysis with him, in response to Klein. She had given a paper to the Society, one of her really heavy numbers about consolidationist theory about schizoid paranoid positions. A number of people – including Bowlby, who was quite alarmed – were concerned at this development, at this extension of the importance of this first three months of life. Now you were at the dinner table or at lunch, table-talk about good and bad nipples, good and bad aureoles. Winnicott too had written a paper. I pointed out to him that what was called the phenomenology of the breast in his 'Paediatrics and Psychiatry' – what a breast is and all the complex of sensations that comprise the feeling of what you would call a 'good breast' – well, it was very difficult to get out of a Kleinian what *they* meant phenomenologically by a 'good breast' in a three-week-old baby. They were arguing that the baby was addressing the mother's nipple with apparent delight but were then saying that it was *really* eaten up by unconscious, constitutional, inherited envy, and was engaged in unconscious sadistic disintegrative splitting attacks on the internal good breast. This was a manic defence in the Kleinian sense of all that unconscious sadism. You can see the splitting because they prefer one breast to the other and there was a differentiation between the skin and the nipple so there were good and bad nipples and good and bad breasts. Well, Rycroft gave a paper which was about someone developing a whole paranoid system, which actually had a remarkable resemblance to the Kleinian psychoanalytic theory. Of course I had no conversation with him except what I said to him on the couch horizontally with him sitting behind.

Neither Rycroft, nor Winnicott, nor Marion Milner as far as I know, or any of the analysts like Sutherland, or Balint who had a Hungarian background, conducted analysis in absolutely the caricature of the classic way.

Classical ...

Mmm, which Freud actually never practised.

Getting back to Rycroft. What did you say to him?

Why don't you get up and say so in the Society? Instead of giving this tangential argument, presenting this metaphor. Rycroft responded by saying that the international psychoanalytic movement was more important than breaking up the British Society over Melanie Klein. I was very concerned about that.

One of Winnicott's more interesting remarks to me was that he had read *Sanity, Madness and the Family* and said that if he had his life over again – and this was also in relationship to Kingsley Hall – he would do what I was doing.

Did that give you pleasure?

Oh yes, I liked that very much.

Did you anticipate him to be the most stimulating man there, and was he?

Well, of them, Winnicott and Marion Milner. Marion Milner wrote a very good book, *The Hands of the Living God*, and under the pseudonym of Joanna Field she'd written one of the earliest 'vindication of women' books, *A Life of One's Own* – there was, of course, *A Room of One's Own* by Virginia Woolf.

I read Joanna Field, it was *On Not Being Able To Paint*, one of the first 'not me possession' ideas. What influenced me more than the false self was Winnicott's 'transitional object'. But again I had this objection that I brought up with Fairbairn who I only met once. I had a conversation with Fairbairn that Sutherland set up in his office at the Tavistock; but I did meet Guntrip, who acted as discussant to my position paper that went into the 'Politics of Experience' International Congress of Psychotherapy at the Central Hall, Westminster.

I can't use the word *object* to say what I want to say about the impact of the other on me. It doesn't seem to me adequate to say that that's a projection, of intentionality from the other, the intentional other. But you can't talk about the intentional other to someone who hasn't got the phenomeno-logical other, the intentional other – I couldn't. I mean you've got a persecuting object, so there is no way you can talk about the other except through the mechanism of transfer-ence in some way, the projection of your internal object onto an external object and a re-introjection of that projection. You've got two games of ping-pong going on against a wall.

I put that into *Self and Others*, in the first chapter. Winnicott was trying to get away from this system, he didn't like that way of talking. The idea of the transitional – Marion Milner and her 'not me possession', neither me not me, in between – the transitional area of Winnicott's and then 'the stage of concern'. It was an attempt to say in a more balanced way what Mrs Klein was trying to get at by talking about the depressive position. Winnicott didn't want to be committed to a Kleinian description of a schizoid–paranoid position but he was committed to trying to work out an ontogeny, a developmental ontogeny of object relations theory. You could not use an object relations theory. The libido model was nothing except ego, superego and id, because the id was an unformed, undifferentiated source of energy, the superego hadn't precipitated yet because the superego was supposed to be a pre-Oedipal precipitate of introjection, of projection onto a primal scene, fused and split parents and that complex system that Freud had modified to pre-earlier stages by Mrs Klein. So it was very difficult to get

a six months, eight months, nine, ten-months-old baby that
gives you something, as you don't want every act of giving to
be a reaction formation against destructive sadistic fantasies,
motivated by envy that are then covered over.

He wanted to try to say that, and I liked that word very
much, I used it in *The Politics of Experience*. Not that he put
his name on it, but I liked 'concern'.

I want to go back to a thing about Bowlby that you didn't
put in your book. He told me – he might have told you – that
a sane society depended on the sanity of its members which
was very much likely to be affected by a wholesome early life
and a wholesome relationship with the mothering, or caretaking, person. If there was enough people, a critical mass in
society that still had it together, that had that chance and
took it and entered into different walks of life, society could
be saved. That was his type of humanist version that he and
Winnicott shared. Carl Rogers is a bit similar.

If there are enough good people bred. Enough 'vitamins'.
That was Bowlby's disastrous comparison of maternal affection being equated with a critical period of being fed a
vitamin and if you didn't get the vitamin then you are lost and
gone forever statistically. It's such a terrible condemnation for
someone who's had an lousy childhood that 'you'll never get
over it'. Also completely unscientific, for that to be said. Well,
Bowlby and Winnicott in their own ways felt that these
institutions – The Institute of Psychoanalysis as an institution –
were important, not a stray straw guy like R.D. Laing.

One of the things that Bowlby said that impressed me was
that at the end of the war – did he tell you about this? –
there were thousands of displaced persons, thousands of
children who had lost their parents. Well, he was involved
with the World Health Organization at that time. It was
sitting wherever it was and was considering from the committee room desk what governmental policies should be put into
effect in relationship to rounding up these children. Should
there be camps, temporary camps and so on. What bureaucratic procedures should go into operation to try to find the
parents of these children and what should be done with them
in the meantime and what should be planned for them. There
was always the kibbutz method. Should the priority be of
uniting parents with children or not, or bringing these children up as wards of state. Bowlby took it for granted that the
first thing to do is find the mother – there's the baby and put

the two of them in each other's arms again. The question was raised, is there any *scientific* evidence that the biological mother of a child is in any way the best person to be sought to nurture that child in the early years? There was *no* scientific evidence, and there still isn't. So he reacted to that very much in the way that, I remember years later, Robert Lifton did, with his research into Hiroshima victims. I don't think Bowlby used this phrase but Lifton used it, advocacy research. If there was something you believed to be true and important science couldn't back it up if it was challenged, but the decision had to be on scientific grounds. Well, a way of reconciling your beliefs, sentiments and values with scientific rigour was to look into what the scientific evidence is in the hope that it will support you and if it doesn't then you'd be entitled, still using the scientific method, to say, well, maybe there is something wrong with the scientific hypothesis or the scientific data and the interpretation of it, and I'm going to look further into this. So we're not being neutral, we're hoping that science will come up with what we think is the best thing to do.

Bowlby would never admit that to many people because he wants to be seen as absolutely rigorous. Another thing Bowlby said was that he thought *The Divided Self* was a very good book but couldn't I cut out phenomenological and existential and ontological ...

As words?

As words. Yes. I didn't need to use the word ontological and he thought phenomenology would put a lot of people off. With *Self and Others* he thought I should cut out the word existential and talk about existential science rather than objective science. It was rather like someone saying that's a great melody but I just think you should take out the F sharp, and that's the end of the whole fucking thing .... [laughs].

Did he want to keep the book within the Freudian fold and thought that words like existential would take it somewhere else?

Bowlby, I think, saw me as a very bright young man and one that he had great hopes for but was always a bit anxious about the wild side of me, or another side of me that he

didn't understand. By the wild side I mean an intellectual wild
side, which to him was phenomenology and this existentialism. He said – this was in response to one of the chapters in
The Politics of Experience – there is no point in preaching to
the converted. He liked to believe that he was a sort of
bishop or archbishop in almost a secret society. We didn't
have to talk about these sorts of things – like my mother
would say, you know, you don't talk about these sorts of
things, that is understood. Bowlby thought we had to address
the scientific mind in scientific terms and that I was blowing
it with this sort of sentimentality as he saw it or by not being
objective.

But at the same time, over a period of years in repeated
seminars and in terms of the research designs that I proposed
– the interpersonal perception design and the outcome study
in Napsbury and Shenley – I influenced Bowlby a lot.
'Intervention in Social Situations' was another influence on
him. But in the research for *Sanity, Madness and the Family*,
he was always pressing for reliability and validity in communicational variables. After a while I found that what I needed
was a systemic theory which would get me off the hook of a
scientistic, not genuine scientific methodology. I would say
that we have got no units of measurement. I mean, what is
the point of talking about measurements when we've got a
ruler and we've got an inch, and I can rule that. But when
someone that you can pick up only on a one-way screen
blinks at someone in the first two minutes of an interview is
the controlling signal for it, well shut up about that? Well,
Bowlby would read a family transcript and say, well, the
mother is hounding, and I would say, well, what's the use of
you saying that to me after what you've said. In a research
design that he wanted to regard as scientific you couldn't use
the word hounding as this was completely a non-objective
behaviouristic variable. Everyone was involved in this type of
problem.

I felt that this medical scientific approach was not going to
get the wain washed, it had to be communication. You see
that was my problem with object relations theory; where were
the conditions or the possibility of an actual transit between
one system and another within the context of a system
comprising two elements not one? There was only ego and
another ego, there is no *you* and there is no word for *we*. In a
family nexus, whereby you could position, as in a multi-

dimensional chess game, people were caught or moved within positions of relationship to other, but one interpsychic psychology couldn't say how you felt when you were in a false position as defined by other people. Paula Heimann took me to task for that. I remember in one phrase she said you'll never be able to develop – using psychoanalytic language – a psychopathology of psychosis and perception alone. You see what she meant because in all this I wasn't bringing in the dynamics of libido.

Was there any time when you thought that people like Bowlby just didn't understand?

Well, they didn't understand what I was talking about. I was quite well aware of that. [laughs]

Even though they were charitable about The Divided Self, *basically they didn't really understand?*

No, they really didn't see the point of it. Rycroft said that it was very good but rather repetitious, that was all he had to say. So you know he's given me about a beta plus for a first ambitious effort.

Did anyone say that it simply wasn't psychoanalytical?

I didn't pretend it was. It was a sort of soft edge between psychoanalysis and existentialism. The nearest similarity was to Binswanger, who was a friend of Freud. Yes, Binswanger. But that was out of their immediate horizon. But I was in very respectable company: Medard Boss, after all, had a psychoanalytic training. He certainly was a friend of Binswanger's and so there was that honorary eye. I mean they were big European guns, they could have accepted that I was bringing in another frame of reference, but they were too anxious. But I mean, it wasn't as bad as being Jungian!

Did any of them say, 'I'm really interested in the concept of engulfment and implosion and this is the way forward'?

Not a single person. They didn't say nice things, they didn't say anything. The book was turned down by everyone, no one was interested in it. It wasn't the talk of the town or the talk of the Tavistock. One registrar, I forget his name, said 'oh I don't know why you took the trouble to write all that, there was nothing in it that I haven't thought of myself'.

Was it partly to do with the fact that they never saw those kinds of patients?

Oh no, these people had psychiatric backgrounds. They just didn't see these clients at the Tavistock Clinic itself. But it wasn't only just that type of client because one of the main appeals of *The Divided Self* was to people who weren't in mental hospitals but who nonetheless found it addressing them.

Your time at the Tavistock ... was it suffocating?

I didn't find Winnicott, Marion Milner or Rycroft suffocating. I'd grown accustomed to feeling that the world where I carried out my intellectual conversations was actually between ideas or with people that I'd never met and didn't expect to meet – and didn't even realize that in practise I *could* meet. If I just took a train and an introduction that I had been given I could have met Merleau Ponty, for instance. Let alone Sartre, Jung, Heidegger and Jaspers.

In the car this morning you were scathing about Melanie Klein and the way that it was, in the end, just nonsense. When did you realize that?

Oh, when I was there. Melanie Klein was giving clinical seminars on four-and-a-half-year-old boys. I haven't read the book that was subsequently published, quite a big volume of a case of child analysis. Well, she was going over this material at the time and I realized that this was a woman who couldn't say anything to me because of the way she treated people.
  If anyone raised a point which they ventured, or dared to give some possible alternative interpretation or something, it was simply impossible to disagree with her. She would simply say take that up with your analyst, for analysis. 'Your analyst will give you a personal interpretation of how you want to suck his penis or rip off her nipple, which you are displacing onto me'. That would be her interpretation. *Literally*. I mean you've read these Kleinian interpretations, that's what you got.
  I wanted to be supervised by Melanie Klein just for the

experience so I asked Rycroft and he said he would try and arrange it.

Did he know your reasons?

I wanted the experience of Melanie Klein acting as my supervisor on a case. I wanted *that* experience. It was reported back to me in the analytic session that Melanie Klein had refused to have me in supervision because Rycroft wasn't a proper analyst and therefore I wasn't having proper psychoanalysis with him. Because Rycroft had been analysed by Melanie Klein's *bête noire*, I think, Sylvia Payne.

There was Ella Sharpe – who was not there then – Susan Isaacs and Sylvia Payne, they were the female queen bees. Anna Freud was at the Hampstead Clinic and turned up at Society meetings but I didn't have much of a glimpse of [her].

This morning you really did suggest that you thought Melanie Klein had lost her way considerably. Not in touch with reality ...

I've got political reservations about what is explicitly said about what I felt about a number of the characters of that time. It might be put this way; I wasn't inclined to dismiss Melanie Klein lightly because what she was saying seemed to fit a phenomenological description of quite a lot of the stuff that I had seen, because in psychosis the unconscious becomes conscious, so the psychotic phenomenology would be the unconscious of a lot of other people.

You should read a paper by Edward Glover which is a virulent denunciation, a sustained denunciation of Melanie Klein's theory, claiming that it was a secular re-done-up version of the old Calvinist and Augustinian Christian doctrine of original sin. He said we had gone back to the constitution of genetic original sin with her idea of constitutional envy. It was against the evidence, there was no warrant for it in psychoanalytic experience, and it was a complete projection of her mind. However, even if it was projected onto hapless infants, she did project a remarkable personal world view, which had some profundity about it. It might be profoundly psychotic or profoundly odd but it was of a serious engaging interest to anyone who was interested in that sort of thing.

And there are other sorts of minds like Bion's with his *grid* and his idea of the disanaporocolis of the differentiation of different elements and the splitting of different elements even down to syllables and phonemes. Very intelligent stuff.

The point is, in a place like the Tavistock Clinic or the Institute of Psychoanalysis, there are different sects of people. Some possess limited viewpoints however much they might think their particular world is the absolute centre of reality in that field, without realizing that all sorts of other frames of reference just as establishment, just as traditional, exist. Someone in one sense as way out as Melanie Klein, and also as far in, was within the same Institute where you had people like Rosenfeld and 'Transference Psychosis' and Bion in particular, who spent years and years and years thinking about very refined situations. Like eight people sitting in a room; exactly how the space is, where the chairs are, where you are, how you move everything.

In the end was there something that all of those people shared that you no longer did, or was the diversity too great to share anything?

Well, I think that what I'd already decided on when I was at Gartnavel and certainly by the writing of *The Divided Self, Self and Others* and *Interpersonal Perception* was this idea of *relationship*. Actually, in 1958 Bowlby gave me some advice on that; he said read that paper by Jackson and Weakland and Bateson, 'Toward a Theory of Schizophrenia'. But I had already got that message.

When you were under analysis with Rycroft, how did you conceive of that?

I was *involved* in it. I met Rycroft in one or two interviews for the Institute of Psychoanalysis, acceptance or screening interviews, and I think once in relationship to his position as consultant to the Tavistock whereby staff of the Tavistock could have psychoanalytic training as part of their training. When Rycroft was in the context of a psychoanalytical session, I would begin to have the experience of what I imagined psychoanalysis was like. Namely *quasi*-Freudian or *quasi*-Fairbairnian or *quasi*-Kleinian or some sort of eclectic mix of interpretations that I imagined was the psychoanalytic job of relating what I was saying in this respect and that respect to transference to him.

I was very interested to see what would happen in that respect; to discover what sort of transference I would be expected to develop in relationship to Rycroft and very interested to see what personal illumination of my life that this experience could contribute. I didn't feel that there was anything the matter with me, only small things, like a bit of chronic wheezing. But I wasn't incapacitated. Rycroft in fact had very few things that he allowed himself, or that he felt like saying. He did say after about a year and a half that he wasn't sure what to make of it but that I didn't seem to manifest much of a transference to him, and this might be because of my particular phase of life. That's a point that was considered somewhat among analysts but not discussed terribly much in public – was there a right *time* for analysis? ...

Were you cynical at this time?

Cynical? What do you mean by cynical?

Well, I mean Karl Popper would just have laughed aloud, wouldn't he, at Rycroft's excuse?

Yes, sure. But Rycroft regarded that he was putting his intelligence and sensibility at the availability of someone else's life as expressed through this analytic situation. That could reflect back his personal viewpoint to another person that that person might not have himself, and that might be a useful contribution to their life. In other words Rycroft was using his intelligent, educated, urbane, civilized faculties to give attention to you for this period of time.

At the Tavistock you wrote books, but presumably you could have written them anywhere?

No, I couldn't have written them anywhere. Well, I don't know whether I could have written them anywhere.

But you never developed friendships, for example?

I don't think any members of the staff had personal friendships. It was an *institution*. People came there to work, did their work in a friendly professional manner, and went away to their separate middle-class suburbs, scattered all over

London. Sutherland lived out north and Bowlby lived some-where else and I don't think any of them had personal friendships with each other. I don't think any of the registrars and senior registrars – Bowlby, Peter Lomas and others – seemed to have any personal friendships with each other any more than I had with any of them. I didn't, as far as I know, make any personal enemies, or theoretical enemies.

Sutherland suggested I spend some time with Michael Balint's family GP group and I was happy to do so. Balint said I would have to spend a minimum of four hours of my week working in his unit, that I would be simply a dilettante in terms of his approach if I spent only one afternoon of two hours. I said I hadn't the time to spend four hours, so Balint didn't want me.

Ezriel had got hold of James Strachey's 1934 paper, which is still influential, 'The Nature of the Therapeutic Action of Psychoanalysis'. Anyhow, Ezriel was one of the first people to use a tape recorder at the Tavistock and record a group and get them to transcribe it. He was doing this research; if he gave one group 'wrong' interpretations and another group 'correct' interpretations, then he ought to be able to compare and contrast the *outcomes* of the two groups. I didn't think that Sutherland should have allowed that research to be done as I considered it unethical research.

One thing that separated us was a complete lack of camaraderie or rapport with the people who were patients. I mean Ezriel was dealing with patients suffering from some-thing. 'He' should get worse, whereas someone who he gave the right interpretation to should get better. He did this for years, and published a couple of papers.

At that time there was 'waiting list' research being done. I don't think any of it was subsequently published. The Tavi-stock discovered that their waiting list was over a year for groups. People who were on a waiting list got better *better* than people who came to the groups. [laughs] Of the people who came to the groups after a year, 80 per cent left after six weeks. The 80 per cent who left after six weeks, after 18 months were better than the others who were still there. People got worse who stayed on, whereas people would get better who had never got taken on in the first place or who had left immediately. [laughs].

Of course, you couldn't whisper a word of that outside the club because the Tavistock was terribly frightened that the

National Health Service, the Maudsley, would find out about
them. Also, if you did a group of eight people you could mark
up eight attendances, separately one after another, you hid
the fact that they had all been in the same room together at
the same hour. So it gave you time to do other things.

I said to Sutherland one day, this clinic is very white, why
are there no, you know, black people? He said 'transference is
complicated enough'. [laughs] Transference is complicated
enough!

*So presumably you realized one of the problems with that
approach was that it was apolitical?*

The work was completely useless to me. Worse than useless
in terms of the politics of experience, the politics of micro-
social situations, the politics of larger socio-economic contexts
in which all this was carrying on, the politics of the ideological mystification formations that occur, determined by class
and socio-economic factors. These notions did not exist at the
Tavistock Clinic. However, you must remember that I was
coming from medicine, and neurology and mental hospitals
and a department of psychiatry at a university. Things like
that were totally outside of their frame of reference too.

I mean there would be something like the Manhattan
Project – the incidence of obsessional neurosis or anxiety or
phobias or schizophrenia or borderline cases, in certain
socio-economic classes in certain urban or other areas of
cities. And how did these environmental factors relate to
genetic factors. But that was it.

When did it occur to you that you had to jump ship?

Well, it occurred to me from the beginning. I told you in a
rather extreme tone of voice that I'd fucked myself.

From my experience at Gartnavel of the patients that had
got into the day room instead of the refractory ward and who
were all out of the hospital in a year and then back again, I'd
had a thought. It had absolutely dawned on me then that I
should report back to the rest of the society what was going
on. So I cast a research proposal to John Romano, Professor
of Psychiatry at Louvain University.

He had read *The Divided Self*, and was the only professorial ranking person who was positive. 'I've read this with

instruction and pleasure, why don't you come over to America? What you ought to do is get a grant and have a look around, you can get a grant to travel around America'. What I wanted to do was my version of studies of the micro-social, psycho-social interior of families. On-site visits to families. I think Elizabeth Bott had already done something similar, and Willmott and Young had touched on it. Then Ted Lidz at Yale and his wife, and then, in 1956, Don Jackson, Bateson etc. were involved. Murray Bowen had written about three generational families already, and there were one or two others. Ray Birdwhistel was writing up his research.

So I went over to America for the first time – it was either '60 or '61. I flew over to San Francisco and stayed with a guy who had done work with Bowlby and Robertson, on maternal and infant bonding at the Tavistock, and was now working at somewhere in the Bay area. I stayed with him a night or so and then went and visited the Palo Alto Group where Gregory Bateson was working.

What were your thoughts at the time?

There were these simple contradictions. These people had limitations as to their intellectual horizons as they saw themselves positioned in society, hence there were limitations to the type of theory that they were constructing. On the other hand they were – in a world of people who address themselves to other people's problems and the theories they come up with to make these intelligible – among the best of the European and North American world of their generation. They still have a place in history.

I mean, to write it all off is a bit inane. The type of research that developed really in the '50s and '60s had nothing to do with the media mock-up of the '60s. The Bethedsa; National Institute of Mental Health; the Lionel Wynne research group; Margaret Singer's work as a clinical psychologist there and the other pioneers of family theory and therapy that I met for the first time in the early '60s in America, were all fruitful. I met Goffman on that ground.

What did you do?

We talked.

No, on a day to day basis, in the States?

I did nothing but go around to different places and meet research teams who presented their research. They told me what they were doing, and I presented to them what I was doing. I had already written the *Interpersonal Perception* book so I was searching for an interpersonal perspective theory that might include such elements as hierarchies and a triadic way of conceptualizing a triad, which I still haven't managed to do. Actually I've been working on that just now. Network theory and the problems of communication theory in terms of different types, modes, levels, classes – whatever you want to call it – categories of messages which contradict each other at different levels. Batesonian type of work.

All this was in the process of being worked out and I was trying to find a way of making studies and observations on what was going on which would reveal what was going on. The method of controlled studies with fixed, measurable variables, quantifiable variables that would identify reliably and had validity did not seem to me in some respects a way in which what one wanted to try to bring out what we could see was there.

How did you leave the Tavistock?

Well, it came to an end when the six years of foundation funding for research ended. I had already moved out of the premises of the Tavistock Clinic itself. I had a basement rented by the Tavistock Institute of Human Relations in Marylebone and had an office, two rooms which was where the work was done, where tapes were transcribed.

Was it a time when you had to think about practical things like earning a living?

Oh well, I was earning my living through that job I was doing. But yes, I had to keep an eye on what I would do after that. I would have liked the Medical Research Council to back up the proposal that I put to the Tavistock board, through Bowlby and Trist and Sutherland who put it to the North West Regional Hospital Board. And I put feelers out to the Medical Research Council about our experimental household with people diagnosed ill, but where nurses wouldn't wear uniforms, where the roles would not be defined in those terms.

This was quite unique?

This was *totally* unique. I don't think there's ever been any precedent for this thought before. And I said, wouldn't that be interesting?

No one thought so?

No one thought so except me. One person on one of the boards that I presented this to said – I had already published *The Divided Self, Self and Others, Interpersonal Perception, Reason and Violence* – you haven't got enough status yet. You do not have enough weight to get that amount of money from the Medical Research Council. You'll have to go away and do some more work to get the status, and to get the funding.

Well, this was before *Catch 22*, but I said, how do you expect me to do the work without the money when I need the money for the work? If I hadn't got status now when will you think I'll ever get it? I've got these books, papers, monographs, *BMJ* article, and so forth, what more can I do at this time? *Well, nothing.* He was very happy to show me that 'ha, ha, ha, you're stymied, you're checkmated' and you know, what could I do?

So I saw the writing on the wall, that I was never going to be able to do that. I also tried to persuade the Tavistock Clinic to develop two things that would still keep me in the Tavistock. One was to develop a new style of family intervention based on my research. At that time the Tavistock never got families. I think Ackerman in New York would get parents and the child, Winnicott had the mother and the child, Bateson wasn't interested in therapy, and Don Jackson was in a strange space. I was interested in a combination of research and therapy. I was interested in this idea like the equivocal figure. As I said in the introduction to *Sanity, Madness and the Family*, it is a shift, *not* in what is seen but in the way you see it. If you see the experience and behaviour of those people that are seen and construed as suffering from a disease and an illness and experience and behaviour is construed as symptoms and signs of a disease, this is what you see. If you see this in terms of the interactional communicational process between other people and drop that, then something else comes into view – what are called the signs and symptoms of a disease process are seen to be much more socially intelligible than has come to be supposed by most psychiatrists.

That was my statement. It wasn't that families caused schizophrenia. Furthermore, the genetic evidence so far is a lie, or an extremely misleading situation of the evidence so far available and in fact I wrote a paper that was turned down by the *British Journal of Psychiatry* and three other journals. It was eventually published by Richard Evans, a professor of psychology at Texas University, who did a series of books in the early '70s called *Men and Ideas* in which he did Piaget, Jung and me. And as an appendix to that book, included a paper I wrote that was turned down by the *Journal of Nervous and Mental Disease* on a critique of the genetic theory of schizophrenia. No one was interested in my negative criticism, no one was interested in what I had to try to propose intellectually and no one was particularly encouraging in the direction of research that I wanted to go on. No one was interested in changing the intervention model, such as let's visit the families on site instead of having them come to our office, which is an entirely artificial situation. Also, let's include children as well as parents in the total system.

I argued that splitting child psychiatry from adult psychiatry and the child department and the adult department at the Tavistock Clinic, they lost the relationship between the parents and children. No one was interested. Would they be interested in that type of visit which general practitioners did anyway, or an in-patient department, a residential unit where this sort of thing could be cultivated. No, *no*. It was politically *out*, it had been wiped out by all the mental hospitals and the Maudsley. But I wasn't fully aware of all these considerations.

Did you get the impression that there were some people there who wanted you to stay?

Well, I never heard a single word from anyone, after my grant ran out. I moved to Wimpole Street and I can't remember how much that – in terms of months – grant overlapped with starting up Kingsley Hall. I could have gone over to America and the NIMH. I probably could have gone over to Palo Alto, I'm sure they would have said 'great, join us, be one of the boys', but it never seriously occurred to me to emigrate to the West Coast at that time.

I even thought I might go back to Scotland, very much so, and there was Eskdalemuir and my feelers were now all out. There was The Open Way. I persuaded Eric Graham Howe of The Open Way Psychotherapy Clinic to change the name to the Langham Clinic because I thought The Open Way Psychotherapy Clinic was a non-credible title. He saw me as very much in the mainstream of psychotherapy, psychoanalysis, existential Buddhism. The mainstream for him. He was eventually very glad to get me to be the director of the clinic there.

So there was also The Open Way, which opened up possibilities. Anyway, none of the things that I mentioned came off but three openings did open up – the Davidson Clinic in Edinburgh, the house in Dumfrieshire, and Kingsley Hall, owned by Muriel Lester.

Before this there was the private practice in Wimpole Street?

From about that time on I was keeping myself going on the private practice I had. I wasn't beholden to having to apply for promotion or position. I had five children and I had to drop down to about £850 a year in those days as a registrar in order to have this deducted, to go through the four years of very expensive Institute of Psychoanalysis training, so I said to Sutherland, 'why not put me down for a Distinction Award?'. I mean, after all, who else in the years that I'd been there had done more; 'oh', he says, 'Ron, we don't want to excite. There's a lot of your colleagues who are very envious of you, we don't want to excite too much envy'.

So they couldn't give me a fucking Distinction Award. But that's what a Distinction Award is for! But it would make the mediocrities on the staff envious of me. So the future wasn't there, and the future was not a consultant or an associate professorship, and I wasn't going to get a professorship at that age any more. I had done myself in with the mental hospital establishment by going to the Tavistock and spending the best part of ten years, as they would feel, doing nothing with out-patients. I had done myself in with neurology and mainstream.

So we'd set up a place and we'll pick it up one way or another. We'll just *do* it. So I got the Kingsley Hall building but of course I'd got no money to finance it.

Going back to Wimpole Street. What did you actually do, if you never really believed in the various therapeutic practices you had experienced?

I did a lot of therapeutic work for years and I didn't think I was wasting my time. There are people around the world in all walks of life who saw me as patients. I've got a whole world of ex-patients who came to see me when they were in a hell of a mess at different periods of their life.

What did you do?

I met them in the room and I addressed myself to the best of my sensibility and intelligence to what they were on about. There is a great deal that can happen and can go on and serious help that another human being can find in another human being if it's the right person at the right time and the right place. I was doing that to all sorts of people, all sorts of problems and sometimes developing my work in connection with general practitioners and all this with the families and that network I was starting. I think it was about 10 years before the next person picked up on visiting families in their own home, sitting down with them for an evening and saying, 'well, tell me what it's all about'.

And where did your referrals come from?

By word of mouth, and from the network of contacts I'd developed. I knew a lot of people, and had a certain amount of credibility. People came to see me and I didn't insist on seeing them for a minimum period of a year or something like that, or four or five times a week. Sometimes it was a short time and sometimes it was a long time. Sometimes it was three times a week, sometimes it was a one-off and so forth. And until I gave it up that sort of practice grew and sustained. There were always letters of referral, professional referrals, direct referrals, and when Kingsley Hall started, the word got around about that.

There were a lot of people who were drawn to that in the hope of finding some sort of mental Shangri-La there in the middle of London.

5. KINGSLEY HALL

1965 marked the formal beginnings of an experiment which took place in Kingsley Hall, an East End community centre in London, owned by the Quakers. Laing describes the experiment in the following manner: 'Several of us lived with a number of very disturbed "psychotic" people who would otherwise have been in mental hospitals or psychiatric units and treated accordingly. Among us there was no staff, no patients, no locked doors, no psychiatric treatment to stop or change states of mind'. Kingsley Hall was, he declared, a free-for-all space. However, 'transgressive conduct', Laing added, 'for whatever reason, of whatever kind is objectionable. On this or any other issue we took our chances together'. (1986: xi).[24]

Can we talk about the beginnings of Kingsley Hall? Were you still on your own in relation to other doctors, or ....

Well, let me go back a little. When I first got to London I missed the study group in Glasgow and so I looked around for another. Esterson turned up in London, he'd been to Israel, came back and got a job at Napsbury. I think Eric Graham Howe, who was an important person for me at that time, had got in touch with me through reading *The Divided Self* and asked me to give a lecture at The Open Way. I had a friendly relationship with him and eventually used to spend one night a week round his house and have dinner with his wife in Montagu Square. We'd talk about meditation and consciousness and psychotherapy. He was the only person that I had met with the connection with meditation. He had written the first introduction to the English translation of the *Satisampajanna Sutra*, a Buddhist classic that vied with *The Tibetan Book of the Dead*. A major sutra that was part of people's lives in southern Asia and Ceylon and that part of the Buddhist world. Howe knew Christmas Humphreys and other people in the Buddhist Society.

Being in a very confused state, the Buddhist answer to

everything like that was what you'd call meditation. There were different ways in which you could tune your mind to get it into balance again. You need not be any more ambitious to achieve enlightenment or whatever, just to balance out, or clarify your mind. The simplest way of doing so is cultivating attention on one single object. Things are so complex, so let's take the simplest instance you can and concentrate on it.

I thought, well, maybe if there were a few people who were imbued with this sort of thing, and were living together with people who were in disturbed states of mind, they all might get themselves tuned. They might settle down, and maybe the most important therapeutic factor was the presence of other people in a balanced, wholesome, healthy, sane state of mind. A lot of very disturbed people who came to see me in Wimpole Street and previously in the army, once they came into my room and we sat together, they calmed down very quickly.

What was I doing in Wimpole Street? Well, very frantic people came to see [me] from morning to night and usually went away a lot calmer, with a lot more balance. That was something to do with spending an hour with a guy who *wasn't* frantic, and who was sharing his presence in the way a psychoanalyst didn't do. I was deliberately making my presence as a human being available to other people, for money. But I never turned anyone away because they couldn't pay. I wasn't making very much money, as a lot of people couldn't pay anything, or very, very little. Just a token. I wasn't making in Wimpole Street a Harley Street income. I still couldn't afford more than a twelve-year-old Ford 8 or 10 car.

So you met Esterson?

I had previously met Esterson in Glasgow through, I think, a guy called Salaman Resnick, who was an Argentinian psychoanalyst. Then there was David Cooper, who was working in a hospital in the south of London, who was interested in existential philosophy, and a guy called Paul Senft, who's now dead. Cooper, Esterson, Senft, Resnick and John Heaton, who was secretary of The Open Way and had been a research ophthalmologist.

Through my connection with the Tavistock publishing house and Harvard Watts, the editor – a decent guy who died a few years ago – I became the editor of a series that I had suggested to them called 'The World of Man Series'. People submitted books to that: John Heaton's *The Eye* and David Cooper's *Psychiatry and Anti-Psychiatry* were first published there. We, of course, had a common interest in Sartre and we did a joint book, *Reason and Violence*, and it, too, was published in that series. I think Anthony Wilden had his last book on communication, linguistics, published there.

Perry Anderson of *The New Left Review* got in touch with me in relationship to some paper or talk I'd given on Sartre's critique of dialectical reason. Perry Anderson actually got into therapy with me. For a number of years while he was editor of *The New Left Review*, he had suffered very bad obsessional thoughts that were a great torment to him. I don't know whether his time with me helped him very much but he had a lot of struggle with this tormenting classical obsessional neurosis. Juliet Mitchell was his girlfriend at the time but later they parted.

Anyhow, Eric Graham Howe put me in touch with some of the Quaker patrons, who were friends of his. Then I became aware of Alex Trocchi and this is how I got to know Jeff Nuttall. Jeff Nuttall had attached himself to Alex Trocchi when Alex was putting out *Sigma*, his early 1960s version of Dada and surrealism. That tradition of Breton and Artaud and pre-war France was alive in his mind, a sensibility of a colony or group or a communal idea. Like the Brazier's Park event that Jeff Nuttall wrote up in *Bomb Culture*, with a lot of inaccuracies of detail and substance!

I'm not making a major complaint about it, but the Brazier's Park meeting, at which Eric Graham Howe and Joe Schorstein came to, there were profound differences. Eric Graham Howe walked out, he thought I was making a terrible mistake in seeking a federation of the poet and artist type of mind as exemplified by these sort of people – John Latham, Alex Trocchi, Bob Cobbing, and Jeff Nuttall.

It was quite a dramatic meeting. Alex was very upset at Eric Graham Howe because it meant that if I associated with that crowd as far as Eric Graham Howe was concerned it was going to be very difficult for me in terms of *his* world. And Alex, although he adopted a persona of the crazy poet, he also had his head screwed on the way that few of the others did. He liked Howe and wanted to keep that together but it fell apart there and then. Schorstein couldn't stand Howe and Howe couldn't stand Schorstein and Schorstein couldn't stand

Trocchi and Trocchi couldn't make any contact with Schorstein and Howe!

These people had all come together really because of me. They were all different aspects of my world but when they came together it just fell apart, they couldn't stand each other. The weekend was a very sad experience because I liked them all. This was the time of Allen Ginsberg's *Howl*, and the beginning of that counterculture notion in Britain. But it didn't hang together.

The Quakers were very sympathetic. I went round the Retreat in York and was aware of that Quaker tradition. Then this chap called Cohen, who was a sort of sociological maverick young guy who wrote the occasional marginal paper that *New Society* might publish, appeared. He was very sharp and in touch with all sorts of things and he had spotted the existence of Kingsley Hall which he said was virtually stagnating. It had originally been an East End community settlement, but it had outrun its original function. There was only a warden and his wife living there and the odd meeting happening once a week or so, for a West Indian revivalist group. So the place was hardly being used.

The trustees were not sure whether to tear it down or hand it over, no one seemed to want it. It was quite a beautiful building inside. So I had several meetings with Muriel Lester who was the senior member of the Lester family. I think the name of one of the brothers was Kingsley. In any case it was called after a child who was dead.

She was the only member of the family as far as I know who was still alive and was the chairman of the board of trustees administering the building. I went to visit her in her cottage in North London and explained to her what my idea was, which she was quite unfamiliar with but which she picked up on very quickly. I explained that I felt that there was a serious gross violation of primitive human decency in the way we treated people who were mentally out of it as far as other people were concerned. There was just a rampage – lobotomies and electric shocks and comas and incarceration and everything, and that no one cared. Psychoanalysts didn't really address themselves to that wavelength, the nearest people they dealt with were competent businessmen and managers. Basically they had no time for people who couldn't straighten a tie and put on a white shirt and collar or polish their shoes.

Mary Barnes, who was an assistant matron at that time, got in touch with me and said she had a younger brother who was in a mental hospital. A chronic hospitalized schizophrenic. She very much wanted something done about him and also felt she herself wanted to make a break. Mary was a very devout Roman Catholic. She would write to me almost every day and come round and say 'you've got to get this place together, you've got to get this place and I'm going to be the first person that goes into it', and you've got to do this. So there were all these questions: would it happen here? Or would it happen there? I was determined it was going to happen *somewhere*.

Kingsley Hall was a historic building. Gandhi had stayed there and Mao Tse-tung was a friend of Muriel Lester's. She had been on the Long March with Mao Tse-tung for part of the time, and she knew Asquith. She knew people in world politics and knew world figures. She was a very remarkable woman. There was absolutely no fucking nonsense about her; she had that sort of clear, searching, no-nonsense intelligence, and with no prejudice. So she proposed we had a year in which we would hold some evening lectures and meetings – David Mercer came, there was Indian dancing. So we got familiar with going around to the building in the evenings. Then there was a board meeting of the trustees at Kingsley Hall, which formed the Philadelphia Association, and that consisted of John Heaton, Sid Briskin, Esterson, David Cooper, Clancy Sigal and Joan Cunnold who had been a chief ward nurse in William Sargant's unit at St Thomas's. She had got in touch with me because she was the nurse in charge of all that electric shock stuff that Sargant would do. She thought Sargant was mad.

The Philadelphia Association was formed for that sole purpose?

In my mind for the sole purpose of having an organization that was a charity, a non-profit organization which could negotiate with an organization such as the trustees of Kingsley Hall and receive Kingsley Hall from them. Muriel Lester asked me to come and talk to them and I did for quite a long time. Mary Barnes talked – I mean this was all ideal – this was all just an idea, a fantasy. She was talking as a professional, as an assistant matron, I was talking in my capacity and Sid Briskin was talking as a social worker. Our position was represented by the three of us.

So they came up with a proposal that they would rent Kingsley Hall to us for five years, 1965 to 1970, and would hand the building over to us subject to them coming around any time they liked and approve what was going on. So this is what happened, with their blessing and goodwill for a shilling a year, as nominal rent. We were to maintain the upkeep of the building.

What are your memories of Kingsley Hall in the early days?

I had at that time separated from Anne and my first family and had fallen in with Jutta, who was to become my second wife. After Kingsley Hall had been going for some time, Mary Barnes moved in and was working in her hospital at the same time. Joe Berke and Leon Redler had come over from America, and Leon Redler was working with Maxwell Jones for six months. Joe Berke was hanging around trying to set up a free university set-up and trying to use Kingsley Hall for that. He put in his book – or that book with Mary Barnes – that I was arrogant in stopping him from using Kingsley Hall for a fucking free university. Alex Trocchi came round to Kingsley Hall and pulled out a needle in a public sitting-room and started turning on to heroin – *no*, I said. What we were doing was far more important than you fucking-well making a political demonstration about drugs and consciousness. *No way.* There was a tremendous influx of that sort of thing with Trocchi and his crowd and Joe Berke and his idea of a lower eastside New York commune.

There was also John Layard, who was in his 70s. Raymond Wilkinson, who had become one of the lieutenants in the Richmond Fellowship Organization; oh, I should mention at that time, Elly Jansen of the Richmond Fellowship. I had met her on a number of occasions and we looked over different properties together – we had thought that we might do this together – including Addison Road in Kensington, which has now become the centre of the Richmond Fellowship. We agreed to try and develop that. But then we went our separate ways because Elly had not the same attitude that I had. I mean she was perfectly correct, her mind was set on the halfway house idea, but I was thinking of a whole-way house.

Jutta and I had a room and shared a sitting room with Noel Cobb, who is now the editor of a Jungian journal called *Sphinx* that he formulated. Paul Zeal came round early in the state of affairs. Joan Cunnold and Esterson made a point of being at Kingsley Hall every two or three nights a week. So several of us were there who were more or less coherent in our right minds but all feeling at that time very strange and baffled. Then people started to come round, one way or another and asked to come and stay. There was a completely informal procedure, some people just simply came and hung around and there was a consensus among those of us who were staying there that this person could or could not join. Soon the place very quickly filled up, and remained filled up until I left it.

Jutta got pregnant with Adam, just a few months before the Dialectics of Liberation Conference in the Roundhouse. I had then moved from living in Kingsley Hall to living in Belsize Park Gardens and visited Kingsley Hall. I can't remember when Morty Schatzman appeared on the scene, but he went to stay there for a year and there was a chap called Ben Churchill, who had been a television producer and moved into psychotherapy via John Heaton. He involved himself there to some extent. So there were a number of people there or around, a number of people living in different states of discoordinated states of minds, going through all sorts of numbers of which Mary Barnes was simply one of about 12. I didn't keep any systematic notes of what was going on. There was no captain's log of our ship.

Noel Cobb wrote a fictional book about it, actually. He is a very sensitive poet, he published a book on *The Tempest*, and is now a sort of Jungian-type psychotherapist. David Cooper had nothing to do with Kingsley Hall at all. I think he only entered the building once, he was completely ensconced in Shenley. I never visited Shenley – Villa 21 – maybe I visited there once. There was nothing particularly to see.

I was living in Belsize Park Gardens and had the practice in Wimpole Street. Joe Berke, Leon Redler, Morty Schatzman, Jerome Liss – all Americans, all from Albert Einstein College – were involved in the Dialectics of Liberation Conference which brewed up over that year and took place in August. Kingsley Hall went round another year after that with Morty Schatzman very largely being the person who was living there and who was most together. Then the following year Morty Schatzman left and there were fewer people in Kingsley Hall. James Greene – someone you might have come across – was a son of Sir Hugh Greene and a nephew of Graham Greene and had published a translation of Mandelstam's poetry as well as a couple of books of poetry of his own. He had been in therapy with me and he moved into Kingsley Hall. That took us to the last year.

Well, by that time I was not going round to Kingsley Hall very often and it was due to end. I said, I'm going to India, I'm all played out, I've got to go and have a rest, clarify my mind, take stock of the situation and get out of it for a bit. Then I'll come back and see what happens. We were all searching for other places. There was another place found before Kingsley Hall ended, then there was another place, and when I came back from India after a year I think there were three places altogether. Over the '70s this developed into seven places as well as a farm outside of Oxford – Ascot Farm – and a place in Shepherds Bush. Also there were several houses around London under the Philadelphia Association, and then there was the Arbours Association as well. The most that ever was going at any one time was seven under the administration of the Philadelphia Association.

The Philadelphia Association was now a loose federation. Anyone who wanted to try their hand at that, on the understanding that we were all in the same enterprise in some way or another in trying to develop an approach to this sort of thing, were encouraged to do so.

I think I withdrew into myself more in the late '70s, with a conviction that the side of this that I had seen as a possible example that other people could pick up was actually picked up by John Perry and in the West Coast by Loren Mosher with Soteria House. That was funded for some time by the American National Institute of Mental Health, and there was of course Bethedsa, and this or that initiative here and there. It wasn't going to break through the concrete of the existing state of affairs, especially with the new wave of biological psychiatry and the propaganda that these guys were consistently putting out to discredit everything else except that.

I thought for myself, the time had come to retreat in good order. What I thought was going to happen was what I think *has* happened. That they were going to either drizzle out quietly, fade out, or develop a relationship with social services which would be another version, addressing itself to more extreme forms of disturbance and with less medication than the Richmond Fellowship. But similar.

Reformist?

I found that the other members of the Philadelphia Association did *not* want to teach R.D. Laing. They weren't going to use my work, which was strange in the organization I had formed. Rather, they would use Winnicott and Maxwell Jones and that liberal-therapeutic-community-revisionism mixed with Lacan and object relations theory.

Did Kingsley Hall soon cease to be what you thought it was going to be?

I thought after about six months to a year that this could be *inspiring*. But that in itself this wasn't going to last and seed itself into society's strategy for responding to the situation that was described in *Sanity, Madness and the Family* and *The Divided Self.* Society was not going to stand it. The local inhabitants of Tower Hamlets did not like it. Eventually the place was like a battleground; pubs at night would throw stones at the windows, break the windows, kick the front door down and be jeering about 'loonies'. The neighbour would complain to me, 'it's an absolute disgrace, Dr Laing, these poor people ought to be given proper treatment and not be allowed to walk in the street in the winter-time without any shoes or socks on'. You know a guy had walked out the door without putting his shoes and socks on. I mean, I did my best to say to people like Francis Gillet, you know for fuck's sake, I mean you are gonna blow it for everyone if you walk out in this street without putting your fucking shoes and socks on.
   Historically, Tower Hamlets had come down in the world. It had been depressed, of course, in the '30s, then there was the war and they were now trying to get working-class respectability and be clean and tidy. And this was just a sore spot that they couldn't understand. Elly Jansen, with every new halfway house that was set up, would go round every house in the streets around her house, knock on the door and explain to them and so forth. I hadn't got the energy. There were one or two people who took I up relationships with; I went to see the local town council, and there was an occasional relationship with the fire service. Mary Barnes went out on the roof once covered in shit and danced, she did a sundance, *naked*, and someone phoned up the local fire brigade. Take this woman off the roof. [laughs]
   The drunks in the pub would break the windows and then

the neighbours would complain to the trustees about the windows being broken. But there was hardly a window broken by the people on the inside, they were broken by stuff coming through from the outside. It was an embattled situation, there was no money, and of course these theoretical contradictions that I was aware of didn't suddenly resolve themselves because they were now being confronted in practice.

Everybody had to be able to get enough money to buy food, or scavenge for it. And had to pay for the telephone. There was one guy, Robin Farquharson, who was about 16 stone, he didn't like walls, so he went on a rampage, smashing and ripping anything, trying to knock doors and walls down – what are you going to do with someone like that? There was very little of that but when it did happen what were we supposed to do in a context like that? Also *decibels*; the neighbours very seldom actually complained about the noise they heard coming from the building. But they weren't friends of the building and their ideology was that of the medical establishment – these poor people are suffering from some tragic disease and they ought to be given proper treatment and attention, given a bath and kept clean and not allowed to disgrace themselves.

Is the fact that you've never written much about Kingsley Hall a sign that it was a great disappointment for you?

... I haven't written about it for a number of reasons. One is that I've still got it on my list to write about. The other thing is what do you expect? Under the circumstances, it seemed to me that you could call it a draw, in a way, as far as it went. The thing is still in progress.

I mean, who would know which way the wind would blow, if anyone was prepared to lather the thing with a bit of social oil. NIMH and Loren Mosher, and Soteria House. It wasn't a foregone conclusion in the mid-'70s that the beginnings of an alternative practical serious approach could be adopted elsewhere. I didn't realize that the Italians had not the slightest interest in this, they were only interested in decanting their mental hospital population, making no provision or response to that distress or any other kind. I thought that if the Italians had picked it up, then ... but no, they made no effort and they still haven't developed any effort to work a model like that. There was Basaglia, who developed a place that could have developed. He convened a European conference at Louvain, and the Italians came to it. I couldn't get a fucking thing out of any of the Italian psychiatrists except why is it being held at a Roman Catholic university? You know, was this some Roman Catholic Papist plot that I was lending myself to. One of them said to me, 'don't try to colonize us'. This was an Italian; don't try to colonize us. I'd no thoughts of anything like that.

Guattari in Paris, he was the director of the so-called therapeutic community, and on the one hand he was playing this as a development of a Cooperesque anti-psychiatry sort of thing. But in *practice* it was fuck all, it was just like any other psychiatric clinic. He was using electric shocks. He just said, they pay me the money, I never go there, they can't sack me and I can't do anything so I just leave them to themselves.

So that's what had happened in terms of the French and the Italians. A lot of people talk about using this household, a small scale strategy as an alternative way of addressing the whole domain of psychiatry. If the Italians were going to deinstitutionalize it all, I thought they would have to do better than that. Kingsley Hall was something that some guys had started up without any money, just got a derelict house in north London and so forth. Basaglia had the whole Italian government behind them to pick up on – let's show the world how you can do it – but no way. But this is still on, the game hasn't ended.

Were there more problems than you anticipated in terms of who wanted to determine policy at Kingsley Hall, and issues of who was in charge and who was not in charge?

I don't think problems like that dominated individual PA houses when they got going. Somehow they found their own modes of energy. Each house ran itself in its own style, its own way and still does as far as I know. I think there are about three houses in London still going but it might have petered out. But that has evaporated from my immediate horizon.

Esterson left, David Cooper left, one of the major people who ran a house for 10 years or more in Ascot Farm, Hugh Crawford, died. He had a heart attack. He was about my age. John Heaton was never interested in households. The people like Noel Cobb had lived there but, like me, didn't sustain it.

Paul Zeal got out. Sid Briskin couldn't get on with Hugh Crawford. Other people came in without what I could recognize as the vision that I had had in the first place. So with a lot of soul searching and wrenching, I let that go. I felt I could better employ my energies in some other way, whatever it might be.

There was never at any time, except, I think, when Morty Schatzman and his girlfriend lived there, maybe at that time he ran it on *his* own authority. *Maybe.* Maybe that ran in a way without conflict in the high command as it were. When I was there I gave up in despair. The contradiction was that without an authoritative structure anyone could do almost anything. But everyone was so daft! I remember on one occasion, Noel Cobb, after putting up with one guy in the middle of night who had a thing between two and three and four o'clock in the morning where he would spend about two hours walking in a door and out of a door slamming it as hard as he could, as he walked in and out beside Noel's bedroom, well Noel just had enough. So the decision-making process at that time was everyone who was living in the building would come together in the same room at the same time to discuss the situation that he was bringing up. Noel said that he wanted to get a night's sleep. So, this guy who was doing this was articulate enough to argue that 'time and space' belonged to everyone and why should he impose his silence rather than him having the right to make a noise and by what token were these hours reserved for his sleep and silence if he was awake? It was all evens, if he was awake and wanted to make a noise and he was asleep and wanted silence then why should he not slam the door.

And people would agree with this. So if someone couldn't live with walls then it was – I mean, what were walls or barriers that separate individuals, why shouldn't you knock a wall down? Considerations that you were answerable to the trustees for this building did not belong in the same realm of discourse. I couldn't see my way personally through it.

Can I read you a quote from Elaine Showalter's The Female Malady, *concerning Kingsley Hall: 'at nine-thirty at night' you would 'expound on philosophy, medicine, religion or mysticism. About midnight the table was pushed back, and impromptu unrestrained free-form dancing to Flamenco or the Rolling Stones continued to dawn'* ...

I'll tell you why that is a lot of nonsense. Kingsley Hall was built by these post-Webb, do-gooding, rich philanthropist, passivist, ideological socialists. It's licensed as a chapel, the lower part of it is a chapel and it's got a small room beside it which I was told technically is a refuge, in English law. You can get into a certain room and can't be arrested for anything. The upstairs first floor was a games room with a large billiard table in it occupying the middle of the room. So as you go up the stairs there is this full-scale billiard table and we played a lot of billiards there, or snooker. Then you go through a door and there is a dining room. The dining room stretches from let's call it the window [here] to the full length of the building and there is a long, sort of baronial, heavy oak table with about 12 seats on either side. There is hardly any space in the room except that long table. That is it.

Then there is a door into the kitchen and the other side of a small passageway and a couple of rooms, and then a stairway up to the third level. One, two, three. That dining room was where we always ate. For most of the time that I was there, we had a regular evening meal and we made a practice of commonly inviting some people who didn't live there. People who might be interested, we'd invite for the evening meal. Maxwell Jones came, Ross Speck came and Loren Mosher, Alex Trocchi. Quite often a few people were round the table and we were in the habit of having a convivial meal. You couldn't move the fucking table, there was no question of pushing the table to the side and starting free dancing. [laughs] That was the dining room.

I don't remember the Rolling Stones *ever*; I think one guy may have had some Rolling Stones' records but Bob Dylan and The Beatles were the favourite music. The account that she gives must be from someone who has never been there.

Another thing she says here is that 'although Laing made the most of Mary Barnes's "recovery", I suspect that her voyage was disappointingly unlike his expectations. It was one thing to relive the dangerous exhilaration of his mountain climbing experiences in Scotland, and to be the manly physician-priest leading another explorer to the heart of darkness, or the top of Everest, five days in and five days out. It was quite another to spend three years changing diapers, giving bottles, and generally wiping up after a noisy, jealous, smelly, middle-aged woman. The image of the schizophrenic voyage that Laing had created drew upon his own

*heroic fantasies; it was a male adventure of exploration, conquest –
scarcely the reality of Mary Barnes's experience. Faced with the
obligation to play mother on the psychic journey Laing seems to
have lost his enthusiasm for it'. You've seen that book before?*

I was presented with that by a journalist in Philadelphia a
couple of years ago. I haven't read the book. It is total shit
from beginning to end. We can take it sentence by sentence;
lets start off with the first sentence.

You made 'the most of'...

In what way did I make the most of it? There is nothing I
have written about Mary Barnes. I've never gone around
propounding Mary Barnes as an example of anything *ever*. On
two occasions, once in Paris, Mary asked me to appear with
her – she had been asked to appear as Mary Barnes and I
was in Paris doing something else – a panel with her about
'Mary Barnes', which I did.
   Mary Barnes and I could have gone around the world as a
double act propagating Mary Barnes' trip. I never wrote, I
never asked, I never wanted to write an introduction or a
preface, or a review or anything of Mary Barnes' number. The
only time I ever referred to Mary Barnes was in a paper I
wrote before the Mary Barnes and Joe Berke book was
published. It was a paper I gave in Rochester in upstate New
York in about 1966 before Mary Barnes was *known*. So I've
never made anything out of Mary Barnes. I've never used her
as an example or a paradigm case or set her up in anything
I've written or in lectures I've given.

*Showalter also says, 'I suspect that her voyage was disappoint-
ingly unlike his expectations'.*

That's not worth talking about. I never had any close affinity
with Mary Barnes – you ought to speak to Mary.

I will do.

Yes, but I never had any sort of number about her or wanted
her as a personal patient of mine. I never took her on as a
patient of mine. I told her after some time at Kingsley Hall she
had to leave if she was going to carry on the way she was doing.

OK.

You know it's absolutely all made up. You can ask Mary, ask Joe, ask anyone.

The idea of 'three years of changing her nappy' ...

I never dreamed of changing a nappy of Mary Barnes. I had nothing to do with that. You know Mary Barnes was in her room in Kingsley Hall. I was involved in all sorts of numbers and if Joe Berke was doing that, and if anyone else was, that was fine with me. It was OK. I'm not trying to distance myself, I can't take either credit or discredit for that except for being the main guy of holding it together whereby she could go through her number. *Fine.* And I'll back her up any time in terms of the human respect that I have for her.

'The image of the schizophrenic voyage that Laing had created drew upon his own heroic fantasies'?

Well, in *The Politics of Experience* I give an example of what Jung and Jaspers would have called a 'metanoia set of modulations and transformations' which at that time and indeed still are called a 'schizophrenic episode'. Before the advent of tranquillizers and the use of electric shocks came in to stop that.

Let me elaborate. I was *conservative* and [Morris Carstairs] had looked up the records of the Edinburgh Royal over the years before tranquillizers came in. He said if only we could have a way of knowing how it's going to come out before you start, that one-third of the people diagnosed as schizophrenic would go through a schizophrenic episode and be all right again in six weeks if you didn't do anything; one-third would be in after six months; and one-third would still be going chronic or in and out of first admissions. It was something like that.

Now if I wanted to put it in clinical terms which I wasn't doing, let's see if we can change the paradigm, *à la* Kuhn, though I didn't get that from Kuhn. Kuhn's *Structure of Scientific Revolutions* came along just before I was about to publish a collection of papers I had written over the last five years, which were mainly from lectures that were to go into the collection for this series on the pathology of behaviour that Morris Carstairs was the editor of, but which eventually came out as *The Politics of Experience*. Part of it came out of the *Interpersonal Perception* stuff, and there was the 'us and them' part of it, my free verse and all the rest of it. And my feeling of the two sides that I wanted to integrate. I was aware of shamanism, I was aware of Eliade – maybe he should have got more credit – but the anthropology of egoless states, losing the ego, going into death-like states and the disintegration of the body image, disintegration of the world, perceptual transformation, going through all that and coming back again reconstituted, that was a standard model of *what happened*. In our society maybe this thing was still happening, but we were culturing it out and calling it a clinical form of psychosis? Maybe we could pick that out and change the metaphor.

Jesse Watkins came into my ken, in his 60s, through his sculpture. I became quite pally with him and he told me that a number of years ago he had been through this and he'd have been completely fucked if he hadn't been an old Navy man. The consultant in charge of his case had been a lieutenant commander in the Navy, and because Jesse had been in the RNVR, the guy let him hang out in a padded cell for 10 days, otherwise he would have got electric shocks. I said would you put this on tape. I gave him £20 to do that. I said I'd like to publish this, as this is a perfect example of what I've got in mind. He talked into the recorder, I got it typed, edited it, cut it down and then I showed it to him. He said that's fine. So I put that out as 'A Ten-Day Voyage' and I said I didn't know how often this happens. I don't know how often it can happen but it does happen sometimes. And it looks as though from what anthropologists tell us that that sort of stuff has been going on for a long time and in our society the only place for it is a padded cell.

Showalter's final remark 'faced with the obligation to play mother on the psychic journey' ...

Not obligated, not obligated, no obligation.

'Laing seems to have lost his enthusiasm for it ...'

Total nonsense.

Can I ask you again. Did you conclude that Kingsley Hall was a failure?

That's not the right way to put it, that it was a failure. I don't even know whether it's even in the past tense.

Considering all the criticisms ...

It's certainly *not* a failure. Look, it was not a failure in this respect. That for the time it went on, people lived there who would have been living nowhere else – except in a mental hospital – who were not on drugs, not getting electric shocks or anything else, who came and went as they pleased. There were no suicides, there were no murders, no one died there, no one killed anyone there, no one got pregnant there, and there was no forbidding of anything. Well, that in itself is a demonstration that if other people had been prepared to back that up more, even under those conditions, something was shown there. You might have thought that everyone would have died of starvation or pneumonia or by killing themselves or raping each other or beating each other up or wasting away on drugs or overdoses. But people didn't do that.

A lot of the criticisms were just that this was a place where anyone could do what the fuck they liked ...

No, that wasn't the deal, that was *never* the deal. You could be in any state of mind you liked but you had to behave in a certain way. We had to work that out as we went along. My dictum was *no transgressive behaviour.* Just because you are fucking out of your mind doesn't mean you can take a hammer and bash someone's skull in. If you think you can do that then I'm phoning the police. I don't care what world you're in or whether you're in the sixth dimension or the 27th dimension, *don't do that!* I wasn't encouraging people to walk over each other and make a mess.

However, my attitude in that respect wasn't shared by other people who were actually there. This was the era of doing your own thing, you know if someone needs to smash a door backwards and forwards for several hours every night and keep everyone in earshot awake, well he's doing *his* thing. If other people want to sleep, well that's *their* thing. I couldn't negotiate with what I thought was a complete loss of fucking

common sense. If there weren't enough other people who had
that common sense, it wouldn't work.

If someone came who wanted to work *at Kingsley Hall, what
would they have to do?*

They hadn't to do anything. They were living under the same
roof and making a life together, on an *ad hoc* day-by-day basis.
There were no formal duties. Simply sharing the same situation,
sharing a kitchen, sharing the arrangements to buy food.

Robin Farquharson had a bright idea that what we needed
in order to develop Kingsley Hall was to buy about 300 acres
of desert somewhere outside of Adis Ababa in Ethiopia.
[laughs] He was a very strange guy, as you can imagine; very
intelligent and totally out of his fucking mind. While phoning
up places all over the world – in the course of about two or
three hours – he rang up two or three hundred pounds' worth
of long-distance telephone bills. I said you can't use the
phone unless you are going to pay for it, he wasn't about to
pay for it. 'No, don't worry. The Ethiopian government is
going to pay for it'. So I tell him he can't use the telephone.
So he rips the telephone out; if he can't use the telephone, no
one else can. You can see that if someone got in the building
who was determined to conduct himself in that sort of way,
what could you do?

*Was what you felt based on the theoretical belief that as madness
is actually intelligible, there was some sort of moral responsibility
involved on the part of the so-called mad?*

No, no, it wasn't an ideological belief in that sense. There was
the ideological, if you want to call it that, policy of *non-harm.*
The Marxists completely fell away from this, which they saw
as reformist bourgeois idealism. David Cooper said every
schizophrenic son or daughter of a bourgeois family that went
on drugs or kills themselves is one bourgeois less in the class
war. We want to kill them all off. Or help them on their way.
He saw these people as psychic terrorists, guerilla terrorists
who would disrupt the bastion of capitalism from within the
family. Blow it apart.

By this time I was tired out. I'd been at this without a
break since I left school and university. I'd already got seven
children, then there was the Dialectics of Liberation Confer-

ence, the impact of all the mêlée of that, and of course acid was around.

I thought to myself that Kingsley Hall was certainly not a roaring success. But it is providing lessons that we can learn from *anything*, even if it simply shows that this particular way of doing it is not the way it is going to work. That should percolate through and maybe lessons can be learned. I thought maybe it could start again; actually I still get letters from people starting up this house, or that house, or this place or that place. All inspired by Kingsley Hall.

I was sadder but hopefully wiser. But my contribution of harmlessness and compassion but without at the same time finding a tactical, workable, pragmatic, operational down-to-earth nitty gritty sort of thing that could work for other people was becoming a black hole for me.

Did you feel at the time that both your psychoanalytic colleagues at the Tavistock and the psychiatric profession generally rubbed their hands with glee?

No, I wouldn't put all these people in the same bracket. I think that quite a number of the psychiatric profession whom I never knew except glancingly had a two-fold attitude. If they had been asked they would have said, 'well I told you so, what can you expect', it was a foregone conclusion. It was a quixotic, ill-advised, ill-conceived, sentimental, inadequately planned, and it was a foregone conclusion. On the other hand, I could say, well, people lived without the aid of the psychiatric division as far as I could make out, and although there is no evidence, perhaps they did no worse, maybe better than other people on *your* treatments.

I think the sooner it was ended for psychoanalysts the better, as it was an embarrassment.

You said to me that someone said to you that you were committing ...

Professional suicide. Yes, that was reported to me. Someone had said that that was Jock Sutherland's remark. He was the director of the Tavistock Clinic and, when I didn't re-apply for a job within the National Health Service and moved into Kingsley Hall, he remarked that if I did so I would be committing professional suicide.

They did not approve because they thought people might see Kingsley Hall as something of a psychoanalytical project?

Yes. And another thing that Sutherland said to me was that 'nothing succeeds like success'. If I'd managed to pull it off, everyone would be glad. That's what he was implying. There would be people who'd be glad to jump on the bandwagon but if I couldn't establish a kind of credibility, people would wait and see and not give support, financial or any other. This was purity and danger. This was not applying psychoanalytic theory to the treatment of psychosis, this was God knows what! This was *not* an official application of psychoanalytic theory but insofar as I had a reputation it was partly psychoanalytic. But no one ever got in touch and pulled me in front of the star chamber.

Did anyone come round there to see what you were actually doing?

Oh yes, at the beginning. But never came round again. I think Ross Speck came round. He kept in touch with what was going on.

Did Winnicott?

Winnicott never came round. Winnicott said that as he was president of the Psychoanalytic Society at the time, he hoped I would understand why he was saying this but as president of the Psychoanalytic Society he had to be very careful to whom and to what he lent his name.

You know, right up to the late '70s there were always people being affected by the Kingsley Hall ideas. For instance, a mental hospital in Spain would engage an aikido teacher to teach aikido to staff and patients together. It actually was an idea that I suggested to them and I mean that was tremendous for a psychiatrist to go on the mat with a patient.

Was the criticism – that your Kingsley Hall 'patients' were hand picked – one that irritated you more than anything else?

In terms of the reign of rumour, hardly a day would go by when I wouldn't hear some sort of report on something. That I'd committed suicide, that I was getting electric shocks, or that patients were raping each other. I mean a criticism that the patients were hand picked was the least of it. The criticism that patients were hand picked was and is beneath contempt. What are they talking about, what do they know about how people got to stay at Kingsley Hall? It's simply a phrase that would circulate round.

I might be in Manchester, giving an evening class to a group of social workers, or at the Royal Free Hospital and I'd be asked, 'I believe, Dr Laing, that you allow schizophrenic patients to talk to you'. That was one question. Indeed, one school of psychiatry thought that it was a bad thing to allow schizophrenics to verbalize because it sets up a forest fire of toxic stuff in the brain, that incites the psychotic process. So the best thing to do would be to inhibit verbalization.

I got a phone call from one consultant psychiatrist who had *heard* that I wasn't actually giving people *any* treatment and he said, 'how could you do this, Dr Laing? Would you refuse to give someone who had a haemolytic crisis a transfusion, would you refuse to give a diabetic insulin – that's what you are doing, these people are going into a schizophrenic coma and you're refusing to give them tranquillizers. They are hallucinating and you are refusing to give them treatment. Are you actually encouraging them?'.

Well, in actual fact I never had any theoretical objection to any tranquillizers or anything like that. I would tell people if they were tormented, well you know you can take this and try it out. They might say 'but doesn't it damage the liver, this heavy-metal lithium?'. Well, there is some sort of price to pay, I'd say, but there's plenty of people I know who have taken it. If you do, your eyes will be focused enough to be able to read and make up your own mind. There was a whole array of disreputable rumour which, you name it, I was doing it.

That you fucked all women, you were always drunk ... that kind of gossip.

Oh, I was either always drunk or I was fucking everyone, or I was on whatever drugs that were going round, particularly acid. Or I was mad, *or I was dead*. I heard quite a number of times that I was a ruined, tragic figure, who had fallen into the clutches of my own profession and been wiped out with electric shocks.

Some people who didn't know that I was R.D. Laing would

tell me these things about R.D. Laing; they'd think I was fucking crazy if I said, well, actually, *I'm* R.D. Laing. No, you're having me on, you're a nutcase. At one point it could have become a nightmare of being edged out of reality. One guy wrote a letter under the name of R.D. Laing to *New Society*. I phoned them up and said that I didn't write that letter. They said, how do you know? *How did I know?*

Did they actually publish the false letter?

Yes.

What did it say?

It was picking on some review in *New Society*, arguing in a third-rate version of my rhetoric, signing it R.D. Laing. And *New Society* wouldn't say that that R.D. Laing wasn't the R.D. Laing who actually wrote the books. They said 'well it reads quite well, doesn't it'.

I didn't enjoy that. It seems to have faded a little in the last 10 years, but in the mid-'70s and in America I had a raging reputation. I mean it wasn't all bad. I was idealized as something like a saint by some people, but then there was the other reputation – alcohol, drugs, psychosis, rampaging sexual conduct, and an image that kept quite a lot of people going, like when you had a bone to gnaw at and fight over. A sort of minor discussion point you could talk around at a cocktail party.

6. CONTEMPORARIES

Unlike some of his contemporaries, Laing's work and influence did not result in a 'Laingian school' of thought and practice, although many individuals did see themselves as his disciples.

David Cooper was one person who was often spoken of as the co-founder with Laing of the so-called 'anti-psychiatry' movement, an observation which consistently irritated Laing.

Another group of contemporaries Laing discusses are those psychologists – Perls, Maslow, Rogers *et al.* – associated with 'the growth and development' and 'humanistic psychology' movements.

One of the things that Peter Sedgwick talks about is the 'shadowy figure' of Esterson. He also talks about David Cooper ...

Ah, well, absolutely completely different kinds of people. Esterson couldn't stand David Cooper at all, and David Cooper – I don't think he had anything against Esterson but Esterson wasn't David's cup of tea.

Were you disappointed that your writing and Cooper's began to be seen as one and the same thing?

I don't think David ever intended to encourage people to misunderstand me. I don't know whether he has ever referred to me specifically in anything that he has written. He was writing his own thoughts and, though I don't remember ever having a conversation about it, I think he must have been pretty pissed off at what *he* said being attributed to *me*. Because I was really pissed off when people attributed Cooper's position to mine. We were almost completely different creatures.

There was both an area of overlap and a big difference, and we always realized that. David was a trained Communist revolutionary, and was a member of the South African Communist Party. He was sent to Poland and Russia and China to be trained as a professional revolutionary. When he completed his course he couldn't bear to go back to South Africa, though he was expected by his organization to return. But he was frightened that he was a marked man and would be killed. He knew that South African intelligence knew all about him, so he didn't go back. He stayed in Paris and there he met his wife, who is the daughter of a South Vietnamese real estate dealer, [laughs] a very beautiful woman, a very nice woman. David then got a job in south London as a psychiatrist and was beginning then to ferment within himself his own completely surreal distillate of revolution. He could not in any way by then be described as a formal Communist or a formal Marxist, or a formal anything. He was simply a one-off character.

David did his best to articulate his own vision of things and I'm not going to try to interpret it. I never found anything that he actually wrote of any particular use to me; in fact, I found it a bit embarrassing. I think his account of himself in the Argentine – I think it was in *The Grammar of Living* – I didn't particularly like. We were both interested in Sartre and French intellectual culture and David had a much better command of French than me. Marcelle had been my first serious girlfriend and I had been in France a little, but he had an ordinary working, speaking knowledge of French. I was very interested in Sartre's Genet book but I wasn't reading it with absolute fluency, but *The Critique of Dialectical Reason*, which a lot of people think is a very difficult book, didn't present any problems. So we cooperated on writing *Reason and Violence*.

David's idea of Villa 21 – which I'm told doesn't exist anymore – his idea of that sort of procedure wasn't mine and my idea of Kingsley Hall wasn't his. So, as I said, I don't think he ever came to Kingsley Hall. So we ourselves had, until his death, this friendly respect for each other's extreme differences. We met over things that we were interested in and I enjoyed his state of mind, because there were very few people who understood me. He was very quick, and was several degrees past most people. I don't meet many people like him and he didn't meet many people like me. So for the short times that we were together we enjoyed each other's company.

However, if there is one person you are particularly associated with, it often seems to be him. When people talk about Laing they often mention Cooper in the same breath.

We never worked in common research together like I did with
Esterson. We never did anything together except belonging to
this very theoretical intellectual study group, the Sartre book
and, yes, he was on the original PA board. He had no
connection with Kingsley Hall and I had no connection with
Villa 21. I had absolutely no connection with his political
alliances.

At the time of Cuba, David got an invitation to go over
and I think he met Castro. I don't know whether he met Che
Guevara at that time, but subsequently he always kept up a
South American connection. He asked me if I wanted to go
over and I said no fucking thank you! This might shock you –
I don't know – but I had no sentimental attachment to either
side in that. I wouldn't dream of accepting his invitation at
that time because everything was construed so politically. I
would have gone over, you might say, as a friendly anthro-
pologist just for the experience.

*Can we discuss that whole group of people who were then seen as
your 'disciples' – Berke, Schatzman, Redler and so on. How did
you view them – as writers, practitioners and friends?*

They were never friends.

*Because you called Schatzman 'Morty' ... perhaps I've read too
much into that?*

Morty Schatzman was never a friend of mine. I don't think he
ever came round to my house, or hung out with me or
anything like that. Nor was Joe Berke ever a friend of mine.
For maybe five years or so in the late '70s, I think I would
have called Leon Redler a friend of mine. I wouldn't say that
he's not a friend of mine now. But there was a time when I
went round to his house from time to time and he came
round to mine and we sang and played some music. We went
to the same parties.

So these people are marginal to the R.D. Laing story?

Oh, very marginal.

I went over to America, again in something like '63 or '64,
and when I was in New York I met Joe Berke, Leon Redler
and, I think, Morty Schatzman and Jerome Liss. They were

four medical students of the Albert Einstein College of Medicine who applied, as part of their post-graduate training in Europe, to do part of it in Britain. Leon spent some time with Maxwell Jones and then he came and joined me in London as Joe Berke did. I'm not certain whether Jerome came from the same medical school but they were all 15 years younger than me. Straight out of medical school, or still in medical school.

They were very American and I couldn't use them for any research. I was at that point the director of a research team at the Tavistock Institute. They were very sort of brashly-declaratively-American in the worst sense of the word, especially Joe Berke and, to a lesser extent, Leon. They were very imbued with this very white mentality – the Yankee, New York number of going to Montgomery on freedom marches on behalf of blacks they had never met and didn't know anything about and had no idea what the blacks in South Carolina felt about this discovery of their cause. This was some completely inchoate vague sentiment that they felt, and of course there was the Cuban Missile Crisis. This was simply a sensibility that I had very little time for.

They were unusable for research into the normal families that I was working with in Britain. I would have had to explain to them how to knock on a door and enter a house and sit down and have a cup of tea with a family.

They were simply students of mine that I adopted at that time – what you might call apprentices. I let them hang around a bit more than usual – not more than you might if you were working in a laboratory – in my office in Marylebone. Joe, or Leon, would come in and look over transcripts. And of course there was John Layard. He was a really cool guy and with great talent, impeccably English. John Layard took Joe Berke on in therapy, for training, and John Layard was coming to see me in therapy at this time because he had been secretly and quietly schizophrenic. And at the age of 72, he had been to see Jung, who hadn't helped him. Jung's wife had helped him and he thought that maybe at the end of his life I could too. Well he took on Joe, he said – I mean it was a bit like John Bowlby being in therapy with *me*, 'cos he was about 50 years older than me [laughs] – he was so bored by just about everyone, and the only person he would take on, to relieve his boredom, in therapy would have to be someone he absolutely hated. Poor Joe.

Elaine Showalter argues in The Female Malady, *that the only full case study you have – and it is mediated of course by Berke – is Mary Barnes. What did you think of Berke and Barnes'* Mary Barnes?

Well, I've got nothing to do with that. I never saw the manuscript. They made sure that I never saw it until it was sent to me *as a book* ... They don't pretend that I had, except that I was the lynchpin of the show, the context of what was happening there.

Mary had no idea of what was going on around her, or didn't care to have. After about three months of Kingsley Hall, when John Layard had Joe in therapy with him by then, Joe went to Paris for a weekend and when he was away Layard said to me, 'it's either Joe or me, Joe's got to go, because he is absolutely insufferable'. I took objection to that. I thought that Joe had to go *anyway*, but I took objection to John's way of going about it. So I said OK, I'll call a PA meeting, but before Joe gets back I want to talk about it with the members of the PA that are here: Esterson, Raymond Wilkinson and Sid Briskin. I said I agree we have to do something about this. Then John said he wanted to come to the meeting and I said, no, you're not coming to the meeting, stay out of the fucking meeting, this is a PA meeting, you're not a member of the PA. He said 'oh it doesn't matter, come on now', But I absolutely insisted and then he insisted on walking in and sitting down in the room.

At this time I was seeing John Layard in therapy each week. So I said, OK we're not going to have a fight about this but we're going to go out of this room, into another room, as I want to talk to these guys about the situation and you are not included in that conversation. Well, he absolutely wouldn't accept that, so the outcome of it was that *both* of them left. Joe was told to leave immediately in coming back on the Monday and John left on umbrage, on his interpretation. He just thought that this protocol was inappropriate to what we were trying to do and so didn't want to stay at Kingsley Hall anymore. But he continued to see me in Wimpole Street. Actually, he didn't like the rest of the company either.

The only time that Joe had any connection with Kingsley Hall after that was when he was allowed to come round for the express purpose of seeing Mary Barnes. So that's what he did but he was expected to come and see her and get out the door as soon as possible. That wasn't my decision particularly, but he was not popular with a lot of people. Subsequently he has developed a following of his own.

I set them all up in Britain by referring people to them; but as soon as they had got enough together on their own they fucked off. Then I think they have done their best to give the impression that they were close to me in some way over a period of time. Practically all that they published they stole from me.

Schatzman's book?

Yes, Schatzman's book [*Soul Murder*]. After the seminar I did, the next thing I knew was that he had written it up without even a mention of that fact. He got the whole thing put together with Niederland or whatever his name was – a New York psychoanalyst who had written several papers on Schreber's father, with some photographs of the instruments and so forth.

I had taken that and put it together in terms of mapping theory and had an idea of writing a book on Schreber which would have gone much further than that in terms of his idea of being a complete man and woman of both sexes as such, having intercourse with himself. That sort of thing. I actually gave a paper on that which David Mercer and Michael Henshaw (the accountant who was part of 1960s London) attended. I don't think I've seen Morty Schatzman more than once in the last 20 years and that was just when I happened to see him in a restaurant.

I don't think I've seen Joe Berke for over 20 years except walking along the street once. Jerome Liss deviated from them and went to Paris and then Rome and got himself involved in some practice that he's developed as an American in Europe. Specifically, in the 'growth and development' movement in humanistic psychology. I don't think Jerome ever used my name when it suited him or put me down. A lot of people who had been with me for a while would then go away and try to make something of themselves and used their relationship with me in a double way. On the one hand, it gives them credit but, on the other hand, to account for the fact that they are not around me anymore and don't know me anymore, that's because there was something the matter with me.

Did you publicly review or speak about the Mary Barnes *book?*

No, I don't think I've ever reviewed it or talked about it in public.

So what did you think?

Well, it's a long time since I've read it.

You're being surprisingly diplomatic! Was it helpful for those people who wanted to understand what 'Laing' was all about?

Well, I always found Mary Barnes a bit of an embarrassment. She is and was an evangelist for a certain type of trip – going down and coming up. This is what she needed to do, she needed firstly to go down, which meant taking all her clothes off, curling up and pissing and shitting herself and being taken care of like a baby. Then she would come up again and she had been doing it periodically for the last 20 years or 30 years. She made an international reputation about going down and coming up.

I had a great deal of concern for her brother who was the real – you've got to say this with double treble irony – the *real* schizophrenic. He had no time for Mary's sort of thing. He was in real despair and was seriously struggling for a way out of it. He took up meditation after a number of years and that helped him. He didn't want to talk about these things particularly but Mary had a mission to save him. In that respect, she was right; absolutely, absolutely right. We completely agreed about mental hospitals and the use of heavy medication. It was like they were simply pouring cement into someone's system to straighten them up, and zonk them with electric shocks and so forth. Her missionary zeal and her sustained enthusiasm I respect. I got a letter from her last week and she's now living in St Andrews and is continuing to persist in a project that she and I were enlisted in a number of years ago, about setting up a place in Scotland. She was saying – 'don't give up, it's still going to happen, you were right to see him'. This was the Earl of Falkland, or the Duke – is he an earl or a duke?

Interruption (Marguerita): I think he's an Earl.

The Earl of Falkland in Fifeshire. Falkland, the Falkland

Islands presumably – anyhow, his family. He became a social worker and worked in London for Shelter; I think it was Shelter. You know that aristocratic do-gooding number among the working class. You know the sort of thing – let me find on a map a really run-down area and get me a flat in it and take away any chairs that look decent and put in second-hand ones [laughs] ...

(Marguerita): Ronnie, you are being terribly scathing about people.

Marguerita and I went up there to meet him at the castle where, having done his field work among the poor, he was going to set up a spiritual community. Anyway, Mary thought that, since he was a Roman Catholic and she's had these Roman Catholic connections, she would put the screws on him to give some money or maybe a few cottages for something to happen there. That was a number of years ago and she's still got it brewing.

I think that what *she* wrote in that book, as I remember it, really pleasantly surprised me. What Joe wrote I can't remember but it didn't impress me at the time. I was just turning over the pages to see if he was ever going to say something interesting. But Mary was seriously baring her heart and soul and her experience to try to convince other people that there was something to be said for the way she did it and I quite respected that.

When people talk about 'anti-psychiatry', they talk about Laing, Szasz and Scheff. I thought that Szasz' early work might have appealed to you, with his use of anthropological and historical data.

Well, you haven't read anything from me in all these years attacking Szasz, *at all*. I met him on three occasions. I think the first thing that came to my notice was that Szasz had an 'attitude' about me that he's modified a little bit.

In a paper in the early '70s, that appeared in something like *Encounter*, he attacked me for being a very unreliable character, *dangerous*. Not so much because of what I said but for the fact that so many people took it seriously. I was a Communist, in his book, a base rhetorician, one of those who uses words for the effect of rabble-rousing – whoever the rabble may be. I was irresponsible and hopelessly confused, as I was on the one hand saying that mental illness didn't exist, like him, and on the other hand treating it as though it did. That was, as I remember it, the gist of Szasz' criticism.

I was very sad about this because I thought that, although I could well imagine that Szasz had things that he would disagree with me about, that basically we were ...

On the same side?

Something like the same side. I could take exception to his association with the John Birch Society and his version of the free society, rampaging capitalist, post-capitalism of cold war. I could make some allowances because he was a Hungarian and no doubt hated the Russians. But fuck it, if he could put out with such intense vehemence this thing about R.D. Laing, I wasn't going to give him the credit of replying to it.

I wasn't going to use his name for the history books. He wasn't going to get anything out of me at all in response to that. Maybe it was a love letter in disguise? But I thought someone had better reply to it, so Leon Redler wrote a reply which was good enough and there it remained. I put out feelers through Ross Speck – what the fucking hell is Thomas Szasz going on about? – and I got word back that some of his friends had tried to tell him that he'd got it wrong about me. But apparently he'd got a fixed idea about me.

I thought my stance in relationship to Szasz' argument that I'm inconsistent is totally wrong. As you know, I've never denied the existence of mental distress, mental misery, confusion, suffering and so on but I've tried to show that this was more socially intelligible than most people supposed. Having said that, out of – actually maybe sentimentally or of some schmucky compassion for other people – *I actually wanted to help*. I thought it would be a nice idea to spend my life to be respected by one's fellow man, make enough money to live off and do something possibly that would make a contribution to the commonweal such as casting some light on this dark subject.

You've made a point constantly of not replying to criticism, haven't you?

The only letter I ever wrote in reply to anything was of a

review in the *New York Review of Books*. It said that I had
recanted everything. So I just wrote a few lines to say that,
if the reviewer could find any sentence [in the book] that
supported that statement, I would be very interested and
that I would take it out if it was there, but I would bet it
wasn't.

I'm sorry that Szasz has gone that way. Everyone [at
that conference] was asked to nominate who they would
like to actually ask to be a discussant to their paper, I
acted as a discussant to Bruno Bettleheim's paper and I
nominated Szasz to act as the discussant for mine. I gave a
talk that – the two pieces of it didn't hang together – they
hung together in what I said, but I didn't think they were
going to *publish* it as it stood. The two halves of my paper
didn't seem to be particularly connected. So Szasz got up
afterwards to discuss it and said that the nearest thing he
had ever come to what it must feel like to be subjected to
involuntary incarceration in a mental institution was having
to sit through Dr Laing's talk.

From there he went on and on in his own manner and
tried to tear it *absolutely* to pieces. What he fixed on was what
he called my relativism and that I was just unrigorous, sloppy
and a dishonest nihilist. It was nihilism in disguise; he was
dismissing me as a nihilist. He also tried to make out that
what I was saying was fashionable *salon* nihilism and that it
had nothing to do with science. So I wasn't going to reply to
that. You know, fuck it.

He came and shook my hand afterwards. Having done this
performance of destruction he came on the stage and offered
me his hand in front of about three or four thousand people.
So I shook his hand. What I had *actually* been talking about
was not so much what would technically be called perspectivism as radical constructivism – but you know, this thing about
whether you can believe your eyes or other people. The
problematic of quantum physics or what to believe with two
possibilities in everything. The undecidability observer paradox, that what you observe actually disturbs the system. This
was a problem *we* confronted; the same terminology which
was used to express *our* dilemmas was being used to express
the world of quantum physics. It was this sort of thing that
was mind-boggling for some people, but you wouldn't have
thought that there was anything mind-boggling if you read
most journals and stuff about psychotherapy. But Szasz got

up and that was the first thing he said – that he had great difficulty in stopping himself from saying that it was like listening to an incoherent schizophrenic psychotic.

He was definitely *boggled* and he couldn't get his voice. Literally his throat was croaking and he said he had flu and apologized for this. Eventually he ground out his accusation of nihilism.

Did you talk to Szasz afterwards?

No. Well, I was prepared to talk to him but he wasn't prepared to talk to me. He had changed his attitude later at a Richmond Fellowship conference, we met standing for cocktails at lunch time. You know that sort of thing – a glass of wine – and he was very affable and professionally friendly.

Foucault. Were you interested in his historical work on the asylum or were you interested in him because of his structuralism?

In my capacity as editor of the 'World of Man' series for Tavistock, I published Foucault in English for the first time which was his history of madness and civilization.

Could you claim to have brought him to the English-speaking public?

Well, the British yes, not the American. An abridged edition of the book had already been translated for Pantheon, I think, but I don't think I knew that. I had come across Foucault. I hadn't read it, I wondered what was in it and I put out feelers through the publishing house and got the manuscript of *Madness and Civilization*. I don't know whether I would say it was a great book but it was one of the books that I would consider to be a really major book. His name was totally unknown in English. I wondered if Tavistock would be able to get it but anyway they did and that was the only book of Foucault that I read until the next one came out and was translated, *The Order of Things*. That must have been about '66 or '67, the late '60s. What I was writing at that time – and I was heavily involved in both of them – was *Knots* and *Politics of the Family*. Actually, nothing I've written has been particularly influenced by Foucault's sensibility, except part of *The Voice of Experience* in terms of Foucault's drawing attention to and doing that historical analysis of the panopticon. It was that objective look of Foucault which I was on to.

Jules Henry and Gregory Bateson?

Jules Henry and Gregory Bateson. I met Gregory Bateson for the first time in Palo Alto in '60, '61 when I went over to America for the first time and met him on a number of occasions thereafter. On one of his latter visits to London, he stayed with me so I became a friend with Gregory Bateson.

The paper of his ... that was the influence presumably, nothing else, none of his other work?

Well, that particular paper which introduced the formal concept of the 'double bind' wasn't a great deal of influence for me either. Because the influences that were influencing me can already be read in the last chapter of *The Divided Self* – about the attributions, first of all about being bad and then being mad on Julie, and in the *Self and Others* where I took that work of Harold Searles' of 'driving the other person crazy'.

So it was a confirmation more than anything else?

Yes, it was a confirmation and the stimulus to think about it in formal logical terms. I'd already come across the Russell Whitehead calculus in use. A completely different way of looking at it was in Warren McCulloch's work in relationship to synaptic transmission where this nerve impulse can be regarded as a proposition; it's an on/off switch, it's a binary thing, it's yes or no. When you've got 30,000 of these things going at once, you've got all sorts of possibilities of multiple messages and the new type of supercomputer, the type of logic you can use is no longer binary. Far from it. I was impressed by Jean Gabel – *False Consciousness* and his European critique of false consciousness which Bateson had no idea about. Bateson was a bit like Bowlby; he too could not see the point of phenomenology.

The last time I met him I'd heard that he had taken up tai chi (which was not the case actually), but I said, 'I hear you are dancing' and he said, 'oh no, I'm still digital'. I asked him on one occasion where did he think that I stood in relationship to him? He said, 'well I think you've got a 10 per cent edge on me'. *Ten per cent.* [laughs] But the point was that he knew that I knew what he was talking about and I could talk about it too. The first time I met him was at Palo Alto and that was in itself a very interesting meeting.

Jay Haley and John Weakland and Gregory Bateson gave me a piece of chalk in their hang-out think tank, Palo Alto, they put me right on the spot. Let's see what you're made of. So I gave them quite a detailed run-down on the theoretical work that I was working out in terms of meta-perspectives and meta-meta perspectives and different disjunctions between perspectives and different patterns and how we could plot that. There was a guy called Herder who had tried to develop a symbol system that might be able to do that. It's very complicated, you know, that work, and there is something to be said for being able to condense it by using one letter for what would take about a couple of pages to write down.

So Bateson accepted me immediately as did the rest of them on the basis of that. With Bateson there was never any uneasiness. He once made this rather peculiar remark to me, he said, 'I've heard that you are having a hard time being accused of being too much influenced by me' ... [laughs]

For you, did the volume of existential psychology, Existence, *edited by Rollo May, lack the social dimension or was there something else you weren't too keen on?*

You mean the absence of the social dimension as, say, manifested in 'the case of Ellen West'. Well, it's not that the social dimension isn't included there as there isn't in fact a clinical psychiatric history, rather the amazing complete unconsciousness of Binswanger arranging with the husband to hypnotize the wife and that in the realm of the immediate relationship, the unconsciousness or unawareness or unrealization or unappreciation. One of the variables is the enormous cliff of power between a husband who will hypnotize the wife and she is suffering from anorexia. Either she's free to kill herself or go back to hospital.

All this is reported, but it's reported after the manner of a colour-blind person giving some minute and accurate description of a colour that they are not seeing. The description is there but there is no realization of it which I find a bit frightening and there's a bit of that sort of thing about Rollo. He's a very nice guy but I don't think he sees these things easily himself. One of the films that you are likely to look at is an interview with a homeless person in Phoenix, Arizona, that caused a lot of controversy and is still reverberating in some circles. The professional reaction to it was extreme. Rollo May saw that video in Amsterdam, at a conference we were both at, and when he saw it he invited me to invite him up to the stage to say something about it. He lavished praiseful epithets to it, saying that this showed what a meeting between two human beings could be like. And that every department should have that as teaching material.

Well I've met him about three times since and he keeps referring to the film. He's an 'American type' like Bowlby is a 'British type', he's an East Coast patrician type. He used to be in the cavalry, and his criticism of Ronald Reagan is like Von Rundstedt's criticism of Hitler – he's not a gentleman. Rollo May thought Reagan still thought he was in the cavalry, leading a charge against the Cherokee or something like that.

You're not impressed with Rollo May, are you!

American academia has not, so far, been able to host that European sensibility and they'll never develop their own home-grown variety. Not in my book. I mean who is a great *American* philosopher? Well the greatest American philosopher I would say is Mark Twain, in his essays. Emerson, William James and Pierce and Dewey. But the whole thing gets terribly thinned down when – what a turning of the wine into the thinnest, thinnest milk trash – you compare Sartre or Camus with Abe Maslow. There's no tragedy, there's no irony. I can't imagine Nietzsche in America. But Rollo May is one of the best of them. There is no doubt of it.

Did you at any stage in your career get involved with people like George Herbert Mead?

The Social Self?

Yes, and Cooley ...

Yes, I read George Herbert Mead but didn't find too much there, like Sullivan talking about the 'generalised other' and 'significant others'. I don't want to write more than a first chapter of *general* statements about that sort of thing, I want to get down to the nitty gritty of *You and Me*. That's how I left the last sentence of *Wisdom, Madness and Folly*. That's what I'm taken up with just now, what I'm into just now.

George Simmel?

Yes, George Simmel, Max Scheler, Cooley, George Herbert Mead, and the rather English, stilted intersubjectivity of Schutz. Maybe I should go back and read these guys again. I haven't read them for such a long time. I never found in them the sort of thing that you haven't thought about before. You know when you stop and you make a mark there and you write down that sentence and that stays with you. I mean sentences like that crop up for me every year or so. One of them was in that passage: We are a We, and what is a We. *We* is not the same as *you and I. We* is an *Us*.

Eddington says when you think of two and you think you've explained one and one you've got to remember you've forgotten the *and*; what is the nature of *and*, what is the connecting link between *you* and *me*, is there anything between you and me except the words that come out of my mouth and go into your ear? What is the nature of the relationship between you and me? You can cut that with a knife and you and I don't die. That relationship is not a physical body. There is a difference between the game of tennis and the tennis players but it's very difficult to say what that is apart from a ball going across the court. We, and, the connection between you and me – how do you find a place for all that?

What's the possibility of developing that connectedness in any sort of object-relations and psychoanalytic theory apart from just repeating *ad nauseam* that we have to have a socio-psychology which must be contextualised and situation-alized and embedded in the social, and that we mustn't forget about roles and the self.

What is the self for Buddhists, for instance, there is no self, there is no ego, *there is no me*. But then you have to say, well, there is a me that comes into appearance or even illusion – are you going to dismiss that? I mean when people fall in love, it is interesting the way you see the person you fall in love with. Everyone remarks – it's one of the oldest observations, Freud made it – that consists of seeing one woman as different from every other. Bernard Shaw has a remark like that as Freud has that ... You do actually see this person – while you're in that relationship – as actually different from how you saw them before you met them. And after you've finished the relationship you look at the woman that you used to live with and though you can recognise her picture, you somehow see her differently. That's very curious. So what is the phenomenology of that and how do you express it, how do you describe it, what is the process? There are some phenomenological components of that which go into the nature of that intimate bond. There is a bond of intimacy; there is a curious observation that Norman Mailer made, that the first time you meet your wife is in the divorce court. You certainly see this woman in a different way than you did a year before.

You don't merely want to synthesize Cooley, Mead and the others. But are you also saying the project is just too large to produce a unified theory?

No, I'm working on it at the moment, when I'm not talking with you just now! If I've got enough energy before I go to sleep I'll have a go at writing the next piece that I'd put off until you go back to London and I go to Vienna! [laughs] ...

Eric Berne and Transactional Analysis. He tried to formalize relationships within families. Did you see his work as interesting? Or was he too concerned with therapy and not with science?

Well, I wasn't interested too much in his therapeutic side of it, it is merely an interesting schema; you can put all of what I got out of Eric Berne on a blackboard in two diagrams. You know: father, mother, adult, child, son, daughter, and we are all of these things and each of those interact across. So it's a contribution to that sort of schematic layout that helps you to clarify who is going on about whom at any point in time.

People like Rogers, Perls, Frankl, Maslow. Is it important for you to separate your work from that whole 'fourth wave of mystic psychology' because they are not really very interested in 'sick people'?

No. You might say that the success of Carl Rogers is a terrible reflection on American society in that a guy can make his reputation (and maybe justifiably), for saying that 'I'm a person and you're a person and I'm a person and I'm hearing you' and merely echoing back to people what they say. After he said that, I don't know what else he said about life or about meaning or heaven or hell. Or what it's all about.

He came over to London 10 years ago and he and I did a joint workshop at the Hilton Hotel in London. His group and a few of my network had a meal together in a restaurant around Primrose Hill the evening before and I couldn't make any personal relationship with him. Well, my son-in-law, Tommy Heenan – this chap that is married to my daughter Karen – he's got an expression for a guy like that, he wouldn't last two minutes in a Glasgow pub. He just wouldn't last two minutes. At the meeting I was badgering him about this ridiculous thing of marketing himself as a 'person'. You know the last commodity, you might say: *I'm a person, I'm a person.* [laughs]

In the course of the meeting at the Hilton – about 350 people came along – I did an interview with Carl Rogers which was taped and published in one of the human potential journals. One of the most amazing things was when I asked him what he had to say about evil, he said he knew 'nothing about evil in himself'. The only data he had on evil was from his clients. That everyone was born good and stays good if they have a proper upbringing like him. He simply wouldn't admit to a trace of evil in himself or knowledge of it or sensibility of it, and thought that all the tragedy that playwrights have gone on about was pathological.

I felt from the moment we were introduced and shook hands that I had nothing to say to him. He was one of the least personable people that I'd ever met in my life and that's saying something. I asked him about his relationship to really disturbed people and he said he had no experience of psychosis. He did say that he had had one psychotic client who drove him crazy. After six weeks or so of seeing her he was driven so crazy that he took a car and just drove north up to Canada and then took another two months to recover. Apparently it was a major event in his life. One of the remarks that he made in being interviewed by a journalist, was that what he was most proud of in his life was introducing the tape recorder into the client-centred interview. [laughs]

Frankl?

... Victor Frankl never touched me particularly. Logo therapy. It is again one of those terrible reflections of the world we live in that, like Carl Rogers made a reputation out of saying that we're persons, Victor Frankl makes a reputation out of saying that the reason why many people are disheartened is because they can't find any meaning in their life. So there's no meaning in your life but somehow or another by going along to therapy you'd find meaning. There was meaning to be found just by lying there as it were, if you just looked out, you could find that life was meaningful. So you just go on being a middle manager in a marmalade factory that manufactured fragments of wood to stick in the marmalade to make it look like real twigs and go along for logo therapy and find it all meaningful.

This was one of the things that George MacLeod had complete contempt for. If you were going to be a real Christian you had to lead a Christian life, it wasn't just a matter of going to church on Sunday, in which you went along as a totally mechanised robot and then had a belief that Jesus died for you and that it all means something. That you're all right and all the blacks are unconverted and hadn't had the benefit of Scottish missionaries and Roman Catholic priests and who don't know how to say the Hail Mary's.

Horrifyingly and terrifyingly, Frankl had been in the concentration camps and if you had an inner persistence of being able to last that out – as they could surround you with a completely enclosed horizon of total meaninglessness and total negative environment that you were not wanted in this world by anyone that you could see or hear or anywhere around you – I don't know whether I might not have pined away and died and given up under those circumstances. Victor Frankl obviously had a great thing that kept him going, and maybe people who came to see him got a bit of that whatever it was. Santayana; the animal vitality that's going to persist anyway even when you are reduced to nothing, just hopelessness and despair. But all very thin compared to Tillich's *The Courage to Be*.

I think you are particularly irritated by Maslow, aren't you?

Well, after the real thing it's just watered-down, thin, diluted milk, *self-actualization*. Just American bourgeoisified Nietzsche. Egalitarianized too, so anyone can self-actualize. Actually just vacuous when it comes down to it. A few corollaries that you could put on a blackboard that students could learn and then repeat in an examination. I mean, if you have to teach something about human beings rather than rats in Brandeis or another university like that, you could always include Maslow on your reading list and set him as an exam question. You have to remember the six things and you get a beta minus if you don't remember them all.

I mean, I'm not impressed by all that stuff on growth and development and human potential weekends where you go through a hero's journey in 72 hours – and *be here now*.

Perls?

I'll have no friends left by the end of your six-hundred pages, but I'm not asking for them.

There are two aspects to all these people; one is any personal contact and any personal impressions, and the other is an intellectual opinion. I met Paul Goodman on one occasion and that was at the Dialectics of Liberation Congress. I never came to know him in detail at all, and the side of him that had led to his invitation there was that with Jules Henry he had written *Communitas*. This was, you might say, in the tradition of that solidarity of Kropotkin, anarchist, anti-bureaucratic state, that the totalitarian state had a perfect instinct for separating people from their solidarity at this level and forcing them to relate up the tangents of a pyramid to the top. So they all did the same thing because they all took the same orders from a source, and their immediate relationship between each other was separated and fragmented. A perfect instinct which prevented pairing off and friendship and love between people. I liked that perception of that trend in our society.

I didn't have any relationship to Paul Goodman's work in relationship to Perls and Gestalt. As far as Perls was concerned, he looked us up in Kingsley Hall and came along one evening. I didn't meet him in detail and, when I was over in Esalen for the first time, Perls was around and again we never clicked at a personal level. He was a character that I didn't take to. By this time he was playing the role of some sort of liberated secular rabbi who had a great propensity for pawing and making physical contact with any woman in sight. He didn't seem to be able to stand there for a moment without grabbing someone and hugging and slobbering all over them. You know this 'do your own thing' number, and that was his thing so he was doing it. Again it was a terrible reflection on the state of affairs that an energetic slob like that could have people around him who would adore him and that he would have such influence.

The elements that have gone into the practice of Gestalt were things that were a codification of awareness that I took for granted, you might say, in my own awareness. The 'empty chair' technique, for example, and I suppose the overlap between Gestalt and Moreno's psychodrama. I mean, that just seemed like a thimble compared to what I felt was the real thing that went on in mental hospitals and the PA houses. *Twenty-four-hour living.*

Perls' main clients seemed to be psychotherapists themselves. Rollo May said that in the West Coast you can't hit a stone without hitting a therapist, that everyone was sorting out everyone else. They are all desperate to find something you could give some name to and could market. Then formalize qualifications that you could again brand, that would give you some pretext for making money.

Because they were Americans predominantly, there is no real background of Marx, European literature or the 'authenticity' issue of the existentialists. Is that the difference?

Yes, I think so. It's a philistine barbarism with an amazing arrogance, and of no depth of European culture. The only way that they could relate to that would be to *intellectualize* it. There was no *feeling* of the Marx of the economic essays and Feuerbach and Buber. When Buber says, 'when I think I think with my toes and my fingertips and my whole body, thinking is not something that goes on out of the top of my head', or Nietzsche's comment that people talk about thinking as a sort of snake that comes up and makes you sick from your guts and through your throat. That it is a real physical activity that implicates you totally.

Not only Marx, but Weber and Töennies and the precursors of German and French sociology. In one mood it evokes contempt and in another mood, well, I feel it serves them right. I don't think that *anything* that I've thought or written about seriously has been affected by them except that they [the Americans] are part of my environment.

From time to time people obviously say to you 'what is your model of man?'. Does that mean anything to you or is man either too free or too constrained to think of the idea of a model of man?

There are too many things I would have to work through to disencumber myself of the word 'model', which implies already that man is a particular sort of being or creature. So the constraints start already.

Whose essence? I'd have to disencumber myself of all the misunderstandings of the word essence. Existence can be expressed in the mode or manner of a model of that, but then it's a very awkward question because I don't want, in the impatience of refusing to answer it, to give the impression that I am some anti-intellectual who doesn't regard it as a worthwhile question. The question is like a question I was asked in America at about half past eight in the morning in Salt Lake City, Utah, on American television – 'Dr Laing, what is your message to the American people in 40 seconds flat?'.

7. THE DIALECTICS OF LIBERATION

In the middle- to late-'60s Laing was internationally known and enjoyed considerable success. It was a time of experimentation and exploration, including the use of hallucinogenic drugs. Most notably, three Harvard academics – Drs Leary, Alpert and Metzner – had been sacked for such activities and had acquired the Alte House at Millbrook, where with paying guests they continued their LSD experiments. Laing paid a visit to Leary.

And in 1967 Laing organized the Congress on the Dialectics of Liberation in London at the Roundhouse in Chalk Farm. It *was* to be a forum, a unique expression of the politics of modern dissent, in which existential psychiatrists, anarchists, Marxist intellectuals and political leaders met to discuss the key social issues of the future. The roll call included Herbert Marcuse, Stokely Carmichael, Gregory Bateson, Allen Ginsberg and many others.

In Bomb Culture, *Jeff Nuttall describes his meetings with you and, I must say, it all sounds like sex and drugs and rock and roll with maybe a bit of intellectual discourse in between.*

I wasn't in a culture like that. That was a culture that Jeff Nuttall, who had attached himself to Alex Trocchi, was in.

I got in touch with Alex Trocchi when I read some *Sigma* papers that he had put out. We met and developed a friendly camaraderie. We had a lot in common; he came from Hillhead in Glasgow, and was a very cultivated guy with a very good literary critical sensibility. He had a very good ear for poetry. It was the people at Brazier's Park that thought of putting that crowd together – which included Joe Schorstein and Eric Graham Howe and Alex and Jeff Nuttall, and the crowd that Alex brought along.

From the point of view of the possibility of something gelling there it was, in fact, a total fiasco. I was about the only one who could stand all the different sorts of people that were there. Jeff Nuttall, I think, was round to my house only on one occasion, ever. I never was in Jeff Nuttall's house, I never met him alone, except on two or three or four occasions with Alex.

At the time I was practising medicine in Wimpole Street, I was engaged in research. These people were part of 'the crowd'. There was the sculptor John Latham, Barbara Latham, Alex, Alex's wife, Jeff Nuttall – who was an *aide de camp* to Alex's machinations – and a very curious guy that Alex knew who turned up at Alex's flat a number of times. I used to go round to Alex's flat quite often and hung out with him after Wimpole Street for an hour or so before going home. I was living in North Finchley at the time with Anne and our five children. Michael X, the black guy who was later executed in Trinidad, having been accused of four murders, was a hench-man for Rachman, the property dealer, and he would turn up at Alex's. Alex kept all sorts of company.

I never knew Michael X closely, but he got into the Dialectics of Liberation Congress through Leon Redler. Leon had a New Yorker sensibility about black liberation and the rest of it but it didn't cut any ice with a Scotsman or an Englishman or a Londoner. I mean, that sort of colour thing meant fuck all to me or in a sense to Alex or to Michael X. But it was a big number to Leon Redler and he knew how to exploit that. He wanted to get into Stokely Carmichael who was coming over.

Michael X had set himself up as the black guy in London, but was fucking a white woman. He had to chuck her out of the house and get a black woman in before Stokely came over because he didn't want Stokely to realize that he was sleeping with a white woman. When Stokely came over, all Stokely wanted was to get white fucks and he couldn't get out of London fast enough to get to Sweden because he wanted to have some Swedish fucks. [laughs]

Anyway, Gregory Bateson took not more than one or two looks at Michael X and said, 'you've got to get rid of him'. I said, 'how do you mean?' and he looked at me as though he was surprised that I didn't know what he really meant. He said 'that man is evil, so I'll make it easy for you, Ronnie; unless he is barred from the Congress I am leaving. It's either him or me'. So I said, thank you very much. The only thing I could say to Leon and to Michael X was, I'm sorry but you have to absent yourself because Gregory Bateson has said it's either you or him. So I'm very sorry but you have to fuck off.

*At the Dialectics of Liberation Congress did you also have
conversations like that with people such as Marcuse?*

I never had a single conversation with Marcuse. As the sort
of director of the Congress I met Marcuse in a friendly,
affable, diplomatic way, but we never talked about anything. I
never got on with him, we never clicked. I didn't like *Eros and
Civilization*. I thought the dialectics of it creaked, the pages
creaked with the intellectual apparatus that he used. That
Frankfurt school of sociology never appealed to me particularly. But Joe Berke was a particular enthusiast for Marcuse. I
did like *One-Dimensional Man* – I quoted it in *The Politics of
Experience* – but the man himself was a very dry German
intellectual and I respected him as a dry German intellectual
but that was it.

   We rented a big terraced house, and also used a hotel
down in Knightsbridge. We housed Gregory Bateson, Jules
Henry, I think, Paul Goodman, their wives and families. And
I think Allen Ginsberg stayed there. There were various
behind-the-scenes dramas going on. The talk between Jules
Henry or Paul Goodman or Gregory Bateson was nothing
about theory or Freud.

What do you mean, 'behind-the-scenes dramas'?

Well, Paul Goodman was a raving – well, not a raving – but
what we would call, *completely* gay.

Promiscuously gay?

He was *completely* gay and one of the people who was part of
the scene at that time was a wild woman who was a friend of
a number of us. One night, I think it was after Jules Henry
had given a talk, Paul Goodman was absolutely played out
and went to bed. But this woman got into his bedroom and
threw herself on top of him with the idea of getting him out
of his 'fear' of women and he very much objected to this.
There was a whole fracas in the house. I started to blow my
cool, I started to yell at her, you know, 'you stupid fucking
cow', that sort of stuff. Paul was trembling, and Jules Henry
came down from upstairs, where he was trying to get to sleep.
Allen Ginsberg was also there. That sort of thing would
happen.

I spent some quiet moments with some people, with Gregory Bateson and Ross Speck and Jules Henry. I got Jules to tell me about some of his work. He had written *Pathways to Madness* and was the only person I knew who had actually gone and lived in the houses of these autistic or schizophrenic children. He said he was absolutely blasted by the experience, he couldn't do it again, that it was just absolutely awful but no one wanted to know about it.

So there were a few deeply heart-felt and human touching encounters and I don't know what other people talked about. But in that nuclear group we were not talking about Marcuse's interpretation of Freud. Gregory Bateson or Joe couldn't care less about that. I mean that was *his* number.

Can we talk about the disaster or the chaos of the Dialectics of Liberation Congress. What was so dreadful about it? Was it the final straw that led you to your Indian sojourn?

I wouldn't exaggerate the aftermath of it. I wouldn't quite call it a *final straw*. In any case, I didn't feel that going to Ceylon was as drastic an action as people thought it was, even though I had never travelled around the world.

The Dialectics of Liberation was my idea which arose out of the turmoil of the '60s and my immediate network of that time. The intellectual context went from a sort of parallel meta-Marxism of latter-day Sartre and the intellectual sophistication of the *New Left Review* type of mind, the Batesonian communication research and the world of Kingsley Hall.

The Dialectics of Liberation occurred in the second year of Kingsley Hall, and at the beginning of the advent of Haight Ashbury and the acid scene. Also at the same time as the very frantic and fraught politics that were seething away, particularly among students, and which blew out in Paris and which in other forms went around American campuses in terms of Vietnam and the Civil Rights movement. I thought, what about availing ourselves of that excellent structure of the Roundhouse – I think I had met Arnold Wesker who had acquired it – and convening a forum and inviting those people that appealed to us to make presentations all around the clock. There could be all sorts of things from Marcuse, Bateson, Ross Speck, David Cooper, myself, Stokely Carmichael, Jules Henry and so forth and we formally released the idea and expressed it in the form of the Dialectics of

Liberation. We got Jane Haynes to act as secretary from my home in Belsize Park Gardens and Joe Berke and Leon Redler acted as lieutenants and organizers with her. They were the secretariat. We put out details of the Congress and the word got round Europe and the world and people started to fly in over the period of two weeks that it lasted ...

Anyway, I had a sort of hope or fancy that some of the people who turned up there would in some way get together and consider that there might be some value in forming a long-term network of people who were interested in an unprejudiced, in-depth, nitty gritty examination of what seemed to be the most important critical areas in the state of the human species. But nothing slightly like that entered anyone's serious mind. [laughs] I mean, most people came along entirely in their own shell to propagate their own propaganda of their particular point of view and butt up against other people somewhat and then go away again. So I realized that that was a lost cause for the time being. As a contribution to the situation I thought I'd better think again and I'd better think more about Kingsley Hall.

Can you clear up the matter of acid and the so-called connection with The Bird of Paradise? *Was the first contact with Timothy Leary an intellectual one?*

No, no, for fuck's sake. Come on. [laughs] Albert Hofmann had synthesized silosebo in 1927, at Sandos Laboratories. Hofmann doesn't like LSD to be called acid because it is not an acid at all, it's a base, so call it a base not an acid. However, LSD had percolated through into the psychiatric world through what is called the field of psychopharmacology. We were trying to find out what are the chemical things that change mental functions, like perception, and memory, and wondered which drugs induce something comparable to a psychosis, produced hallucinations and different other shifts and so on. This had started to be studied in Europe in the '50s and if I had stayed on in Glasgow it was one of the things that Professor Rogers was interested in and there was a possibility of putting me on to doing work on this.

I don't think Rogers ever did anything with this, but there were some people who were starting to fiddle around with acid in different mental hospitals. The staff at Shenley were tentatively trying out acid on themselves and I think they were giving it to one or two patients. But I'm not certain about that. There was a psychiatrist there called Gelfer – he's still there I think – who was a friend of mine from medical school in Glasgow ... So he was working in Shenley, this was in 1959, '60 and he had taken acid, and I met him from time to time. He was in analysis with Marion Milner as I was (in supervision), and he thought that I would find LSD interesting.

Gelfer had a flat in Hampstead and there I tried out a dose of acid in his flat and I thought that this was definitely an extremely interesting substance indeed. I don't think I took acid again for about a year, but I was curious about mescaline and got hold of some from a London hospital laboratory that had it. In some ways mescaline was even more in the direction that acid was. About this time – it was before going over to America for the first time – I had met Alex Trocchi and I had turned him on to some acid. I think I had said that this would be an 'interesting thing'. I went over to America some years later, in '63 or '64 and this was the time I met Leon Redler and Joe Berke.

Joe told me about a chemist they knew called Ralph Metzner who was imbued with a couple of guys called Tim Leary and Richard Alpert who were at Harvard and had done some acid experiments. At that time Tim Leary was Professor of Psychology at Harvard, as was Alpert, and they had got hold of this LSD 25 and published a paper on it. Joe knew Allen Ginsberg and, as I had read *Howl*, I asked him to introduce me. So he took me round and introduced me to Allen Ginsberg and Ginsberg had taken acid. He said, look, there is a guy called Metzner who will put you on to Leary. They've got a place in Millbrook where they are using it. So through Metzner, I don't think I actually met him, I was put on to Leary. I was given the Millbrook number and I phoned up Leary and said that Allen Ginsberg had given me his name. He said, 'well, come over', so I went over and met him ... I've got a clear memory of the meeting we had in the kitchen of the house. It was a bit *sticky*, we hadn't very much to talk about. He showed me around the Millbrook installation. Upstairs they had about six or maybe more bedrooms, each of them furnished and painted up to be a whole different trip. One of them painted in a wall of fire, with flames, and another was a chintzy bedroom for romantic couples.

Leary was in the process of inviting people round to

Millbrook and giving them a room of their choice and giving them acid. Leary had a very enthusiastic belief that everyone was completely crazy, that we were all going to blow our-selves up very, very soon, that we were all on a crash course, that everything had been tried – reason, politics, and wars – but nothing worked. Here was a drug that he thought altered people's minds, that once you tried it, nothing was the same again. He thought there was something to be said for getting this out and marketing it.

Wasn't it illegal?

No, it was quite well known. The CIA subsequently admitted they were playing around with acid and it was becoming known to people like me and Leary. So Leary wanted to put this outside of the club, in the general population. He wanted it to be marketed as an available drug and I just said, *uh huh*. I did not think it was a good idea *at all*. I said I didn't share his enthusiasm for doing it that way because people were crazy enough without being driven even crazier. It was too abrupt to be given to people in general and I thought it would be a fucking disaster. But I didn't insistently argue that.

I suppose he looked on me as rather a stodgy conservative Scotsman, but he did give me credit for being where he had been on the acid world. You know, there is a sort of esoteric world of acid takers, and by the time I met Leary, there was nothing he could tell me about acid. He knew that.

I think he told his pal Richard Alpert about me, and Alpert came over to London some months after that to meet and talk about acid. I got him to give a talk to the staff at the Langham Clinic. I don't think he met Howe, who regarded this whole thing as essentially trivial, but Blaize Maloney – who might still be the director of the Langham Clinic – was on the staff, and I think John Heaton was at that meeting. It was quite an intelligent staff, but they practically all fell asleep. Alpert gave a brilliant lecture. He was a great speaker, fluent and articulate, like *Be Here Now* [written when known as Ram Dass]. In his fluid, facile language he described what he saw were the psychotropic properties of this chemical. He gave a very good talk, but it never cut any ice with anyone.

I'd never taken any acid with Leary, but Alpert and I took acid together and spent some hours sharing this – I don't like the word trip – but whatever acid does; we spent about six or

seven hours together. There was very little conversation but
there was a sense of exploring each other's presence in the
state that acid puts you in.

He went back to America, and I met him again when I
was over at Esalen when I gave a series of seminars about the
transformation of consciousness as it occurred in psychotic
states, so-called, and compared this to states accessed
through meditation and through different chemicals. One that
we knew of was certainly psilocybin, and also mushrooms and
peyote, mescaline and acid. One of the guys said, 'have you
heard about Haight Ashbury?'. I hadn't. So he said you ought
to go there and you ought to hang out there just to see what's
happening. I think this was '65 or '66. So they got me a place
to stay just at the corner of Haight and Ashbury where a
chap called Murray Kongold, who was a psychotherapist, had
just blown. It had just been going on for about six weeks, and
I was absolutely appalled by it.

Appalled by what?

Well, I'll tell you. Leary and Alpert had thought out this plan
to distribute something like 300,000 acid trips within a
24-hour period to late school, college, and first-year university
students. They had picked on this particular zone in the Bay
area and Berkeley and around and distributed this stuff, 300
units of acid apiece for free. They viewed this as an experiment on this zone of the population to see what would
happen.

How much stuff?

I don't know how many got round but they had 300,000
available. They got a Zen master over from Japan, put him in
a room in Haight, in a Zen meditation centre there, and got
him to keep his mind pinpointed. They thought: what will
happen as people take it? What happened was that they did
blow a critical mass of people that had acid in other parts of
America, which they had released with a view to blowing the
mind of young America. They were hanging around, spaced
out, painting the buildings and putting on clothes and robes
and flowers. I thought it was all absolutely fucking ridiculous.

You returned home?

Yes, I was only over for a few days.

Some time after that Alpert came over to have a chat and get my reactions to things and he put to me – this is worth a book in itself, because this has never been released by him or me. He said that they regarded Europe as my territory, and Britain in particular. They would like to do this to London, what they had done in Berkeley. But, he said, we regard London and England, Scotland and Europe – but they had no real concept of Europe, they were thinking of Chelsea – *as your territory* and if you say no, that's the end of it. There will be no argument, that's fine, we don't do it unless you think its OK. So I said, well, if you are asking me, well, *no*. They said fine, OK, and that was an end to it. So they never carried out that operation they had done in Berkeley and San Francisco on the schoolchildren and 17-year-olds of London.

But of course acid very quickly became widely distributed in London, not exactly at that time, it was a few years later when it hit London. It wasn't part of *that* operation, but there were other operations. You've probably read a book, *Operation Julie* – what's his name, the guy who wrote that, the drug squad guy, *Lee*. He came to see me at Eton Road a few months before [the trial] came up. He phoned me and said that he would like to come round with his second-in-command and talk about acid because although he had done a lot of research into the background of acid he thought that I might be prepared to tell him something that he'd like to be filled in about.

He came round and we spent one night, from about six o'clock in the evening to about six o'clock in the morning talking about acid. I told him quite a lot about what I knew. He said he wasn't sure whether I was a member of American intelligence, which was quite possible – *I* wasn't sure whether I was a member of American Intelligence or British Intelligence. I am still not sure. But he had checked me out in depth, he said. I had said to him before we started talking that it was very interesting to me how he knew that I had nothing to do with the various things he was interested in. How did he know that? I said I'm not going to ask you how you know that, I know that you can't tell me that, and he said no, I'll never tell you that, Dr Laing, you know that.

So I've got my thoughts about how British intelligence knew that I wasn't involved in the following. There was a crowd, that Leary started off, that called themselves The Brotherhood. This was a group of wealthy Americans, million-

aires, who formed themselves into this organization called The
Brotherhood. The initiation into it consisted of going into the
Mojave desert and taking 10,000 units of acid with them.
They were engaged in international manufacture, they had
factories all over Europe and elsewhere manufacturing LSD.
They also distributed it.

The head of that organization visited me in London just
before I went to India and said that they had checked me
out. They offered me the directorship of The Brotherhood,
with an invitation to go to the Mojave Desert and take 10,000
units of acid. They thought that I was the Pope and they
would take it from me if I would take that on. So I said no,
thank you very much. But Lee, the detective, knew that this
guy had turned up at my house, even though the guy had
taken about five taxis and came at about half past three in
the morning. He knew that he had come to my house. The
only way he could have done that was to have had a
permanent observation post across the road from me. Or this
guy was, in fact, bugged.

This guy was very security conscious and was, at the time
that Lee was talking to me, residing in an Italian jail on a
14-year sentence. But Lee said he didn't think that the guy
they had got was the real guy, that it was someone else. And
that the guy that had come to see me was still at large.
Anyway he said, that's the Italians' problem.

I met Alpert in London when I came back from India,
when he was visiting Samye-ling and when I was up to see
my family in Glasgow. We had a six-hour chat about things
and I never met him again until a couple of years ago in
Vancouver, when this film was being made on me and they
filmed a meeting with me and Baba Ram Dass [aka Richard
Alpert]. I met him glancingly again last year at a growth and
development place called Omega in upstate New York.

And Leary?

I've never met Leary since the '60s and I really thoroughly
disapproved of Leary and Alpert's attitude of mind and
strategy for a number of reasons. Even giving them full credit
for their good intentions, I thought it was an incredible
arrogance to think of themselves as some sort of world high
command. I mean on unsuspecting people without telling
them what they were letting themselves in for, and to

missionize this. I thought it was just another symptom of the
disease that they were purporting to address and to cure. But
because of the complexity of everything I never felt I wanted
to make a public statement of denunciation, I just never said
anything about it, never wrote anything about it.

I gave a lecture in those days at the ICA, when interest was
aroused. So I gave a talk on LSD which was reported in *New
Society* and elsewhere, in which I tried to give an account of
what LSD did and that was that. I've never talked or written
about it since.

I thought it was another fucking disaster because I considered that, if one had time to go easy on this and really work
it out, it could be a really useful therapeutic agent. But it
needed quietness and a lack of hysteria over a period of time
to begin to get the hang of how this could be employed. I
used it in my practice in Wimpole Street for several years.
I got into a habit of giving it to some patient of mine or
someone else every other week. I incorporated it into my
whole work. It was about six hours for an acid session. I
never handed it out to people. I actually wrote to the Home
Secretary who put me on to one of his civil servants – chief of
the Drug Squad in an office in Scotland Yard – and he had
no idea, acid hadn't registered yet. But I wanted to tell them
that there was this cloud on the horizon and I thought that
they ought to anticipate this. That the whole thing was going
to fall into the hands of international criminal groups who
would seriously fuck up people if it went that way. I didn't
really want to speak to a policeman, I wanted to speak to the
Home Secretary.

I was quite upset about this prospect and I was already
taken in as a confidant. I knew more than I wanted to know
about what was brewing.

Can you see why people came to the conclusion that you wrote
The Bird of Paradise *on acid?*

It had nothing to do with acid ... I regard that as a prose
poem of the genre of Aurélia or Gérard de Nerval and that
19th-century mystic sensibility. Balzac's *Séraphita* and Her-
mann Hesse, *The Magic Theatre* and so forth. Through my
own meditation experiences and through taking acid – though
acid was not a revelation at that level – I was aware that
there were all sorts of states of mind, all sorts of states of

consciousness and that acid definitely was a very powerful chemical agent that transformed one's state of mind.

There was a lot to think about in the relationship of the altered states of mind that acid put you into and the way people got confused and lost and shipwrecked in psychotic states of misery. How could they get out of it? Was there a possibility if someone was stuck in a sort of hell world – which I felt was too socially risky to try out in any depth, but I asked myself this question – was there a possibility that acid could release someone from being caught in this hell and allow a movement to occur, which they might, in the presence of other people, move themselves back into a balanced, sane world, if they've ever been in it before?

There is one page in *The Bird of Paradise* that I don't think I could have written without the experience of mescaline, which with some hesitation I put in and incorporated it into the text. But practically all of it was made out of my own dreams and states of mind that I accessed between sleep and waking up from sleep. Sort of altered states, that with a bit of meditation you get into. I could wake up very early and spend some time in a state that was a half-waking dream state; I'd never *not* been in these different states of mind. It was only when I grew up that I became aware that this was very unusual, as I regarded this as a normal range of imagination and phantasy and reality that all children live in. Most adults forget and grow out of these states by the age of four or five in our society.

You mentioned American Intelligence with a smile. That whole thing's quite bizarre, isn't it?

Well, it is *very* bizarre. I don't spend much time addressing this question mark, but it goes like this: when I was in the British Army, stationed at Netley, I was operating as the hands-on officer-clinician-in-charge. I'd come from Killearn and I'd been sent up to the Dumfries Royal by the army to spend some time with Mayer-Gross who was *the* psychiatric authority on insulin comas and electric shocks. I went up there and I'd been given the option of whether I wanted to go into psychiatry or neurology in the army branch. I found out that what they wanted me for was in virtue of my technical experience at Stobhill and at Killearn in bringing people out of insulin death comas.

Well, one of the things with Schorstein was that he was

extremely interested in brain death and he had taught me techniques of keeping people who were brain dead physiologically alive. People with head injuries sustained in battles. He had been right through the war as the number one surgeon to the eighth army – Montgomery – right through Africa up to Italy, he had been in charge of the neurosurgical unit accompanying the fighting. He would be operating for 18 hours a day doing nothing but operating on battle casualties, brain casualties. So at that time he probably knew about as much as anybody in the world about extreme head injuries and comas, and he taught me the techniques of keeping people alive who were brain dead and in coma. So I was a specialist in that.

Well, I was in Netley, and Marcelle, my French girlfriend, was in Paris. I had written to her and I had bought a train ticket to Paris but before I went on leave the lieutenant colonel who was the Commander of the hospital asked me to come to his office. He said, before you go to Paris, 'A branch' would like you to go to such-and-such a room in London. They want to have a talk with you. So I cancelled my ticket to Paris and I never went to 'A branch'. But I wondered how they knew that I was going to Paris? I asked him, I said is there anything wrong in going to Paris? He said no, no, no, it was nothing like that, absolutely not. But what I put together was that Marcelle's older sister's boyfriend – who I don't think I ever met – was a member of the French Communist Party. And at that time Marcelle's mother had bought a flat in Montmartre which she had offered Marcelle and me, a beautiful flat looking over Sacre Coeur just in the heart of Montmartre. Her sister and her sister's boyfriend were living in the flat at that time so I would be meeting this guy. So this is what I thought, there must be some connection and they must be wanting me to maybe find out something that I could tell them. I didn't want to have anything to do with it.

But I mean, how did the British Army know that I was going to Paris, why would they want to know, or did they do this with all officers? They must have opened my letters to Marcelle. So if I was picked up then, they would never have dropped me since. So at different times I've wondered, how do I know that this conversation isn't bugged? Anywhere I go, they must know where I am if they want to. *Obviously.*

8. BUDDHISM

In 1971 Laing travelled to Ceylon [Sri Lanka] and then India to escape the practical and existential impasse he found himself in and, more positively, to explore further his long-standing interest in yoga and certain Buddhist meditations.

Peter Sedgwick, for one, was not impressed: 'We can observe Laing's extraordinary state of dissociation from the left which enabled him to sit meditating in a monastery which was part of Sri Lanka's landowning Establishment, while peasants, students and trade unionists were being slaughtered and rounded up by the government's forces of repression'. (1982:267).

Apart from the odd reference that I've found here and there, I cannot find much about your journey to Sri Lanka and India.

... I haven't written *anything*, I haven't published anything on this domain of my life and very few people know anything about it.

I want to get away from the cynicism of people like Sedgwick.

Well, I don't give a fuck about that ... at the age of 12, I refused to play the organ at the Crusaders summer school because I thought they were a bunch of hypocrites. You know the Crusaders – Scotland Covenanters. They would hold school camps and have Bible meetings and prayer meetings during the week and try and teach Christian boys to lead a proper Christian life.

Well, I took religion very seriously as I took science and poetry and music as important things to do with life that I wanted to explore and partake of and understand. Scientific endeavour, what did that mean?; the rhetoric of religion, what was that?; and music very much so, and the sensibility of poetry, literature, song and all that. In terms of one's spiritual, intellectual, emotional, social and physical aspects of life, I don't regard them as separate hierarchies or levels.

What is called the spiritual is the way the spiritual interfuses one's ordinary life, not what happens specifically when you pray or when you read the Bible or when you go to church.

So I was involved with this from as early as I remember, from the time I was taught to say my prayers at night and through school and university. I'd as much dissatisfaction with organized religion as Kierkegaard, Nietzsche or Marx had. I hated the abuse of it. Like the abuse of science and the abuse of words and truth in order to bedevil people and confuse them and subject them and use them for their own purposes. I disliked that very much from as early as I remember. I also wanted to be as much on my guard against being caught up without knowing it, as being hypnotized in a spell like I saw other people being hypnotized. There were all sorts of subtle deceptions taking place.

I'd look around and of course you eventually come to Buddhism and Hinduism, Sufism and other faiths and other religions. What the Chinese have been at, what people in non-industrialized places think and believe. I read *The Golden Bough* and the usual sort of stuff that you do if you follow your nose. I was interested in ideas that were existentially relevant to *me*. Not as an object of interest but *existentially concerning me*. So I don't know whether God exists or whether Jesus Christ ever lived or whether it was all a myth that grew up over something that is completely shrouded in darkness. From the Buddhist tradition, the first thing that I remember that really gave me that sort of click was Ch'an Zen ... At that time I was a university student and among other things I wanted to find out was something about the basic tenets of Buddhism – the Four Noble Truths and The Eightfold Path. The Four Noble Truths – I can't even remember what they are now – were to do with the suffering, the origin of suffering, the arising of suffering, the cessation of suffering and so on. The Fire Sermon. I mean these are standard handbook Buddhist teachings. There is no theology, at least in Mahayana Buddhism, and no insistence on having to believe unattested historical facts in order to get at the immediate truth of one's own life. So that seemed very reasonable. For me it was a major weakness of Christianity that it insisted on you having to take the word of other people that a man called Jesus said certain things some time ago in some circumstances. What is the relevance of that?

Whereof one cannot speak, thereof one must be silent. I

was also attracted to the perennial philosophy as mediated through Victor Gollancz' *A Year of Grace*. He had quotations from all over the world, from people purporting to be on the same wavelength. Aldous Huxley did the same thing, putting together things from all over the place in a very engaging manner. Then there were the Max Müller translations of *Vedanta* and the *Upanishads*, tremendously complex Hindu classics.

You were into these as well?

Yes, a little bit. In talking about my reading range, you must remember I was brought up on a history of the world, so Europe was a very small part of the globe. We've got historical records in Europe going not very far back, bits of stone inscriptions going back to Sumeria and Mesopotamia but a hell of a lot going on before Christianity. Complex social organizations that seemed to mould peoples' belief systems a great deal simply to justify the people in power.

There was a period in which I saw the whole of religion like Freud did in his latter days as really an epitomizing example of a human psychosis. The prime delusional system was the belief in one single God who created everything and who would absolutely smatter you if you didn't do what he said, and what he said was simply what people said that he said. I wasn't about to buy that version.

There was a particular book that I read when I was 16 that is still in print, I think, and which gave me a fully fundamentalist version of christianity. It was called *Who Moved the Stone?* It pointed out that in Matthew and Mark and Luke there are three versions of people discovering the cave that Jesus had been put in after the crucifixion. In one there was an angel and in another there was two angels and in the other there was a man. In Mark it is a man and in Matthew it was two angels. I thought to myself, it can't all be right. Was someone seeing double? It was very sloppy reporting. I mean, if you seriously expect me to believe in the Resurrection on the basis of that sort of evidence, forget it.

So what came out of the Buddhist texts, like the notion of the Eightfold Path? Well, get yourself together and be your own light. The Buddha is your own mind, but clarified. This obviously fits perfectly with Nietzsche, you know, if you haven't got the nerve to take command of yourself, if you can't believe in yourself, don't talk to me about believing in God. And David Hume's critique of causality, because something always comes before something else doesn't mean to say it causes it. Correct speech, correct conduct, correct way of seeing things, correct livelihood, correct conduct, correct prajna, and Sana Prajna and Sana Samadhi often translated as correct wisdom and correct concentration.

What is meditation? You have to find a text which *describes* meditation, not talks about it. There was practically nothing, there still is very little translated about the actual practice of meditation. But there was one book that had been translated by a guy called Nyaponika Thera on the heart of Buddhist meditation, a translation of a particular sutra. A sutra is supposed to be a spiritually inspired piece of writing. When I was writing *Knots*, my aspiration was that it would be a sutra and quite impeccable. I actually thought of calling it at one time, 'a sutra on knots'.

And of course there was yoga, an inescapable word that crops up. What is yoga? Well, you can read about what is yoga – Patanjali yoga, classical Indian, Hindu and all branches of yoga. The classic text is Patanjali, which defines yoga as control of the mind. Very interesting. Well, who is controlling the mind and what do you mean by control, what do you mean by the mind? Well, yoga and Buddhist meditation refused to answer any of these questions. The way they go about it is in effect to say here is a recipe, do this and do that and if you do that for 48 hours you'll have got to this stage and then do that and do that.

Well, I scouted around those areas and I came across classical Hatha yoga, and the different limbs of yoga, the different jhanas, different yoga's – Bhakti yoga, yoga of devotion, karma yoga, allowing the wheel to turn, of karma. I had read this stuff with *The Divided Self, Self and Others, Interpersonal Perception*, so I was beginning to realize that the cultivation of any of this in practice could entail different decisions. I might want to find out where the best meditation was, or the best yoga training group. And the martial arts teachers might be somewhere else. I thought I might give up everything, and go off with the family for a year or two and undertake that and see where it took me.

Well, I found one text that was very simple and very clear on what is one of the mainstream Buddhist practices called *Satisampajanna* which has, of course, got various nuances –

but the basic thing I subsequently learned to read in the original, in Pali. A Tibetan will demur, perhaps, at any offer of a word for this but it had something to do with *bare attention* – the cultivation of attentiveness without presupposition. That immediately clicked into place with Husserlian phenomenology and to some extent with Freudian suspension of the direction of thought in free association and the complementary side of free association; you know, the other side of the patient's free association is the way the analyst would listen, without projecting onto what you're hearing your own thoughts.

Well, that is pure *Satisampajanna*, the cultivation of being aware of what's going on, without projecting your own fantasy system upon it. And if you *can't* stop, the attention to that fantasy system, to mental events, to emotional events, to bodily events and to one's conduct. The four domains of attentiveness. It's very difficult to be clear and simply attentive to anything and you don't have any idea of how much of a blur one's mind is in until you clarify it. Until you see a bit of the dust that's on that mirror it never occurs to you that it might be a good idea to wipe that dust off – then you might see what the Ch'an people talk about, the mirror wisdom, where you see things more clearly as reflected in sight, sound, taste, touch and smell. In doing that you're aware that, for every sense, there is that which you see, there is the organ of seeing and there is the mind behind the seeing that puts it together; sight, sound, touch and smell as objects of sight, sound, taste, touch and smell; as organs of sight, sound, taste, touch and smell and as constants of sight, sound, taste, touch and smell, and the 18 domains plus the sixth sense which puts it all together. You get 18 components and you can start anywhere with objects of sight and cultivate special attentiveness to what you actually see, the manner in which you see it and the consciousness behind it.

What is called the *Abhidharma* system goes through the whole course of attentiveness to every possible domain of experience including altered states, non-egoic states, states that you could term transcendental, so called, meditation – every conceivable state is documented and you can access them by doing this, doing this, and doing this. You are advised not to talk about it to other people because it's an open door for anyone who wants to take it, just get on with it. And if you get on with it and do it, sooner or later, sooner

– in a flash of Satori – or later it will dawn on you that what you thought it was all about or not – when it does, you'll find that it's not what you expected. A river is a river and a tree is a tree and a mountain is a mountain [laughs] but you never realize that until you actually see it.

Sure ...

And the elements of Hatha yoga. I became aware of what they were, the Chakras, energy systems and Chi lines of subtle energy, subtle forces, subtle bodies, subtle colours, all sorts of weird and wonderful things. I was aware of these things existing and I was engaged in practice of a certain amount of Hatha yoga postures. I quickly became particularly aware that one of the central things about the whole thing is the breath. In fact the breathing was one of the practical things that drew me to this, particularly in terms of my asthma. The analysis with Rycroft hadn't touched my asthma at all, in theory or in practice really, he had nothing to offer really of illumination to me from the psychoanalytic point of view.

So breathing in Hatha yoga is *pranayana*. In the Buddhist world there are a number of breathing meditative practises and in particular in the tradition of what comes to be the same thing, *Satipitana*, the bare attention to the breath. There are different ways in which you can cultivate that and I read in one of the Buddhist editions that the Buddha's own favourite form of meditation in the latter period of his life was said to be the practice of what is called *Anapanasati* which is the attention to in-and-out breath.

Then there are mantra yogas, mantras, and I was starting to engage in some of these practices. *The Satisampajanna Sutra* as translated by Nyaponika is a very clear text – I think it's still the official text of the Buddhist Publications Society – and when Eric Graham Howe got in touch with me I hadn't realized that he had actually written the introduction to that text.

Howe cultivated a particular form of meditation directly on the heart Chakra and he convened a group of a few people that he knew who meditated with him for about 40 minutes a week. He invited me to join and I did. We never talked about it; at the time we simply convened together at 14 Wimpole Street and sat down in chairs and proceeded to meditate in whatever way we imagined we were meditating, on the heart Chakra. There were about eight of us. I can't remember who the others were and I don't think we ever met personally. I was also getting involved with The Open Way and went round to see Howe once a week for dinner. He was one of the very few people in my life that I've ever talked about those sorts of things with. He had been to Ceylon and he had been to northern India and it made it a bit more real, let us say, that there was an actual person who had actually been, and who was involved in that world.

His version of meditation and spirituality was what he called 'the open way'. When you talk about dhammas or ways, pathways or spiritual pathways, he would say keep on putting one foot in front of the other, *all* ways, *all* roads. You couldn't pin him down to anything and that suited me fine because I mean I wasn't interested in becoming any system's disciple. In the world of gurus and spiritual maturity, he was a significant figure. Henry Miller – author of *Tropic of Cancer* – wrote a book called *The Wisdom of the Heart* and the first essay in that is an essay on Eric Graham Howe. Quite a sympathetic essay.

Howe knew people – Alan Watts, who came from the same Episcopalian English background – and one of Howe's brothers was a bishop and in all respects he was an interesting man for me to become a friend of. He had also been the first Secretary of the Psychotherapy Section of the pre-Royal College of Psychiatry and he was absolutely and totally supportive of me having such a mixture of exasperated contempt for the world of psychiatry and psychoanalysis.

Howe once described Ernest Jones, whom he knew, as a man shrouded in darkness. He had phrases for quite a lot of people. I asked him, like I had with with Gregory Bateson: in his range of things how would he place me? And he said two things. He said that he thought I was older than him – a double-edged term – well, it was a compliment of a kind, and that I was a priest after the order of Melchizedek. Do you know what that means?

I think I do ...

Well, if you read St Paul's Epistle to the Hebrews, he's trying to explain to the Hebrews who Jesus is, and he says there are two types of priest: there's the priest after the order of the Levitical priesthood and there are priests after the order of Melchizedek. Melchizedek in Genesis ... Abraham after the slaughter of the kings comes back and hands over a tenth of the spoils to Melchizedek, King of Kings, King of Salem, King of Peace, without father or mother, beginning of days or end of life. The nearest you get to, I think, a biblical statement of what a Buddhist would call a Bodhisattva. So no credentials.

Let's get back to how you thought your life was shaping up.

Well, I had been through a grammar school, I'd got at least a touching access to classical literature though I hadn't completed what I wanted to do on my course of self-education in European culture and literature. That involved poetry and the humanities and music and medicine and psychiatry and psychoanalysis and social research outside of the commitment to the medical work. And by that time I had a touch of the Christian religion and a touch of acid, which I don't think was a major component of the soup. I was now really doing this every day and there was Kingsley Hall, the chaos and the confusion and the Dialectics of Liberation and the mêlée at the time. I was now of my age group one of the guys who was right in there as much as anyone else.

I was having dreams in which I was driving a very fast car and couldn't see out of the window and the brakes wouldn't work but I was just going and I thought it would be a good idea to at least know how to stop. I was travelling very fast, but I couldn't see where I was going and I didn't know how to stop it. That seemed to be an indication that it might be a good idea to step off and take a year off.

How old were you?

Forty. I was a bit late in keeping to my timetable. I'd still got this chronology: divided into fours and threes and stages and the pacing of one's self and so forth, but decades didn't quite fit with my birthday which was 1927.

1957 took me up to 30, 1960 to 33, so I had opened up my publishing career with *The Divided Self* roughly speaking by 1960. At 33 I hadn't quite finished, but I was working on the Canadian broadcast series that went into *The Politics of the Family*, and the manuscript of *Knots* was maturing. There was nothing else immediately within me that I wanted to write about. I wasn't going to write about Kingsley Hall, it was still on but it was too confused, and the Dialectics of Liberation had largely been a complete fiasco.

So I was putting together a package in order to go away for a year. Eric Graham Howe knew Nyanaponika Thera who was alive and well in Ceylon and living in Kandy. He was half-Viennese and half-Singhalese. A Singhalese mother and an Austrian father who had adopted Buddhism and had gone to stay in Ceylon and stayed there. I was aware of other Indian figures and people. By that time I had cultivated *Satipittana* and *Anapanasati* in-and-out breathing for about seven or eight years. I was beginning to want see Kingsley Hall through. I didn't want to leave London until the end of the five years' lease of Kingsley Hall, although I had disconnected myself from the immediate machinery of the place. I owed it to Muriel Lester to see it out, but at the ending of Kingsley Hall I would go off to Ceylon or India or wherever. I would seek out situations where serious meditation was going on, and do that for a year and see what happened. I made an arrangement for my Wimpole Street to be wound up and I got Mary Duhig – who was an ex-nun who had become a patient/student of mine – to act as my secretary. I left the affairs of the world in her hands.

You were married to Jutta at this time?

Yes, Jutta.

And children?

I had Adam, and Natasha was about a-year-and-a-half old. I had a lot of people around me then, or trying to be around me and coming and leaving and there was a tremendous amount of rumour going on about me and all around me. I detested it, because none of that had really anything to do with what I thought was really important. There was all this frantic stuff of the mind, of that world of the late '60s which just seemed to be more and more total nonsense. There were people who called themselves Laingian and were propounding that sort of thing and I couldn't stand any of them. All of them knew that they never got into my house, or that I had anything to do with them.

So I was ripe for moving out but I left behind a skeletal structure which would be there when I came back. I went off with Jutta and Adam and Natasha and a woman called Brenda, who was a companion for Jutta, and would help Jutta look after the children.

As far as Jutta was concerned, this was a terrifying experience because when I went off I said, 'I'll see you in three months or I'll see you in six weeks', but God knows what would happen in six weeks so she didn't know whether she was ever going to see me again. So we went to Colombo and quickly moved up to Kandy which is the main town in the middle of the hills of Ceylon. It was in what is called a jungle, but really it was just an unspoiled sort of forest area. Nyanaponika had got his house, very simple and full of books. He lived a contemplative life, the life of a scholar.

What was the reaction of your other children about you leaving?

Oh, we had a very tearful parting. There were restrained tearful hugs. They were in Glasgow by then and I had told them that this was in the air and then went up to Glasgow and said farewell. That was that and then off I went. There was no big drama, we were all pretty attached to each other, I mean it was a big wrench for me.

I had wanted to go off on my own but Jutta pleaded with me not to do that, she didn't want to see me disappear because she thought that if I really went off on my own in the mood I was in she might never see me again. I might disappear into the depths of God knows where, and certainly a side of me felt like doing that.

I wanted to get away from people and from thinking. I wanted a rest, and for me a rest was *solitude*. Anyway, if I'd had more money I might have been able to take my whole tribe with me and they could have lived nearby, as Jutta and Brenda and Adam and Natasha did. I mean, they lived within two or three hundred miles from me but not on the other side of the world. We eventually found a house up in the mountains in Kandy which was owned by a guy called Ratewatte. I didn't know anything about Singhalese politics, although Perry Anderson in the *New Left Review* had done a run-down of the various sinister states of affairs going on in Ceylon.

Ratewatte had a tea plantation and we lived in a coconut tree plantation house. In Singhalese society everything is completely hierarchized and he came from a traditional hill family, he was like a Scottish clan chief you might say. I think he was a cousin of the prime minister. It turned out there was a whole Singhalese network of people who were all inter-related to each other.

The Prime Minister of Ceylon had been assassinated a year or two before I got there by a Buddhist monk. There was a civil war going on which wasn't reported which we walked into. The rebel headquarters were about six miles from our house. Anyway, I fucked off to a spend a few weeks with Nyanaponika and the meditation I wanted to get into *undiluted* and that meant 24 hours a day. There were two places I could go to, one place where a guy had cultivated that particular form of meditation for about 40 years and he was the most accomplished practitioner of this sort of meditation. So I went there.

Which was where?

Well, it's a Buddhist monastery – well, the nearest thing you could call it would be a monastery, they are not actually monks. They were Bhikkhus, people who take the robe. I did not take the yellow robe, but there is a special name for being sworn in to the system and I lived in that state while doing this *Anapanasati* meditation which became more and more rigorous. Eventually I wasn't sleeping at all; for 24 hours a day for several weeks I was sitting in a lotus position, apart from the precise meditation on the breath.

He eventually put me into a regime after several weeks where there was no single movement of my body, not even a blink or a knuckle movement, no single movement whatever, such as blinking my eye or gulping. Any movement that was to be done was to be done without prior awareness of it. I remember on one occasion sitting in front of him and he noticed me making a flick of – what I don't know – I was facing him, making a thumb movement without being aware of it, without anticipating it or directing it.

Did the Order have a name?

Singhalese Buddhism, the Buddhism that exists in Ceylon and is called by the Tibetans and the northern branch of Buddhism, *Hinayana*, which means the lesser vehicle. The small vehicle. The type of mind that is cultivated in that system is regarded as a preliminary state of mind. The *Anapanasati* – the meditation, practice – is done by Tibetan Buddhist monks in exactly the same way. I didn't regard myself in the least bit committed to Hinayana which is also called Theravada – vada means the way and thera is someone who had taken the vows, taken the robe and the bowl.

So it was Theravada Buddhism, the Singhalese version. The first place I went to did that, then I came back to Kandy to Jutta, and then went off to another place. That was a place in the south, an inland swamp, with an inland lagoon with an island inside this lagoon crawling with alligators and mosquitos. It was really tropical, no fucking nonsense there, where there was a Buddhist monk colony. In both places I was the only European, the others were all Asian monks. I spent some time there and then I rejoined Jutta and we took a plane to Delhi.

And how long were you on your own at this colony?

A number of weeks. I was a number of weeks in the first place, a number of weeks in the second place, about six weeks and the civil war was going on in the middle of all this. I arranged to have a meditation hut near the house, where I spent most of the time sitting in the lotus position continuing pretty well uninterrupted the meditation practice and this system of consciousness. The whole body becomes like a puppet so that you are deliberately moving everything. Very complex, it was very, very difficult to take a step or move the soles of your feet, there are so many muscles and you've got to be conscious of them all, penetrating the consciousness of the whole system, of which the muscle system is only part. Also I was moving in slow motion, very slow motion, so it would take me about 40 minutes to move as fast as I could from here to [there] to have a pee.

How was Jutta coping with all of this?

When I was with Jutta I was conducting myself normally. I wasn't mixing it up with my ordinary life where I was perfectly urbane, properly dressed, and sane and clear and urbane and talking and moving. I was wearing native Singhalese dress.

Anton Ratewatte was a Singhalese aristocrat and he got me in front of his major domo and showed me exactly how to wear a skirt and exactly how to tie it and exactly what sort of haircut and shave to have. He was very, very precise about presentation. There was no question when I was with Jutta or when I met people of conducting myself like some guy who was spaced out. This was a real thing and dignity was very important. I was to behave with courtesy, correctness and clarity. For one thing there was no question of disgracing the Sangha, the Buddhist Order of which I was a member.

Jutta has got her own story about that and she found it very difficult. I mean, that's probably when the end of our relationship began because it was too much for her, it stretched her range of what a relationship was. At that time she had no interest in any of it and I never tried to convert her or lay that on to her. It was available to her to pick up whenever she wanted but that wasn't her world. She is a bit more interested in that now than she was then. But she was a sane, healthy, normal European woman, in her 20s.

So you flew to Delhi.

We flew to Delhi ...

This was part of the previous plan anyway ...

That we would spend six months in Ceylon and six months in India and planned to be back within 12 or 14 months of leaving London and we kept to that timetable. We went to India and Delhi. For the Indian trip I'd deliberately not laid out anything in advance for myself. In Ceylon I'd met a guy called Ageha Barathi who was later Chairman of the Department of Anthropology at Syracuse University who had found out I was in Ceylon. He was staying in a sort of Graham Greene type of hotel in Kandy, a colonial hotel in the middle of the hills. I think he was actually a member of American intelligence. He was an Austrian originally, and had written a book called *The Ochre Robe* that you may have come across. He had a very, very strange life, where he'd gone to India for about 10 years and passed himself off as an Indian. Became an Indian, a priest, and still is.

He suggested I should take the route from Delhi to the centre of Indian classical religiosity around a place called Rishikesh and then northwest, the northwest Himalayan territory rather than to Benares which I thought of going to (we went to Benares later). Anyway, we checked into the hotel in Delhi and I decided that I wouldn't eat anything, I would take a taxi, take some money and get on a train to go north and follow my instincts. I would find a place for Jutta and Brenda and

Adam and Natasha and come back and collect them and then go together to that place. Well I took a train, sat on the train for 12 hours, eventually got off the train, had no idea where I was going or what I was doing and went from one town to another town up past Rishikesh for a couple of days. I was beginning to get a bit lightheaded. I was staying wherever they put up visitors in small villages and taking a bus or thumbing a lift or getting an Indian taxi from this place to the next place. I wasn't trying to live without a penny in my pocket, but I hadn't very many rupees that I was carrying with me and I eventually met a guy who told me about a place.

I went to this place called Almora where there was a guy who was reputed to have several houses that he might have for rent. I got in touch with him and stayed at his place overnight and he took me to a place which was about 40 minutes or so away from the town, past where there was any telephone or plumbing, or electricity or motorized roads. There was a house on a ridge which had just been vacated a couple of days before by a guy who had been there with his wife.

He had been one of the translators for the Dalai Lama, an American Tibetan scholar who had spent some time in Dharmsala where the Tibetans and the Dalai Lama were stationed. So he'd just vacated that house. It was a very simple two-roomed cottage, clean and simple and on the ridge. It seemed perfect. So I went back to Delhi and went back to the Japanese hotel in Delhi that we had booked into. We had just gone from the airport to that particular hotel. I went to collect Jutta but she wasn't there and the hotel had no trace of her. I hadn't eaten since I left the hotel, I had been all over the place, it had been four or five days now, and my family had disappeared. So I got hold of a taxi driver and said I wanted to go round the best hotels particularly with suites of rooms, older Indian hotels – there can't be all that many in Delhi – on the supposition that she might have moved there.

He took me to what was, I later discovered, quite a well-known rather old-style residential hotel and there they were. They *had* left a letter for me. She couldn't stand the Japanese hotel and she had found this other hotel and got themselves a couple of rooms. It had an old-style fan and so on, it was a nice place. It was about half past eleven in the morning by now and I hadn't eaten. The only Tibetan restaurant that was in Delhi was just round the corner from the hotel, so we went round the corner for lunch, the whole lot of us. There was this guy, I forget his name, a guy that I had met a number of years ago in Majorca and a woman who was the ex-wife of Tim Leary.

... So we went up to Almora and settled into that house and I then went off, looked around as to what action there might be in this pursuit of 'non-Buddhist Indian' versions of yoga and discovered a guy who went by the name of Gangotri Baba.

There were a number of Europeans around and among the contacts I made was with a Swiss woman whose husband was a doctor with the Swiss Red Cross. She had been dying of cancer and had found this Indian Baba who was of a special branch of Indian holy men who lived up in the snow and ice of the Himalayas without any clothes and who never shaved. *Naked wild men.* The only thing that they carried with them was a trident, a six-foot-tall trident with three points. Shivite Kali priests put ashes on them and paint them. She attributed to him the fact that she was now cured of cancer.

He was living in a place not far from a town called Nanital about nine thousand feet up, there were nine lakes up there, it was the place of nine lakes. It rang a bell for me because Nanital was a traditional Indian town that is known all over India as the home of Ayurvedic medicine. There was a congress about 10,000 years ago of Indian holy men who laid down the basis of classical Indian medicine. He was living about 10 miles outside there in an underground cave, then he moved to the outskirts of the town and he moved up a ravine. This was in the middle of winter, there was absolutely thick ice and snow – about a 40-minutes climb from the nearest road up to this ravine, up in what are called the Kumaon foothills of the Himalayas, 8,000 to 14,000 feet mountain ranges.

He had just started to ensconce himself in a ravine which sloped down this river; he had found a rock and had put some tree branches over to cover him like a human bird's nest. There is a special branch of this type of Sadhu or Baba, where fire is a major feature of their lives. They sit on fire, walk on fire and eat fire and put the dust of ashes of fire over their bodies. Very strange creatures. Anyway this guy spoke perfect English [laughs] and he couldn't stand people; he could smell them from extraordinary distances away. Human beings were not his cup of tea. Anyway he tolerated this woman and she introduced us. He and I got on very well and he invited me to join him up in his nest.

He didn't like people?

He had absolutely no time for Buddhism or the Tibetans. He thought that they were riddled with superstition and small-mindedness. Anyway, he invited me to stay with him and so I did. First I went back to tell Jutta. The Baba had a guy who ran a Shivite temple school behind a little teashop that was a station for the local Indian village bus, and behind the shop he had a tabla for the school, to play sacred temple music. I went and lived with this guy for a bit and went up and down there, and went and stayed in the nest when the snow and ice and sleet came down. No one could get up there.

So I was right up there for three weeks without any other human beings, only the occasional leopard, monkeys – it was up in the ice mountain jungle – and we sat in front of the fire. He had made a human nest with arching trees, and there was a fire the size of [this table] and about that depth. Anyway, my life depended on that fire being on all the time fuelled by tree logs that had to be got and carted up there. I had the job of getting the wood to keep the fire going. It was a major physical effort and we just had enough rice and grain to maintain supplies. There was a river that was just down the ravine that was running. It wasn't iced over so we just had enough to keep us going. He had just a loincloth on, and I had a Scottish pullover and a loincloth and that was it. So we sat in front of this fire, we hardly had any conversation or talked about any-thing for several weeks and at the end of that time he told me a few things about his life which we needn't go into just now. But he was congenial company.

I was particularly drawn to, you might say, the spiritual sensibility of Kali, in one of the respects of Kali which you could maybe relate to the Christian mystical tradition, the Pope's tradition of the black virgin. Before I left he convened a meeting up on the cave as the snow and ice had made it accessible again. This was a ceremony initiating me into a particular hierarchy of Kali initiates. It consisted of a massive cake-like substance; this cake was supposed to be me, my body, and this was burned and eaten by everyone. So I left there and went back to Almora, and we stayed in Almora at this house for six months or so where I learned some Sanskrit from a professor of Sanskrit and also got to know a Tibetan Lama who lived there.

Getting back to Sedgwick ....

Well, in one sense he's got a perfect right to say what he fucking well likes [laughs]. On the other hand he's got a perfect right to make an absolute fool of himself because those people who know what he's talking about, know that he doesn't know what he's talking about. The people that do know what he's talking about know that he's just a little naff who doesn't know what he's talking about, he hasn't met any of the people including me that he's talking about.

He doesn't know anything about Singhalese politics, he could have asked Perry Anderson, a friend of mine, or he could have found out, and I could tell you now what I found out when I got to Ceylon about Singhalese politics. Singhalese international politics are involved with North Korea, South Korea, China, Japan, the American Pacific Fleet, and then there is the Russian naval interest in the global situation. Ageha Barathi was researching all this when I was over there. He told me that 84 per cent of Buddhist monks in Ceylon were Marxists. The assassination of the Prime Minister was done by a Buddhist monk who was a member of the Communist faction or Marxist faction that were allied to China; that is a very ironical thing. The Chinese sent over 50 so-called workmen who were all in Chinese intelligence who built his centre. [laughs]

Anton Ratewatte, who I was staying with, was a member of the family of the then Prime Minister Mrs Bandaranaike who was like a sort of Indira Gandhi. He looked in on us on one occasion, when the place was surrounded by rebels. There was said to be 10,000 people killed, the place was cut off. No access by road. A curfew. The place where we were living had the headquarters of the army about four miles away while the rebel headquarters were about 10 miles away on the other side. Guys with knives were all around the house. The local colonel came to check out that everything was all right and the only way to get from the south was by military helicopter. Post offices had been blown up and he came back by helicopter. He said he had been at a dinner party with the head of the revolution who was another cousin of his [laughs].

You know, this is what Peter Sedgwick was talking about. The local population had taken their knives out and were settling old feuds. I mean, ostensibly they were complaining about the price of rice – rice was free in Ceylon but the government was going to put some price to it so the local people were going to have to buy rice and this had never happened before. This had to do with very complex issues about people struggling for opportunities and advantage between Asian merchants and families and politicians and lawyers. It had *nothing* to do with this simplistic thought that Sedgwick referred to.

In Dodondawa, this southern meditation centre which was right in southern Ceylon where it was very hot, there was the sea and a lagoon and an island in the middle of the lagoon that you could only get across by a rowing boat and on the island was this place. Not far from the lagoon, in the nearest village – I *think* the name of it was Dodondawa – there were several hundred people. The chief monk there had lived on the island in the swamp for about 40 years, he'd only once or twice ever come off it. This is what he said – I wasn't completely immersed in meditation, I was also learning Pali from the monks – we were talking a bit and this is one of the things that they told me. This was *apropos* a discussion about the state of the human mind and desire and aversion and the ignorance and the state of the world as far as they were concerned. Twelve years ago one Saturday afternoon in the village, the Tamil Indians – dark skin, not Singhalese, Tamils in the village, – were rounded up, several dozen of them, men woman and children. They then tied them all up, laid them down the road and a steam roller went over them backwards and forwards while they sold coca cola and the kids and everyone turned out to cheer them being squashed into the ground. That was the end of the Tamils in that village.

Well, I don't know why the Tamils live in Ceylon, I mean they regard this as their island also, but every so often the Singhalese do this to their next-door neighbours.

The monks regarded the human race as absolutely psychotic, as a species; the Buddha was the great diagnostician of the psychosis that had beset the human race. In his terms the human mind could not clarify itself and *see*; if it saw what it was doing when it was doing that it would see that what it was enacting was insane. Because that's what they were doing to people. The utter farce of madmen. I remember one discussion – with alligators not terribly far away – they said, why don't you stay with us? Well I said, I've got two children; 'what's that got to do with it?'. The Buddha had set an example, he'd fucked off when his child was born and didn't turn up again for seven years.

Pima is family affection which is regarded as one of the worst afflictions that can get beset you; affectionate attachment to your own children and to your father and mother. It's the same tone as in Luke's gospel, where Jesus said unless you hate your father and mother and follow me, and your husband, wife, brother and sister – and yourself of course – you can't be my disciple. That's terribly like Theravada Buddhism.

Then one of them said, it's not as though your wife is an Asian woman. I don't know whether you get the point of this. 'She's not Asian, is she?' I said, no, she's European. Well, they said she's half a man already – do you get the point? If I was feeling that, as an expression of enlightened compassion, I ought to go back to the world for the sake of the children then there was even less reason to do so as she was European and not like an Asian woman who would be helpless in effect, widowed at that stage, without a husband.

How does the Ceylon and Indian experience fit in with everything else?

You could compare it to going into analysis. A training analysis as part of the course. I chose that particular practice. I wasn't particularly imbued with Theravada or Hinayana Buddhism, but there was a very specific course that they were known to favour. Between – however long it took – three weeks to six weeks of this total immersion. When I came out of Kanduboda and went to Dodondawa and went back – before I went to India – I discussed this with Ageha Barathi who did not like the type of meditation I'd opted for. My impression was that he hadn't much time for it and he just took my word for it that it was what I wanted.

I particulary wanted to accomplish the meditation on *Anapanasati* and that sometimes did take a lifetime to *never get there*, or it could take three months, or it could take three weeks. It certainly takes more than three minutes. Your mind has got to fix on a certain very subtle set of sensations and remain without deflecting from – because that breaks it – continually for several hours on end at least to go through different stages that the mind goes through and changes as you maintain that degree of attention without any break. You pass through various levels of mind as you go through that and then you go through more and it takes maybe a minimum of 10 days without a break of any kind to travel in the mind.

I wanted to do that without the telephone ringing, and they provided a set-up where a guy came round at five o'clock in the morning with a bowl of gruel. Everything you were doing was in slow motion. I would pick up a piece of rice and put it in my mouth and chew each grain of rice 50 times before swallowing it in slow motion. You can't do that under ordinary circumstances. So this place provided that service and, of which maybe two or three people in the world at a time were availing themselves of – no one was queuing up to do this. [laughs] There were other members of the Singhalese Buddhist hierarchy who didn't like this practice and one of them told me that the reason was that about 20 per cent to 30 per cent of people who underwent this went completely crazy and they were sent off to get electric shocks and tranquillizers by the Buddhists [laughs] ...

Were you doing all this primarily so that you could pass this on in one way or another?

Oh both. I have to be have to able to do it in order to pass it on.

In literature or in practice?

Well, in theory and practice, whatever the best, most adroit, skilful means of passing it on might be under the circumstances. The Theravada tradition believed that there are two types of what they call Buddha minds; they regard that one person became completely sane in the last 2,500 years, I mean totally sane. He got his own ordinary mind perfectly clearly, and broke through this cloud that he had got into for God knows what reasons. But there are others called arahats who do go through a process of purification, clarification, and reach Nirvana. You could reach Nirvana and there are various stages of Nirvana. I was credited with what is called a *Sotapanna*.

I was credited as having come to a consciousness which they called a Nirvana consciousness. There's no labels or certificates and it depends on your karma and your destiny and anyone, I mean you or anyone might, the local postman or local landowner might be in Nirvana consciousness and who is to say? They don't expect very many people in a generation to be *Sotapannas*. That is in the Theravada Buddhist tradition. You may arrive at that position and adopt the view that there is no point in talking about it to other people who haven't accessed that state of consciousness. If you access it, you may or may not feel that you want to facilitate other people accessing. There would be no fun for me if I was the only one.

Is this another study of the mind?

Well, in this case, one of the things about the 'study of the mind' is the realization that the words we use, the syntax in which the words are expressed, the phonemes that are mapped with meaning, are an inadequate vehicle for communicating mind to mind. When you get to a certain point you have to speak paradoxically and take the chance of being regarded as arch or stupid or ultra-clever or fancy. Zen at that point of Nirvana say, 'no mind', the Zen doctrine of 'no mind'. So if you conduct this conversation into this zone, I can't go along with words in an ordinary way. I've got to explain that we are now talking about Nirvana and that cannot be expressed in words and the word 'mind' now becomes an inadequate term for what you access through the mind.

Anyone who has accessed Nirvana will not use the word 'mind' to describe the state that is accessed. And people like Ken Wilber don't have very much idea about what they are trying to talk about. They may have an *idea* of it but they don't give me the impression that they have accessed what they have an idea of. The idea doesn't give you access, you've got to lose the idea before you can access what the idea is about. You've got to have the idea probably in the first place then you've got to go through the idea like a ladder, that evaporates, and then you have no idea. You don't enter into a state of idiocy however when you've got no idea, and you have very clear ideas that come back to you, but ideas are like the rain falling through the sky and what you, or what other people used to call 'mind' is the rain, not the sky.

So, in a way this is compatible with all your life in the sense that it's another exploration of human experience?

Yes, and the source of suffering and the way to eliminate suffering if there is a way, *if there is a way*. Looking into the Buddhists of that tradition, how they went about it, I was taking it very seriously as a world strategy. It's one of the global strategies in the world, something to do with perplexity and confusion, vacillation and different sorts of states of mind that even the best of us are in most of the time. It's a good idea to really make an effort to look into the clarification of one's mind if nothing else.

So reading Kierkegaard on suffering in the Glasgow library ...

Direct line.

I can understand what you got from the meditation, but what was it you got from being with the Baba?

Well, at the simplest level it was a boy scout course of survival and I was in the mood for that sort of thing. He had a very clear mind, he said he had lived up in the jungles of Nepal for seven-and-a-half years without seeing a single human being, completely naked and just living off the fruits of the earth and had returned to civilization just in the last couple of years.

He said to me we were both half crazy, I was half and he was the other half. Put us together and we were either completely sane or completely crazy. But he thought I was crazy to go back again to human beings because they were all completely crazy. [laughs]

When you left there, and drove to Delhi to get the plane home, were you looking forward to getting back?

Well, Almora was a most delightful place, absolutely exquisite. Primitive in a sense but very civilized in another sense. I mean there was no plumbing and no electricity, no telephone or no road but we were embedded in a comparatively intact and not impoverished embattled Indian civilization there. Lama Govinda – who was, I think, in Europe at the time – was living a couple of miles down the road. I wouldn't be entirely surprised if one day Jutta went back to stay there for some time.

Had you missed reading and writing?

Well, I was learning Pali and Sanskrit. I was reading things at the time when I wasn't meditating and in any case meditation is something you can get very addicted to and attached to. There was one guy in Ceylon, one of the monks in Dodondowa who was a Frenchman who, after two-and-a-half years was still slow-walking and he didn't appear ever to want to come out of it. There were certain qualms about that; because even for them that wasn't the whole of life. It was a thing you went through and came out of.

At any rate you moved around as a monk. Of course as far as they were concerned he could do that for the rest of his life and it did get some people that way. There are different states of very, very, sweet bliss and you are warned against taking that bliss to be Nirvana. And there are all sorts of altered states and these constitute subtle and more subtle temptations, that's what you've got to remember. You've forgotten that, but that's what you've got to stick at. Just that. And you're aware of all these fantastic zones of phantasy or experience that you've got to keep walking through. If you step off into one of these then you can stay in one of these heavens for the rest of your life.

Can we talk about your return from India? Apart from giving talks at various communities, there were no great institutional changes ... no post-Kingsley Hall developments?

No, oh no, I was generally drifting away from any institutional connections such as I had. I was giving talks and becoming a focus for a number of years to our network of people who were looking me up and coming around, and hanging around. Some of whom have gone off and done something with it, like Andrew Feldmar who's got quite an on-going centre going on in Vancouver; Theo Itten who's got a place in Switzerland and another two or three guys. I saw a lot of people during these years, up to two-and-a-half years ago from morning to night.

From Eton Road?

At Eton Road and Belsize Park Gardens. That's how Marguerita met me in the first place. She had six years in an office in Eton Road adjacent to my consulting room. She's got any amount of reminiscences, a book of reminiscences of the people who came through the door and would sit with her when she was supposed to be typing *The Voice of Experience* and *Wisdom, Madness and Folly.* She was typing and chatting to them and having a cup of tea.

Going through the '50s and '60s, through existential philosophy and phenomenology and Marxist-orientated thinking and psychoanalysis and so forth, meditation was something that I've never written about. It is difficult to write about, I've *talked* about it, and I've got notes about it. But there are different things I've got for the next book after this and I've given some quite coherent taped talks on what I've called 'The Yoga of Everyday Life'. I've done seminars in Copenhagen and Sweden, in Berlin and Munich and Frankfurt and places in Switzerland. And in France and Spain.

Consider what you were interested in, in your earlier days, namely building a bridge between neurology and individual experience, communication theory, all those sorts of things. Do you now feel that you've completely lost the 'body' in your theorizing?

No, no, absolutely not. I'm aware that I sometimes give that impression in what I've written. There is a danger in writing about what you find difficult and not obvious and what you take for granted, and forgetting that other people don't necessarily take for granted; it's not obvious to them what has become obvious to you, so obvious that you forget to write about it. If I, in the next stage of things, could put together with some people a way of incorporating the awareness and physiology and understanding of the presence of the body in relationship to the way that we communicate and imbed that in a coherent integrated theory or descriptive generalizations of what goes on between people, I am very interested indeed in contributing what would be a serious and major contribution to that side of things if I could.

But you can see why some people might have thought ...

Oh yes, every reason. But between ourselves it is also obvious that it doesn't necessarily mean that out of all these hours of 24-hours-a-day and every day of the week and every year, the tiny little two or three hundred pages of text represent – I mean every book to some extent is an opportunist occasion. You write what is the pathway of writing at a particular moment, it doesn't mean that that represents a continued unbiased sampling of where one is at and what one is engaged in.

The main part of my active professional non-writing life has been sitting in a room with other people, and I've never written about that *ever*. It's not because I haven't thought about it, haven't been aware of it; I've got plenty of notes and I've talked about that. I've got piles of tapes, some of which are circulating around, some of which I've played back in some quarters to study groups here and there. I've hoped that some people along the way would seriously consider some ways of communicating these ideas.

For instance, in Naropa I did a seminar on what I called 'Co-Presence'. I was saying that Tibetan and other forms of meditation were all solitary activities that you do, you can sit in a group and meditate but that's only for encouragement but when you go into your own concentrated number you cut out other people. Well, what about the possibility of addressing one's attentiveness to the other person and what is going on between you; for instance, one of the things that one can tune oneself to be aware of is the other person's *breathing*. A lot of people who come to see me are terribly frightened, they're uptight, they're not aware of being frightened, they're out of it and they are exhausting themselves by not breathing properly especially if they are not breathing *out*. All talking is done on the out breath, so you've got to remember to take a breath in – all talking is, you breath in and you breath out. Most people are quite unaware of what they are doing with their breath and people breathe autistically.

Most normal people have got their own rhythm of breathing. However once open to the presence of someone else – and this is completely unconscious – you start to breathe, and I use this expression technically, *conspiratorially*. The word inspirations – con – you start breathing *together*, like a mother and a baby are breathing together. There is a rhythm of breathing which is a duet of breath. Well, people can be completely changed around in about 20 minutes if you tune into the way they are breathing, and without saying anything to them you entrain your rhythm and your movements and everything else to where they are at in their vital functions and breath, and without them knowing it they go away feeling much more relaxed and they don't know what's happened to them.

You set yourself incredibly high standards to begin with. Kierke-gaard was a guide, Nietzsche was a guide, Jung was clever but not in the same league and so forth. Have you in any way, and to what degree, been disappointed with your own output so far? In particular in relation to the fact that the big guys have already asked most of the questions.

No they haven't. The main theme between, say, Kierkegaard and Nietzsche – and leave Freud for the moment and Jung *out of it* – they never made it with women. So they are not in a position to talk about what it feels like and what it means to live with a member of the other sex. What goes on in that respect is completely unexplored by them. I think that's true.

Freud's and Jung's stuff in relevance to this is very important and very cogent but it has by no means wrapped up that old story. Neither of these four or Sartre or Foucault or Reich broke through into an understanding of the co-presence of people in other states of mind and the presentation of themselves that are perceived within the parameters of craziness, madness and psychosis. They never got into that. Freud never really got into that, he never got into that directly and intimately in terms of the co-presence. None of them have spent anything like the same amount of time that I have with actual people. I don't know anyone who has spent as much time in the 60 years that I have in daily, in actual practical relationship with people in a professional capacity.

If you are a psychoanalyst you can't see more than eight or nine people at a time if you are seeing them five times a week, that's your limit and that's absolutely exhausting. There's very few people you can see in a lifetime. The sampling I have of people – I've seen far, far more people in the last 20 years in particular – that's more or less all I've been doing apart from writing and hanging about and reading. *All that is unwritten about.* I might go to my everlasting bonfire without writing about it but that is in hold to write which hasn't been written about *at all*. I'd have liked to have written about all I've seemed to derive from the households and my time at Kingsley Hall, again that has so far defeated my capacity to give what I – by my standards – regard as a satisfactory account of this, bearing in mind that what I've written so far has been so amplified into misunderstanding.

David Cooper was very good about that – that the essential ambiguity of language means that you can't beat it. Nietzsche was on to that as was Kierkegaard: that from now on in, no writing cannot be at least doubly ironical because you can't say the truth in a straightforward way any more, if you ever could. Well, that is a decisive argument for someone like me; trying to write about You and Me, who is You and who is Me and who is She and who is Her, what do you mean by the simplest, most basic terms? How do you talk about I love You, who is You? You know Apuleius in 'Cupid and Psyche'; Psyche to Eros 'I love you whoever you are – I would love you if you were the God of love himself, I ....' ['I love you, I adore you desperately, whoever you are; even Cupid himself can't compare with you'.] So what do you mean by I Love You, who is the You that you say you love? Well, Klein and Freud would say that it is the heap of your projections, well that's not true, there is a You there but it's not easy to explicate who You is. Well, that's my sort of problematic of language.

9. THE DIVIDED SELF

The Divided Self, first published in 1960, gave Laing international credibility as an innovative and compassionate analyst of madness. It was his first attempt at making madness and the process of going mad comprehensible.

If you're seen as the Antichrist by traditional psychiatry, Sir William Sargant represents the other end of that continuum. Did you meet him, or communicate with him?

I never really communicated with him. I met him as far as I remember on three occasions, the first one was in Queen's Square when I went down from Glasgow when I was about 28 to sit my exam. This was before the foundation of the Royal College of Psychiatry. I took an examination called the Diploma of Psychiatric Medicine in which I had to be examined on psychiatry and there was also a neurological examination. The neurological practical exam occurred in the wards of Queen's Square in Bloomsbury. There were two or three consultants hanging about while we examined people of the kind that Oliver Sacks writes about – neurological, neuro-psychiatric niceties, complex problems of clinical diagnosis. Macdonald Critchley was the main person there to discuss things with and Sargant was hovering around.

I remember Sargant, he turned up at the time when Joe Schorstein and I went down to London to show this film to the BBC. There was a viewing room and Sargant, Joe and I sat down to watch it and Sargant thought that it was an extremely interesting clinical film but he didn't feel it appropriate for general viewing. I remember his expression, 'it was too depressing'. I can see what he was thinking about in that respect but there was nothing ideological or whatnot about these two encounters. The only other time I met him was – is it Anne Brackwell? She is around now but at that time she was in her early 20s, she was one of the leading television interviewers ...

Joan Bakewell?

Yes, Joan Bakewell. Yes, it was an early Joan Bakewell talk show in which, just after *Sanity, Madness and the Family* had been published, I took part in a debate, with her as moderator, between Sargant and myself. At that time the usual way you met was in a lounge and then go on and then come out again after the interview. I hope I've got this, this is pretty close, that way a general addresses a major, a junior officer, and Sargant said, 'Ronald, we are both on the same side, you shouldn't talk like that in front of the children'.

Did you say anything?

I didn't say anything, but that perfectly epitomizes the major criticism from the Sir Martin Roths of this world to the extent that they had to take me seriously, but I shouldn't talk like that in front of the children. There was another thing he said – I think he said this on camera – his argument at that time was, well, we completely disagree and my whole approach was a load of shit, while his was the scientific one and we shouldn't pay any attention to him but *he is a doctor.* You know, I'll vouch for him as a member of the club, but I shouldn't make the criticisms of psychiatry that I do in front of the children.

When you consider his constant espousal of ECT and psychophar-macology, was it alarming to you that he was the most significant figure in psychiatry for a period?

Within the psychiatric world Sargant was regarded as a bit over the top. There were rumours that he gave himself electric shocks and that he was manic depressive, and that he had parties in which orgies occurred. I mean, I'm talking about the rumours that John Bowlby might circulate. He was not regarded as entirely sound in mind or body. It would be like the Pope having to distance himself or a rather over-enthusiastic bishop or archbishop who was involved in these things, but he *was* well into them. He was a fucking examiner for the pre-Royal College of Psychiatry! He *was* one of the boys, and could hang around Queen's Square and speak for that tradition.

But people felt that he was a bit excessive and no one took him really seriously. Joan Cunnold was one of his chief charge nurses but she left saying it was awful because he would breeze in in the morning, do his ward round and of course after someone had had electric shocks they were terrified of having another one – he would say, 'how are you today, are you all right?'. And if you didn't click to attention and say, 'yes sir, fine, I'm OK', you would get another set of electric shocks. So he got a 95 per cent immediate remission rate.

Like that guy who I wrote about in Glasgow who'd give people a touch of hellfire, 10cc of turpentine injected into their arse. Now see what they were complaining about – give them something to be really depressed about.

There is the establishment and the *establishment*. Francis Huxley is a friend of mine. I met his father, Sir Julian, via Henry Dicks in the first place, because Julian had been given a number of electric shocks for his depression and I think Sargant was somewhere involved in this. Huxley was a world intellectual figure and I was asked to put my mind towards helping him. I don't think that in the long run William Sargant will get much of a place in the history of psychiatry.

You've written that when you lived in hospitals, you found a 'great deal of human warmth and camaraderie in them'. People have forgotten about that viewpoint, particularly since Goffman's Asylums. Presumably the whole British policy of closing mental hospitals is just another example of people not really thinking clearly about it?

Well, I'm not close to policy making in that respect but my impression is that for them what is appealing about community care is that it doesn't cost too much. Hopefully, it's more cost effective. I mean that was the argument, wasn't it? In the California Reagan administration they were, as they called it, 'decanting' mental hospitals because they were old-style institutions that were just too costly to keep going. Just to keep the central heating going. It was nothing to do with anything else but that. The human warmth in these places was completely forgotten about.

And by implication, we've therefore got to find some safe houses for people who want to escape into themselves and into friendship rather than be stuck out there in the world?

Well, one of the contributions I've made is that the discussion about safe houses and asylums (in a genuine sense) was a rhetoric that I introduced into the debate in the '60s. It still stands to me as a very simple, possible programme, if it was really backed up and taken seriously. It has never been really taken seriously in this country. Neither have the Italians, who have abolished the *hospital* but who are not prepared to address themselves to setting up small scale asylums.

Jenner, the professor at Sheffield, one of the pioneers in the introduction of lithium, wanted to try it out in his region, and Ivor Brown in Dublin wanted to try it too. Jenner wanted me to join with his research team in designing a research project doing that very thing. But I did say I don't know why you are asking me anything about research design, it's all perfectly simple. It's the same as Loren Mosher did at NIMH; you flip a coin for each random entry into your system (a patient) and one of them goes to the left and one of them goes to the right. The one that goes to the left goes to a safe house, and the one that goes to the right gets the usual treatment in your wards. You have people tactfully hanging around and you regard these as two black boxes so you don't have to do detailed research as to what goes on inside one. But in A they are not getting any intervention that is rated as treatment, they are just being sheltered – and if it's too much for you with this or that person you can take them out. Then what you do is to *follow up* the results. That's the most important thing. How is everyone in one year, two years, three years, four years, five years afterwards? Couldn't be simpler. So what is the problem?

Well, the problem concerns two things. There's just not enough professional people in any department of psychiatry who have got the nerve just to try that out, even if the professor wanted it done, as people panic immediately. Ivor Brown said that it would be great if he could invent his own staff, but the staff that he had are the people that actually come along and apply for jobs. They want to give his patients ECT and he can't forbid them to do that.

Why is psychiatry so reluctant to let go of its ineffective techniques and theories?

They are not all that ineffective. They are only ineffective from our point of view, but are effective from *their* point of view. Jenner put it to me very clearly one evening round at Francis Huxley's house: he thought that I was going on and getting a bit worked up about this so he said, 'it's perfectly simple Ronnie, what we psychiatrists do is that we stop undesirable perceptions and experiences and undesirable conduct. And what is *undesirable* is what society says is undesirable. We are the people that society appoints to stop people seeing things and hearing things and feeling things that society thinks it is undesirable for them to see, and hear and feel. Right?'. It has never been so clear to me. We use a medical model because that's the tactic that is currently most acceptable to justify this activity in our society.

The corollary of that is that we're not saying anything about making people happier?

No, no, we're quite glad to have a happy set of drones. I mean, if they're happy they'll flutter their wings in time better. It's like insects and bees. There are so many people, billions of people we don't want. Anyone who is out of order creates disorder. There's too many people in the world and a few million people who'd be better dead or cost as little as possible to be kept alive while they are alive. They'd be better dead.

There is not the slightest desire to have any empathy with them, it is simply more efficient from their point of view. It works better from their point of view – you've got to put yourself in their vector to see that it's not totally efficient but they are working at it. It's becoming more 'efficient', picking them up with blood tests pre-natally and that sort of monitoring. In [that last page] that you referred to in 'hatred of health' I used the term *psychophobia*; if the psyche is the soul and the soul is the world of our experience as Aristotle argues, we are afraid of it. We don't want too much of it, or too much variation. We want it trimmed down to mundane perception and imagination, no dreams in colour. *Any* unusual perception is a criteria of mental disorder in DSM3. In other words, sanity is statistical and lets keep it that way. We're talking about health and happiness in a metaphysical sense here.

I was thinking about Max Weber, and the disenchantment of the world, the bureaucratization of the world and the decline of myth and magic and so on. He ended up with a great sense of pessimism, and his own life fell to pieces ...

Well, I think that the world has changed already – the dreadful has already happened. Change is a feature of our century and we're moving into another world and we can either make a kirk or a mill of it. Either give up or make the best of the circumstances whatever the best of the circumstances might be in the light that we see it. However, the world is going on and some people are still into it and some people are still involved in keeping themselves more than physically alive, in keeping our souls alive in a world that doesn't believe that a soul exists. Trying to convince people that there is a problem between faith and reason when no one has any faith in reason or belief in reason or see any reason for faith. There is a a contemporary cultural world-wide trend of which the psychiatric number is the operational expression of the conditioning and grooming of people: let us all agree that any unusual perceptual experience, the sensing of the presence of a dead person in the same room as one like your [B.M.'s] mother felt about your father for example, well it might not be worthwhile to bother about an old woman who still feels her husband sitting beside the fire with her. She's crazy.

Well, I don't think there is any serious conversation possible or any conversation possible with people who have made their minds up in that direction. But there *is* something to be said to people who continue to feel these things, and to offer one's reflections, out of one's own life and out of one's own reasoned faith of how to keep on living and how to bring our children up as best we may.

How did the symbiosis – if that's the word to use – develop between your compassion and your theoretical and intellectual development?

Well, it's reason in the service of faith. Let me go back to these discussions I had with that ex-Franciscan when I was 18 or 19 who was trying to save my soul from damnation of getting caught up in atheism. Well, a few years ago, for the first time, I actually read Anselm's proof for the existence of God in an edition that was annotated and commented on by Karl Barth. I was inclined to agree that it's absurd to try and prove the existence of God to someone who doesn't believe in the existence of God, it's almost a blasphemous endeavour from an orthodox theological point of view. But, reason can be, as it were, the handmaiden; you attempt to justify your compassion with your intellect. You can't say with the intellect with anyone who's got no compunction or compassion for anyone that you ought to, but if you have it you can try to show that it's not totally unreasonable to be compassionate.

What was your direct experience with ECT and psychosurgery?

It was standard practice. When I went into psychiatry from neurosurgery, insulin coma was the standard practice everywhere with electric shocks sometimes being given in the middle of the coma. In the army and at Gartnavel there was the usual range of treatment from the pre-tranquillizers of paraldehyde and barbiturates and bromides to electric shocks and insulin, and to lobotomy. And until I, in my view, wised up to what was going on in that respect, I carried out my duties as any junior doctor does. That was the treatment for this or that condition.

I began pretty quickly in the first encounters with that, however, to feel a gut reaction against it and was helped along by Schorstein who refused to do lobotomies. The other two neurosurgeons at Killearn didn't see any reason not to and besides it was good practice for a beginning surgeon. It was such a simple operation and who were they who weren't psychiatrists not to perform an operation which the psychiatrists requested them to do?

So you saw them being done?

Well, one of the consultants at Killearn went round to Gartnavel once a week and did a lobotomy. I was revolted by this practice on sheer clinical grounds, and with the utter casualness with which it was done. When I tried to find out by combing through the case records of patients who had been lobotomized, you would turn the pages and find maybe a line that a lobotomy had in fact been performed. The nurses weren't sure themselves who had been lobotomized and if someone didn't remember to put a note for '3rd of February 1950, frontal lobotomy', they weren't sure whether such and such a person had had one because the hair grows over it again. It just didn't seem to be a decent sort of thing.

This is the reason why psychiatry had the reputation of being the 'dregs of medicine' as a whole, because if anyone was clever enough and dedicated enough and ambitious enough, he wouldn't go into psychiatry. So the quality of psychiatric staff as caretakers of these people had the reputation of not being the highest quality of medical graduates.

And ECT. We know nothing except that it 'affects the electrical activity of the brain'. Is that correct?

Yes, it was very rough and ready and crude.

The Royal College of Psychiatry did a survey of ECT about 20 years ago and found that the electric shock machines were not actually precision instruments and so the manufacture was re-adjusted so as not to give such a high shock and for a less period of time, about a tenth of a second less. They generally felt that it was simply too much.

I don't know whether too many psychiatrists would be happy imagining themselves getting – I mean they keep on saying that electric shocks don't damage the brain – but I don't know how many of them would like their own brains or their own wives' or their children or their own daughters' or sons' at university or at school to have fun with an electric shock. Both in terms of human feeling and on the grounds of clinical rigour and precision, it just seemed pretty crude and barbarous.

Bearing in mind that you've never addressed yourself directly to developmental psychology, there is nonetheless a kind of implication and understanding in your work about how the infant comes into the world. Could you comment?

There's an unpublished paper of mine that has been quoted in some books as an 'unpublished manuscript' on 'the ontogenesis of the first eight months' which was going to be a chapter in *The Divided Self*. I took it out of the *The Divided Self* and was then going to put it into *Self and Others*.

The Divided Self and *Self and Others* at one point was going to be one book or one book in the form of volume one and volume two. But the publishers wanted them separated as two books. It would have been slightly different, but I think it turned out perfectly well as it was.

I was influenced by Winnicott's 'formal relations' in that respect and wanted to propose that there is an initial formative period where the main cognitive-emotional task is to develop a set of primary distinctions – the words that we later give to the primary distinctions before me and you or before I or before self and other, would be here and there, now and then. In other words, distinctions of space and time, and a distinction between space and time. Sorting out space and time from a primal space-time continuum which might be more real, as it were, than the distinction we make between space and time. A continuum, a space-time continuum, a pre-distinction of here-now and there-now and there-then, because as soon as we move we are not in the here that we were then and maybe inside and outside, not necessarily in terms of containers, like the inside of a cup or the outside of a cup, but rather thresholds. It's very remarkable that from the very beginning a baby in crawling might stop at a door. It seems to mean something as soon as there is movement ...

Gibson's visual cliff?

A visual cliff, and I've confirmed this many times. Left to itself a baby does not fall off a table. It's an ability to determine 'here' and 'there' together with something to do with lived space. It might well be genetically determined, to do with sophisticated perceptual clues that are immediate or absolute of the visual cliff. There are also distinctions which become remembered – like those between hot and cold. Most mothers are frightened to let their children touch hot things. Marguerita is frightened to let Charles touch the stove when it is too hot for him. But his fingers don't stick to it, there's just a touch and they come away. There's a delayed cry but there's no burn. It's just a touch of pain and he's never done it again.

So there's some very specific memory, and it must be integrated. There's acceptable sensation and non-acceptable sensation. Maybe dangerous sensation and safe sensation is a better way of putting it. This is integrated into the whole gestalt of a world-forming into which what we later call me or self and other become stabilized as a certain clump of all that is. There seems to be a pretty sharp distinction between what we recognize as a person's body and what isn't. It doesn't seem to be a fuzzy area. I don't think Charles is, as it were, confused between whether the pillow or the bed or the blanket on which he is lying are part of him or belong to the world outside him. I think there is a sharp edge, like the cliff edge, where the sensation begins and where it isn't, between what is me and what isn't.

So I think the whole Kleinian position of schizoid–paranoid positions and working through of that into a depressant position is entirely a fantasy projected onto the infant by the adult mind. I don't think that these distinctions are operating. I don't think that Freud's proposals about erotogenic zones is operating. I don't think the child is focusing particularly on his mucous sensation of the mucous membrane of his mouth in order to re-establish contact with something that has previously given him pleasure there. Still less do I think that his anus is going to be a buzzing erotogenic zone, nor do I think that there is an erotically activated penis area or a female genital area that comes up vividly and has to be integrated with the rest of the complex of the body and then has to be repressed in relationship with the object relationships that are formed in relationship to these sensations. I don't think any of this is a mainstream feature of the development of a healthy child.

You were writing The Divided Self *in Harlow 'in a duffle coat' and then publishers consistently turned it down. Can you talk about that?*

I *started* writing the book in Glasgow. The first typescript was typed with the assistance of the secretary of the Department of Psychological Medicine at Stobhill, Glasgow University. I came down to London from there with the primitive manuscript of that and the Tavistock Clinic gave me one of the secretaries in the secretarial pool who did the rest of the typing. It was finished in the first year that I was in London and I presented it to publishers. That manuscript didn't have an agent – I never thought of an agent.

I thought of the publishers Gollancz, first of all.

Did you share the manuscript with anyone?

Not very much. I shared it with Karl Abenheimer and Schorstein. Karl Abenheimer was a Jungian psychotherapist in Glasgow who had originally been a lawyer and had been a student of Karl Jaspers and Jung. Jung was apparently in the habit of sharing his patients with his wife and he had referred Abenheimer to his wife.

Abenheimer was a thoughtful Jungian man with a legal training and philosophical background and a relationship to existentialism and a relationship to Jaspers in particular. He was Jewish and originally came from Germany and went to Switzerland to get away from the Nazis. Sitting with Jaspers in his study he said something about his problem of being a Jew and he said the door was slightly ajar and, when he said 'Jew', Jaspers quickly got up and shut the door.

Abenheimer thought it was immature. He thought I wasn't ready to publish something like that and that it wasn't sophisticated enough.

Was that manuscript the one with Self and Others *in it?*

It had components of that. As soon as I got to the Tavistock and went into the British Psychoanalytical Society I ran into a barrage of Kleinian thought and opinion. I mean, that was the most active theoretical development – the so-called Viennese. The people at the Tavistock called the Freudians were those whose lineage was one direct from Freud and from Vienna. Willie Hoffer, the Secretary of the Society at the time, had been a student of Freud's, maybe even in analysis with Freud, I can't remember. There was Anna Freud, and in a sense Ernest Jones, who to some extent, and to their embarrassment, had given support in the Society to Melanie Klein. She herself was of the lineage of Karl Abraham in Berlin.

The most active theoretical thinking was Melanie Klein's and Herbert Rosenfeld's. There was also Bion, who had been in analysis with Melanie Klein, but who wasn't in such an obvious way Kleinian, and Hannah Segal. There were three streams of thought, each with their own seminars but also with some shared seminars. The challenging thing was the development of the 'object relations' thinking on the one hand and the Kleinian thinking on the other. Apart from Joseph Sandler, who was quite clever, but a dedicated Freudian, I didn't find anything to particularly challenge me because it was just sort of repeating Freud.

These various people all seemed to me in particular to have no sense of challenging the theory of intra-psychic objects. Whether it was Fairbairn or whether it was Klein, everything was an intra-psychic object. It was made very clear that, whether it was the good breast or the bad breast, it was the breast that was the original object. Original not necessarily in the sense of originally integrated but original in some un-integrated or pre-integrated form; it was the original force of sustenance and pleasure. The libidinal object didn't exist as an object until the advent of the depressive position. Fairbairn hadn't much to say about the origin of the thing and Winnicott was very unhappy about the way that this was being put. There was the problem of making contact with reality out of which he wrote two papers. He had just come out with the formulation of a 'transitional object' and Marion Milner had also just written a paper. So there was a big gap there and there was no one who I could talk to about this at the Tavistock. Both *The Divided Self* and *Self and Others* were totally ignored by everyone. No one ever said anything.

Can you go through who turned it down ...

I can't remember all of them, but I think I sent it to Gollancz first of all because of being attracted to his own *Year of Grace*, and I sent it to Penguin because I thought, why not? Let's go for it. It just came back after about three months. Allen and Unwin. I sent it to Pantheon who turned it down.

Were there any interesting responses?

No, just that they hadn't a place for it. There were no intelligent, helpful or encouraging suggestions. Oh, I sent it to Kegan Paul and they turned it down of course.

How disheartened were you at this time?

Well, it was quite a few turn-downs and Schorstein rather shared Abenheimer's view. I think he thought of it as a 'private PhD thesis' which would be good practice for later mature work but thought I was a bit pompous thinking that I could get it published.

Well, one thing that gives that book the heart that it's got was the relationship I had with Edith Edwards who was the schizophrenic woman of the last chapter. She was very beautiful and was wasting away with no chance of ever getting out of it. Her parents were just a total disaster, there was nothing else for Edith but the ward or going home. When she went home she would just last a weekend. There was nothing outrageous about her at all, she just sat and didn't say very much to anyone, but would talk to me when I gave her the opportunity. I was very imbued with that and I didn't think there was a book on the market that put that out and, compared to innumerable books that I had read, I thought it *was* good enough to be a book. So after it had been turned down by these people I offered it to Tavistock Publications who were glad to get anything, particularly from a member of the Tavistock. However, they were out of business temporarily and so they held it until they got themselves together. So it was another year with them.

Self and Others?

Self and Others went to them automatically, so did the other books. *Sanity, Madness and the Family* mandatorily went to them. They took 50 per cent of the royalties of that until about 1976 because they had provided the basis for it. They were actually going to take the whole lot, they were not going to give me *anything* for the publication of it because they said it was based on research that was funded by them. So I had to object for them to let us have 50 per cent.

By that time I had two books published, *The Divided Self*, *Self and Others* and then Penguin approached me to write a book. I was now a research fellow, I'd written a number of papers and had these two books published. Penguin asked me to write a book on the 'pathology of behaviour' for a series of the same name. Carstairs was the editor of it.

In the course of the years before, I had given this or that lecture which I then worked up carefully on paper. I made efforts to write a book on the pathology of behaviour but it was already too much of a contradiction for me to separate out pathology and non-pathology. And I was being affected by the Americans – Goffman's book *Asylums* had come out – and I was becoming aware of the logical extension as it seemed to me of Sullivan's interpersonal psychiatric work. I was also hearing of the work that was being done at NIMH.

Lyman Wynne, who was the director of research into schizophrenia at NIMH, started to publish this or that thing on pseudo-mutuality and this seemed to dissolve the sharp distinction between pathology and non-pathology. If you were going to call some behaviour pathological, what was the word for the opposite of pathology. Well, in medicine it was physiology. So I couldn't go through with that so I put together this collection and I added to it some work composed out of the freer writing that went on all the time and had gone on since my schooldays. Largely of dreams that I wove into the text of *The Bird of*

Paradise and sent them that, and they accepted that to my surprise. That was *The Politics of Experience* ...

But didn't they say that it wouldn't go in the series ...

Well, they were going to put it in the series but I refused to have Carstairs writing his patronizing introduction, his back-handed put-down. When I said no to that, they had the option of rejecting the book or taking it out of the series and publishing it separately, which they did.

Was the title The Divided Self *an easy thing for you to get to?*

How did I get that title?

Because all your titles are significant ...

I can't remember how. I've got a temporary amnesia about that, I've never actually thought about that question for years and years. It wasn't by any means the first thing I thought of. I think I was going to call it 'The Ghost of the Weed Garden' at one point. It wasn't *The Divided Self* until the last minute.

But that was your title?

Oh yes, that was my title. I don't remember anyone else suggesting it.

And Self and Others *was your title?*

Self and Others was my title, yes. The idea was first of all that the first volume was going to be *The Self* and the second volume was going to be *Others*.

You mean The Divided Self *and* Self and Others?

Well, it would be an overall thing. The first one would be about the self and the second one about others and this would be a comprehensive whole. I hadn't come across Jean Genet in Glasgow, but I'd reflected on the focus of *Crime and Punishment* for several years, and I'd written things that my mother destroyed on Gogol and Dostoevsky, and I'd been very affected by Chekhov's *Ward 6* and of course Kafka.

I had a piece on Kafka that I wrote as a student and pieces on Nietzsche and Plato. There was also a piece that won the first prize in the Glasgow Student Medical Society in my first year 'on being a medical student', and there is a piece 'Health and Happiness' that the Psychoanalytical Society have in their library unless they've torn it up or burned it or taken it out of the library, which they are quite capable of doing.

But there was one piece which I would have carried forward which was an essay on the symbolism of the sea, or the ocean or water – the sea in Camus and Kafka. Kafka never mentions the sea coming as it were from the depths of the inland of *The Castle* and all these corridors and so on. There is no fresh air from the sea breeze, but in Camus' *L'Étranger* there is the desert on the one hand and there is the sea. I was also at the time taking exception to Jung; I mean his stereotype of the archetype of water and the sea as always being an expression of the unconscious, whereas in Camus the sea is fresh – fresh air comes from the sea and it's blue, and it's breezy. I've never been to the African side of the Mediterranean, but there is that sense that freedom was there. There was *Moby Dick* also, you know, where the sea is the place for adventure and free spirits and Vikings.

This is another point that might be interesting. In the first printing of *Wisdom, Madness and Folly*, I said that there was this family mythology that I was related to Robert Louis Stevenson via my mother. I then put a note in that in later editions; it should be said that this was in fact a myth. Someone from Edinburgh wrote me a letter saying that this was not the case that I thought it was. Robert Louis Stevenson was an only child or something so he couldn't be my mother's great-uncle or whatever it was. This myth was entwined with another myth and related to one of my earliest memories, of being in a lighthouse off the coast of the west of Scotland. John Duffy actually identified that lighthouse for me. It's a lighthouse that a guy called George Stevenson built. I had been taken there by my mother and father. There was a vast reflector, it seemed to be the size of a whole wall like a big lens and I put my finger on that glass – I would be about two-and-a-half or three-years-old – and got into a row for the imprint of my finger on the glass ...

Have you ever felt that you could have written in a more fictionalized manner?

I never felt that the professional pathway that I took could be used as an excuse by me for lack of creativity in literature. I felt after writing these interminable medical case histories that I had to watch it because I felt that too much of that could have a dulling and constraining effect. I did not want it to affect my literary style.

I was aware that Somerset Maugham and Chekhov and the Scottish playwright James Bridie had all been doctors and had still managed to weather whatever the difficulties are in terms of still producing good literature. I don't know what the history of literary criticism would make of the contribution of people who had been to medical school to literature, but I don't think it's particularly a blight. No, I don't think that stopped me from being more fictional, it just hasn't been part of my repertoire.

How conscious have you been about wanting to write well?

Oh, well, from the very beginning when I picked up literature I had an intuition which became more critically sophisticated that it was a false distinction between content and style anyway. There is some doubt about whether there is any other way to formulate the sort of thing I was talking about that I've written about, in any other medium than language; that is to say the alternatives would be some symbol system or symbolic logic or mathematics. But if you try and say it in language – and I *was* trying to say everything that I've tried to say in language – that criterion of good style is the same as the criteria of clarity of thought. Eventually, after I'd got a manuscript or paper or article or chapter or a whole book, I'd go through it with a view to, among other things, having an eye or an ear for – can what I want to say be said in words of fewer syllables or fewer words? Do I need a complex construction if a simple one would do?

Going back to Morris Carstairs and The Politics of Experience. *Did it surprise you that he could say anything about the book because it was not quite his ken, was it?*

Oh, he said it was a book of creative imagination. [laughs] He said what you might imagine what Morris Carstairs would say. He stretched himself as far as he could as the editor of the series to say something – he patronizingly, benignly and mildly recommended it as a work of creative imagination.

Another way from his point of view was more or less saying it was a load of shit, scientifically, or medically speaking.

I was told that there was quite a number of my colleagues in America and Britain who were alarmed and concerned when *The Politics of Experience* came out, especially *The Bird of Paradise*, because they thought I might have ruined my brilliant mind. That I might be moving into a schizophrenic form of paranoid psychosis. Eric Mishler at Harvard got a federal grant to do a linguistic analysis of *The Politics of Experience* to see whether it showed any signs of mental disorder and he actually published a paper on it! A number of years later I was up in Glasgow and I was talking to one of the psychiatric consultants, Arthur Schenken, who is still alive in his 70s at the Department of Psychiatry at the university, and I can't remember how it arose but I said do you think *The Bird of Paradise* showed any signs of schizophrenic disorder? And he said, well, he did at first. When he first read it he thought there might be some signs of a loosening of association in it, which is certainly a bad idea to suffer from, but the second time he said he thought it was 'coherent'.

Do you think that when people have looked at your work they have forgotten, because of its style, that you are still pursuing 'the science of the person'?

Oh well, if you read the technical literature of human relations for the most part it is written in absolutely exorable language and that horrible scientese which they think is scientific. I mean I can imagine Richard Feynman, who had absolutely, of course, no time at all for psychiatry as a scientific discipline, and other real scientists certainly don't believe that you have to write badly in order to have scientific credibility. The first condensation of the first and second chapter of *Self and Others* I gave as a paper at The Royal College of Psychiatry as 'Existential Psychiatry', and I added a bit more technical stuff referring to existential psychiatry and Binswanger and Minkowski and Manfred Bleuler ....

And you sent it to the British Journal of Psychiatry, right?

And they turned it down because it wasn't well enough written. They said, it was 'badly written', that there were too many quotations in it and was badly written.

10. SANITY, MADNESS AND THE FAMILY

In the 1970s Laing gained the reputation of being opposed to the traditional nuclear family and of blaming it for the psychic disintegration of certain individual members and of enslaving them into a life of conformity.

Part of this reputation arose from books written at the time, like David Cooper's *The Death of the Family*, and with particular readings of Laing's own analysis in *Sanity, Madness and the Family*, co-authored by Aaron Esterson, and *The Politics of the Family*.

How did you organize the actual research and writing of Sanity, Madness and the Family?

Well, there was this procedure of interviewing every member of the nuclear family – singly, dyadically and triadically, the whole family. We visited their homes with a tape recorder and then a full-time secretary would transcribe the tapes. For the first year I was doing this work while writing other things. There was Esterson, David Sherritt and Peter Lomas, and we agreed to call this a team and give it a name, the Tavistock Schizophrenic and Family Research Unit. But Lomas quickly resigned. He wrote me a letter saying that he didn't want to be pulled into it and that he was going to remove himself from that and that was that.

David Sherritt was given the job of seeing that the tapes got transcribed. After a year – well, I was preoccupied and hadn't turned my attention to going over the transcripts at all – I asked him for the transcripts and he had done fuck all. They were all stacked in his office, and I was absolutely furious at this and he wouldn't apologize. So I told him to fuck off and went into his office – and he tried to stop me getting the fucking tapes from his office though he had done nothing with them – got the whole lot of tapes out of his office and took them to my office. I shut the door on him.

I caught up on the tapes rather quickly. One of the cooperations with Peter Lomas at the time that led him to be *nominally* part of the project was that he had approached me in the work that he had been doing with the Balint group to help him go over tapes that he was working on concerning interviews. He wanted to check out whether his memory of a session was accurate. He was doing interviews without the use of a tape recorder and then from memory, was adopting a policy of enumerating about one to 20 of what he called 'issues' that arose in the course of an hour's interview. So an issue would be something that was talked about for two or three minutes and the nuance might change and he would give another name to it, and to summarize the interview he would have, say, 20 sections. Lomas wanted to establish some credibility as to the reliability of his memory. So he asked me to go over some transcripts of his interviews and by reading them he asked me to think of about 20 categories as to what was being talked about, then we would compare my categories with the 20 things that he had. So we did that and his memory was remarkably accurate.

Jacky Cradd, who worked with Carstairs and was a research social worker, also worked with Esterson and myself. So we had these transcripts and there was a lot of pressure on us to establish reliability and validity. So we had to try and produce an independent agreement that could both identify the same thing with the same name. Where something arose, for whatever reason, that we found mystifying we put an X there. A mystifying area or a double bind that you could actually write down.

In *Sanity, Madness and the Family* the descriptions there are descriptions of the actual kinesics; there was one occasion where the schizophrenic designated individual was sitting in a chair and while her parents kept on talking this woman, who was thought to be catatonic, slowly tilted over in the chair. Eventually she was sitting there on a straight back chair at an angle of about 45 degrees! Suddenly the mother and father said 'oh, were you asleep dear?'. [laughs]

Comments like this were from memory alone. So I went over some of these things, and Esterson and Jacky went over some of them to check them. Things like misunderstanding, gross misunderstanding, gross tangential communication – two people apparently talking about the same thing but talking at complete cross-purposes, or a complete confusion as far as we knew what the hell they were talking about. As these things occurred, we would note them without any attempt to quantify the intensity of that. We wished to compare the density of these things which were found in the families of schizophrenics with the families of normal people to see whether we could really say that there was more of this in the families of schizophrenics than the families of *normals*.

The families of normals were deadly dull but they didn't contain these elements of misunderstanding at all, and of course then the argument was to what extent the mystification processes were a secondary induction of the fact that there was a *diagnosed* schizophrenic in that pathology in the family. Supposing a normal family has the misfortune to have a genetically disordered person, then might that not induce those mystification processes in *any* group of people? That's an impossible question to answer, there's no way of getting behind that. You know we can say it was already there, and that was that. There were a number of difficulties with the work. I could never get Bowlby to get the point that I *wasn't* trying to do a piece of research that would be decidable; the issue wasn't the decidability of whether the pathology of the patient induced the pathology of the family or whether there was family pathology. I didn't want to talk about the family pathology but you could never stop them talking about 'family pathology'. I was interested in the communicational phenomenology that went on in the families of diagnosed schizophrenics.

That was specifically what you were interested in?

Yes. Of course we couldn't keep on doing research into what was going on *around* the family because it extends endlessly. We'd be examining the whole global social system if we didn't draw a line somewhere. We had to stop somewhere and so decided the cut-off point was to be the nuclear family. We had to cut our losses and be specific and get something done and limit our claims.

At the time I had five children and I wanted to spend time with them. I'd take Anne out for a meal at least once a week, on our own, and once a week I'd supplement my income by seeing two or three private patients. Then I'd be reading research documents and listening to the tapes and going through transcripts.

I didn't know what form the research would take. The original thought was that it would be a series of papers about the presence of different sorts of peculiar communicational things taking place in the original family systems of people diagnosed schizophrenic. The idea that it would be an ideographic study of depicting the family life of a number of people was not the original aim. It was going to be itemizing tangential communication – a study of communication *à la* Bateson rather than a study of families.

Tangential communication?

I wrote one paper that was published in a book called *Mystification, Confusion and Conflict*, and the aim was to produce a whole series of papers on mystification and confusion. Tangential communication was a term that had been used by someone else and there seemed to be a lot of tangential communication and tangential communication taking place. It interests me a great deal. When you hear people in a railway compartment having a normal ordinary conversation, they are both talking and looking at each other and one person is talking away about something and the other person is talking away about something entirely different. But to their own satisfaction they are bonded in a conversation. That seems very peculiar to me, but since that sort of communication went on so much I didn't believe the idea that this sort of thing *caused* schizophrenia. I tried to be critical of that prevailing way of talking about the so-called pathology of communication. Even Bateson came out with that type of idea. But he was tarred with that a lot, he never gave it up really.

There was a meeting at the Tavistock Institute to which one of the Menninger brothers came – Karl, I think – when they were in London, and I gave a short talk in which I argued that the logical extension of the way he was looking at things was that he had to abandon the metaphor of pathology. The pathological metaphor indelibly came out of pathophysiological research into the body and this was not a paradigm that was useful for that. Menninger couldn't take that at all, he said I was throwing the baby out with the bath water. I remember he said ... these Americans, like when they're talking to a young officer, they feel they are entitled to call you by your first name although it wouldn't be on for me to say Karl. Anyway, he said, 'come over and work with us, Ronald', you know, putting his hand right in there and I didn't move my leg. I just looked at him. I didn't even contract my muscle. I just looked at him and he took his hand away.

Although I was a really bright young man this 'come over and work with us' was a terrible insult to the whole Tavistock as well. As if he knew everything that we didn't.

So to keep on the track, how did you proceed with the communication research?

Well, in order to get everything done, I made out a 24-hour schedule divided into 15 minute segments, each of these themselves being subdivided. I was so engrossed in this research, absolutely from morning to night. I mean 24 hours round the clock. I was aware that my relationship with Anne seemed to be absolutely awful, but I had no time really to take stock.

So I made a one or a zero for every five minutes I spent with her. I put down a one or a zero in terms of whether it was tolerable or impossible. After several weeks it was zero, zero, zero ... [laughs].

And how much time were you spending on writing ...

There was a zero for time that was pure self-indulgence, where there was no constructive outcome and a different notation for that time that I was actually at it and not just meandering and thinking about it. I realized that I was never going to be able to do all this on six hours sleep so I cut that down by five minutes a night until I was down to four hours or less. Four hours, absolute maximum.

The main time I was able to get this research written was between about four or five in the morning and seven or eight o'clock, that amount of time was enough really to ... get through this mass of hundreds of transcripts. The transcripts were far too long but I had to keep the original transcripts. I then established with Esterson and Jacky Cradd, it was Peter Lomas who had given me the idea, that as a starter, we were picking out a sequence of tangential communication, or mystification or double binds, radical misunderstanding, cross purposes or any number of things that were particularly sensitive. I could then mark that. That would mean that the material was much smaller. The original was now gone but still there in my memory ...

I realized that we were into paralinguistics. I was going to go into that, but I couldn't do such a finely honed thing without another research grant. I was aware of these fucking French intellectuals on semiotics and of course I had to learn all this for myself. Saussure and phonemes, the organization of phonemes and the mapping of signification on to phonemes – all that had to be worked out. Unless I was going to work with headphones I had to have an annotative assistant to identify phonemes, and I think I did approach someone in London who was working on phonemes.

I was feeling quite a lot of agony. I wanted to get this work done but there was a whole insistent urgency to develop a model of a real safe asylum, live-in place, where people would be able to just to live without being fucked over with all this psychiatry. I couldn't do it all, so I had to abandon working primarily with the *sound* together with the transcript. I made a tentative research application to see if someone would pay me enough money to have a complete studio and one-way screen and sound and filming. A whole equipment set-up so that I would have a way of processing this and be able to carry further a whole theory of communications in different directions. I was finding my limits though. There were the limits of self-tutoring in the sonic and paralinguistic semiotics of communication. There was a limit to the relationship of the sound with the sight because of what I had to say about the way people reacted to the interview. For instance, I was very impressed with one interview. I saw that when the family came into the room, it was the father or the mother gave a sort of a blink on the side of the face to the patient, which just meant 'you fucking well watch it, we don't want you blowing the gaff'. I just saw that, and, well, I could see that something like that could determine the course of the whole interview but it could be missed. But how could you quantify the weight of that flash? How could you quantify that reliably? How could we all agree that this was some sort of preliminary secret order or command, a private signal that was not available to others and could be a family sign, a private sign within the family? You know how parents control their children, they learn what the slightest thing means.

It was a lost cause, a hopeless case. Esterson was able to listen and sit and absorb but nothing came from it. There was no one I knew in London or in America who could help, not even the very best of them, like Bateson. Ray Birdwhistel was an exception but I couldn't work with him in the long term so I was on my own. I thought I've got to cut my losses and make the best I can of this pictorial representation of as many families as I could put together and depict. I thought it might be two or three volumes, as we had about 100 families. I didn't analyze them all to that extent but I analyzed closely maybe about 20 of them. I wasn't sure which way to go though.

I decided to cut my losses and make the best of the circumstances. I wasn't going to have the energy and skill without more of a background in paralinguistics and semiotics. I didn't know whether I had the energy to do a comparative study with the normal families; we'd already done them, but I thought I could get back to that later. I had a very strong instinct of wanting to *complete* something. I also had to maintain a foot in private practice because I had to do that to make a living, as there was not enough money coming in from books. That was not an income.

I wanted to be my own man, I didn't want to be answerable to these characters *any more* and if I applied for more research money I'd have to fill in all those forms, but no one would give me the money to develop the new type of empirical research I wanted to undertake so I'd have to fund it myself by keeping the private practice going at Wimpole Street. So I thought I'd put all the chips down on going for Kingsley Hall and on working on and getting out what I eventually got out in *Sanity, Madness and the Family*.

Was there much of a decision involved in deciding to do the book with Esterson? Or did it just come naturally out of the research that you sat down and did it?

Well, Esterson was a very envious character in a number of ways. I always felt embarrassed by what I felt was his envy of me.

I did a paper that was published at the *BMJ* which I was very sensitive about. I was absolutely furious at Cameron, Freeman and McGhie who, in their work that they did at Gartnavel, incorporated – in their book on chronic schizophrenia that came out before *The Divided Self* – my work, swallowed it up and made it out to be their own. I was absolutely furious at that and I spoke to Professor Rogers who said he completely agreed with me. He thought it was disgraceful and that I ought to write to the General Medical Council and complain about this and have them disciplined. I thought well, fuck you, you're the guy, you're giving me the runaround, you're the professor, if you had said no to them doing this it would never have happened. I thought what a two-faced bastard. Having to think about all that was a factor in getting on with finishing *The Divided Self*.

Then there was the paper in the *BMJ*.[25] Because of the politics of the North West Regional Hospital Board where Shenley and Napsbury were located, Esterson mainly, and to a lesser extent Cooper, helped me – through the permission of their consultants – gain access to families. So they got their names first on this paper – although I had designed the whole project and written all the paper – as the primary authors. Everyone in the know knew that they hadn't written it, or had thought of it, or had anything to do with it except helping me with access. But to soften up the Regional Hospital Board who were very sensitive and wanted to get their own people credit for work done on their turf, that's what happened.

How did you and Esterson organize the writing of Sanity, Madness and the Family?

He never wrote anything. *He never wrote a single line of the book.* I wrote the whole text of the book from beginning to end, there's not a single word in the book that is his. He got an honorific title as a joint author for the part he played as my companion in endeavours.

That's not made clear though, is it?

No, no, I thought I would give him that as a present because the Tavistock wouldn't give him any money. I wanted to get him some research money for the time that he spent interviewing people, being involved in this in the middle of the night with me and all the rest of it. They wouldn't give him anything and so I thought he deserved that credit. I wouldn't do that now, actually. Also, I didn't want to give the impression that this was a one-man band. I wanted to create the impression that there was a movement going on, I wanted to give the illusion to other people that there was some stirring in British psychiatry in our direction though there wasn't any of course. I succeeded only too well, and then Cooper gave the impression that there was a whole anti-psychiatric movement going on, but there was nothing! It was all on paper. [laughs]

So volume two of Sanity, Madness and The Family *never appeared. If the study of normal families had been published perhaps there wouldn't have been this idea that all families 'create' pathological relationships. What were your plans for volume two?*

There should be two sets of material, one residing with Esterson, and the other one in a warehouse in Yorkshire. All the transcripts and tapes must still be there. It was all transcribed and a good deal of it was examined. I went over quite a bit of it in detail on a number of randomly sampled sections in which I made an effort to compare and contrast the texture of the communication in families of schizophrenics with the families where there were no schizophrenics. There was a strong expectancy to find a way of putting the two sets of families in contrast that would suggest that there was a difference.

Well, it petered out. It didn't go further than that for three reasons; one was that there was a sudden and unexpected PA meeting which didn't involve everyone – it involved Esterson, David Cooper and myself.

I had absolute contempt at David Cooper for – as Esterson had – it couldn't have been *Psychiatry and Anti-Psychiatry*, it was the book before *The Grammar of Living* ...

The Death of the Family?

It must have been *The Death of the Family* in manuscript form. Neither Esterson nor I were against the family. We never thought in terms of pronouncing 'the death of the family' or wanting to. It seemed that David and Esterson were incompatible and unable to be in the same room together. I had very mixed feelings. David had walked out never to return and I made a extremely violent attack on Esterson for his attack on David. Esterson and I fell out. So all three of us fell out.

I never lost my contact with David but I lost my contact with Esterson completely after that. There had also been

other things that had been brewing between Esterson and me.
I'd relied a lot on Esterson in the *Sanity, Madness and the
Family* research, he was the only person I could talk to. I
would quite often go round to his house in the middle of the
night when I was writing that book. We were both extreme
characters in that we had no considerations of sleep. I mean,
if I felt like speaking to him at three o'clock in the morning I
would phone him up and be round there in about 10 minutes.

This argument with Esterson completely disrupted everything. I had never found anything in the families of schizophrenics to make allowances for the depressing nature of the
material, but after all that's what you would expect. When it
came to looking at the families of so-called normal people,
there wasn't anything to redeem it. These families of normals
were like gas chambers: the reciprocal effect of deadening.
Every member of the families *totally fitted* – getting up and
going to work and going to school and coming back and
watching television and doing nothing and going to bed.
Nothing to say really. To get them to say anything about
anything was almost impossible. They thought about nothing,
they said nothing very much, they were just fucking dead and
there was no edge or no sharpness or no challenge and it was
very difficult to keep awake reading this. Just fuck all, an
endless drone, about nothing. Nothing was happening.

It was like Samuel Beckett, reams and reams and reams of
nothing. No one was particularly happy, no one was particularly up, no one had achieved anything or crashed in anyway,
they were just going along in their own way. This was the
silent majority of the population. I knew that anyway I
suppose, although as a doctor you're called out in an 'emer-
gency'; but I realized I knew nothing about how people
actually live in these endless streets that a John Osborne
movie would show. How these actual human beings lived in
these houses and these were the people we were going to
study, who were *not* in despair. If anyone thought that you
could mobilize the masses for some social change, forget it.

I thought, how was I going to dress it up to publish it? I
really couldn't publish a whole book of transcripts of people
talking about margarine or fuck all. I could take on a
particular family and characterize it but there was nothing
really to characterize. You know, someone had died at some
time or another, and someone had been born and in between
they just did this and did that. The most colourful family was

one which, something had happened, it was like Eric Heller, *something happened* ...

Joseph *Heller*

Joseph Heller. You know something happened. A girl of 17 or 18 had got a stomach pain which her parents related to the fact that previously she had been warned not to go out with a boy who was in a pop group because it would make the other boys in the band jealous. Well the girl completely agreed with her mother, mother was right. So she had been a bit ill, she'd lost a day at the bank where she worked but she thought that her mother was completely right. Her father said 'you know, she's so romantic'. How do you mean? I asked. Well they'd seen her on a Saturday afternoon in Chiswick High Road with her boyfriend looking at bedroom wallpaper. I mean that stood out for me as a glittering moment of wit. Well it wasn't meant to be.

I finished the families of the schizophrenic study, completed the empirical work on normal families, got it all transcripted, analyzed or at least read over a good deal of it and was on the verge of launching into it, when my marriage finally came to a crisis. The marriage was still on but it was pretty miserable all round.

Have you ever thought about going back to that material?

A few years ago, about 10, more than 10 maybe, 12 11, *10 years ago*, I had always felt like taking it up again. It always kept on bugging me that I never finished it and I phoned Esterson and asked him if he was interested in reviving that project and he was prepared to talk. I invited him round to Eton Road and then he phoned back and said – he was now living with Mary Garvie (who was involved in the real story about why David Cooper got the sack at Shenley). Jutta couldn't stand Esterson so Esterson didn't come to my house; I had to go in the middle of the night to his place.

So I hadn't the intensity of impulse to reopen the question, to finish the second volume and that's where it was left. It could still be reopened, if someone raised a few thousand pounds to go over that material and make something of it. A number of normal families interviewed in *exactly* the same way we did families of schizophrenics; there is a whole wall full of cardboard boxes with typed transcripts of the tape cassettes.

Thinking of the mundaneness that you saw in the ordinary families – you know birth, school, work, death, that sort of thing – didn't you want to say something about that?

What's the alternative? State intervention? State planned social engineering to break up that family system and design another type where children are brought up not by their natural biological parents, but by some state approved appointees or experts in child rearing? Well, my quasi-rational anarchism – that a lot of people confuse with socialism – of freedom for the individual makes me oppose that idea. I mean, this is not a coherent rational social philosophy I'm talking about, I'm just digging into my total gut prejudice against interference in people's lives by organizations on the supposition that they're doing people good.

That sort of dead family is absolutely essential for the function of the type of society that we still have. So I had a lot of sympathy with David Cooper and *The Death of the Family* in one way, but I couldn't see my way through it into a constructive statement. I've never seen myself as any good at being a strategic policy maker, never seen myself as any good at coming up with constructive-affirmative-bright-suggestions. I don't know what the fucking answer is, I wish I did ...

Do you think that if you had written volume two it would have made it more crystal clear why a normal family could end up being a family which houses a schizophrenic?

No, I think, like everything I've written, its *unfinished*. I just wrote to that extent in that direction.

If I could have put an energized double shadow of myself into my body to get me to do that and complete that, in that direction of a sustained theoretical analysis of a family system with reference to empirical data, I would have done so. Trying to clarify all sorts of questions of a fair kind that I could answer if asked, I could put together a coherent and consistent theoretical framework of step-by-step contexualising the individual in a triadic, quadratic, intra-familial network interwoven with the other networks that each individual participates in networks, intervening with each other. If I could have

coherently systematized a theory that was better than any
existing theory as it existed I would have done so, otherwise
there would be no point to it.

If I could have put a supplementary R.D. Laing into my
own system to do that job, while I was doing other things, I
would have been very glad to do so. But I was very much
caught up in the hope that by continuing to see people in a
room in Wimpole Street who were very upset and distressed –
giving up the psychoanalytic model of the couch, giving up
the medical stance of the clinical psychiatric interview – day
in and day out, month in and month out, year in and year
out, that I might be able to contribute something to what was
called *therapy*.

I felt blocked for a number of reasons in the marshalling
of this research but how about a theoretical thing? So I
worked on that hard in that I thought there was some sort
of matching of 'sets'. So I spent over a year spending a lot
of time tutoring myself up to what was the end of first year
university mathematics, grade and set and map theory, and
made notes and eventually this came together in two series
of things. One was a series of six lectures that I gave in
New York in '68 or '67, about that time, which were very
influenced by networks and that sort of thing. I tried to
develop a theory of that, and that eventually got pared
down, down and down until they were summarized in *The
Politics of the Family* and *Knots*. *The Politics of the Family*
and *Knots* in a way is the second volume of *Sanity, Madness
and The Family*.

Husserl once made a remark about transcendental reduc-
tion. He said that when he was about five or six years old, his
father gave him a present of a pocket knife and he kept on
sharpening the blade of the knife, it was so sharp, and he
kept on sharpening it until he sharpened the fucking blade
away. Well, I kept on working on that, and what ended up
really was about two chapters maybe, on mapping and
families and intervention in family situations, that went into
The Politics of the Family and *Knots*. That's the best way of
putting it and it somehow missed being volume two.

*Before I forget, you were telling me about Carstairs ... what was
he telling you?*

Carstairs? What was he telling me?

Yes, you recalled an incident. What would it have been about?

I mentioned Carstairs to you in relationship to the numerous considerations about me becoming the director of the David-son Clinic in Edinburgh. In the course of studying the families of schizophrenics I went over to the Maudsley several times for discussions with the people there who were doing their own work on families of schizophrenics. In a paper that I wrote which was published with Esterson's and Cooper's first names on it in the *BMJ* on the outcome of treatment of schizophrenia, I acknowledged a number of people who had been consulted, either giving them credit or damning them with having any responsibility for the paper. Morris Carstairs wrote a letter to the *BMJ* more or less disowning any implication – that could only remotely be found in the credits at the end of the paper – that he had anything to do with it.

About that time he became Professor of Psychiatry at Edinburgh University. Scotland is a very small space, and Edinburgh University holds a very strategic position. I could-n't work at the Davidson Clinic unless there was a real, friendly camaraderie between the Davidson Clinic with me as the director of it and Edinburgh University. It wasn't anything that Morris actually said at the time, but I discovered that his attitude was absolutely uninviting. Keep off my turf.

However we never actually fell out, in fact far from it in latter years. One of my daughters – my eldest daughter – had her ups and downs, a sort of manic depression and she was getting a lot of drug cocktails from psychiatrists in Glasgow. I sent her to see Morris, for him to use his authority and handle that situation. They wouldn't have taken it from me, but he was very tactful and very useful.

We were virtually neighbours in Primrose Hill in London for about 10 years and we occasionally met socially.

Turning to Interpersonal Perception. Your joint authors, Phillip-son and Lee, they are even less well-known figures than Esterson ...

Phillipson was a senior clinical psychologist at the Tavistock Clinic and when I got to the Tavistock Clinic he had devised an object relations theory *test* which may be still in use. After the manner of Rorschach, it was a projective test of shadowy figures that people looked at and projected their fantasies onto and discussed what was going on between them. Russell

Lee was an American psychiatrist of my age who had come over to work at the Tavistock for a year.

I was a junior psychiatrist on the staff and Lee was another member of the staff. I was going through the papers in the Tavistock library and asking Phillipson and Bowlby about similar material to *Self and Others*. At the Tavistock we got journals sent to us from other research groups from all over the place and a routine practice every morning was that the librarian would draw my attention to something that had come in. For example: the Palo Alto group work; and an influential paper in the object relations theory world that had been written a number of years before by a guy called John Rickman on a critique of what he called one-body psychology in contrast to what he called two-person psychology.

There was a potential psychology that hadn't been developed that had to do with how people related to each other. But it didn't exist.

He wasn't coming from a background of phenomenology?

No one had heard the word phenomenology at all. I think my first thought was that you felt different when you agreed with someone than when you disagreed with someone. Suppose we are talking just now and you're doing your thing and I'm doing my thing. Supposing we disagreed, that sets us off internally, it might be quite upsetting emotionally. Disagreement can't be expressed in terms of one person, it takes two people.

Joe Schorstein had given me this phrase that no one's been able to trace, 'the dreadful has already happened', from Heidegger. Also, somewhere in the Bible – I can't remember where it is – a statement Joe had read was that the truth begins with *two*. Anyway, agreement and disagreement, there is a different feeling about being in agreement. There are different sorts of tangents that your mind goes at and different ways to organize things when you're in disagreement with someone. When you're in agreement with someone you can go together on something ... there's a synergy factor, or a dysynergy factor of energy.

Margaret Singer [at NIMH] had the idea of giving Rorschachs to two people at once and getting a joint Rorschach. A joint Rorschach is not the same as giving a single Rorschach – and agreement and disagreement and understanding and misunderstanding, these are at least two-person numbers. The

Tavistock Institute had no interest in this sort of thing. There was a guy called Fred Emery and also Eric Trist, who were interested in conflict resolution at the time of the cold war, and also game theory.

Object relations theory, when it was expressed in a coherent formalized theory, was always the object relations of *one person*. At the Institute of Psychoanalysis there was one occasion, I think it was in my second or third year, when Rosenfeld gave a theoretical seminar. He had written some papers on transference psychosis, and he gave a presentation in which one of the things in it was a dream of a psychotic patient which he presented as an example of a schizoid split in a patient's mind as depicted structurally in a dream. The dream was that the patient dreamt of two vertical cliff faces and some way up out of one vertical cliff face a hatch opened and out came a mechanical cuckoo that went cuckoo, cuckoo, cuckoo, three times and went back in the hutch. Shut. And at the same level out of the other vertical cliff face another hatch opened and out came another mechanical cuckoo that went cuckoo, cuckoo, cuckoo, and shut. This showed the split in the patient's mind, both were psychotic, both split parts of the patient's mind were psychotic and this was shown in a dream.

Rosenfeld is on the top table at the Institute of Psychoanalysis and there are budding psychoanalysts including myself sitting round the table and I said to Rosenfeld – as a complimentary interpretation to that dream – do you think that it could be a depiction by the patient of his perception of the state of affairs in analysis between you and him? And he just sat absolutely impassive, and made not the slightest movement and said nothing. There was silence for some while and then someone else said something 'as a proper question' and he responded to it and that was that.

I never went back again – I thought, oh fuck you! – and I never went to his seminars. Some time later I was summoned to an interview. Rosenfeld had complained to the organization committee that I had not attended the last three of his seminars, and I was asked to account for this. Well, I accounted for it by in effect saying – which I said very politely – that I had better things to do. Or other things to do. One hundred things to do: I had two other seminars to attend and I had five children. So they let it pass.

Returning to the potential of two-person psychologies ...

The imperviousness was another variable. It affected both people and it affected the system. You couldn't express agreement in a formalization of a one body, one person intra-psychic object relations theory. You couldn't express the product of two perceptions in the perception of one person, whether it was agreement, disagreement, understanding or misunderstanding, or imperviousness or tangentialness. Then it occurred to me that agreement wasn't the same as understanding, they overlapped. I mean you can't agree unless you understand, but to understand someone you had to see someone else's point of view. So the word for seeing someone else's point of view is understanding and there are two quasi-technical terms – Scheler and Simmel – *empathy*, empathy?

Let's say there were two equivocal figures that I was caught by; this woman, the Vase woman – that's her nose and you put that there, that's a mouth and a chin and so on. OK, well all right, you (A) are looking at that, and I'm (B) looking at that at the same time. Do you see a vase or do you see a face? Well of course you can see both. Supposing there's a stopwatch, might we *synchronise*?

If two people are very much in tune with each other – if Marguerita and I were looking at that would we both see the same thing at the same time or would it be random? Or would there be any variables that we'd both tend to see – the old hag or the young woman or the old hag and the young women as we were looking at it? But that research is something that has never been done and something that I might do.

So I thought, well, could I guess what you see in something, how would I answer this if I was you? How would you answer it if you were me? Then I had this flash; I was using the word perspective for point of view, you are a point of view, not your point of view. Someone pointed out in the phenomenology of *Erfahrung*, translated into German in the phenomenology of perception, a person is a point of view.

I mean, I don't know whether I could back that up rigorously but the point of view in German is translated as each person has their own point of view. But I wasn't substantializing a person who has a point of view, but I'm saying the person is the point of view. The point of view which is both the point of emergence of you and what you see, the point of view isn't predominantly meant to be a spatial perspective. The point through which one perceives – perspective. Another line of thought that started then that I still haven't completed or written about is the problem of not splitting time and space. The time that we are in unites us, we are always in the same time, we're in a different space and location, but we're in the same time. So there is a thought that some people are split more; time and space for some people are frantic because they are not in the same space with each other. They feel separated by space whereas some people feel that they are always connected. Once they have made their relationship, they are always in the same time so they are never really apart, spatial difference doesn't really matter.

I realize that actually I'm very spatially synchronized. I don't miss people greatly simply because they are not in the same space as me. We're alive together. Although we might be on the other side of the world we're in the same time. What we have in common is that we're in the same time and I think that's one reason why I've got on so well with some terribly disturbed people. Analysts say 'don't they keep phoning you in the middle of the night?' and all the rest of it. But they don't, because we're together, even though we are miles apart. It is very difficult to say what the validity of this is. There are apocryphal stories about how someone's dog may start howling when their master has had an accident or you may have a sudden start if, if Marguerita had an accident and she and Charles died, there might be a sort of ...

Crisis telepathy.

Yes. Same time, different space, something transpersonal. I began to wonder whether this factor might be one of the components that some people go crazy about, if others can't understand or accept it. If it's highly developed and totally invalidated, then you tend to go crazy about something that you seem to believe or perceive or a sensibility that you have that no one else validates. *Imperviousness.*

I was pursuing this sort of line and feeling very uncomfortable about the otherness but I thought, well, I'll have to wait until I mature a bit more. Maybe 20 or 30 years or so but for the time being as a stepping stone I'll stick to a location of the self in relation to others because, after all, I do experience the other as others and maybe there is some sort of schema there ...

So who did what on the book?

Well, I did the whole conceptual structure without any contribution from anyone else. Russell Lee wrote the main part of one of the first two chapters. Phillipson and I sat down together and worked out the items. I think they were called items. Phillipson did all the clinical testing and the statistics of it as far as it went and I think Phillipson wrote two or three pages of the text. But they were edited by me, as was Russell's stuff up to a point. Both of them deferred to me particularly in terms of the English.

Do you think it's one of the more underrated of your works?

Well, I always thought that neither Russell Lee nor Phillipson were cursed with brilliance. That's as far as it went. I always thought I would take up this stuff and carry it forward and incorporate it into a deeper theory. Some of it might go into this book I'm writing now about the *eternal triangle* – to handle a three-people situation is terribly complex. But yes, it's not an easily accessible book, it's a difficult book.

Is that why Penguin didn't want to do it?

Yes, I didn't think it was quite a Penguin book. It was somewhere marginally in between, possibly, but if I took it up and added more of the work that I'm doing at the moment it *could* be a Penguin book.

Do you see Reason and Violence *as being outside the mainstream of your work?*

Oh, I think it's within the mainstream, although it's not so obviously in the mainstream you might say. I wanted to give Sartre credit by 'translating' his work. That stuff of his hadn't been translated – it has subsequently been translated – but it didn't look as if it was going to be. It's an impossible text in certain ways, footnotes of footnotes of footnotes, and very involved. I thought that the distinction between praxis and process and the distinction of nexus and series that he makes, once they were presented to English readers, they might be taken up so that then I could use them in my own work.

11. Knots

When R.D. Laing's *Knots* was published in 1970 not many people knew what to make of it. Was it poetry, or descriptions of patterns of interpersonal communication, or what? Laing himself described what he was describing as 'knots, tangles, fankles, *impasses*, disjunctions, whirligogs, binds'. The following is an illustration:

> Jack tries to get Jill to see
>   that Jack can see
>   what Jill can't see
> but Jack can't see
>   that Jill can't see that Jill can't see it' ...
>   (Laing, 1970:57)

You were saying ...

As I said, when I got to London, I was missing the Glasgow study group I was part of. I fished out people who were in London. There was Paul Senft, now dead, editor, for I think over 10 years, of an interesting journal called something like *The Journal of Human Sciences*. Paul Senft, Resnick, David Cooper, John Heaton. We met in each other's houses in order to do exactly as we had done in Glasgow – to carry on this conversation about existentialism of one kind or another. I was very thin on the German and French background. Paul Senft had grown up in Germany and was into Husserl in particular so I used him in the way that I'd used Abenheimer and Schorstein to go over German books of Husserl's ideas. I got the original German expressions and original German sensibility for some of that stuff. Cooper was very intense, an abstract theoretical mind. He was thin in those days with his hair cropped and very, very ...

Severe ...

Yes, severe. He had the French connection. I'd read Genet. I

was fascinated by Genet's sensibility and writing. Then
Sartre's book on Genet came out. There was also Merleau-
Ponty who was giving lectures in child development and there
was a chap called Peter Hildebrandt who is probably still
around if he's not dead. He was a psychologist at the
Tavistock who'd actually attended Merleau-Ponty's Sorbonne
lectures on child development.

Merleau-Ponty was lecturing on phenomenology and Piaget
and Melanie Klein child development – this felt like home to
me. Merleau-Ponty was putting it all together and I read his
lectures. There was a year course that Peter Hildebrandt gave
me, a collection of about 12 Merleau-Ponty lectures from the
Sorbonne. The whole text has never been translated.

I had read *L'Être et le Néant* when I was in the army and I
wasn't sure whether I was making some of it up because, you
know, that if you never actually write it down and if you've
got no one to talk to about it it's very difficult to remember. I
wasn't quite sure whether I was making up my own phantasy
about what Sartre was saying. I wanted to get that anchor so
I started actually making notes and summarizing *The Critique
of Dialectical Reason*. I did this for the study group. The
Genet book was rather formidable, the language and vocabulary was more complex for me. David could do it with facility
so he agreed to do the Genet while I worked up the *Critique*.
There was another paper, the critique of analytical/regressive/
progressive method that I think he did, and then we both
wrote an introduction to it. Most of that was written by me
and it forced me to come to terms with this Hegelian dialectic
of *aufheben*, of, what do you call it, 'transcending', that Sartre
used. *Aufheben* meant going beyond in the thesis/antithesis
number, it pushed you beyond into *dépassment*; *dépassment*
was Sartre's translation of *aufheben*. It was specific things like
that which were a goad to get the terminology that I wanted
to think of in English.

From Sartre's *L'Être et le Néant*, this freedom of the individual and the critique of dialectical reason, I could see
immediately that he had taken on this business of trying to get a
synthetic theory that combined a theory of the societal impact
on the elements that comprised it, a sort of existential systems
theory and the distinction between the type of group where all
people were united, say, in a queue waiting for a bus where no
one gave a fuck about anyone else or knew anyone else but
where there was a tremendous group coherence. In the absence

of interrelationship between the members of this sort of group this coherence seemed an important point. I'd already got the distinction there between *gemeinschaft* and *gesellschaft* but I hadn't got the English words for them and that is what I wanted. It was like working at the Tavistock and then going home to the family, it was moving into a different world. The type of relationship one had within one system was different from the type of relationship one had within another. At the Tavistock a number of people were united by a common purpose but with very little personal affection or personal relationships between them. This would contrast to the kind of thing that one has with friends where the thing is the enjoyment of the relationship that one has oneself and where any common purpose is a sort of pretext to have each other's company.

There seemed to be a whole different individual personal psychology according to the type of group that one lived in and there seemed to be a balance in life between living in different groups. There seemed to be a remarkable split between these two in the modern world. One was the one you went to and the other was the one you came back to.

Presumably Tavistock was surprised with that book?

I don't think they even noticed it. Harvard Watts, who was the publisher, was an educated man. I had already talked with him about the absence in English of the type of European literature that was important to me and that could be useful in psychiatry. I did the best part of a translation of Minkowski which was never published. It was a paper summarizing Minkowski and another book of Minkowski on spaciality. There are some manuscripts of mine for that, but Minkowski never came to be translated because they thought that not a sufficient number of people would buy it.

Which came out first? The Politics of the Family *or* Knots?

They came out about the same time. I was working on both at the same time. There was another thing that was never published. It's still in manuscript and possibly could be published if I worked it out but I had just to leave it as it was because out of *Sanity, Madness and the Family*, and the normal family studies, two big theoretical things cropped up in my mind. It was an area that I didn't know had been developed and don't think it has been developed even now. I wanted to try to do it – it was generational.

There was an analogy between one person's psychology, two persons' psychology. There was an idea of transference between them that I developed. Transference in time. It's like I am trying to do now – talk about the past without projecting onto the past my present position. The best way is to talk about the past without erasing where I've got to in the present. Transference and counter-transference, there's no difference. There is space and time and there is transference across that. There is transmission from generation to generation. There is a horizontal line of reciprocal transference of something that is happening at the same time and there is a vertical line of time going from the past into the present. It's projections across the generations. I project on to you my image of my father, but I internalize his projection on to me. People treat their children like their grandfathers, so I take after my grandmother. My father's projection of his projection of his response to his father's projection on to him is projected on to me, internalized by me and I project that as part of my self on another, right?

So that was one of the theoretical problems you were grappling with?

Yes. We've got this system here that is already two generations away. Two generations away is determining what I'm laying on Marguerita, what my mother's mother laid on her about her father etc. ... and the final product of all this, which goes how many generations back, is laid on Charles.

What is involved is not a transference, it's a whole set of relationships. They were obviously set, interlapping sets, so I had to find an algebra for this. I had to go back and teach myself some mathematics, to find out what mathematics there was. I discovered set theory and I discovered transformations of set theory. There was set theory, group theory, latticework theory and in particularly there was the theory of mapping, of mapping one set onto another set. That's what we're talking about – products of mapping and degrees of density interlaced with one another and undergoing transformations, and so forth.

So I went to the Island of Pátmos, I spent six weeks there the summer before I had to write these ...

Greece?

Yes, Greece. It happened to be Pátmos for other reasons but actually that's where *The Book of Revelations* was written, in a cave on the island of Pátmos. I never actually did the tourist visit to where John was chained up in a cave and supposed to have written *The Book of Revelations*. We found a place that you could only approach by a boat, there was no road to it, it was a completely deserted beach with a shepherd's house. I spent six weeks working all this out and it was going to be published as the *Pátmos Meditations*, a manuscript which is still in existence.

I had to do this because simply thinking about all these ideas is very complicated. I can't stand it once you get the scent of a thing, but I had to get a clear basis in order to do a series of broadcasts for Canadian Broadcasting that I had been invited to do. So I went away for six weeks to prepare for that and did so with this set of manuscripts.

They were given that autumn and winter [1968]. The last book I had really written was *Sanity, Madness and the Family*. *The Politics of Experience* was a case of polishing up and putting together stuff I had been thinking and writing about since 1958 through to 1964. *The Politics of Experience* was a backlog, then I was running into all these theoretical issues. And the Kingsley Hall experience was also a tremendously complex operation and situation. So I hadn't written anything and indeed wasn't trying to write, but I *was* trying to find a system that could facilitate my thinking about the complexity of this material that I was trying to organize in the form of symbolic logical systems. Have you come across a guy called David George Spencer-Brown – *The Laws of Form?*

I only came across him when I read Wisdom, Madness and Folly.

To some people he's one of the 12 most important mathematicians alive. His *Laws of Form* is a very elitist book but it's right in there. He's one of the original minds behind computer theory. The first monograph he wrote is still quoted by mathematicians on the theory of random numbers. Well, he was writing *The Laws of Form* at this time and was a patient of mine, and this is 1968, '69.

He was a patient of mine at Wimpole Street, he hadn't any money, and was working on his book. Of course we had now dissolved this distinction of 'patients'. I mean he was consulting me for the state of his mind and, since he hadn't any money, we did a deal that he would teach me mathematics if I would teach him what I knew about him, as it were. So we used to have a two-hour session on him and then a two-hour session on mathematics which started with zero and then 1, 2 and so on. I remember on one occasion I asked him to prove – I mean I could not understand how 1+1=2. Since in his theory of numbers 1 is supposed to be a *real* number and the distance between 1 and 2 is the same as the distance between 1 and 0 yet both are infinities, so how can two infinities be the same? So we were still there at 10 o'clock at night, he was on the floor with sweat pouring off him [laughs] anyway he eventually to his own satisfaction proved to me conclusively that, in terms of systems of axioms.

There is a thing in *The Politics of the Family* – 'we're a happy family' – well, he applied his logical system to that little vignette and he said it cancelled itself out on his system perfectly. He also checked out a number of 'knots' in terms of the operations that were entailed. So I had three years when I was immersed at this level, and I put a popular exposition of the background of that into *The Politics of the Family*, a collection that first of all were these lectures. I expanded them into the book and threw in a paper that I had given to social workers on intervention.

Knots intertwined with this and I think *Knots* was published first, then the Canadian Broadcasting Company talks, and then I was asked to expand that a bit more into a book that became *The Politics of the Family*.

Was there a particular publishing response to Knots, *because a lot of people talk about* Knots *as much as they do* The Divided Self?

Oh well, Tavistock were not going to publish it.

Really?

I thought *Knots* was a very special thing and my second wife, Jutta, she had had the distinction of being a designer for a major German publisher. So I insisted that she had the chance to design *Knots* and her design of that was very influential.

The white on black?

The white on black. They didn't want to take it, in fact it was delayed for a month because they would not get the font. She was absolutely set on those long white letters and I think a line that was two-thirds up the page, a white line across [like that]. They came back with just a thick line and she wanted it exactly that thin but they said it was too expensive, and I think that the print was one which they had never used before. They weren't very keen on the book. They didn't know what to make of it, it wasn't like anything else they'd published – it wasn't poetry. So where were they going to slot it, it couldn't go into this bracket or that bracket?

What did you think when you were writing it?

I didn't know what I was writing. I knew I was writing something that I hadn't written before and I didn't know anything else that had been written like it. I had been getting these precursors of 'knots' for years; I began to get one or two, but I had no idea where these would lead. Maybe I'd send three or four things to the *TLS*. I think I did send one or two of them.

 I didn't know whether it was going to go on and on, until it was clear it would be a book or a slim collection. Perhaps a number of thoughts like that I might put at the head of chapters? I mean I had the idea I was going to use them in *some* way. Also, of course, I didn't know they were going to be called 'knots'. I didn't start off with the idea of writing 'knots'. I started off with writing things that I didn't understand and I collected them together and put them in a folder over a period of five or six years. The first of them went back a long time, so it seemed that here was something I would keep and add to as it happened. Then before going to Pátmos and sitting down to write what I thought would be the grist out of which I could develop six half-hour talks for this contract that I had already signed to do that winter, the first draft of the first collection of these things that later became *Knots* arrived by a rowing boat from the harbour off the island of Pátmos!

 When I returned to London I wrote out the text for the Canadian Broadcasting Company and in doing so refined the collection that now became *Knots* and I think they leapfrogged on each other. I think *Knots* came out first and then the Canadian collection and then the English edition, expanded as *The Politics of the Family*. I can't remember.

And the title? Was it going to be anything else first?

I can't remember the original. I was looking around that bookshop just opposite the British Museum, Luzac's. They have got all oriental material but particularly Islamic and Sufi literature, but I mean it's not populist. I was also looking around libraries because I wanted to find out if in the world literature there was a *genre*. For instance in the case of *Do you love me?*, after that was published, two people told me that in that genre I had written there are Bengali street lyrics quite similar to it.

I was looking to see if there was anything like that genre of *Knots* that I hadn't come across in English. I found in an annotation of some book, which I never traced, it was in some other language, some Parsee or some language, a sutra 'Knots'. A translated sutra, 'Knots'. *Knots*.

Can you talk about collaborations with David Mercer and David Edgar?

I never met David Edgar until about 10 years ago in New York when the Mary Barnes play was being performed by the New York acting company. He never approached me about the play, I never met him, I never saw it, that's the first time I *ever* saw it. So I've got nothing to say about David Edgar.

After the play I think we went out and had a Chinese meal in a local restaurant with a friend of mine. I think I ventured to say, did he think of getting in touch with me when he was writing the play because I thought it was a very dated piece even then? I don't suppose the play did any harm but I didn't particularly like it. It was far too long and didn't work *as a play*. I don't know, as something like documentary-social realism it had some bearing on what the scene was like. It wasn't very depictive of Kingsley Hall, it was Joe Berke's perspective really. 'Oh' he said, 'I thought of doing so but I thought that you would have made it too complicated for me'. David Mercer, I didn't like the *Wednesday's Child* ...

That's what it was called in the States?

What was it called?

Family Life.

Yes, *Family Life*, that's right. I didn't like it ...

But you worked on it ...

No, I advised him. I got paid for it but I said I didn't want my
name on the credits. I was only prepared to have my name on
the credits if David had been prepared to be influenced by me
slightly more. But I've got no complaint about it.

I was brought over to New York for about a fortnight by a
guy who was the American distributor of the film. The film
was discussed for about 10 days at midnight cinema sessions
that were packed, off of Central Park, in a cinema by The
Waldorf. It was a piece of propaganda and, as a piece of
propaganda, I had to say to David Mercer and Tony Garnett,
well, maybe you know better than me what propaganda
tactics are but it's not the sort of film that I would I have
stayed at very long. I know these things are terribly painful
and very earnest so I've really got to be even handed; it was a
fair, absolutely fair piece – the last thing in the interview with
the girl in the medical context as you probably know was
absolutely real. A lot of people thought that it was overdone,
but that was exactly what it was like and people should see
that. In every respect there is nothing incorrect about it, it
was just that David Mercer's sensibility I suppose was too ...

Too clear cut?

Well, you see I would say that myself and then would have to
take it back because it *is* terribly clear cut. It *is* just like that,
it is an either/or. You could be sent this way or you could be
sent that way and it *is* clear cut, black and white, and it is as
bad as that. So it was a pity that there wasn't a film done at
the time that I could have been really wholeheartedly enthusiastic about in all respects.

Were you more involved in the various productions of Knots?

No, I wasn't involved in the productions of *Knots* in detail. I
went to rehearsals and made suggestions about this or that; I

made a suggestion in the first place in that I thought it was mime, a cabaret. A sort of Marcel Marceau – particularly the 'there must be something the matter with him', that skit. In the film I gave them the little boy with the arrow idea, the little boy comes and aims an arrow that pierces the mother through the breast and mummy says, 'mummy isn't angry, she's just very, very disappointed'. They used that in the film, it wasn't in the book.

I wanted what's his name – Petherbridge, Edward Petherbridge? – the way I would have liked him to go more was in the direction that I was most happy with, a kind of commedia dell'arte formal clowning or formal miming.

I think when it came to *Do you Love Me?*, I think it could really have had something. But it never worked in London. I was very disappointed in that because I thought there was the makings of a cabaret theatre in the text of *Do you Love Me?* that could be sustained and I was disappointed that that didn't work. I thought that he should have let himself spend a bit more time with me. I saw it as a unitary thing but it ended up as a lot of fragments. It didn't have the theatrical momentum, and when it came to the West End after a regional trial it just flopped.

Was it a medium that you enjoyed and wanted to do more of?

It didn't change my life. It didn't draw me into attempting to write other things for the theatre. I never forced myself to try against an absence of inner inspiration or compulsion.

Do you Love Me? was actually played successfully in Paris, Rome, Munich and Frankfurt and different parts of Europe, for several months on end in small theatres, and did quite well on that basis. If it had done better in English I would have been drawn into using the time that the money from that would have given me, to see what would have happened if I addressed myself to developing a form which would be something like the form I had in mind.

I would have had to stop doing everything else and sit down and take my chances for about a fortnight, fully concentrated to do so. I saw it as something between a one scene and a one act play, but it would be one scene; but the scene itself, it could be like Genet, or you could have different levels of reality being depicted on the screen at the same time, one above the other or at different distances or different choreographic zones. But it wouldn't be as long as an act and it might be as long as 20 minutes or half an hour, and it wouldn't be appropriate to call it a playlet or a novella, it would be a very, very short story. A couple of fables in *Do you Love Me?* – absolutely true stories – could be done exactly as they are. I wouldn't know whether to call it a play or a ballet. There would be music in it, and there would be words, but it wouldn't be an operetta, it wouldn't be a one act operetta with a libretto. In other words, I have got in my mind a form that one of the reviews of *Knots* by the then, what's his name, Professor of Poetry at Oxford, in *The Listener* ...

Levi?

No ... A rateable English poet, I think the professor after Robert Graves [Roy Fuller]. Anyway *Knots* got a lot of ridicule when it first came out. A well-known poet wrote a piece that he seemed to have volunteered for *The Listener*. In effect it was the only decent review of *Knots* that I remember that really gave it some credit. Maurice Richardson, in one of the reviews in *The Observer*, said it was a ridiculous waste of paper on the publisher's part, just for a trivial few pages of words. The positive reviewer said that Laing might have invented a new literary form, which doesn't happen every day.

If I had felt that I had not been under an internal preoccupation to spin other things or if at any time from now on, I felt that I could devote two weeks to nothing else, to see if something like this, which I sense might be in me, could come out, a literary form, a theatrical form that isn't quite in any existing forms, comparable to what *Knots* might be ... I might do something.

The Politics of Experience ... the publishing history of that?

After it was published by Penguin, which was all routine, it went automatically to Pantheon in hardback and then probably became their bestseller in Pantheon paperback. No one particularly liked it in my immediate circle, and I remember the Penguin editor said that it was a 'rabble-rouser' and I don't think the USA publisher, André Shiffrin, particularly liked it either. I mean he didn't like any fucking thing that I said, I don't know *what* he liked. He eventually rejected *Wisdom, Madness and Folly*, so it went to McGraw-Hill.

Presumably most of your psychiatric colleagues saw The Politics of Experience *as nothing to do with psychiatry?*

I can't remember a single comment from anyone about it. I think they felt I'd really blown it and finished myself completely. Not a single British psychiatrist that I remember mentioned it. Well, by that time I had drifted away anyway from actually meeting them but not a single one that I remember said anything to me about it. I think they regarded it as a *disgrace*.

And presumably that bothers you because you don't want to be defined away, do you?

No.

12. THEORY AND THERAPY

In this set of conversations Laing talks about what he has never actually written about – his therapeutic practice. He discusses what he actually did with those people who came to his consulting rooms over a 30-year period.

Also in a most complex and lengthy yet illuminating manner, he explains what he actually *believes* in. What his philosophical world view consists of. In particular he specifically describes the context of his opinions and beliefs, and the complex inter-relationships between them.

Let me read you a quote from Elaine Showalter: 'In London in the late nineteen fifties, Doris Lessing, Ronald Laing and Clancy Sigal, formed a circle of almost incestuous mutual influence.' But you weren't really influenced, were you ...

Not at all. I met Doris Lessing on one occasion. She had been Clancy Sigal's girlfriend. Clancy Sigal got a grant for writing and he came along to see me professionally although he didn't want to regard himself as a patient. I had already written *The Divided Self* and *Self and Others*, and he had picked this up and wanted to consult someone about his life and he thought I might be able to do that. So I agreed to that and he saw me for about once a week for two years.

I don't think he was speaking with Doris Lessing by that time, I mean it was absolutely finished. I never heard her side of the story. It wasn't in the late '50s it was some time in the middle '60s.

This is a quote from the Female Malady: *'although he never directly discussed the connection of sex roles and schizophrenia, Laing's exposé of the assumptions about feminine dependence, passivity, chastity, dutifulness, obedience and docility that governed the behaviour of his eleven families towards their daughters [in* Sanity, Madness and the Family*] gave feminists important ammunition in their analysis of women's oppression'. Do you feel that you didn't discuss the connection of sex roles in schizophrenia?*

No, I didn't. I've never had an explicit feminist vector. I've never done so, in a coherent piece of theoretical writing. No, I didn't. I've never taken that up. I mean, you don't have to ask me that, its an objective statement about my literary corpus.

Do you feel now that it's something you should have done?

No.

Because women are human beings and persons first, and women second?

I still regard myself, and regarded myself when I wrote that book, as a social scientist. You have to allow me my own idea of a scientist which I adumbrated slightly in the second chapter of *Self and Others*. There's a correct appropriate knowledge of a certain domain of reality which we can call that knowing, or science.

My field is the psycho-social interior of family life, having a bearing on how it comes that some people come to get themselves in the position of being seen and treated accordingly as card-carrying schizophrenics. And I'm not talking about labelling theory. In order to make a scientific statement of that, I would have had to do a comparative study of male and female schizophrenics and families and compare and contrast what happened to them. Not global theories about gender-linked issues. Certainly there are statistics. There were at that time more women lobotomized – a three to one ratio – a definite preponderance of more women than men being diagnosed schizophrenic. And all sorts of other studies. But that wasn't my domain.

Sanity, Madness and the Family was simply an account of what happened in eleven families, out of about 100 families that we studied. As I said, the reason why it was only eleven was that I was exhausted after reading through all the protocols. So 1, 2, 3, 4, 5, 6, 7, 8, 9, 10, 11, that was enough to make the point that I was making, namely, that schizophrenia is much more socially intelligible than has come to be supposed. So if anyone wanted to make some kind of scientific statement about how this linked up with what sex you were, they should go ahead and do the work.

Having said that, do you feel that you have written enough about the relationship of sex roles?

No. I haven't written anything about it ... When I left London, two and a half years ago, I thought I was going to write a book about sex and gender, about the emotional, intimate love life between men and women. It would also be an occasion for me to put my two cents piece in about all the feminist controversy. I read the major things in the field, some of the French feminist and American feminist literature and got myself up to date on the generation of feminists of the '60s and '70s. Also the second thoughts that some people were having, and how the whole feminist stance is not one monolithic thing. For instance, there's a whole lot of controversy between Dinnerstein and Chodorow. I've got a manuscript on that, but I'm not going to publish it because I didn't finish it....

I've got all sorts of private opinions about all that, of course, as you can imagine. Including the women I've met in that respect. What's her name, Doris Lessing is not one of them, I mean she is not an influence. Germaine Greer is not an immediate influence. She may well have attended a lecture that I gave in Vancouver in 1976, but she could have mentioned that the only time we *actually* met that I ever remember was on a strange advisory board of Longmans when they were doing the first computerized dictionary of the English language. They appointed an advisory board to meet two or three times a year, of about 20 people. Asa Briggs was the chairman of it and Lucien Freud was, not Lucien, the MP ...

Clement ...

Yes, Clement Freud. Germaine Greer and I had a glancing – I was quite keen to say hello and meet her. She, I felt, reacted to the point of rudeness and I wondered what the fucking hell she had got against me. I just wanted to say hello. I thought *The Female Eunuch* was a sort of bashy book, it was very Australian you might say. But it had a lot of energy and spirit.

How serious were you when you talked about Kierkegaard and Nietzsche 'not knowing women'?

I was very serious. I don't mean to say that what Kierkegaard and Nietzsche have got to say about women and femininity is not profound – and it is understood that I put them in a totally different bracket from these other people that you have mentioned. Nevertheless, I would say in my own life, a relationship with a woman whom you live with, in some sense something happens between you whereby you might say you get married and have a child and grow up together. There is something about that experience that neither of them knew at first hand which is a limitation on their range. You've got to live that to know what it actually is about.

You don't experience that from a single sample of human life as a child with parents, because you only experience the relationship between a particular man and woman and that's a sample of one, and one's experience of a child of *theirs*. You have to grow up, you've got to see other men and women, you've got to realise that not everyone is like one's own father and mother. That one's father and mother is not – although it is an embedded model – a reliable model. It is not a model necessarily to emulate or copy. Also it is not on to believe the Bowlbys of this world that what happens to you by the age of two and a half is critical or that you can't love unless you've been loved, which is a horrible idea, and quite untrue. It is certainly a good idea to love children and it's unfortunate if you've had a bleak, unloved early beginning to life, but life hasn't ended; it is not that you can never grow again, it is simply not true. There is not enough scientific evidence to back it up so you shouldn't say that sort of thing as though it was scientific truth. You should not say that love is like a vitamin deficiency and that there is a critical period in life which unless you get it like a dose of enough vitamins, you are marked with a deficiency disease for the rest of your life. It is a really scientifically irresponsible statement to say that.

If you want to say such a thing in order to encourage people to dose out love to children that is not the way to do it, it will boomerang back because then you'll have to market love as a professional commodity, like vitamins for children.

Well, what was I saying about Kierkegaard and Nietzsche; well, Kierkegaard said, if I had had more faith I would have married Regina, well, Regina might not have married him!

I was thinking about that book by Podach, *The Magus of Nietzsche*, and, as I said, that's one of the things I've got on my immediate list to do. There is a German television producer and another guy who I thought in the springtime of going with to the Engadene where Nietzsche spent a lot of his time before he flipped and was taken off. The Engadine is not very far from here, where he walked and wrote his last stuff.

Apparently the walks he took were very exacting, 20 kilometres from one place to another. I thought I might do some of these walks and take a few critical texts of Nietzsche with me and if I had a couple of companions who were thoroughly imbued with German and who knew of Nietzsche's work, maybe put together a paper on what might have happened between Nietzsche and Elizabeth.

What experiences in relationships have you not had?

I can't talk about the gay experience. I've never been attracted to men, or sexually aroused by them and I've never had any experience of that with men. I mean, it doesn't crease me up or anything.

I haven't got the experience of celibacy. There have been times in my life when there hasn't been a woman in my life and I've lived alone for a while, but not for over a year. I don't know what it is like to live the life of a completely celibate virginal priest or monk or man or woman who really does live that life and who regards it as out of order even to imagine sex or masturbate, or who deliberately erases that side of life. I can't talk about any direct experience of that.

And women?

I know more about that, I would say, than Freud did at first hand, but maybe not more than Jung. He seemed to – I don't mean this in a snide sense – womanize quite a bit. Whatever Freud did about that he kept very, very secret and probably we'll never know. You got the impression that Freud was not talking out of the top of his head, and he could say things about all that that men like Kant and Kierkegaard couldn't. I don't know about Spinoza but when you read the chapter 'On Human Bondage', you get the feeling that he knew what he was talking about from direct experience and so did Socrates and Plato. So did David Hume as did Sartre and Merleau-Ponty.

Michel Foucault couldn't talk about that, which is a pity because I think it tells in his last book, *The History of Sexuality*. I never talked with him *specifically* about it but I'm sure *he* was aware of that; so there is a limitation in everyone.

Obviously no one can live every kind of life in the one lifetime, you can't live a celibate life if you're living a sexual life and you can't live a sexual life if you're living a celibate life and you can't live the life of a promiscuous ambidextrous character if you're a living a heterosexual life. You can't lead the life of deception in the formal sense of what you call adultery if you don't actually go in for that.

Are there a set of central concepts you want to take to the grave with you and want people to write about when you're gone? I mean concepts other than implosion *and* engulfment *and* petrification?

Well, the way I would like to respond to that, very important, critical question is to take a break for a couple of minutes. But I'll give you a response before taking a break if you want to; well I just say this, that I feel that the response to that question is that it is unfinished business. I always find it difficult reading R.D. Laing without knowing him from his books to say what these are; if I got a hold of R.D. Laing's books and read them all through, because Laing's writings don't directly take on these Kantian questions – what is man, who are we, what do we do – he doesn't take these questions or respond to them, I haven't done that in what I've written.

I would like to have a go at taking on that sort of issue in writing before I die. I mean these are the sorts of questions that I've been at all my life. If I've got a type of inspiration in the manner that Jung got when he wrote – what was that book, when he felt, he sat down and it was channelled, dictated to him? – I mean if some inspiration like that came I wouldn't resist receiving it as an oracular statement, and I might publish that and say this came to me. I'm channelling it, on the one hand. On the other hand, I haven't done so. So it's not likely that at this very moment I'm suddenly going to be able to epitomise for you and myself what I haven't been able to epitomise. You see to draw all that into the scope of what is called a model has been responded to by a number of people who have said that reality cannot be modelled ...

There are statements about the society that we live in and the socio-economic conditions and material things and how these form, and the decisive factor of division in modern society into class. There's a class of people who do this and get exploited for doing it and there's a class of people who –

I'm a Marxist in that sense, but I think that is too broad to justify the word Marxist in the world at the moment because it has been so done-over. But there is a hard core of analysis in that respect that can be brought into the present day; but that isn't a model of who we are, that is a statement about our socio-economic organization, and the biological and theological and imaginative thought forms and everything else embedded in this situation, and the illusions you can somehow get out of that.

I also reject a deliberate subjectivist idealist idiocy. The worse type of, you might say, bourgeois intellectualism in it's Marxist critique of it. I mean, Adorno's critique of existentialism made me very cautious about using a word like 'authentic' any more, or his critique of immediacy made me very chary about calling myself a phenomenologist in the Husserlian sense that somehow you can pare away all the sort of thing and see an immediacy. I don't like in referring to our species as Man with a capital M. I would prefer to talk about us as human beings and I would like to regard *us* as a bisexual species that comprises men and women and we reproduce ourselves by – at the moment – committing sexual intercourse with each other and conceiving new human beings that way. We've just discovered in the last hundred years how that happens and that's amazingly recent that we've actually discovered how we keep on going as a life form.

I don't feel obliged to believe *anything* – which doesn't mean to say I don't – but I don't feel obliged to believe in evolution, say, as expressed in either some neo-Lamarkian version of it or the Darwinian descent of man version of it. I feel obliged to accept anything that I regard as a fact and I will use *my* critical judgement, and no one else will tell me what a fact is. They can tell me but I will be the last judge for myself of what a fact is. Anything that I call a fact is something I agree that I've got to admit is the case, whether I like it or not. An ordinary fact is that we are sitting here. In that sense I adhere to the Scottish philosophy of common sense. There is a very good book written about that by an Australian guy who summarizes the Scottish philosophy of common sense that flourished in the beginning of the 19th century, and which has intersections with Sir William Hamilton and John Stuart Mill. Thomas Reid has a place in 18th-century philosophy and is listed sometimes as a precursor of 20th-century phenomenology. As a seam in philosophy

– I'm footnoting just now, as a reference point – it is a very uncommon common sense; a refined, cultivated common sense; an attempt to steer away out of solipsism or, on the other hand, crude materialism.

I have to say that we are spiritual and physical creatures and the one doesn't reduce to the other and there is a problem of saying what we mean by these terms and how these domains are seen to live together in our existence as a multiplex unity of different aspects and wholes. When it comes to the words we use, including the word spiritual, all such words are so used and abused and prostituted that I can't use any of them without having to disclaim their current usage. Similarly, the way they are understood apparently by most people who use them, and that includes the word spiritual and such words as divine, God, love, charity, compassion, time, eternity, space, a priori categories, a posteriori categories, all of the terms that we use to express what we think about when we say what we are thinking which refers to the whole lot.

I'm very sensitive to the – in the physicists' sense of the word – discovery of the physical world in the last two hundred or hundred and fifty years. Until then we only had our senses and the extension of our senses through microscopes and telescopes. Now we've got instruments. Everything comes back to what we can pick up with our senses but our instruments seem to pick up all sorts of stuff going on that are non-sensory, and these things seem to go on as a necessary precondition of what we sense but it is difficult to know what the relationship of that is. How come the nerve impulses in our brains happen in such a way that only after, according to this doctrine, these happen, do you see me and I see you and we see everything, is unsatisfactorarily explained at the moment.

I reject all dogmatic positions of dualism, monism, and interactionism; none of them feel to me as a thinking and intuitive person, using my intuition and cognitive faculties, none of them seem to be a satisfactory and adequate account of the system in which we live and partake of, and so in that sense I'm a provisional sceptic. Being a provisional sceptic I have to disassociate myself from what a number of people would then immediately say is the necessary outcome of scepticism, which is dogmatic nihilism. I reject that too. So I reject dogmatic materialism, dogmatic evolutionism, dogmatic objective realism.

Vistas of relative perspectivism and radical constructivism are very cogent. I reject positions of randomism and God playing dice and what I think are just inverse superstitions, like the ideas of chance and necessity. I find, from a point of view of formulating cognitive coherence in the situation we are in, that the expression 'meson cosmos' which has been introduced into the debate may be an inescapable concept. That is to say, that there is a world of middle dimensions in which we live and which is our homeland, our sensibility, while beyond that there is infinity and the unknown in both directions into the world of astronomy beyond what we can imagine, into the world of quantum physics beyond which we can imagine and all these directions that go outside of the meson cosmos which we have to infer from the meson cosmos. The categories of thought that we have got are inadequate for *that* domain, that we infer from the domain that we ourselves are in, namely; contradiction, paradox, the existence of two possibilities that are both necessary and incompatible at once.

Leibniz, *Monadology*, non-compossibility, seems to be the order of the game at the present. For an ordered set of events to exist as a cosmos, everything in a cosmos such as the meson cosmos in which we live (and love) must, by the fact that it exists and is not a self-destruct system, be able to compossible together with everything else. If your thought and feeling and whole being runs into a state in which the world that you live, the elements of which seem to be – not *seem* to be, but from your point of view become non-compossible – then you are living in a self-destruct system and you will probably appear to other people to be mad. The compossibility of the world that we live in doesn't seem to be accidental to me and I don't believe it's an illusion or a delusion necessary for survival as it were, a lie that enables the species to survive.

On the other hand I have to reject Nietzsche's criticism of 'truth'. That whatever we call truth is simply what we need to make our beliefs compatible with our existence and our existence compatible with being. I have to resist out of sheer instinct and common sense and intuition the pit into what is called dogmatic nihilism if you go down in that direction. The world is coherent, the cosmos blows one's mind with it's consistency and coherence; the main domain of incoherence in this universe seems to be the human species in the way it conducts itself in this cosmos.

There definitely seems to me to be something seriously the matter with the human species in it's reckless and wanton destruction of other life forms, and our collective lack of companionability. The name of the game of survival doesn't seem to be the ruthless destruction of everything else except ourselves in order to survive, rather there is some profound law of symbiosis of co-existence and living together that we are missing which is our main species mistake, as it were, at the moment. I don't feel that that is an adoption of pessimism for the future. The fact that we are a bit ZZZZZZ at the moment seriously doesn't mean to say that we are always going to be like that as we might come to our senses very quickly. We're going to have to.

Mortality is one of the existentialia or one of the components. We are finite, and we have a beginning in life and we have a death, our physical life lasts for a few suns and a few moons and we dissolve and we are mortal creatures. I think we've got every reason to suppose that the human species, like every other species that we imagine, that we have indications of, is mortal that a hundred million years from now I do not expect that in this cosmos there will be any human beings. There seems to be some indication that life forms arise – however they take the form that they do, they take the very specific form and there is an inference, I wouldn't say it was an absolute fact – but there seems to be an inference that what we could call species, identifiable forms of life of which we are one, as humans, *come and go*.

There is some inability to accept that and we go into states of despair and listlessness and can't take it if we have to admit the inevitability of species extinction as well as personal death. Some people find that difficult, they don't mind that they're going to die themselves as long as they've got some phantasy that human beings are going to go on forever. We are not, I don't think. As a species we are maybe a flash-in-the-pan in the vastness of universal cosmic time.

I cannot define what the point of it all is but it seems to be so coherent, so beautiful – *everything* – so cruel, so tender, and everything is more than anything we can imagine in every direction. That doesn't reduce everything to nothing and meaninglessness, rather to more than we can imagine, whatever that may be. I mean if we admit our finitude then we've got to admit that infinity is something that we can just about glimpse but which is beyond us. The immanence of what is beyond us or the immanence within us of the transcendental, if you want to put it that way, is also beyond us.

If you work further down, so to speak, what comes next? The world is not meaningless?

Well, if the world within us and outside us is *beyond us*, in both directions, then we are reduced not to nihilism but to an abject humility in the face of all this and the undecidability, uncertainty, may have something to do with the deepest wisdom.

But I can't see beyond the beyond of that, so I don't know whether I've got a positive statement that isn't in effect a negative criticism of different sorts of negativity.

There is a Marxism that is a materialistic historicism. I have to reject that. There is a sort of stupidity that is a crude sort of evolutionism, I have to reject that too, as I have to reject scientism. I have to accept Marx, evolution, science, art, the spiritual and the divine in such a way that there isn't built into that acceptance an *ism* that closes it off into a dogmatism and exclusivity. I've got to accept that coherence and pattern that I don't want to forget or leave out of that statement. I've got to bear that in mind and at the same time not paint that around with contours in such a way that it can justifiably be accused of being another closed system. So at that edge between exclusion and inclusion and openness and closedness there is an edge of paradox all the time. At that edge of paradox, it can again fall into a paradoxical mannerism, an intellectual mannerism. I have to avoid that.

I'm fearful for sounding really stupid. But is it in any way possible to talk about what individual members of the species can do?

I don't think it's possible to answer that question that you put to me or you put to yourself or I put to myself or we put to one another from what you might call a standing start. You've got to spend some time taking that question and making it, shall we say, operational.

The question: is there any sense in what individual people can do? All right, well it's a serious enough question to question the question a bit before we go into action in an attempt to answer it. I mean what are we doing just now, this is what we're doing, what can we do, well this is what we can do and are doing, so what are we doing? It's a very hairy pursuit to go into the labyrinth of sorting out that question into a non-trivial, pragmatic response.

Well, let me put it another way. For Freud, 'man' lives for love and work. In your model, what can he or she live for?

Oh, he quoted Scheler, who said that hunger and love make the world go round. Well that is a sentence made out of Scheler, sure, OK. Carrying round a pocket book of little sentences like that that sort of stop one from getting pissed on a plane by a feeling that you know something that one's hanging on to. *Love* and *work*. OK. Well, fair enough. [laughs]

We are creatures, as has been said, whose being is in question to ourselves. I want to say that *that* gets close to the sort of creatures we are – we are our own question mark. That what the whole of one's life becomes is the question mark one is, and explicating that question mark either attempting to clarify the nature of the question or venturing some answer to a question when you get a question that you think there is something of an echo back of the answer of the question – but maybe all questions like this are in a sense their own answer. That there isn't a question and answer.

The existence of this question is itself something we should see as a very central aspect of who we are, that we are questionable to ourselves. That can drive one frantic, that sort of questionability of one's own existence or in it's own existence to itself, of itself, for itself, to one another and so on. We are social creatures, tremendously so, essentially social, there is no you or me and so on without each other. The individuality of ourselves has always got to be interlaced with the others of which we are in a dialectical relationship to, and that has to be seen within the whole of the societal structure, and our response to that doesn't seem to be adequately expressed by the immanence of the conditions in which we are formed. So we are getting to the paradox of so-called freedom and determinism and whether they're expressed theologically or sociologically, you can't give up either.

You've always got to struggle with it and struggle against it and admit it and accept it. There are some values that I won't give up concerning basic human decency which can sound so sloppy that one can hardly dare use the terminology. But I revolt against the idea that if I can get away with it and just happen to feel like it at the moment proceed to cut you up in little pieces and eat you, or use you for the fire tonight. The sensibility of Camus in *The Plague* is very close to mine. The sensibility of the writer of Ecclesiastes in the Old Testament I have found very close to mine. The sensibility of some parts of the New Testament is very close to mine, and the sensibility that comes across in some of the Buddhist and Sufi writings I find heartening. The sensibility of even the phrase 'the Courage to Be', produces a reverberation, a resonant effect in me. The heart and sensibility and coherence and intelligence and affirmation in some music from humanity like bird songs produces a resonance in me. That resonance is not philosophically or metaphorically trivial. It may be the most important thing to me when it comes to the bit. There *is* that resonance and it's an affirmative resonance and it doesn't fall into sentimental sloppy optimism or sentimental sloppy pessimism. It means that you can't do it alone but you've got to accept the solitude of one's social being, and one's individual solitude which doesn't necessarily mean pining away with loneliness. There is both. There is an amazing species component as well as the disintegrative alienative components of the human species. There is this amazing coherence in our species life as witnessed by any moment in time; just look around and ask, where does this come from, how is it all kept together and put together? It's all absolutely mind boggling at any moment as soon as you start thinking where does all this come from and where is it going to and how does it all come round? Some guy in North Korea in a hundred years time might pick up a satellite of this conversation, you never know, it's absolutely amazing, I mean not just trivially amazing. And 'a collective human spirit and mind' – leaving all that para-psychology mumbo jumbo behind – there is something that is eluded to in that, that maybe we're going to get it together and find a way of co-existing in this planet that is fundamentally wholesome and happy for all creatures great and small.

Apart from the fact that it is you, R.D. Laing, who is the therapist with all that that means, and bearing in mind the variety of things that you've done with patients, what is it about your therapy that you would claim to be different?

Well, I've been taking a spell off since leaving London and thinking and wondering whether I should try to formalize in theory and practice what I have done. At this moment in time, while I'm here, I'm not obliged to have a coherent answer to your question; I am thinking about whether I will or won't or what will happen by the time I, in a sense, re-enter things in September, as I see it.

I don't know at the moment whether I'll try to put a package together which would be communicable to other people and learnable, teachable, adaptable and formalizable and identifiable as a Laingian – like the Alexander Technique – method. It will immediately be subject to unbearable corruption and misunderstanding as I see it. It will immediately get out of hand, so I will be squirming with embarrassment and unhappiness about how this goes as it drifts off in the world. Like NLP and Milton Erikson. It will be ripped off immediately by the sharks and my name and my method will be taken up and used by other people that I will find absolutely detestable. That's a fair prediction I think.

When did it become apparent to you that what you were doing was something which was not the kind of thing usually done?

Oh, that became apparent to me when I was in the British Army when I was taking Peter home with me or sitting in a padded cell. I couldn't have done that sort of thing unless I was ahead of the game. I was aware that I was doing things that were extremely unorthodox, and only because I could conduct myself in relationship to other people, convinced them that I wasn't a total nutcase myself that I could get away with that. I mean the data that is in *The Divided Self* couldn't have come from orthodox relationships with patients.

From pretty well the very beginning, I *was* interested in learning the clinical method of a psychiatric medical examination. I felt that I had to internalize and make myself competent in what was going on. I never had any temptation to be swallowed up by it, but I also didn't have a simplistic contempt for everything that serious and intelligent people had brought to bear on this subject.

When you eventually went to the Tavistock, was there a time when you saw clients as a classical psychoanalyst?

Oh, of course. *I was in psychoanalytic training.* I spent four years as a student at the Institute of Psychoanalysis undergoing a classical analysis by the British Psychoanalytical Society, five times a week for 50 minutes at a time on the couch of Charles Rycroft and was supervised doing classical analysis by D.W. Winnicott and Marion Milner and peripherally with other people, like Sutherland. I was in supervision and presented my work at clinical seminars at the Institute of Psychoanalysis and at the Tavistock clinic, did classical analytic group work à la Tavistock for a number of years. For over 10 years I spent something like 12 hours of the week doing this out of about 90 hours a week in which I was seeing people one way or another, within the formal framework of a couch and a chair. The formal framework – you have an appointment, you come in, you lie down on the couch, I sit on a chair and then a transaction develops. Most of my time was spent in a room with people sitting in one chair and me sitting in another chair until two-and-a-half years ago. Twosomes, couples, families, in their own homes, in my place in Eton Road, going out for walks eventually – perhaps – sitting on the top of Primrose Hill, looking over London while they talked about themselves.

I mean these were very intelligent people, people like Henry Ezriel and Winnicott and Balint and Rosenfeld and Paula Heinmann and Melanie Klein. People of high IQs who spent all their life addressing themselves to the psychopathology of other people with a view to making some kind of contribution to their lives of a positive kind. I didn't write all that off. I was learning how their minds worked. I could very well see what a Kleinian would take out of that, what Fairbairn would make of that, what Balint would make of that. And so on.

My 'patients' would want in a sense to get from me my view of them, well, they *would* get it, and they could go away and make the best or the worst of it. I mean, 'I'm not saying that this is going to do you any good, but if you are coming to see me and if what you want to get from me is how I see your life and the situation you're in and you think that will help you well I don't mind giving you that. But I am not promising you that this is going to be therapeutic. I don't know whether you can take this, one thing just one thing, don't kill yourself on my doorstep. If you can't take what I'm going to tell you, just fuck off in good order, and if you're going to think of that, give me a promise that you won't slit your throat until you've stopped seeing me for at least six weeks because I don't want any responsibility for what you do with your life'.

I might say that to somebody, I might not say that to someone else. With someone else I might be tender and gentle. But I mean I *have* said that to people. You can't then codify that and say this is what you say. That would be my response to one person, but there would be a completely different response to another.

So I am responding. What I am offering is my contribution and my availability to them if they feel that a touch of *me* in their life would be useful to them. Well, they can have it for a fee because I've got to live too and they've probably got a lot more money than I have, so if there is any side to that, then 'I'm not twisting your arm, you are paying me to put up with you for one hour, at the very most, at a time'. [laughs] Well, I had a bit of a severe tone just now, but you know what I mean.

When did you stop using the concepts that the Tavistock would have liked you to?

I was never imbued with any Tavistock concepts. I never started using, in their manner, their idea of it, I was never a convert. I never had to be deconverted.

So transference was not a thing that concerned you?

No, I had my own idea of transference. I had written *The Divided Self* before I went to the Tavistock, and the *Self and Others* was written in the first year at the Tavistock. I still have my own idea of transference. Transference is a very good idea. Transactional analysis is also a very good idea, if it helps you to clarify your mind. If someone is coming to see you and laying on their mannerisms, their kinesis, their tone of voice, their other person, you ask yourself – it's a very good question which you are trained to do in object relations theory – who is this, who are they are talking to, who do they think they are speaking to, their mummy when they're two-and-a-half years old, or they are treating me like a little baby, who are they addressing? Who is the unconscious object relation or part object that they are projecting on to me?

Well, that's easy. I didn't have to go to the Tavistock to get that. I'd got that. Very useful indeed, and some people are so imbued with that that you've got to point it out to them, in the best way you think it will get through to them, instead of making an interpretation to them. I might say 'do you realize that by virtue of what you've just said that you are treating me like your father. Now I want to point out to you that I'm not your fucking father'. [laughs]

Right. I'd go on: 'You are probably doing this to everyone you come across who's wearing a tie', and so on. One guy comes and accuses me of being his father because I'm wearing the same type of tie that his father wore. 'If you think that I'm the same as your dad because I'm wearing the same tie you've got another thing coming to you, you'll find that out very quickly'. I cut out about two years of transference interpretations: 'You can't get any further as long as you keep on going on at me as though I was some aspect or part of a component of an original internalized transformed projection projected back on to me, that's all you can see of me'. You have to say that to some people. So it is useful if this person is able to see that himself; therefore, I've got to mediate my manner and my way of saying it and my way of putting this across with tact or without falling into being caught up with being his father. Maybe I'll fall over backwards not to overlap with his father image projected on to me or mother projected on to me or good or bad breast.

Presumably you were much more directional and, unlike Rycroft who said very little, you said a lot?

No, well, it depends, it depends. If what I felt someone needed was to hear themselves, to hear what they were saying I would maybe say something. I've gone into what Marguerita would call my severe mode just now, [laughs] this is coffee and nicotine in the middle of the afternoon without any breakfast! I would say without an edge, 'I mean you're wanting me to say things to you, start off with listening to yourself, you're not listening to what you are saying, now would you like to repeat to me what you are just saying?' Can't remember what they said: 'well, I'll tell you what you just said to me, I'll repeat to you what you said to me, I want you to listen because I'm not going to say anything to you except what you've just said to me. You've just come out with this, to me, amazing statement', and I'd repeat back to them what they've said.

I've had some people who wouldn't believe what they've said. 'Well, next time you come you bring a tape recorder with you and you take it and you go away and listen to yourself talking to me', and I had people who would accuse me of saying things I never said.

With a client that came regularly, did you plan what might happen?

No, not at all, though I didn't go into the thing mindlessly. The regular arrangement would be that someone would write or telephone. In the last six years, Marguerita would answer the phone and her instructions would be if they wanted an appointment with me they ought to write me a letter. Although some people were far too gone to write a letter.

If a doctor wrote to me I would explain to the doctor that you are referring someone to see me, but that I was not offering anything that is called medical treatment. 'That means you're not going to get any reports from me couched in medical terms on the outcome of this treatment, do you understand that?' Someone might want a psychiatric opinion in which case I would be prepared to give a psychiatric opinion in my capacity as a trained psychiatrist.

So someone comes to see me, the appointment would be, say, from two o'clock to three, or it might be half a hour and they would come in the room ... the word therapy has got an etymological meaning that I favoured ... the etymology of the word means attentiveness, so the name of the game is cultivating tactful attention to each other, *attentiveness*. 'So I'm offering my attention and my response in my judgement of what is appropriate, of how to respond to you. I'll be attentive to you.'

So there's a room in Eton Road – that you came to – and the encounter starts from the moment I meet the person. I'm in my room, probably sitting. This is all part of the technique which has been endlessly argued about. Rycroft, for instance, never opened the door for me, he sat in his chair, rang a bell downstairs, and when the bell rang I – like a trained rat – went upstairs, opened his door, he stood up from his chair, I lay down on his couch and he sat down out of sight and *that was it!* The second after 50 minutes he would say 'time's up', and I would get up, walk to the door, turn round and say 'good-day', shut the door and walk out. Five times a week, for 50 minutes.

I developed the practice that the meeting ought to be

conducted within the form of civilized courtesy. Courtesy. So that meant a handshake. Most people would say, 'where do I sit' and I would say, 'well, that's my usual chair, that's where I'm sitting and you can sit where you like.' There were two chairs so they'd usually take up a position, sit there and I would sit in my chair. I had a side table beside them, which usually had an ashtray on it and they might say 'do you mind if I smoke?' or something like that. Then the first opening would usually be 'right, you've come to see me and I know nothing about you except what you've put in your letter – or nothing at all – so maybe the best way to go about this is for you to convey to me in any way you like what leads you to come here. Why you've made this appointment.'

This would then launch the person into starting off. They would often fumble around. 'It's very difficult to say'. So I help them out to get into their stride and they would start to tell me what it was that had brought them to see me and this would lead into me asking this or that. Not taking a formal history at all. Some people would go into whatever it was and not mention anything about their original family, brothers and sisters and if they didn't mention that, I wouldn't. I'm not taking any notes, I'm just listening and asking this or that question.

This would end after an hour, or earlier if the appointment was for half an hour; this would be the opening presentation of them to me and then towards the end of that we'd consider where we would go from there. I'm making my mind up in the course of listening to them. Is this someone that I'm going to take on myself or is it not? Am I going to see this person again or am I not going to see this person again myself? Sometimes the whole thing that seemed as though it might take five or six years of therapy would be resolved in one hour. Sometimes the issue that was bringing someone to see me might be extremely diffuse – someone couldn't say why they had come, they just felt they had to, and couldn't put their finger on what it actually was. Well, all this would be taken into consideration and I would then have to consider what I felt I could say or recommend to them in their best interests. Would it be a good idea for them to make a few more regular appointments with me, would it be a good idea for them to go off and do something else, would I not feel that I could really be the person for them?

By this time I was in no way committed to the idea that they had come to see me for *psychotherapy*. They had come to see me for a consultation as to what I could contribute to their life positively, which might not be a recommendation to get into therapy, it might be anything, absolutely anything.

Meaning what?

They are out of tune, they are an instrument that is jangled and is out of tune. What would be the best way for them to get into tune, let's say. Well, one person might be a physical disaster, they might be in a terrible mess physically and might be completely unaware of that. So I might have to point out to them that smoking 20 cigarettes before breakfast is unhelpful, that they couldn't get anything straight unless they addressed themselves to that sort of thing.

Or I'd say I think you should go along and see so-and-so and take their advice on how to get yourself in shape and if you do that in about a month or six weeks you'll be in a completely other space than what you are in. Then come to see me again when you've done that. And we'll see where we'll go. One woman, who was living with her father who for years had been in the habit of beating her up, I said, 'I mean *you* haven't got a problem'. 'But I can't even lift the phone up', well, I said, phone up someone. 'When you walk out of here, we will get a car to come round and pick you up in 20 minutes and you just go and stay with that person. Don't go back into that house, that's the end of it, right? OK, so do that'. This particular woman was absolutely at the end of her tether so I said just get out of it, and when the dust has settled and you are able to calm down you'll be able to see what you've been living in. Then we'll go over all this. So you see, it might be anything.

One of the mythologies that surrounded you was that you would take people back to birth. Why do you think people thought that?

No, never. I never, never used a feeding bottle and never cuddled. I can't remember any case where I cuddled a patient or a client in my life except, perhaps, in a workshop where I might put an arm round someone. No feeding bottles, no changing nappies, nothing like that. I mean I'm a Scottish male chauvinist pig who has got very little time for the business of changing nappies of babies. Marguerita doesn't expect me to do so. I've changed a few nappies of Charles, and that's as far as I go with changing nappies. I would never dream of anything like that with anyone in therapy with me.

I mean if they want that, go and see a David Cooper type of person, but not me. And I'd also expect them to have a bath before they came to see me, I mean I wouldn't let them into my room if they were smelling. Absolutely no way.

Anna, the David Reed book, about the breakdown and suicide of the young German woman. Elaine Showalter makes a lot of this, and she talks about Anna in the context of the problem of 'Laingian therapy' for schizophrenic women. Can you talk a bit about that?

In about 1971, when I was living in Belzize Park Gardens – and I'm saying this to you without any commitment on my part that I am remembering all this accurately – but to the best of my memory he came to see me about his wife who was in a terrible mess, there was no doubt about what the clinical diagnosis was. I wasn't prepared to take her on at all, but I said I could refer him to Leon Redler. So I told Leon. I wasn't keeping case notes any more, this was simply a consultation, and I can't remember whether I saw her first of all, whether with him or alone or at all. Anyway I referred her, in a straightforward way, to my colleague Leon Redler and that was that. Some time later, a few months later, I met him in the street, I was out shopping ...

Leon?

No, Leon lived a few streets away. I saw Leon from time to time, and I can't remember what was happening with this woman I'd referred to Leon but I remember meeting this guy [Anna's husband] retrospectively, because when Anthony Clare reviewed the *Anna* book there was an episode in it about meeting me in the street with a shopping bag, and this guy was asking me about the outcome. In his review Clare quoted the fact that I put the bag 'up and down' several times. I was out shopping and met him on the corner with this shopping bag and he button-holed me about his wife who was no better, who was getting worse and that it was all pretty hellish. I think she had moved out and had a flat of her own, and was living in pretty broken-down circumstances. I don't know whether she was seeing Leon regularly, or whether he was visiting her on the southside of London.

Anyway, he asked me if we should persist in this, what do you think? I said I had no way, I wish I had, of saying how something like this will turn out. 'I'm sure Leon wouldn't mind if you wanted a second opinion'.

Anyway, some time after meeting the husband, Leon said he was not happy about her because she had refused to see him and didn't want him to visit. I think he said to her husband that he wanted me to visit her.

So we did. We went over to the other side of the Thames, where I think she was staying in a flat in Greenwich. She was living alone, as I remember, in a pretty chaotic room and wasn't interested in saying anything to me or to Leon. So we hung around for a bit and then left. Leon felt that there was a special sort of taut to this situation she was in. She was the grand-daughter of General Rommel and she had made out there was some double-take on a number she had about Jews. She thought there was some conspiracy that had enveloped her and which was still going on, of which Leon was a part. It was all to do with Rommel, the Nazis, the Jews and this and that. As I said, I think it was something to do with a Jewish plot to kill her and Leon was involved. Anyway she saw Leon not as a possible benign guide and friend and helper and therapist, but as a sinister figure that her husband had materialized through powers that be.

In the face of this, Leon was feeling pretty checkmated or stymied in his relationship to her. Well, I hadn't any words of wisdom or advice to offer to Leon – you know, use your own judgement, play it by ear and do what you think fit and obviously if you think that she might kill herself, then maybe it comes down to the husband who has to make his decision about whether he wants you to go on in this capacity or whether you want to tell him that you're going to throw your cards in, or whatever.

I don't think I heard from the husband again. Leon was an ex-student of mine, was now a younger colleague of mine, so he was a big boy. He could always talk to me about these things.

Anyway, she was not having anything to do with me. So there was no Laingian magic that could break through her attitude of 'just fuck off, the whole lot of you'. The next I heard was that Leon's wife, Liz, was going through a very bad patch. Leon had got me round to his house – I'd arranged for her to get into therapy with another psychoanalyst.

So Leon was in a very, very stretched state and I think the next thing I heard was that they'd gone on holiday somewhere in the south of England and 'Anna' had – I mean Leon did have a therapeutic relationship with 'Anna', but it was a very ambivalent one on her part – gone on holiday with them, and on Liz's birthday she had made a bonfire of herself and burnt herself to death.

Both Leon and Liz were pretty shattered with this, it was terrible. I can't remember the details, I can't remember whether they found her half burning or not. I think they rushed her to hospital, and then, half charred, she died in hospital. The kids were also involved and all the rest of it. So it was a disaster all round, a catastrophe all round.

It was just a case of life goes on, and the next I remember, apart from the talk between ourselves about the reverberations of this human bonfire – I can't remember whether it was Hiroshima day, but it was all very symbolic – and the next thing I remember about that saga was the appearance of this book called *Anna*, in which this obviously very embittered husband, had written this quasi-fictional story. I never read it, I think the publisher sent me it and I saw what it was, and I thought, well, I can do without this.

True as he saw it?

The whole thing was without keeping to facts. So it was fictionally true as he saw it. I could give him credit for that immediately. But some of it involved turning over the pages and getting to things that actually happened while other things were made up as fiction. It was a bit like Clancy Sigal's book. It purported to be a novel. It claimed itself in a way that you couldn't attack it for libel. It was fiction/faction and it had a terrible taste to it.

So Anna is nothing to do with 'the problems of Laingian therapy' really, is it ... her case is about a woman in distress, I mean that's all there is to it?

In the course of each year in every psychiatric unit – whether out-patient, in-patient, clinic or hospital – there are a certain number of people who commit suicide that come to see psychiatrists. There has been no particular epidemic or rash of people who have killed themselves who've come round to my neck of the woods. She was one person who did. I don't think it proves or disproves anything at all.

Were there any patterns to how people ended up coming to see you? How many people came because they had read your books?

I think it was about half and half. Half were through the books and half were word of mouth. And half of the people who came *via* the books were through *The Divided Self.*

I read all the incoming correspondence, secretaries took the telephone calls, and the occasional person turned up at the door. I received letters from all over the world, more from America than Britain, but Britain as well. At one time I thought of publishing a book or selection of their stories; people would write me lengthy sagas about their experiences. I didn't answer all of these, I answered some of them, and some of them would seriously want to make an appointment and so they did in the formal way and then came to see me.

The Facts of Life got a lot of people. *The Politics of Experience* – the trip, the voyage, the psychotic sort of thing – well, a lot of people were wanting me to help them go through it, but that wasn't a consulting room thing.

Some people were referred to the PA, who might want to go and live in a household, and I had by that time a regular contact with one of the PA houses. I maintained a once a week evening visit with one place.

And a certain amount of referrals, less than a third maybe, were from professional psychiatrists, doctors, family doctors, and professionals themselves. Professionals who were not caught up in any mythology about me. When they came to me they wanted to consult me about a problem they didn't want to put to their usual colleagues. Maybe about their own family, or children.

Did you in any way see what you were doing as some kind of – I'm using the word loosely – reality therapy?

Ah well, you have to use the word too loosely to make any sense of reality therapy. No. You could call some of it psychoanalytic, some of it existential, some of it Gestalt, some of it eclectic, some of it psychosynthesis, some of it primal – all these little bits and pieces were all fragments of an integrated whole array of possibilities including reality therapy. Just a 'scream away' therapy and all sorts of bits and bobs and so on, but I wouldn't call it particularly reality therapy. With some people it was a confrontation with reality.

What would make it Laingian therapy in the end?

Laing. Certainly that would make it Laingian therapy.

There were people who came to see me as students or apprentices, like Andrew Feldmar. He came to see me and was particularly into his version of Gestalt and hypnotism and he took out of what his experience was with me and just cultivated his own approach, which I think he calls Integral Therapy. Integral therapy was a term that I wondered about using at one point, but any single term never satisfied me.

Was there too much variety for you to be able to tell me how long or how short people stayed with you?

People stayed with me for one hour, half an hour, or several years. It's really for a life time in a way, for those people who establish that bond or contact with me. They can phone me up or get in touch with me at any time. Years later I might hear from them – can they come and see me again? Some of these people are now therapists. There is one guy who is now a practising therapist in London who came over and stayed here for a few days in November. He was feeling a bit hard-pressed, and wanted to come over and so I saw him in a formal way for an hour in the morning and a hour in the evening. I hadn't seen him for several years and I might not see him again for several years.

If you didn't take notes, did that mean that each client each week was in a sense a new encounter?

No, it didn't mean that. I wasn't suffering from Alzheimer's. I was quite capable of remembering people from a previous time. When I said I didn't take notes, I meant I didn't keep as I had been doing up to the early '70s a file on everyone and keeping notes on every session. That didn't mean to say I didn't write down whenever I felt I wanted to remember something about someone.

No one ever seems to answer the question of why 'talking' should alleviate misery. What are the connections between talking and ...

Well, I don't think talking about things necessarily makes things clearer or better.

But the whole of psychotherapy is based on a version of that fact, isn't it?

Not my psychotherapy.

So what changes then? Insights which will lead to change?

No, I've never said anything about that. When you said why should talking about things make them necessarily better, I can't answer that question because I don't agree with the premise of the question that talking about things necessarily makes things better. Nor have I ever said so or implied so in anything I've written.

OK. Point taken! When you have been with people who have come to you for help and you've taken on, those who have gained help from you, have done so through which mechanisms, do you think?

Well, I think it's fair enough if you're going to ask me questions and I'm going to answer them, that I'm not going to answer anything that puts me in a false position. When you say what are the mechanisms, what do you mean by mechanisms?

What have you done or given to them to make them subsequently feel easier?

Maybe I ought to still be picky on the wording because that is one of the things that adds confusion to confusion. It's not a stupid question, it is a perfectly valid question, but again it has got two implications in it that I don't necessarily accept. For instance, that I've done or given anything to people that have come to see me. I've certainly been there. I think the bottom line is that they've had my company.

And attention?

And attention. They've had my company and attention, my *engagément* on their behalf. They've had my company, they've had my attention. As a matter of honour on my part they've had my attention and I've put myself at their service, and of their life and addressed myself as best I could to what's troubling them. The way that that could turn out could take many different varieties of the range of my presence and attention and my training, and my hopefully refined, trained, cultivated intuition, spontaneity and sensibility. If you want me to package all that in a model, I can't do that for you just now any more than I've been able to do in my own life in writing about this. I've talked about this and it's been a very disheartening experience trying to explain to people what I'm not doing and giving them examples of what I have done. This shit that has been laid on me and all that, it has made me both disheartened about communicating that sort of thing, and *angry*.

What do you mean the shit ...

Bed therapy!

Oh yes...

If I use the word spontaneity, for instance, people think that's getting into bed, jumping into bed with someone. It's their own filthy minds laid on to me. *I don't like that.* My voice of what I hope is reason and sanity and sensibility is drowned out with shits like that. Take the word spontaneity, it's a very good word, well, Freud specifically condemned spontaneity. He used the word and says you must never be spontaneous as an analyst. You have to check out and analyse transference and counter-transference and then come up with a non-spontaneous interpretation. He is very specific about that. So if I say that I cultivate spontaneity people may immediately construe that as jumping into bed with someone, well that's not my spontaneity. I'm a very formal guy.

What you mean is non-preconceived interventions? That's what you mean by spontaneity?

Oh, not just in any way. I said that courtesy and respect are written into the bottom and top line and uncultivated undisciplined spontaneity could possibly lead to anything. I'm not claiming to be Jesus Christ or Buddha. So I'm capable of being unpleasant to you or to anyone else or to myself and striking wrong notes and being out of key myself, and going through ups and downs myself in my life. I don't regard being spontaneous as laying my numbers on other people, so as I said when we try and start to talk about these things, including the words that we are talking about, what is the point of using a word that means something to me that means something to someone else? What is the point of using other words to explain what I mean when every word that I use is being received in a meaning which might be the exact opposite of what I intend?

That argument which I think I've articulated in these two sentences with clarity, is an argument for shutting up and being silent. What is the point of being silent as a means of communication if silence is itself misconstrued? So you start trying to say something again or write something. To speak or write in the face of this interminable misunderstanding because I can't explain what I mean when the only words that we use have double and treble meanings and other people take the meaning or significance of my words to be different from the intended meaning as I use them. So Kierkegaard and Nietzsche say that irony is a tactic or strategy of writing but, again, what do you mean by irony and what do the Americans mean by irony? The Americans, if I may characterize the Americans with a certain amount of irony, are totally lacking in irony. And as you know, when in the company of, you might say, one's own company, the company of friends, the sort of repartee, or the way of speaking that occurs is so impossible to explain to other people you wouldn't care to spend any time unless they were paying you a lot of money to be in the same room as them, it is so different that it is hopeless.

I think too many people do not realize that psychotherapy is excruciatingly hard work.

Since the days in the padded cells in the '50s, what I've been doing is in one sense so different from the understanding of psychotherapy from practically all psychotherapists. Is it psychotherapy, what is psychotherapy? There are all sorts of occasions for two or more people to be in the same room together in all sort of consultations about life. Lawyers are consulted, ministers of religion and priests are consulted.

There's an asymmetry in the room in that the other person has asked to see me for what they want to see me about; I haven't asked to see them and I'm making a living out of this activity. With that disclaimer, what you call psychotherapy *is* extremely hard work because it entails giving one's attention and the availability of one's presence. Listening in the first place is very hard work. You *can* get used to listening and practise listening and then it becomes less hard work very often as time goes on. But if you ask me what have I done or given to people, a lot of people who have come to see me have said that the main thing they have got from me is that I listen to them. They have actually found someone who actually heard what they are saying and listened. That in itself without saying anything can be of critical importance. We are social beings, somehow or other. For many people in their walks of life, there's no one listening to them, no one hears them, no one sees them, they are made up by everyone, they feel quite rightly that they are ghosts. They might as well be dead, as far as their nearest and dearest are concerned. They are other people's phantasy. That can sometimes get someone down, and so if they come to see someone who actually sees and hears them and actually recognizes their reality, their existence, that in itself is liberating. In fact, that's got to be there in terms of what I do or nothing else is there, otherwise they could just as well go along and consult a computer who would do the job a lot better than most therapists.

You are seen pre-eminently as a writer because more people are able to avail themselves of your books than your professional services; however you spend more time actually with people, so how do you rank the two activities?

Most of what I've written has come out of my professional life. I imagine that if I hadn't been a writer, or writing about something in one way or another, that I couldn't have possibly written most of the books. I don't mean if you say professional that you have to include in that what people would call research. I don't think you have to make that distinction because I don't feel at all happy in view of what most people mean by therapy or seem to mean by therapy.

Without that engagement with people in the exploration of their life situations in the manner that I've done so, there is not a great deal of what I've written that could have been written. I suppose *Do you Love Me?* could have been written without that professional experience and *Conversations with Children*, but I mean it's so intertwined with the whole of my life.

The Divided Self; Interpersonal Perception; Sanity, Madness and the Family; The Politics of the Family and most of *Knots*, and quite a bit of *The Facts of Life*, appertain to professional situations. Very succinctly written, but not picked up are the pages in *The Facts of Life*, for instance, about a girl who has stopped eating, who has got anorexia. I don't know whether that is a sufficient response to that question of how do I rank the professional work with the writing. The two are so involved in my life and the writing is an outcome. I mean it's manifestly an outcome of what I've brought to and taken out of the professional situations. I couldn't be sensitized to the diagnostic look and the objective look in the manner that I have been without my training as a doctor. Actually being in that world for so long has certainly sensitized me once I became aware of it. I remember one instance as there are moments that you can remember that are just the flash of a second for all one's life; I was suffering a lot of perplexity when coming towards the end of my first marriage. I invited four of my friends to spend an evening to consider what my wife and five children should do in the circumstances. You know, whether we should separate, whether we should get a divorce – well, what did they feel about it? There was one chap there, I didn't know him, he wasn't so much a friend of mine, he had been a friend of one of my closest friends who had died and so was a friend of my friend, and a child psychiatrist. I didn't want to divorce the children but it was going to be very difficult if I left home and I hadn't enough money to set up a separate establishment so that the children had the option of two homes. As I was mulling this over I caught his eye and he had just turned on that 'clinical look', as he was now looking at me. A number of my colleagues were wondering whether there was anything the matter with me. That it was a terrible thing to abandon five children, and he was just looking at me as if he was looking at a patient, and I thought, fuck you.

You've had quite a lot of that haven't you?

Oh yes.

Well it's outrageous to me that someone can express an idea and because it is not a conventional one that people can then question their sanity ...

Yes, it's a common tactic.

Have you suffered the accusation that you are not sane consistently or just at particular periods, like when The Politics of Experience *was published?*

No, not consistently.   *The Politics of Experience* was the book that blew it. *The Divided Self* is very cool, so is *Self and Others.* When *Interpersonal Perception* was published – or before it was published – I don't know whether it is in the first chapter but I think it is the first sentence of the first chapter, where I talk of the refractions of refractions of refractions that stain the white radiance of eternity. At the proof reading, stain was crossed out by the proof editor and replaced by 'colour' and I was furious. Of course they had never read Shelley. It was just ignorance but we argued about that and again I almost saw red. Don't you dare change a comma or anything or tell me how to improve my English. They thought there was something peculiarly perverse or maybe psychopathological when I used the word 'stain'.

A friend of mine at that time – Sid Jourard who wrote *The Transparent Self* – told me that in those days, the second half of the '60s, that he would say that 80 or 90 per cent of American psychiatrists had made up their minds that I was psychotic. They regarded me as clinically psychotic. Of course they had never met me. The 80–90 per cent regarded me as psychotic, simply psychotic, on the basis of accumulating rumour, confirmed by the text of the book [*The Politics of Experience*]. As I told you earlier, there was this guy, Eric Mishler, who was doing a federally funded linguistic analysis of the words, sentences of the book. He found that there was something to suggest that there *was* indeed something the matter with my mind. The sentence complexity index showed that the sentences had become about two-thirds shorter, the vocabulary compared to earlier books was impoverished, the constructions were simplified, the associations were perhaps loosened. Well this is deadly serious and somewhat frightening.

You've now spent over 40 years of helping people. Was there an initial moment when you decided that this really was the life for you? Or did you kind of lurch into helping people?

I lurched into it. There was something about me at university so that fellow students would button-hole me and tell me about themselves for no apparent reason. I was someone that all my life has tended to be the recipient of confidences and secrets of other people. My conscious vector at the time was some sort of medical research activity in terms of brain and consciousness and mind and body and the psychophysical interface of things. I wanted a field of life in which I could exhaust myself, exhaust my self-actualization impulse, that I couldn't blame external circumstances that I hadn't had a chance to deploy that potential as fully within the circumstances as possible.

It seemed to me at the time in the army that this business of listening to people was something that I couldn't see could help people particularly, but nonetheless, people wanted to talk to me so I allowed them to talk to me. Or if I interviewed a patient in my psychiatric capacity I interviewed them in such a way that instead of wanting to get out of the room as quickly as possible they wanted to hang on and tell me more. That was quite a compliment. Patients don't usually want to stay in an office and go on when the time was up. They realized that I was someone they could talk to, and I was listening. And what they were telling me was not the sort of stuff that it was appropriate to put in usual medical notes. Nothing to do with what was supposed to be the matter with them; like the example I put in *Wisdom, Madness and Folly*. This guy I was asked to see who was referred by the Ear Nose and Throat department and who had a pain in the ear. When I started to listen to him, it was his 'guardian angel' who was giving him a kick round the ear. He told me that, but he never thought of telling any other doctor that – I never asked him, it never occurred to me that he might have a guardian angel giving him a kick in the ear – but it was something in the way that I was open to listen to his reality that he told me what was really the matter. That he was getting this kick from this little creature that he couldn't quite see, every time he turned his head. He said he *knew* it was a she, dressed in white in a long white robe, that was giving him the kick because his eyes wandered to a naked statue when he was going to his work in Kelvingrove Park. [laughs]

Illich says the best psychiatrists are 'latter day priests' of some sort or other ...

Eric Graham Howe would pick that up and say, well, yes, as a priest after the order of Melchizedek, a priest without portfolio or any pretence to any credentials of a priest, and certainly not wearing a dog collar or anything. In that sense yes, and only in that sense.

And you see yourself in that sense?

Yes, in that sense.

Someone struggling with problems of living?

Yes. As one human being to another.

And of course that kind of notion is anathema to the psychiatric profession.

Mmm.

One thing you said when I first met you which interested me, is that you said that you were surprised that people didn't follow up The Divided Self *with 'Divided Self studies'. That a school didn't develop. What kind of things would they have done?*

Well, there are people in Zurich and elsewhere in Switzerland who regard themselves as existential psychiatrists. I think that *they* have followed it up. There is an American journal of – I don't know what they called it perhaps, *Existential Psychology* – that has got completely unreadable gobbledegook in it which they think is following it up. Simply Heideggerian jargonese, drowning the visibility of the other person through their haze of existentialese they regard as following it up.

The sense of placement in the world that we have and our sense of what is real and unreal and our sense of ourselves as embodied people in relationship to other people is intimately related to the life we lead with other people, and so there are all sorts of things that can be said about the relationship between our experience and our conduct. There was a bit of a surprise that apart from the world of literature and novels and plays that there is so little written in that vein. But that surprise is immediately countered by a counter-awareness that there should be no surprise at that since the professional world culture, as Harry Stack Sullivan said, is very largely a training in interpersonal incompetence so the sensibility that could be cultivated to be alert to that is exactly what is *cultured out* of students. Norman Cousins, in *The Anatomy of an Illness*, has got an interesting statistic from UCLA that a clinical rating scale of empathy applied to medical students at the beginning of their medical career and at the end of their medical career shows a statistically significant fall off in empathy. So you might think from the side of myself that is surprised that studies like that would be followed up and people would be interested in checking that out and maybe correcting for that, but no, it's just an isolated thing that disappears in the amnesia of history. For example, James Lynch's work is very seldom referred to by other people, though he is the Director of Neurophysiological Research at the Maryland Medical School. He has written quite a lot of papers as well as quasi-popular books, and he is a particular specialist in the physiology of the heart and cardiology, but you don't find him quoted very much or his work followed up. The interpersonal relations in relationship to the cardio-vascular system is not a subject that appears in *The Lancet* or the *BMJ*. So the other side of that flip of surprise is that there is no surprise. Obviously the system is a cultivated selective inattention to the other side of the coin.

Do you think, when you consider the work that came after The Divided Self, *that one of the problems that prevented people from following them up is simply the fact that they were written in a unique way?*

Well, yes and no. A sort of communicational description of what goes on in a family – as appears in the 'Mystification, Confusion and Conflict' paper that you might have come across but that hasn't been collected – *Wisdom, Madness and Folly*, and 'Intervention in Social Situations' are quite accessible to people. I am told that 'Intervention in Social Situations' has a lot of influence but there hasn't been, as far as I know, a whole collection of professional work that has amplified that genre. It is left to sociologists like, as you say, Lemert or Becker to do that.

But even in that world, especially in the '80s, there hasn't been a whole tidal-wave of people picking up on that very fertile zone because it goes against the sham hypocrisy of the prevailing lies of society.

Perhaps you are in a bit of a dilemma, in that too much acceptance can mean that your message is thin milk, so to speak. I mean, does that place you in a dilemma?

Too much of the wrong sort of thin-milk acceptance is. I don't know what the dilemma is. I've already told you of the dilemma about saying anything since everything is liable to be misunderstood by a lot of people if not everyone and I'm not getting paranoid about that. It's a simple business of the words and syntax and content and form of what I say coming from me on to the page. When it comes off the page on to the other person's eyes and ears is for most people received in *their* frame of reference. The same words are understood in another way by me from the way they are understood by them. There is no way out of that, so I don't know whether you call that a dilemma, that is merely a fact of communicational life. There are actually a few people who do 'get it' and they are the people who are worth – for my sake as well as for them – maintaining a sort of camaraderie through it all.

There is this idea in some peoples' minds that you somehow enjoy the relative marginalisation of your ideas and your position but that isn't the case, is it?

No, there is nothing enjoyable about that *at all*. I've just got to accept that. I haven't, in my English style, in my manner of writing, I haven't gone out of my way to marginalise my writing as eccentric in any way. In fact, very much the opposite – of trying to use ordinary words in an ordinary way and ordinary syntax and say as simply and clearly as I can what I intend to say.

Have you read the book by Anthony Storr called The School of Genius? *It's all about the role of solitude in creativity. He criticizes Bowlby in particular for being too concerned with attachment and love and security, and not looking enough at the importance of work, solitude and so on. Considering the interests you have had in your life which have taken you to being on your own for considerable periods of time – have you theorized about yourself and your abilities in terms of your early years?*

I don't know whether I should say this, but I'm going to say it anyway. Since you've introduced that proposition or issue via

Anthony Storr, I haven't read his book but what I have dipped into of Anthony Storr, I've concluded that he is not cursed with genius himself. I don't think that what Anthony Storr has got to say about genius is likely to have very much bearing on what genius is all about.

John Cowper Powys wrote a very good book on the philosophy of solitude. It has also been said that genius is 95 per cent hard work. There's another component concerned with the difference between would be or could be or might have been or potential genius and accomplished/achieved genius – Mozart, Dostoevsky. I don't think we'd have any argument about completed real genius. I think there are two factors involved in the movement from potential to actualization, and one is good luck: anyone might run into bad luck, or adverse circumstances in life for that person which blight the flowering of their potential genius.

The other thing is that every potential genius might not have the flair to negotiate themselves through the rapids, or the options of life and they might run aground and get shipwrecked and stuck or bogged down or overwhelmed by adverse circumstances and they might not be able to find their way out of it and collapse under it. Or the genius might, in a sense, be wilted or withered or taken out of them.

All my life, I've felt that there is a combination of limited options – like for instance at this stage of my life *I've* burned my boats in many respects. I am not going to be appointed professor of psychiatry at Glasgow University I don't think, or professor of psychiatry at anywhere else. Thirty years ago that was a possibility, there was an option for me to pursue that ambition. You've got to conduct yourself accordingly, and if you make a wrong move there is plenty of competition and you're out. You only have to blow it once and you're out. So say at this stage in my life there are a number of options that I haven't got and there are a number of options that I *have* got. You can always say of anyone, including oneself, the choices that you appear to have are all illusions, that once it happens you can see that it was all inevitable and all written in the stars and in your *karma* before you started, but as you go through life you appear to have bifurcations where if you walk down that road you cannot walk down that other road at the same time, and that road doesn't necessarily go where you thought it did. It might double back but there might be an impassable mountain range, and once you start on that direction then it's too late to double

back, it has got to be one way or another and it can't be both.
There are bifurcations as they say in computer language. There
are essential bifurcations.

One of the considerations as to what I do tonight, what I
do tomorrow, what I do next week, who I spend time with,
what I read, my style of life, where Marguerita and Charles
and I go when our lease or rent of the flat is up in September
– where do we go from here? One of the components of
considerations that go into the calculations of that and a very
important one is to make a choice that will, whatever talent
or abilities or potential that I've got, are ...

Maximised?

Maximised. I could make an imprudent, an unwise choice.
Gregory Bateson said to me a couple of years before he died
that when he was about my age he made a serious mistake, and
I agree. I think that fucked him up for what he had in him.
Instead of it flowering out into a possible major statement of
what he had to say, what he could have said, with his range and
all the rest of it, he just managed to get out – what was it, his
last book [*Mind and Nature*] – which was put together largely
out of his lectures. He couldn't quite get it together.

So one knows when one's got the feel for that, it's a very
moving book and it's a very thoughtful book and it's a very
honest book, *but*. He took a job in Hawaii studying interspecies
communication and intra-communication in dolphins. He said
to me that he felt he made a mistake that in order to get at the
really cutting edge of that work he had not enough mathematics
and physics because it's very, very, sophisticated, the thought at
the cutting edge of that. He said after he had done it that it
would take him about five or six years to catch up and after
about 10 years he gave it up again and he never quite made it.
And he never came out with anything very much out of his
dolphin work. There is a very nice anecdote about dolphins
learning to learn – well, OK, dolphins can learn to learn, *but*.

Well I don't want to make a mistake like that, who would?
So genius or talent or whatever it may be. Solitude – I don't
think for instance, excessive solitude of the kind that Anthony
Storr doesn't know anything about – you've got to design your
life in such a way that you've got the right mix, the right
balance. At one time in your life it might be more of this, or
more of that, and so on.

13. REPUTATION

Laing did not enjoy a favourable reputation in the minds of conventional psychiatrists. Institutional-establishment psychiatry had little sympathy, if any, with Laing's work.

His reputation as a 'radical thinker' underwent a quantum leap in the late 1960s and early 1970s. In that period he was seen to be a charismatic figure and was referred to in terms such as the 'Acid Marxist'.

Laing was told by an Italian psychiatrist that his books were on every student's bookshelf, 'somewhere between Castaneda and Marx'.

Would you like to be professor of psychiatry at Glasgow University?

One side of me would like to be professor of psychiatry at Glasgow University and the other wouldn't. The other side of the one side is that it would be a hopeless quixotic fantasy of being professor of psychiatry at Glasgow University because I would be so pinned down by circumstances in what I could do that I would like to see done I don't think at Glasgow or anywhere. I am not interested in a lost cause, only if there was some possibility that it might not be. A few people – Kay Carmichael, I don't know whether you know her? – in Glasgow would like me to come to Glasgow, if I would consider it, and they would get me a professorship in some capacity. This is Strathclyde University I'm talking about. They meant the whole sort of thing – the west coast of Scotland, 'you could play a part in that' – and they would like to have me. Well at the time I said 'yes'; if we could steer something like that and I could play a part there, I would certainly be delighted to play any part in the practical business of social life that was offered to me that wasn't something that would just grind me down into a powder for no purpose.

So if there was something I could be engaged in and do of that order I would take it up. I was over in America last year, in the Bay area of San Francisco, with Rollo May and Fritjof Capra at Berkeley. Rollo said, 'how would you like to stay here if we could fix you up with a job?'. So I had a few meetings with various people about staying in the Bay area and – this is another epitomizing example – a lunch was arranged with two Californian businessmen of some influence and wealth in California in Trader Vick's restaurant in Emery-ville, just the other side of the Bay Bridge. You have to be careful how you report this; they made it clear to me, this is an offer that if made to me I couldn't refuse, you are not going to get this offer if you are going to consider it after you've turned it down, so you've got to, yes you will accept this, if we offer it to you. Do you want to meet the rector or president of Stanford University? Yes, I said, I have been dying to meet him all my life.

OK, so they give me a rap. Well, Stanford University – forget about Harvard and Yale and forget about the East Coast and forget about Princeton – Stanford is at this moment in time getting the cream of the crop. Stanford is picking off the very best of university graduates. It is more difficult to get into Stanford University than anywhere else. They said they would-n't want me to see undergraduates but after graduation – before they go out into the world – it would be very good for the best of them to be exposed to my mind. They added, you know, that 'in first year of Stanford they have the highest suicide rate of any university in America' ... do you get the point?

Not really ...

They were saying to me, we are going to give you the best, don't worry about having any weeds. Even in the first year they are cropped out.

So the elitism appalled you ...

Well, you are talking about getting jobs and obviously I'm not at Stanford University just now, I'm here in the wilderness.

You haven't been given any honourary degrees from British universities, have you?

Or any universities.

Do you see that as simply the fact that you have been seen as a 'radical'?

Well, that is one side of it, yes. That's a great deal of the story but it's also the case that I've been put out as a radical to invalidate me. To some extent that has been cynical, I think. I wasn't perceived like that by these Californian businessmen, I mean the guy who was talking to me said that he had read *The Politics of Experience* in the '60s and it had changed his life. Both of them said that they were admirers of my writing.

Radical – the way they've ....

Oh yes, well, radical is one thing but I don't know whether the sort of people, you might say these elitist people, in the know really regarded me as a radical in the sense that it is put out. I mean the term is used to nullify, it is a term of abuse. They'll give me an honourary degree when I'm dead, as soon as I'm dead, they are waiting for me. I hear about my death quite often, that I'm dead. They'll love that. Glasgow University has never invited me to give a fucking lecture in any department in the whole of my life. I've been asked to give lectures in pretty well every university – at least a lecture by a society or so on – but not a single lecture in Glasgow. Well, that's my home town. Well, fuck them.

As you are aware, you have a varied reputation: 'oh, he's the one who says things like "it's mad to be normal and normal to be mad"; and that the family destroys everything'. When people say that, does it matter to you?

Of course it matters to me. Why did I write the fucking books in the first place if it didn't matter to me? I thought it was important to me to say the things I said, so it matters to me that what I said seems to be drowned out by what people make up that I said which are things I didn't say. So I don't like that.

I would like to contribute to what you're doing, hoping that what you're doing is putting a bit of factual information into it. And anyway, you don't seem to be having me on, you don't seem to have believed all that stuff, you've actually read what I've written, you can see that there have been ups and downs, I've struggled this way and that way and given and taken, and I'm still at it. I mean I'm still alive, and the game hasn't reached its end.

Who knows, there are a lot of things that are unfinished business. What I actually do, what I did with people, in terms of my practical way of conducting what you would call therapy, I have found it defeats my capacity to give an adequate description of. There's one or two visual records of my idea of how you could adopt a decent human relationship to another human being who is in a state of whatnot, one way or another. There's a lot of the puzzles about the world and the way our society works which I haven't really been able to see my way through into any post neo-Marxist unified theory of a systematic order of society like that. If I could have developed something like that I would be very glad to, who wouldn't? I hadn't either the talent, the genius, the vision to see my way through that. I am just exactly as you find me now.

There is a real kind of moral finger wagging in your direction. That somehow, whatever your intentions, patients have not necessarily benefited from your interventions ...

One of the things that Marguerita has drawn my attention to while travelling, in the last two-and-a-half years, when I have given major lectures to over 2,000 people, and weekend workshops and seminars and so on. Practically everywhere I go I conduct myself just like I am, the professional and so on. Practically everywhere I do my number and then leave, and if I'm friends with the organizer they will tell me always that I left a big wash behind. 'Some people thought you were crazy.'

There is a guy called Theo Itten – you won't have met him – he lives in St Gallen which is outside Zurich. He organised a lecture tour in Switzerland about six years ago and one of the places I spoke at was the Burghölzli, which is maybe the most prestigious mental hospital in the world, where Jung worked for a while and where Eugene Bleuler was the Superintendent there and Manfred Bleuler succeeded him for about 60 years. Well, I went round to Manfred Bleuler's house – he is in his 80s now – and spent a couple of hours talking about psychiatry, and how he felt about his father and about schizophrenia and all that sort of thing.

I gave a lecture at the Burghölzli. a mid-day lecture about 12 o'clock, in the main amphitheatre. Most of the audience were in white coats, and were senior staff. Junior staff were excluded, I was too controversial and dangerous a figure for the junior nursing staff and junior psychiatric staff to be present at this lecture. I was speaking in English, of course, and Theo was translating. I gave a talk on *Gemeinschaft* and *Gesellschaft* and the relationship between the theory of the human relationship disturbances in the condition called schizophrenia. I couched it as best I could in terms of the German-Swiss sociological language that they understood.

Then I had lunch with some consultants and professors, then had a meeting with a smaller medical group after lunch and then I left the hospital. A week later I met one of the people who had been at the lecture, who was a biologist and who was on the staff of the Burghölzli. So he said, you know about a third of the audience in that lecture thought that you were either psychotic or were on drugs. I said well did you think so? He said no, he thought it was a brilliant lecture, you know they had never heard anything like that in their life and they were not going to hear it again, probably.

So what led them, those that had that impression of me, what led them to it? He was a precise Swiss biologist, and he said – 'well, it was mainly your movements. When you stood at the dias, I don't know whether you realized this, you had your notes in front of you, as you started talking you started leaning over the dias and sort of swayed backwards and forwards as you were thinking, as you talked. And at one point when you were making a point you lifted yourself up on the dias and then you moved away. A Swiss lecturer stands there and delivers a talk from a paper and you were animating yourself in a way with your hands and gestures, and facial expressions. That sort of thing led them to believe that you were in some sort of dyskinesia.'

So Marguerita was saying that I probably don't know the effect I have on some people, it's just the way I am. Some people think I am crazy. Well, I don't like that. On the other hand, as long as I never have to fall into their clutches, as long as they don't feel they can get a hold of me and treat me accordingly, then I can live with that.

I just can't open my mouth in public without creating problems. I gave a lecture in New York when I was over recently to the inter-agency federation of agencies and I gave an after-luncheon speech on mental handicap and mental deficiency. I heard after that that some people thought it was excellent, while other people thought it was dangerous, unconsidered, and incoherent and completely useless. Another lot felt the exact opposite. I really would like to find a way of earning a steady income so that I didn't have to put myself in such situations any longer. I mean, I can do without that reaction to me. Of course, there are people who think that I am excellent, 'oh, don't give up, it's great for us for you to come and speak to us and don't be put off by, you know, we'll deal with them, it's important for us, don't go away'. It now depends on the mood I'm in when I get an invitation. Sometimes I think, fuck it, I'm not going through this sort of thing again, even though I should maybe put myself through the mincer.

In New York I thought I would produce an interesting argument for discussion on the subject of incest. Now I had absolute sympathy for the moral indignation at fucking children up literally and child abuse. But incest involved all sorts of personal intimacy and there was very little scientific or clinical evidence that had anything to say about this subject and our clinical decisions in the meantime had to made on our ethical position, not on scientific evidence. They got very very angry about that and thought I was a supporter of child abuse and child rape. My argument was that it is not in the long run going to do any good by kidding ourselves that the reason for stopping people doing this to children is on existing scientific grounds. It's not, it's because it is absolutely outrageous. That is an ethical sense of outrage, *which I have* and I'm not about to give it up, but that's the reason why you say to someone – you can't do that. Well, they wanted to have it both ways.

OK.

Look, I would like to aspire to being even-handed. I was just thinking in terms of between 'then and now', maybe I could summarise it. Leaving out The Open Way and Eric Graham Howe, and completely leaving out contacts that developed in the course of the early '60s with the Davidson Clinic in Edinburgh and the couple of little old ladies who bought a house in Dumfrieshire and gave me first refusal – I actually suggested to them that as I wasn't going to take it, they approach Trungpa Rinpoche because he was looking for a Buddhist centre, and now its the major Buddhist centre in Britain, Samye-ling – and leaving out Murial Lester, and the trustees of Kingsley Hall and Kingsley Hall itself.

All of that said, the professional world I worked in – that's

Glasgow University, the world of the Tavistock and the Institute of Psychoanalysis – were all extremely *constrictive*. Their horizons intellectually were less than arms' length in front of them. They prided themselves in this, but the potential creative invention of strategies of relating to the domain that they were concerned about that would be appropriate to this changing world were completely useless. They were not prepared to discuss alternatives. That, for instance, the formal elements of the relationship between the doctor and the patient or the doctor or the social worker and the clients, should be re-thought out. Like the desk, the inevitable desk, the swivel chair behind the desk, the two, maybe one or two, armchairs or side armchairs or one armchair. I eventually designed my own consulting room, very specifically, and so there were three comfortable armchairs that all were of the same status.

There wasn't a throne for the consultant, there were three chairs, plus other chairs around, and there was a roll-top desk or a desk put away beside the window. It wasn't one of the things that I might surprise you with by suddenly getting up and sitting behind it and starting to take notes from that position about them. So from simple issues like that, right the whole way from research design in the social sciences to therapeutic strategic rethinking, you could put their contributions *in a thimble*. They had no imagination or inventiveness in any of these respects. That was my considered opinion at the time and the fact that it was the best in Britain was just too fucking bad. It was pathetic. That's one side.

Did it therefore disappoint you that Charles Rycroft, for example, thinks there is an 'unspoken affinity' between your work and Bowlby's?

I take that from Charles Rycroft as a very considered compliment that he is paying both to Bowlby and to me. I think he probably means it as more of a compliment to Bowlby than he means it to me because he is stretching a bit more credit in his mind to Bowlby than he is to me. He is giving me credit, which is more credit than maybe Bowlby would give me for being thoroughly wised up.

A lot of this is unspoken of, but Bowlby felt that Melanie Klein was a total load of shit and an absolute disaster and thought that if they had got her in time they would have got her out of the country but they weren't able to do so. And he felt that Joan Rivière was probably psychotic and they didn't know what to do about her. Anyway, only over Bowlby's dead body were any Kleinians going to enter the Tavistock Clinic and the children's department when he was there and still had influence.

So Rycroft would also give me absolute credit for sharing the British sensibility of Fairbairn, Guntrip, Ian Suttie, Winnicott; Bowlby in a certain sense; Wilfred Bion definitely, and Marion Milner, Ella Sharpe and Sylvia Payne; Ernest Jones, not quite; maybe Strachey; Alan Tyson very much so, and Peter Lomas.

After I had been seeing him [Rycroft] five times a week on the couch for over two years, I was going on about something that was taking place at the Tavistock – as I say he didn't make interpretations particularly but he made remarks and comments as things struck him – and he said, 'you know one of the things about when you talk, you appear to mean it'. [laughs] Sort of half joking, I said is that supposed to be some psychopathology that you are writing a paper on, 'he means what he says'. He said 'no, no. But it's very unusual'.

Can we talk about your international reputation?

The United States of America. As I said, in Britain *The Divided Self* was turned down by just about every major company, then eventually taken up by Tavistock and then in the USA taken up by an equally bankrupt or small scale or non-swinging concern called Quadrangle Books. In the first four years of *The Divided Self* – I don't know whether anyone took *Self and Others*, I don't know whether anyone took *Interpersonal Perception;* and I don't think anyone in America took *Reason and Violence* – they sold between 1,000 and 2,000 copies in all. *The Politics of Experience* was published by Penguin in this country and it must have been Pantheon who published it in hardback but I don't know whether it was a Pantheon paperback in America.

The William Alanson White Foundation, where Erich Fromm and Rollo May were, is still the major East Coast American institution that carries on that kind of tradition of Harry Stack Sullivan. It is socially and culturally more sensitive to psychoanalysis and has watered down the libido theory and concentrates more on roles and identity, etc., *à la* Karen Horney.

Maybe the heaviest intellectual in the group was Erich Fromm. Well, I gave a series of lectures there in New York about medicine, which have subsequently gone in to bits of this and gone into bits of other things, but the lecture series itself wasn't published. That was in 1967 or 1968. It was packed out, and the amphitheatre held about 1,000 people. I found myself over a period of two weeks giving William Alanson White lectures and it was most unusual in New York City for that number of people to enrol and come along and I realized with some sort of startled amazement that I had made a name for myself in these circles in America.

This had come through with – not *The Politics of Experience*, I think, as much – it was more the professional interest of *Sanity, Madness and the Family*, and *The Divided Self*.

I was invited over to Esalen after *The Politics of Experience* and I didn't know anything about Esalen. It's a gorgeous setting, and it was a fully attended seminar from people I didn't get any feedback from. But Fritz Perls was there for a time, living in Esalen. He had visited Kingsley Hall and he was in tears while there. He said he was tremendously moved by what we were doing here and nothing like it had ever happened and that I didn't realize how great this was, and how it might change the face of the way people went on about this. He thought it might be a new beginning of the end or the end of a new beginning. He was very ebullient and when he was enthusiastic he was very enthusiastic.

Leary had never heard of me when I met him and I had barely heard of him or Alpert. I wasn't back in America at all until after the William Alanson White lectures, and I didn't know that I had become *known*. When I went to Ceylon no one knew me, but when I came back from Ceylon and India I got an invitation. An agent came over from New York, he promoted lectures, and asked me to do a lecture tour, so I went over to America and there I was lecturing to 4,500 people at Santa Monica. I was on the stage a week after Dylan had been there and I was a celebrity.... So I was now suddenly moving in a completely different space and world. I spoke at Harvard, I spoke at Yale, I met Abe Maslow.

I had acquired a number of people who had come to see me in the late '60s, and early '70s, on a basis of this gush of celebrity status, including Chris Stamp who was the manager of The Who. He informed me that The Who were very enthusiastic about me and that the Beatles had also picked me up. The Living Theatre, who were active, well-known and avant garde or radical in terms of theatre had picked me up, as had Julian Beck, their founder.

Timothy Leary had started to drop my name in a number of places. Baba Ram Dass's very widely-sold book, *Be Here Now*, had included my name as one of his list of enlightened people. So in the early '70s I discovered I was in that bracket. I found it very embarrassing, I didn't know how to handle it; people expected me to make all sorts of pronouncements about Richard Nixon and Vietnam and condemn American imperialism and western society and thought I was either an acid head or a Communist. 'Acid Marxist' was a term that stuck.

I saw 'myself' in a bookshop, a volume in a modern masters' series of paperbacks that a guy called Friedenberg, who I had never met, had written. I now had a life out there as R.D. Laing. It was a completely other frame of reference and what people were picking up on was stuff that when I came back from Ceylon I was terribly unenthusiastic about.

All this altered states of consciousness stuff and I had also contempt for the popular attitude about Vietnam. The Americans – it had very little to do with anything else, they just didn't want their bollocks shot away. When the rich sons of America were themselves being called up, and might have to take some sort of risk on the line, then they burned their draft card and fucked off to Canada and all the rest of it.

And Leary's message of 'Turn on, Tune in, Drop out'. I was mentioned by him somewhere and was spoken of in the same breath. It was very embarrassing, I didn't know what to say.

Lectures really frightened me. I would piss and shit myself, start trembling, lose my voice, lose the track of what I was trying to say, develop asthma on the stage and things like that. I mean I actually shat myself once on stage, so I didn't enjoy it, I didn't enjoy the experience. I wasn't able to get behind it and become a demagogue or be a white Martin Luther King. A lot of people had a lot of hopes for me that I would become a populist, counter-culture leader.

This was America, and *Knots*, according to Pantheon, was a turning point in their publication of me. The publishers were not happy about that book, I mean *Knots* was a funny sort of thing, it didn't look like anything else that was around. It didn't receive immediate acclaim or rave notices in Britain either. There were some long and serious reviews or support-

ive reviews, but André Shiffrin at Pantheon said that it was
selling like hot cakes in Fifth Avenue and Madison Avenue
just before Christmas. They kept getting orders from bookshops for more and more *Knots*. They checked this out and it
was typists in offices, young girls who had gone round and
who were all buying it for their boyfriends for Christmas.
They sold a lot of it, and it appealed to a completely different
type of person than they had ever imagined. It wasn't taken
up by intellectuals. I was delighted, that's what I had always
hoped, that I would manage to write something that didn't
have a passing fancy ideological pop-appeal or only a very
esoteric in-group intellectual appeal to some people, but
instead was accessible to any intelligent person.

What has been the situation since Knots?

The Facts of Life, according to André, held its own. He was
really insulting about *Do you Love Me?* He thought that I was
sending him some shavings from my wastepaper basket or
something or leftovers, and I said to him, *it's a fucking book!*
So he didn't want to lose me as an author, so he published it
in quite a nice edition but I don't think he promoted it. The
Conversations with Children book didn't do anything in
America at all, I think it almost completely disappeared. He
didn't like *Sonnets* and he shouldn't have tried to publish it if
he didn't like it. I would rather have had that published by a
small company – it was a sort of anti-poetry piece in a way. I
was trying to write something in formal sonnet form which
was like Flaubert's dictionary of bourgeois sayings where any
metaphor or anything was just out of ordinary speech, but if
you said it in my Scottish accent, if you got the tone of it
there was a ...
       The Voice of Experience held its own as a book in the same
series as a Foucault book at some university departments, and
Wisdom, Madness and Folly has done quite well. Most of them
are still in print in America. The only one that fell out
completely was *Sonnets*.
       They have sustained me in a moderate reputation, but they
are waiting for another hit if another one ever comes. They
imagine it's there, and my reputation in America is probably
higher than it's ever been. I've become an established European, respected controversial celebrity figure of 61 years old.
I've become a name that is known by any intelligent person,

any well-read educated person has heard of R.D. Laing at least and maybe they might have read *The Divided Self, Knots,* or *The Politics of Experience.* They might have read *Wisdom, Madness and Folly,* they might have read one or the other and they are used in different places – literature departments, philosophy departments, in sociology and anthropology as well as in psychiatry – at least I might be an exam question! Along with Harry Stack Sullivan, I might be an exam question. I was asked if I would be on the editorial board of a journal called *Humanistic Psychology.* In it there was a paper by a guy who had raked around the reading lists of psychology departments for who were the people that were taught in the field of humanistic psychology and I'm one of the few standard names that are taught in American universities – Abe Maslow, Rollo May, R.D. Laing, Carl Rogers and that's about it.

Is it impossible to measure the degree to which you have been influential in the USA in terms of psychiatric practice?

I am one of the 20th-century names in psychiatry in every country now in Europe, I'm one of the *names.* And a common thing that I will be told is that, you know, 'you've had a great influence on us, you've influenced us a lot more than you realize. It might not be obvious, but what you've done is you made us think again and those of us who read *Wisdom, Madness and Folly* or *The Divided Self,* that changed my whole life. I saw patients suddenly in a way that I never saw them before, it's not that it's done this or it's done that but it's made us see, it made us realize that these people were human beings'.

So the next country ... Italy?

There was a guy called Vincenzo Caretti who wrote a book, I forget what the Italian title of it is but it became, if not a best-seller, well known in Italy; translated from German, *I Don't Mind Being a Human Being* [Es stört mich nicht ein mensche zu sein]. He interviewed me, edited it and wrote an introduction. He's a professor of philosophy. He knows about R.D. Laing in Italy. I remember him saying 'you'll find yourself up on a student intellectual's bookshelf somewhere between Castaneda and Karl Marx.' In Italy [laughs] ... Maybe that says it all. I am regarded as a European intellectual of the first order of European intellectuals in Italy.

Have there been peaks and troughs in Italy? Is the graph the same as the USA?

It was quite different. According to my Italian friends, although in the long term I don't know what the distribution graphs of my booksales are in Italy, the book that was the most recently successful one in Italy was *Conversations with Children.* That went into railway stations and the Rome airport kiosk. It was a very popular book. I was introduced on television as the author of *Conversations with Children.* I would never be introduced as that on national television in America or Britain.

What about professionally ...

Every psychiatric professional in Italy knows of me and regards me as a major psychiatric figure of their time, if not maybe the most important figure in the 20th century, outside of Italy.

Well known, too, in Greece. I am considered one of the most important psychiatric thinkers in Europe to the Greek psychiatrists. The professor of psychiatry at Athens University, Stephanos, got me over to Athens about four or five years ago to debate the diagnostic value of DSM-3 at his department with the two editors of it. He had been a neurologist until he was appointed Professor of Psychiatry at Athens University, and he knew nothing about psychiatry at all until then. The Greek government didn't believe in psychiatry so they appointed him!

Glasgow University as far as I know has not yet managed to appoint a professor of psychiatry. Glasgow medical school can't stand psychiatrists, the nearest is a neurosurgeon who is the acting professor, entirely neurological and biological. So he [Stephanos] was reading up on psychiatry and he came across me and said that I was the first psychiatrist that he was reading that made any sense to him. I haven't had much contact with Greek psychiatry but the leading Greek psychiatrist apart from him was very ceremoniously honoured to get me to come and speak to a packed meeting at his major mental hospital in Athens.

People and psychiatrists have turned up at three summer seminars that I did in the last 10 years on an island called Kyos, a cultural centre – semi-supported by the Greek government – particulary interested in introducing Greek culture to Greek third- and fourth-generation Americans. There is a Greek diaspora, about 40 or more thousand Greeks – more Greeks, like Irish live in America and in Australia – there are a lot of Greeks, who forgot the Greek language and don't know anything about Greek culture. They invite people of world reputation there: the last time I was there I was talking about Greek tragedy – I was supposed to be talking about human relationships in the dramas of Aeschylus and Sophocles and Euripides.

OK.

Spain. The major public event that I was involved with in Spain was at Madrid University, it was about five, six years ago, and chaired by the president or rector or chancellor of the University. He took me out to lunch afterwards with a Spanish friend of mine who operates an international consultancy agency for corporate bodies and he said that mine was the largest lecture ever attended in the history of the University.

I was at Barcelona this summer at the Conference of the European Association of Humanistic Psychology. Rollo May and I are on their notepaper as special advisors to European Humanistic psychology. At this conference, all my books were displayed there, there was quite a big display of R.D. Laingiana.

OK. Germany?

Surkamp Verlag, I think, published the first three or four of my books and published *The Politics of Experience* under the title of *The Phenomenology of Erfahrung*. I don't know whether you've got a bit of literary German, but *Erfahrung* is an ordinary German word that is often translated as experience. You could translate it as *Erleben* which is more accurate. But our German friends say that they regard it as a very good book in German but it's not *The Politics of Experience*, they published it without *The Bird of Paradise* because they said it was untranslatable, because a bird in German is masculine and the gender stuff of *The Bird of Paradise* was untranslatable. The last book has done very well in Germany ...

Wisdom, Madness and Folly?

Yes, and *Conversations with Children* has done very well. *Conversations with Children*, I don't know whether it was a good tactic, but there was a hell of a lot of theory behind it. I mean I was being anti-Piaget, I thought instead of writing a whole book full of theory about children I would just publish the vignettes, and intelligent people who were interested in children or had children might enjoy it as a casual book. I wanted to give them the idea that it wasn't a trivial matter for a man particularly to enjoy himself with his own kids and quite a number of intellectual men have said to me that they have really enjoyed that book, especially after having some children.

A very nice thing to read on a train to give them a feeling about their relationships with their own children. That was part of, in fact, the main reason for writing it. In Germany and Switzerland they picked up on *Do you love me?* - it was done as it was done in Britain. The BBC did it on radio and Carl Davis wrote the music for it. It was done very carefully by Swiss Radio, and by one of the German radio stations. It was played as a small theatre cabaret thing in Germany. It was, I think, slightly known in the theatre world of that genre in Germany.

Knots is a well-known German book. One of the people that answered our advert for a baby sitter was a schoolgirl, a 17-year-old, something like that. Well, it came to the notice of the school and apparently there are one or two fragments of *Knots* that are taught locally in German schools on their English course. In *Do you Love Me?*, 'Now if not forever is sometimes better than never' - well that's a useful thing in English for schoolchildren too. 'Now if not forever is sometimes better than never'. And that rhyming thing of just a couple of fourliners as a rhyming *aide mémoire* is a popular, old-standing German convention.

What about German psychiatry?

I don't know whether I've had any influence on the inside of German psychiatry in the way that the Americans said I'd given them a different way that has become ingrained - a subtle but important difference. At the [Hanover conference] there were several major German psychiatrists - they were all neuropsychiatric types. There was a meeting of one group that went on for several hours one evening over dinner, and they had all read R.D. Laing, as would apparently any intelligent German psychiatrist. So I was one of their stock-in-trade figures. They might be cautious about when or in what way they would introduce my work to their students, I think, but they definitely take me seriously at their level as one of them.

What have been the highs and lows in your British publishing career?

For a number of years I got the Durrant clipping service and my name cropped up quite often. I was really pissed off, you might say, at the *The British Journal of Psychiatry* which never reviewed any of my books, I don't think. And they turned down about four papers that I sent to them in my early days. The Maudsley's and Aubrey Lewis's attitude was that I never crossed the portals.

In terms of the real world outside of psychiatry, Philip Toynbee reviewed *The Divided Self* in *The Observer* when it first came out and I was aware that it was a very lucky shot that a guy like him, who was a very well-known reviewer, would pick that out to review. He reviewed it in a favourable and sympathetic way. Julian Huxley invited me to give a paper to the Royal Society in about 1964, the only paper I have given in that company, at a conference on ethology.

Roy Fuller was the name of the guy who wrote a piece in *The Listener* about *Knots*. *Knots* was being put down and I think he felt that he ought to say something about it just to give people the idea that this was a serious literary effort. Oh yes, he said that it was in the same league as the three Eliots. I don't know what that would be, T.S. Eliot, George Eliot or – but that was a sort of accolade. I was friends with Alan and Ruth Sillitoe and he had stayed in Morocco and was friends with Robert Graves. Robert Graves took me seriously as 'the most evil man in the world' apparently. But I met him and he treated me perfectly well.

When I met Sartre, Marcelle, my French girlfriend, was at the long meeting I had with him. I only met him once. I could have met him again, but on that one occasion we had about five or six hours of intense talking about his work. When we came away from that she said that the thing that most impressed her was that he treated me as a complete equal, and he did. In a way I took it for granted that he would, but

I also needed her to remind me that Sartre, who was a big figure, treated me absolutely straight, on the level.

I'm not above reacting as being delighted or pissed off at the way a book is reviewed. Geoffrey Gorer wrote about as nasty a put-down review as his pen could find, I think, in *The Guardian* on *The Facts of Life* when it came out. He was adopting the view that I had been an *enfant terrible* of the '60s and now after a lapse of several years I'd written *The Facts of Life*, and this showed that in effect that I was a played out and damp squib, and that there was nothing there in the first place. And that I – he must have got this from Bowlby I thought, or Sutherland – couldn't even bear the minimal discipline of the Tavistock Clinic, so had fucked off. I'd met Gorer on one occasion, at his house. I wondered what the fucking hell is he talking about, where had he got this from, what was he going on about, what had I done to him? I never met Peter Sedgwick except glancingly in the early '70s after he had contributed to *Laing and Anti-psychiatry*.

What did you make of his contribution to Laing and Anti-psychiatry?

I was very pissed off at Deborah Rogers [literary agent] and Neil Middleton [publisher] over that book. They were both – especially Deborah Rogers – great admirers and friends of David Cooper's. Well, I thought that she and Neil Middleton had really done me a publishing disservice by encouraging my alleged association with anti-psychiatry. I was questioned at different times by many journalists, and sometimes they didn't publish what I actually said, because they were determined to have this mythological storyline of anti-psychiatry and an anti-psychiatric movement that never existed in the way that they said. They had Cooper, or Cooper and Laing, as the joint prophets of it.

Again and again, I had said to David Cooper – 'David, it is a fucking disaster to put out this term.' But he'd a devilish side that thought it would just serve them all right and confuse them. So let's just fuck them with it. But I didn't like that.

Sedgwick?

Oh, I had mixed feelings about Sedgwick because Sedgwick took me seriously and was earnest. I thought Sedgwick was

honest in this respect, namely that he had serious objections
to what he thought I was on about that mattered to him. I
thought of writing to him and saying you're putting some sort
of ideological map in front of you, in terms of which you see
me, but it doesn't correspond. 'Your reading of me going off
to Ceylon is completely wrong, there is no comparison to be
made with the Spanish Civil War of going behind the Franco
lines to a monastery and so on, when one is supposed to be
on the government side. It's ridiculous, it wasn't any declaration of anything, and meditation isn't a betrayal of the cause.
You don't know what you are talking about. How about when
you are next in London, we'll go out and have a walk on
Hampstead Heath and have a chat about these things?'.

Then he wrote something else that he was obviously very
worked up about to do with the so-called schizophrenic
voyage and I was very sensitive to his ideological criticism of
this piece that I had put out. I was sensitive to it in that I
thought that it was doing two things that I didn't like; firstly,
that I was being misunderstood, and secondly what I thought
was important that led to me to write the thing was being lost
by this misunderstanding criticism which was impervious in its
tone really. It was belligerent and polemical. It wasn't the
tone that you could answer in a quiet tone of voice.

Why did Thomas Szasz and Peter Sedgwick from opposite
positions converge on attacking this proposal that I'd never
gone on about, which consists of about four – apart from 'A
Ten Day Voyage' – pages in The Politics of Experience? I never
took it up in The Politics of the Family and I never took it up
in Knots and at that time that was all they had to go on with;
no one ever mentioned 'The Coldness of Death' chapter in
Self and Others, no one.

I mean, people treated it as some sort of salon fashionable
idea and never related it to Jesse Watkins who is about 70
years old now and had been in the Navy and been through it
and was a hard-working sculptor and a very decent guy. This
had been a hell of an experience for him that he had come
through, and there was something to be said for not treating
him as a total nutcase and letting him have a place where he
could go through all that number and come back. And no one
seemed to be interested that this referred to actual people and
that I wasn't glorifying madness or anything. I went so far as
to quote Harry Stack Sullivan saying that when it comes to
the bit that the schizophrenic is simply human, they are as

human as we are, but cracked. I never said that they weren't cracked, and I also frightened some people as well as reassuring them by saying that you and I could crack up also, and how would *you* like to be treated? These characters they could be us, they *are* us. Well Sedgwick didn't respond to that which I thought was in what I had written. Someone said that he had a sister who had been diagnosed as schizophrenic.

My attitude to Sedgwick was a double one, not a personal one because I never met him. I was glad that, although I had these criticism of Sedgwick, that he was a serious sociological observer of this field and was addressing my work seriously and with intelligence, but I was pissed off that he was, I thought, in some blindly woeful way, batting at laying on anti-psychiatry and positions that I didn't see myself occupying.

Was he the most serious critic, in retrospect?

I don't remember, I was missing most of that time. I was picked up by this or that person in California, I was being stolen from extensively of course, and was being marketed like a 'trip' similar to *The Primal Scream*. I was being associated with the wrong sort of people in terms of this 'voyage' idea. I sometimes wished I'd never written those few pages because they were picked up with such excessive dust around them, it was obscuring the whole sober, non-acid, non-trippy, ordinariness of, and misery of, a lot of that sort of thing. The idea that I was glorifying it, or recommending it was ridiculous. Someone compared me to a colonel; I think this was a piece in the *Village Voice*, 'we didn't need people like Laing, like a colonel, ordering the men over the top to be mowed down. He was alright sitting in his base camp at high command'.

The real people who went through different numbers and came to me when they were in distress, told a different story. I never found a way of writing intimately enough about what really goes on or went on between me and people who were patients or clients of mine because the real stuff always still does involve talking about intimate issues. You've got to change details to fictionalize it as obviously Freud did. Jung never wrote any case histories. It's very difficult to do that.

About Rogers and Middleton ... that really bothered you?

I understood that Deborah Rogers and David had been falling apart in London and she, I think, felt very affectionately *engagé* with David. I don't think there was any affair that he and she had, but she was very fond of David. David had an appeal to a certain sort of mind. Neil Middleton also liked David Cooper's mind, and *The Grammar of Living* and *The Death of the Family*. I, myself, liked David personally, but I didn't like his books, although I liked his mind. I thought it was a terribly sloppy thing for anyone to read one of my books and read one of David's books and to muddle us up. If they couldn't see the difference, what *were* they capable of discriminating between? And I like Deborah Rogers too, and so I thought there was no point complaining to her. That was simply her taste. Neil Middleton was more subtle.

I know the difference that *you* were talking about, when you asked me whether my next book would be a *major* book? Well, Neil Middleton would say a *serious* book. He didn't think – maybe it *didn't* work – much of *Do you Love Me?* But I mean, I was really serious. I can imagine if I've got a future and I recycled some things, I could make them more accessible. As well as conventional ordinary English prose I began to produce another type of writing. I mean I had always written in that way but the right-hand-side came out more first of all, and then there was an undercurrent that I wanted to integrate and give expression to. It came out first of all in *The Bird of Paradise* and then that side of it came out in *Knots*. But that's a very dangerous space, *Knots*.

In terms of my literary destiny I liked being included in a few anthologies. There was an anthology of western poetry in America called *The Western Wind* in which a couple of 'Knots' were included. It was a university anthology in which the editor anthologised different genres of poetry and wrote an explanatory critical commentary on them. He took some 'Knots' and said 'here, there is no clothing, there is no colour, there is no content, the text is suspended in a space where you know there are no trees, there is no grass there is no evening, nothing, it's just that, there'. He compared it to Sappho. A particular poem of Sappho that I greatly admire is where you don't know where they are, what they are doing, just suspended in a timeless triangle of space, all you can infer is that there is a woman speaking to a woman about a man who is there – 'how can he look at you, so unruly, he's empty like a God, while I am' – and you don't know whether they are sitting on a park bench or an island or anywhere or what the time and space is.

Well, that was very much what I was hoping would come across the page, something like that would last, too, in *Knots*. I would like to deserve a place in European literature, *a small place*. One of the best compliments that I've had – I could publish an anthology of the insults I've had – was from Christopher Isherwood, who said that he'd include the last two pages of *The Divided Self* in any anthology of 20th-century English prose. There are a number of people that I've come to know who have treated me with great respect as a writer – like Ted Hughes and William Burroughs.

Have you ever felt that a lot of people think that you've done your real *work already?*

As a celebrity in America, when I give a celebrity lecture, I get introduced as *R.D. Laing*. But they actually mean an author who died about 25 years ago, as they've never heard or read anything I've written since about 1962. I got up at one thing after being introduced like this, and I said that a friend of mine had told me a story about Fred Astaire. Well, Fred Astaire said to her – this is a true story – that someone had come up to him at a party and said, 'did you used to be Fred Astaire?'. You know – did you used to be R.D. Laing? Well, that would worry me actually but although I never thought that *The Voice of Experience* would be a popular book, and in fact it was almost completely ignored in America, it's taken very seriously in Germany. There it's called the *Stimme of Experience* and it's considered a serious, major work. This is one of the things about Germany, that the last 10 years of my writing has enhanced my reputation. I've come to be regarded as a deeper European thinker from *The Facts of life* and *The Voice of Experience* and *Wisdom, Madness and Folly*: three books of the last 15 years that are taken *not* as a sign of decline.

The Voice of Experience is better written and more densely thought out and has got some claim to be a serious philosophical text, I think, in a way I don't think any of my other books have. They do not have that dense fibre to them.

Neil Middleton – I can't remember his exact words – but he gave me some upbeat compliment about it as a piece of writing. I don't think he liked anything that I'd written very much since *The Politics of the Family* and *Knots*, but he was unembarrassedly complimentary to me about *The Voice of Experience* as 'a very good read'.

When I talk about R.D. Laing, some people say 'where is he?', or that you're burnt out.

Well, I'm the last person to get direct comments like this. I mean, people don't come and tell me that people are saying that I'm burnt out on the whole, but I sense ....

Do people see the writing of your memoirs as a sign that you're rounding up your life? Do you know what I am getting at?

I wanted to fill in the gap in my presentation of myself, because of so much nonsense. For instance, where did people think *The Divided Self* had come from? I would get terrible cheek from people as though they were telling their granny how to suck eggs. I mean, they were talking to me about R.D. Laing as though I didn't know anything about him. You know I must have done *some* homework before I wrote that book. I wasn't this Acid Marxist type of person, I was actually a Scottish Presbyterian, Trotskyist-phenomenological-anarchist, a religious atheist, and God knows what else, and had been in padded cells in the British Army and all that fucking stuff, and with a mental hospital experience, and came out with *The Divided Self*.

I was wanting to clear my own mind for what I'm writing now, I wanted to get that out and be able to forget about my early life sufficiently so I could go on to what remained of my future. So I *wasn't* saying ta ta. [laughs]. I also realized that I had never written anything really about what I thought about present-day psychiatry.

Recently I had quite a lot of material, ideas about psychiatry, stuff about the '70s, attitudes about obstetrics and Sheila Kitzinger and Leboyer and Michel Odent, to a lesser extent. That resulted in a book that I wrote of about 30,000 words that never got published – *The Politics of Birth*. I don't know what happened to it actually, it was presented as a preliminary text to go along with a picture book on birth and the whole thing got lost somewhere in the Penguin shuffle.

I didn't know what *Wisdom, Madness and Folly* was going to turn out to be, whether it was going to be a full memoir or autobiography, or whether it should have my statement about psychiatry in it. My main problem was putting it together, which is also my main problem about the present book. When I open a book – not a vast book like Spengler's *The Decline of the West* – a reasonable sized book that I can't read in one reading exactly but might take a few days or a week to read, I want to be able to read something that has got a compelling unity and momentum that pulls me on to finish it. It is a false distinction in a way, but there is a certain distinction between form and content, and I think the form of *Do you Love Me?* didn't work. It is so minimalist that you can just read it right through and not get caught in the page. It was like an etching or Haiku, you could get through the whole book in about 20 minutes just like that and you wouldn't see anything in it.

Especially after one writes your first one or two books you get into the deeper waters of the strategy of the interface between what comes from you on to the page to what that page is like to someone who reads it. Sometimes it just falls into place and sometimes there is a lot of work to be done at that, some very conscious craftsmanship. Sometimes you can miscalculate. The effect of that book allowed it to be treated as a trivial, non-serious book that I didn't intend it to be and that was a fault of calculation. Anthony Burgess liked *Do you Love Me?*, that was very nice for me. He appreciated it. I mean it looks as though a sixth-former might have written it in some respects, but it was very encouraging for me that he could see that I had, in fact, put a lot of calculated effort into it.

South America and Australasia, were they the outposts of your influence?

I'm told that I'm seen as one of the major European intellectuals in Latin America, in Brazil and the Argentine. I was over in Brazil, in Rio, eight or ten years ago and I was treated as a major intellectual figure. At Sao Paulo University Medical School, Rio, I was talking to packed audiences as a celebrity. My visit was compared to the visit that Jung made. I'm obviously *R.D.Laing* well before I get there.

And what about the Soviet Union, Eastern Europe, and China? Or hasn't your work reached there?

I have been told by one of my American friends who has spent some time in China that Chinese intellectuals are completely aware of me and that if I ever wanted to go over to China I could go over in some sort of capacity. I've never taken that invitation up. I'm well-known in Hungary, well-known in Yugoslavia; *Conversations with Children* has just been translated into Hungarian, and apparently it's doing very well there and in Yugoslavia. I don't know first hand about Poland; a Russian intellectual who knows anything about who is who in Europe certainly knows R.D. Laing. I was told that I'm 'restricted reading' in Russia. I'm one of those books that if you're a member of the Party you can get, but are not on general sale in bookshops. Intellectual members of the party know of R.D. Laing.

People talk about Ginsberg's Howl *and the Beat literature, and sometimes say that the same kind of romanticism permeated your writing on madness. The notion of romanticism is a very trivial one, isn't it?*

The way it is used ...

The way they perceive your work ...

Yes. I had absolutely or virtually no awareness at the time of the 1950s Beat literature and when I *did* come across Kerouac – I don't think I ever got through a book of Kerouac's – I couldn't stand him. I came across *Howl* shortly after it came out in the Ferlinghetti book and I appreciated it. I appreciated it as a voice from across the ocean, from another world that was a contemporary voice that had an immediate presence. But I don't think it had the slightest effect on where I was going. It was like hearing music coming from a station in a train that went through the station in the middle of the night. I had no particular affinity to the sensibility from which that came and the social context of it was entirely foreign to me.

The first time I was ever in America, I went over to San Francisco in the first place and was going to New York. I flew into Kennedy Airport from San Francisco and the impact of the airport was overwhelming – I got as far as the exit and turned back and got myself on a plane and flew right back to London.

Really?

Yes. I was absolutely terrified at New York airport. I mean, San Francisco was nothing like it, it was another kettle of fish. I had never been anywhere like Kennedy Airport. New York was another kettle of fish – the vastness of it, it was like a Fritz Lang *Metropolis* set.

It strikes me that France is a country that might appreciate someone like you.

My reading of what happened in France is that I was picked up fairly early on. Sartre told me that Simone de Beauvoir had read *The Divided Self* and recommended it to him, brought it to his attention. Then I originally did a piece on *Critique of Dialectical Reason* partly as an exercise in mastering Sartre's French – and the way it came out, it was that it was not quite big enough for a book. In a way it was *en passant* for me, it was an intellectual exercise in translation and condensation. I didn't feel like taking the rest of Sartre and backing up that text with a critique and a more extended exposition.

I sent it to Sartre and I sent repeated letters to him – I think Marcelle actually took one round to him – for about two-and-a-half years before I got any response. In the meantime I suggested to David Cooper that he did a number on the Genet book and then there was the smaller essay on method, so that was put together. I don't know whether Sartre ever read Cooper's pieces. Eventually I met him with Marcelle and a girlfriend of his. At his instigation the four of us sat in the bar of the Palais Royale hotel which he hung out in. We talked solidly, he talked mainly, for about six hours solid. He set the pace. Every 20 minutes or so he would order whatever he was drinking, double dry martinis. I was drinking whisky. The energy he had was quite amazing as was the sustained *engagément* that he had which was quite remarkable. I never met a comparable character to Sartre, in fact I never met anyone comparable to him in that quality of brilliance and absolute concentration.

Though I didn't know anyone else personally, I never 'met' a major French intellectual I felt drawn to seeking out. But from the way he treated me I assumed that, in the intellectual world of Paris, I had come to their attention as a new figure in the club. But I had no contacts with anyone at all. I was told that after the French student boogaloo in 1968 that some of them – after it was all over, after the dust settled – tried to find out what they had been going on about. Apparently they weren't particularly well read, that it was a so-called spontaneous number! My French publishers told me that a couple of my books had been translated, *Self and Others* had been accepted by Gallimard and also *The Divided Self*. I don't know whether others had been published. I think *The Politics of Experience* was, or maybe they discovered it from its American popularity.

It was a campus best-seller at the time and I became one of the reference points for students in Italy and Germany in the late '60s – like Marcuse.

Do you think you influenced French psychiatry?

Yes, I think I became known among French psychiatrists. I became very confused with David Cooper, even more so, because David went to live in France and I think for a few years he became better known than me because of his actual presence there. Every time I read a reference to me in a French newspaper or journal, I would be bracketed with Cooper and insistently referred to as 'the father of anti-psychiatry'. Actually, on the occasion that I was over in Paris once in the early '70s, I was invited round to an evening at Félix Guattari's house and so I went round with Marcelle. She'll probably remember this occasion. I never got on with Guattari. He had written *Anti-Oedipus* with Deleuze and I thought it was just intellectual wanking. But he asked me to give him my autograph and I was just about to do so and turned over the back of the place where I was supposed to be putting my signature and found out it was a petition to the president of France to release a terrorist hijacker. I was very angry and didn't actually storm out of his house but I told him, in my Glasgwegian, that it was an absolute piece of impertinence to ask me to sign something like that that I had never seen. And *had* I seen it, I wouldn't begin to sign it. I thought they were all completely phoney – all the things Szasz might have to say about the phoney radical salon revolutionary left, well this was them, the Guattari crowd.

How influential were Sartre and Camus to you?

I was moved by both of them, intellectually and emotionally, moved by both of them in their different ways. I had to be more influenced by Sartre to take the trouble to do the Critique of Dialectical Reason; I saw that *L'Être et le Néant* was a text which was a fair effort to cover the ground that Freud covered, objectifying and translating the existalia of the person into a meta-psychology of energy dynamics in an attempt to work out all that stuff between the latent and manifest.

Sartre tried to do two things I think that Freud completely had no ear for or no nose for. In *Being and Nothingness*, in his prolonged discussion of object and subject/object and inter-subjectivity it was sufficiently visible that he was trying to do something that was important to do and I found that encouraging. It opened up the question mark; it's always a bit easier when someone at least opens the page, starts the book off even though they don't fill it up.

His theory of bad faith as an attempt to talk about degrees of self deception à la *Psychopathology of Everyday Life*, where you don't have to use a meta-psychology to account for how you can lie to yourself and deceive yourself and other people at that same time. I liked that. A smaller book, *The Psychology of Imagination*, I really read that in detail. I hadn't come across any other text that discussed imagination in those terms and also his theory of the emotions seemed such a breath of fresh air.

I never read any of the philosophy of emotions except the 18th-century work, the philosophy of sentiment, the man of sentiment. The only discussion of emotion I had come across was in medical school in terms of Cannon and 'affect and emotion', and Darwin of course. It woke me up that here was a serious phenomenology of emotionality.

This is the Sketch? [For a Theory of Emotions]

Yes the *Sketch*. It was just a small book, but again it was enough to wake up a dormant centre.

Presumably things like The Outsider *by Camus, Meursault's right to be himself and with his view of the world being completely alien to everyone else's ... that must have stuck in your mind?*

Oh yes, the double, Camus and Kafka, and the stuff that Colin Wilson in effect anthologised, were meat and drink to me at the time. It was a direct and immediate background influence on the sensibility of *The Divided Self*. I don't think there was anything as immediate and as telling – not influential in the form of immediate doctrine – as all that *genre* was. I don't think

I subscribed to *Les Temps Modernes*, but I was at the bookshop to pick it up as every edition came out and I followed it in detail. I was very affected by the prolonged argument that went on in these pages between Sartre and Camus after *L'Homme révolté*. I suspected that if such passion could exist about a fine scholastic point there might be all sorts of emotional sexual politics going on that could colour a philosopher's reason in that respect. This provoked me to write the first unpublished paper for this existential group or whatever you want to call it in Glasgow. It was on the ontology of human relationships, and in it I rattled through Kierkegaard and Descartes, and Kierkegaard and Sartre, Buber and Camus, in terms of whether you could give – as Sartre would argue you couldn't – an ontological status to the We, or whether that was a sort of schmucky sentimental smudge on intellectual clarity.

There were somewhat technical arguments like this that we were having in Glasgow. Arguments about the correct understanding of Heidegger's *mit sein* in *Sein und Zeit*. John Macquarrie was working on the translation which I thought was a total disaster and at times I tried to persuade him that the whole point of Heidegger was totally lost by translating *sein*, which is the German infinitive of the verb to be, *sein*, by 'being'. I mean, the main thread of the whole book is to distinguish the infinitive from the present past.

14. PSYCHIATRY AND SCHIZOPHRENIA

Much of R.D. Laing's professional career, especially in the early years, was spent with chronically disturbed psychotic patients.

The Divided Self's central argument was that schizophrenic behaviour was, in fact, far more intelligible than it was thought to be, if enough time, skill and compassion was expended in trying to understand it.

Laing held strong views as to what the concept of 'normality' actually entailed, and also of what constituted as evidence in the debate surrounding the 'cause' of schizophrenia.

In Psychoanalysis Observed, *the Rycroft book, Peter Lomas argued for a satisfactory language with which to discuss human relationships in a scientific way. He said he was worried about the fruitful channels open to psychoanalysis being neglected by 'the existentialists'. Could the existentialists afford, he argued, to put aside the technique of transference interpretation, and had they paid sufficient attention to guilt, mourning, depression, child development 'or to the fact that there are two sexes involved in human intercourse'? And so on. Has he got a point?*

I think he's got a point in every one of those things. It is something to be careful about. I've only written about what I've written about, and I haven't written about the whole range of all these things, particularly transference. I've never written about transference head-on. What Lomas is influenced by is a combination of Murray Parkes and Bowlby in terms of guilt, mourning and separation. Object Loss. Object loss is what is behind all that. I am sufficiently alert to the importance of object loss in development and in adult relationships and its bearing on transference. It entails subtle aspects of transference in terms of introjection and turning a good object into a bad object and idealisation and splitting and all the rest of it.

Melanie Klein's projection of all this on to children is *bizarre*.

But if you don't do that and simply take all this problematic of projection, introjection and projection and splitting and apply it to transference between adults, as a number of people have tried to do, maybe that's the way it will be carried forward. There's a lot in it. The only book that I wrote that really covers or intersects with that is *Self and Others*.

After that I went onto the two family books, and after that nothing. The fragments in *The Facts of Life* really don't count. *The Voice of Experience* would be, to them, alarming because – without talking about revival of pre-natal memories – the comparison between pre-natal patterns, pre-birth patterns and adult patterns and transformations is very, very strange to this type of mind. So it is a big undeveloped area in the corpus of Laing's work *so far*.

I think it would be absolutely fair enough for me to write a paper on transference. My reason for not writing a paper on transference is as follows. What I've been working on particularly in the last year, is a skeletal ontological framework in which I can talk about triadic relations and from there between you, him and her, or you and me and him and her. Triadic processes instead of an ego. See I want a third; I want to be able to designate the other in terms of you or her, and I can't do this in ordinary object relations theory because – if I project *her* on to you, I'm projecting not the object *her*, it's *her*, if you become a *her*, it's another way at looking at transference.

Or you separate from a woman who has for a number of years been with you, suddenly you are talking about *her*. It's a different experience, suddenly this woman that you made love with and lived with is a *her* in your life and in a sense you know that's the end of it, once she's *her*. I've lost you and you are just another *her*, that's a terrible thing to say to anyone. I mean that could break someone's heart.

Well, that there's that and I certainly want to get to my own statement of transference. Also, Peter Lomas is talking from detailed work that we did together, he was working with Balint when I was working on my own work with families and we would talk about things and he obviously hopes I won't forget these things that he thinks are important. Maybe I'm inclined for instance, in the family side to not bring out into sharp enough contrast the fact that actually men and women are different.

It's a criticism that has been made and it might be right about *Sanity, Madness and the Family*, that these eleven families could have been written up and could have been men. That's maybe justified, and in the arguments about the counterpoint of experience, the Dostoevsky chapter and 'driving the other person crazy' and indeed all through the *Self and Others*. I think now I would sharpen up the colour contrast.

Looking back on it *now*, I think that it is evident that there is an absence of sisters in my life. I had a mother and aunts and a granny, so there was no absence of women in that sense and once I'd got over my initial shyness with girls, I would say that I've had an unbizarre but sort of up-and-down relationship with women. But for a number of years I never had any particular, sisterly, friendly relationship with women.

Sisterly, friendly relationship that wasn't a sexual one you might say. You know I don't know what I actually mean – what is a sister?

In Wisdom, Madness and Folly, *you talk about shamans, medicine men and so on, and say 'a mental healer may be a psychiatrist, a psychiatrist may or may not be a mental healer.' How seriously have you come to believe this?*

You can't get very much from books in that respect. One of the most delightful academic compliments I ever received was from Mircea Eliade inviting me to contribute a chapter on shamanism. I know comparatively little about shamanism except from one or two shamans that I've actually met. Native American, Indian or black African or Mexican characters who were medicine men. We got on very, very well. I mean they immediately accepted me as one of them.

I realised that shamanism is a phrase like totemism, it comes from one location that has been adopted world wide, I think shamanism was originally an Anglofication of an eskimo and Lapland word for their medicine man and spread to cover all sorts of medicine men now so-called, whether they are in the south or middle of Africa or anywhere in the landmass. They go into themselves – egoless states, altered states – they retrieve or have access to alternative states of being or consciousness in which they carry out healing processes which are traditionally embedded in the traditions of the society. Gregory Bateson was extremely interested in this sort of thing and we talked a lot about it. I never witnessed any convincing healing ceremonies, but I felt sufficiently close to it to feel that I knew enough about it to write that sentence seriously.

You say that 'psychiatry is the only branch of medicine that treats people physically in the absence of any known physical pathology', and that it treats conduct alone. Do you think that we will never cease saying that?

Social engineering in the modern technological socio-economic society such as we have is going to have more and more experts in population control and doctors. The medical profession may lose it's front-line position as the most prestigious organisation that does that. It might be transferred empirically or pragmatically to some other group of people. Nonetheless doctors have a monopoly on drugs and other instrumentalities at the moment for stopping and starting conduct and experience, and I don't think it's likely that any other group in the immediate future will take their place. Who is going to do it? Will social workers up-grade themselves and take over? It will be a long time before the head of a mental-health community organisation has not got a medical degree.

The school, the teacher, parents, and corporate bodies and military establishments have got to find some group who they can refer their problem characters to, either to get them out or to cool them or at least do something to them. The Tavistock gained financial prestige as much as anything, by virtue of a paper written by Ron Hargreave at the beginning of the war which went to 'A branch', called the 'Economic Use of Manpower in the British Army'. In a conscript army you have to sort people out quickly and put them into tank corps, put them into a regiment, use them as combat soldiers and so on, and you have to do aptitude tests to see what sort of people are best adapted to do particular sorts of work. All of which is predictive; you knew how they were going to turn out. Well, psychiatrists in the German and British Armies, and possibly the Russian and American Armies, got recruited into that and became the advisors to the military. This gave them a position that they had never had before which carried into the bureaucratic planning of the population in civilian life after World War II.

Do we know enough about the history of western civilization to speculate about a time when people accepted difference?

Well, I think until the middle of the 19th century the mass of the population were not monitored to anything like the same extent that they came to be when it became necessary to educate far more people – to the extent of them being able to read written instructions of obedience. You had to educate people to have arithmetic and be literate for the organisation of society that evolved.

I found Donzelot's book, *The Policing of Families*, very illuminating in that respect. In a book like *Malleus Maleficarum* they are talking about a 17th-century population where most of the people have never come to their notice, they haven't set up schools, they haven't factories to produce a particular kind of human product. The reason for doing that is a consumer demand – the consumers being industrialists – and the government needs some sort of person to service the new technology of production.

You've mentioned that when you took a history of a patient it was like 'a detective investigation'.

Oh, I got absolutely fed up taking these interminable histories where, as you know, you rattle through it and it never seems to be getting anywhere. The data was never going to be used anyway, in a way it might be used nowadays in computerised fashion.

You could say that Oedipus is the first detective in the western world. Something is wrong, something is the matter – what is, who is, if there is someone, who is the criminal? And he investigates that.

Liam Hudson has written papers about the backgrounds and motivation of various medical specialists – for instance why someone wants to become a paediatrician, or a gynaecologist. If I remember correctly, he is scathing about the competence of psychiatrists. Do you think that one of the problems is simply the recruitment?

I'm not in a position to answer that question in a competent way. One of the things that was held against me by Martin Roth and Morris Carstairs in the mid-'70s was that my books having got through to medical students had resulted in a drop of 10 per cent in recruitment into psychiatry. There had, of course, been a few distinguished minds in psychiatry, like Maudsley – I think he was professor at the age of 26 – and some very intelligent people became psychiatrists but until World War II there was only one professorship of psychiatry outside of London, I think. Edinburgh University had a chair in psychiatry, there was no professor of psychiatry at any other Scottish university, and there was no chair in psychiatry anywhere else in England. What was the question?

Recruitment ...

Oh yes, well the top psychiatrists would tend to lament the fact that psychiatry tended to get the dregs of the medical profession. If you couldn't make it in medicine or surgery or paediatrics and didn't want to be cast out into the outer darkness of being a family doctor and you wanted an easy life, you became a psychiatrist. You would settle into a mental hospital. Until the last 20 years or so, psychiatry was basically working in a mental hospital. Psychiatrists weren't out and about. You wouldn't become a psychiatrist by *choice*, you would become a neurologist by choice and then if you were interested in the finer points of the mind, you became a neuropsychiatrist.

Because psychiatry is the most difficult branch of medicine in some respects, is there a tendency for some of them to lapse into an easy way of doing the job?

Oh yes, very easy indeed, and it's very disheartening because in terms of the job you are expected to do, there doesn't seem to be very much point in keeping particularly awake while you are doing it. You are just turning a handle. In some study that was made in America, it found that the length of time it took to diagnose someone with schizophrenia in America was about 3 minutes. The psychiatrists were under the impression it would take them about 20 minutes to 40 minutes, but in fact they came to their diagnosis very very quickly. There was no point in going into more detail. That was it. The outcome was already pre-determined and that meant hospitalization, observation and then treatment. And treatment consisted of about half dozen drugs and half a dozen levels of dosage.

Can we talk about the theories of genetic causation of schizophrenia ...

Have you read a paper I wrote a long time ago which is published by Richard Evans? It looks at the whole of the genetic evidence up to 1960 and, I think, completely destroys it. It was turned down by the *British Journal of Psychiatry* and another couple of journals but was eventually published by Richard Evans in *Laing, the Man and his Ideas*. Well, if you apply the critical apparatus of that paper to any paper you read, then you will realize that any study that purports to offer scientific evidence about the genetic component of the thing has got to meet certain criteria and they don't. They are all propaganda pieces and I think they kid themselves. But there's another way. If you collect – if you get from Martin Roth – I mean you don't have to be polite to Martin Roth particularly, you've got nothing to lose. Ask Martin Roth to give you the hard data that he is basing his statements on, not the blah blah blah but the papers he would stake his generalizations on and give them to me and I'll go over them with you. The leading medical geneticist at the time I wrote the paper is a guy called Penrose; there was also Planansky, there were four of them altogether, and I've got correspondence from all of them in my files. I got letters from all of them saying that they completely agreed with me. That there was this embarrassing spot, there is no genuine reason for what psychiatry says is a genetic relationship to schizophrenia. Mind you, even if there is, all it means is that there is a certain mental style that is hated and cultured out by our society.

Does it appal you that the only kind of initiative in terms of government funding is attempts at further and further clarification of genetic components?

Well, it must have a function for government. Yes, it does appal me but you can see the logic of it. It is just like this IQ stuff and so on.

Can we talk about identical twins?

You have to do two things if the concordance rate is genetic. I mean how high are they going to put it. No one has ever claimed that it is 100 per cent. They can't do that, whether they separate at birth or grow up together. The thing to ask is what is the highest concordance rate that they are claiming in a series of how many? You must take the whole population. You can't take the cohorts from hospitalized or diagnosed schizophrenics and find the other ones that haven't. You've got to have the whole thing from the beginning. It's a completely biased sample if you only take the twin, identical or non identical, brother or sister, of someone who has wound up in mental hospital with schizophrenia. You'll never find them anyway, you can't do it that way. Denmark was the only country for many years which had that sort of data. I think they had something like 60 per cent who were separated and 80 per cent brought up together. Now this is a soft argument from my point of view but lets look at it for a moment. That means that 30 per cent of schizophrenics would have to be said to be non-genetic. That's a hell of a lot – one out of three are not. What happens then is that they switch feet and say 'oh it's a mis-diagnosis' or in the case of [Slater's study] which still crops up being quoted, he made up the diagnosis. I mean quite literally made it up, and I put that in the paper, if someone wasn't diagnosed as schizophrenic he said that they must have been and counted that as a concordance.

All of these studies are looking for concordance, and there is a tremendous bias for saying that a person shows signs of schizophrenia because of the way the whole thing is set up. There is no scientific validity in these studies because there is a bias towards what you are looking for. It is such an obvious biased fault in research design that it's absolutely inexusable in 1989 that anyone should try to establish credibility on a design like that. The only reason they still keep it up is because they haven't got the nerve to put it to a real test. I have never come out with a general theory of schizophrenia because I've said that the whole category and the whole thing is so corrupt in its intellectual first principles and in terms of the design and application of anything to test it, that it is undiscussable really.

Barbara Robb's Sans Everything. *You don't talk in your memoirs about the kind of things that people like Robb talked of; about nurses and auxiliaries being cruel towards patients. Was that a thing that you didn't notice or did you come to accept it as part and parcel of what life was like in those wards?*

I didn't want to alienate the nursing profession any more than necessary.

What, in your memoirs?

Yes. That sort of thing can happen with any group of people. It's not a systematic policy to be cruel to patients, and these scandals are the sort of thing that you keep on reading about. Nurses are tremendously sensitive about that. I thought I would restrict myself to what I knew more immediately about. Although it might not look like it to some people, I was falling over backwards not to needlessly create resistance to the point of view I was trying to make.

Let me turn to Myerson's review in the American Journal of Psychiatry *of Kierkegaard's concept of dread. He says that it is interesting because it presents strong evidence that Kierkegaard himself is a psychiatric case ...*

Yes, and I didn't actually mention Jock Sutherland's name there – he was the Director of the Tavistock Clinic, and now is the director of the Scottish Institute of Human Relations. *Sutherland.* He had this insufferable complacent attitude to anything that he didn't know about, and he had heard of my dabbling interest in this existential literature. So I gave him *The Sickness unto Death* and he gave me it back and he said – I think I've put this in without mentioning his name – that 'it was a very interesting example of early 19th-century psychopathology'.

Did any of these people reflect on what that meant?

That's what they *believed*. That's what Rycroft believed about Beckett and about most of what I was reading. He thought that modern art and modern literature was an organized, institutionalized expression of contemporary psychosis and the schizoid mind. He quotes Leopardi in one of his papers – Leopardi, 'the moon falling from the sky' – and analyses it as an example of psychopathology. I managed to lie on his couch just long enough to get through it....

I mean, they considered without any equivocation that Beckett, Kafka, all of them were examples of psychopathology and that's why you read them. You do pathographic studies – have you read that sort of literature? Pathographic studies of Strindberg, Nietzsche and Van Gogh. That's why I couldn't stand Jaspers. I hadn't read that of his when I thought of going over to study with him. He was one of the founders of that genre, and even Jung does that, on Nietzsche in the Terry Lectures. How Nietzsche was destined to go crazy – a genius gone psychotic.

They are completely on the other side of the barricades and in fact set them up. Oh, it's either them or us and you know they're picking them off as early as possible at school.

The concept of 'normality'. That is the thing that bothers people, it must bother Rycroft, too. It's nothing to do with being a Freudian or a psychoanalyst though, is it?

No, it's nothing to do with being a Freudian. I mean being a Freudian of a certain kind and an analyst and a psychiatrist is an institutionalized corporate representation of that sort of mentality, but no, it's much prior to that. The notion of normality, it's being like everyone else; anyone who is different and in pain at the difference they feel from other people, well they think that that might be genetic.

Are you saying that the minute someone engages in the diagnosis then they have to find something?

Relentless. Relentless. One guy who was up for his DPM examination got a patient – there was nothing the matter with him – and he went on examining him for 40 minutes. He was talking to me about this and getting into a real panic because he thought he would fail his examination unless he found out what the fucking hell was supposed to be the matter with him.

He was a colleague of yours?

Yes. This was a patient that was presented for a psychiatric examination and the fucking bastard was absolutely furious with this guy for being normal and he then described to me how he had to dig in to 'get him.' So he drove him crazy in the last five minutes and passed. The patient was a very fragile guy who felt people were persecuting him and hounding him and all the rest of it, so this guy hounded him and started to get him going.

In a normal situation, presumably, most psychiatrists start from the premise that there is something wrong?

Oh, it's a matter of honour to find something wrong. There is an argument that there must be something wrong with someone or they wouldn't be a patient in the first place. As soon as you are in that chair or in that situation, there is obviously something wrong with you and you've simply got to find out what it is as you wouldn't be in that position in the first place. If you can't see what is wrong – I mean I've heard this question asked – well why are you being examined by me, it only means that you lack insight into the condition that has led you to be in front of me? And of course you can't expect someone with a brain tumour to necessarily know that they've got a brain tumour and if someone has got a psychosis without insight it doesn't necessarily show up on first impressions. And of course some people can put a face on it and be articulate, particularly when the delusion becomes paranoid and the person then becomes cagey, so their normality is an expression of their illness.

Do you think that still happens, even after your work?

What do you mean, even after my work? You think I've cut into the conscience of everyone that Martin Roth teaches? My work has not made the slightest difference – *in fact it's only entrenched them.* There was a BBC programme a few years ago on R.D. Laing. They interviewed a number of psychiatrists about me and some of them made it clear that the main value of my work was to wake up psychiatrists so as *to refute it.* That that had been done. To that extent, by acting as a gadfly, I had done a service in leading them to do more research as to the biological causation of this sort of disorder. They always use the word causation or aetiology, as if the more they repeat the word the more they prove that it's true.

You talk about a woman suffering from 'catatonic mutism' – a 'little old lady wringing her hands, lips moving'. She is 'listening' but there is no one there. You ask, 'Is she an hallucinating psychotic or is she saying her prayers in a cathedral?'. Is that only a bit of rhetoric or ...

Well, my eldest daughter over a period of about seven or eight years – particularly after her younger sister died – got hospitalized a number of times for schizo-manic states. I think the first time that she was taken to hospital she was saying her prayers. She was on her knees on the steps of the Roman Catholic cathedral in Great Western Road, Glasgow, at about 4 o'clock in the morning. She was picked up by a police car and taken to hospital because it was obviously crazy behaviour saying your prayers on the steps of a cathedral. [laughs] The door of the cathedral of course was locked or she would have gone into the cathedral. If the door had been open and she had gone down on her knees in the cathedral it would have been all right. Mind you, she was very frantic and so on but that's what cathedrals are for.

You have argued that drugs can be a great boon to psychiatry and that if you yourself were in torment you might beg for drugs or electric shocks. The point you are trying to make is that this has nothing to do with the causation of what we call illness, has it?

And remember that the causation has nothing to do with treatment. I mean, if a certain sort of mental distress is due to the impact of our culture on a genetically determined, steered style or state of mind, so what? How do you treat that person in that distress? How do you treat someone with a peptic ulcer? It runs in families, and supposing you find that there is a high genetic component somehow or other working its way through the genotype which finds it's way to the phenotype and there is a something like genetic ulcers – more identical twins have peptic ulcers than dizygotic twins – what has that to say about the treatment of a peptic ulcer? It's got absolutely nothing to say about it at all. Absolutely nothing; do you give them milk or do you do an operation or what? Or do you treat them psychosomatically or surgically? It's got zero contribution to the therapy of a condition, whatever the aetiology of it is.

Presumably one of the things you feel is that psychiatrists collapse what they consider genetic causation to be and psychopharmacology into one thing?

Yes. *I'm* not talking about the *aetiology* of schizophrenia, I've always said that. I'm talking about the experience and behaviour that leads someone to be diagnosed as schizophrenic is more socially intelligible than has come to be supposed by most psychiatrists and most people. That is a very embarrassing statement and people can't hear that, and so it means that it is translated into saying that families cause schizophrenia and therefore if you've got a schizophrenic child, you ought to feel guilty about it and that therefore there are schizophrenic associations in families, etc. It's got nothing to do with *them*. The only way it can have nothing to do with them is if it's a virus. Now if it's a virus – as the Russians have been trying to say every other year – well, that has now to be discovered. Well, that would get everyone off the hook: if it's got nothing to do with the genes then they've got no moral responsibility. No one likes to feel that they've got tarnished or inadequate genes, or bad genes that they've passed on to their children or that might crop up in future generations. Anyway, a government might take the wrong turn about it and decide to sterilize them as the Nazis did and that's not very far away.

All these positions are so politicized that, as has often been said in politics, always look for who is to gain. Anything you can't put in a journal headline in a couple of sentences that a bird mind can grasp is completely lost and collapsed into one of these formulas; that it's caused by genetics, or it's caused by society. I mean how ridiculous to say that it's due to capitalism if you're a Marxist – what about China, or what about cross-cultural anthropology? Or the family; well it's bigger than the family so you convene a network of 35 people. But that's ridiculous too, because if you convene a network of 35 people why not 75 people, why not 300 people?

Do you feel that not enough people have tried to get their mind round the problem of what comes first – mental states or chemical changes?

What I seem to find comparatively little of is a schema which relates the psycho and the pharmacology to the social context which has been very well argued by André Laborie. Have you ever heard of him? I've met him on three occasions and been round his laboratory in Paris and he says he feels that he's fundamentally in agreement with what I've written. He said he is absolutely disgusted with the way that his research has been applied. He introduced tranquillizers.

I haven't really got any quarrel with him at all. The way he looks at it is as follows. He was first put on to what he did by seeing sailors jumping off a ship in the Indian ocean when he was a ship's surgeon in World War II. He noticed the way some service men, after combat, found it almost impossible to contain themselves, they went berserk and threw themselves overboard. So when he got back he started with rats to see how he could drive them crazy.

Notes and References

1. The quotation of Rumi is from Badi al-Zaman Furuzan-far's *Kulliyat-i shams*, Tehran (1957–66), and included in A.J. Arberry's *Mystical Poems of Rumi* (1968), Chicago: University of Chicago Press, p. 164.

2. R.D. Laing (1976) *The Facts of Life*, New York: Pantheon, p. vii.

3. Jalal al-Din Rumi (1925–40) *Mathnawi-i Ma'nawi*, edited and translated by Reynold A. Nicholson, 6 volumes, Volume 3, pp. 1259–68.

4. R.D. Laing (1986: orig.1985) *Wisdom, Madness and Folly*, London: Macmillan.

5. R.D. Laing (1960) *The Divided Self*, London: Tavistock.

6. R.D. Laing (1967) *The Politics of Experience and the Bird of Paradise*, London: Penguin.

7. Martin Roth and Jerome Krull (1986), *The Reality of Mental Illness*, Cambridge: Cambridge University Press.

8. Peter Lomas 'Psychoanalysis – Freudian or Existential', pp. 116–45, in Charles Rycroft, ed. (1968: orig, 1966) *Psychoanalysis Observed*, London: Penguin. I borrow heavily from Lomas's description of *The Divided Self*.

9. R.D. Laing (1961) *Self and Others*, London: Tavistock.

10. R.D. Laing, H. Phillipson and A.R. Lee (1966) *Interpersonal Perception*, London: Tavistock.

11. R.D. Laing and A. Esterson (1964) *Sanity, Madness and the Family*, London: Tavistock.

12. On R.D. Laing and the so-called 1960s 'counter culture', see Peter Sedgwick (1982) *Psychopolitics*, London: Pluto Press; and Jeff Nuttall (1968) *Bomb Culture*, London: Paladin.

13. Robert Hewison (1988) *Too Much: Art and Society in the Sixties 1969-75*, London: Methuen.

14. Jonathan Green (1989) *Days in the Life*, London: Minerva.

15. The quote repeated by Jo Durden-Smith is taken from Green (1989) p. 209.

16. Roger Scruton (1985) *Thinkers of the New Left*, London: Longman.

17. R.D. Laing (1968) 'The Obvious', pp. 13–34, in David Cooper, ed. (1968) *The Dialectics of Liberation*, London: Penguin. The Congress was held in London at the Roundhouse in Chalk Farm from 15 July to 30 July 1967.

18. R.D. Laing (1970) *Knots*, London: Tavistock.

19. Shulamit Ramon (1988) 'Introduction', pp. 1–29, in Shulamit Ramon, ed. (1988) *Psychiatry in Transition*, London: Pluto Press.

20. For Laing's own account of his post-1970 work see his self-description in Richard Gregory's (1987) *The Oxford Companion to the Mind*, Oxford: Oxford University Press, pp. 417–18.

21. R.D. Laing (1976) *The Facts of Life*, New York: Pantheon.

22. R.D. Laing (1982) *The Voice of Experience*, London: Allen Lane.

23. The major unpublished work remains the tentatively titled *The Challenge of Love*, 'completed' in 1989.

24. The quotation of Laing's concerning Kingsley Hall is taken from *Wisdom, Madness and Folly*.

25. The paper Laing refers to in his discussion of *Sanity, Madness and the Family* is, Aaron Esterson, David Cooper and R.D. Laing (1965) 'Results of Family-oriented Therapy with Hospitalised Schizophrenics', *British Medical Journal*, December, volume 2, pp. 1462–5.

The following source books have been invaluable:

Richard Gregory, ed. (1987) *The Oxford Companion to the Mind*, Oxford: Oxford University Press.

Geddes MacGregor (1990) *The Everyman Dictionary of Religion and Philosophy*, London: Dent.

Charles Rycroft (1972) *A Critical Dictionary of Psychoanalysis*, London: Penguin.

J.O. Urmson and Jonathan Rée, eds. (1991) *The Concise Encyclopedia of Western Philosophy and Philosophers*, London: Routledge.

INDEX